THE ADOPTION RESOURCE BOOK

THE ADOPTION RESOURCE BOOK

Fourth Edition

Lois Gilman

An Imprint of HarperCollins*Publishers*

HarperCollins books may be purchased for educational, business, or sales promotional use. For information please write: Special Markets Department, HarperCollins Publishers, Inc., 10 East 53rd Street, New York, NY 10022.

FIRST EDITION

Designed by Interrobang Design Studio

Library of Congress Cataloging-in-Publication Data

Gilman, Lois.
The adoption resource book / by Lois Gilman. — 4th ed.
p. cm.
Includes bibliographical references and an index.
ISBN 0–06–273361–3 (pbk.)
1. Adoption—United States. 2. Intercountry adoption—United States. 3. Adoption agencies—United States—Directories. I. Title.
HV875.55.G55 1998 98–21174
362.7′34—dc21 CIP

06 07 ❖/RRD 20 19 18 17 16 15 14 13 12

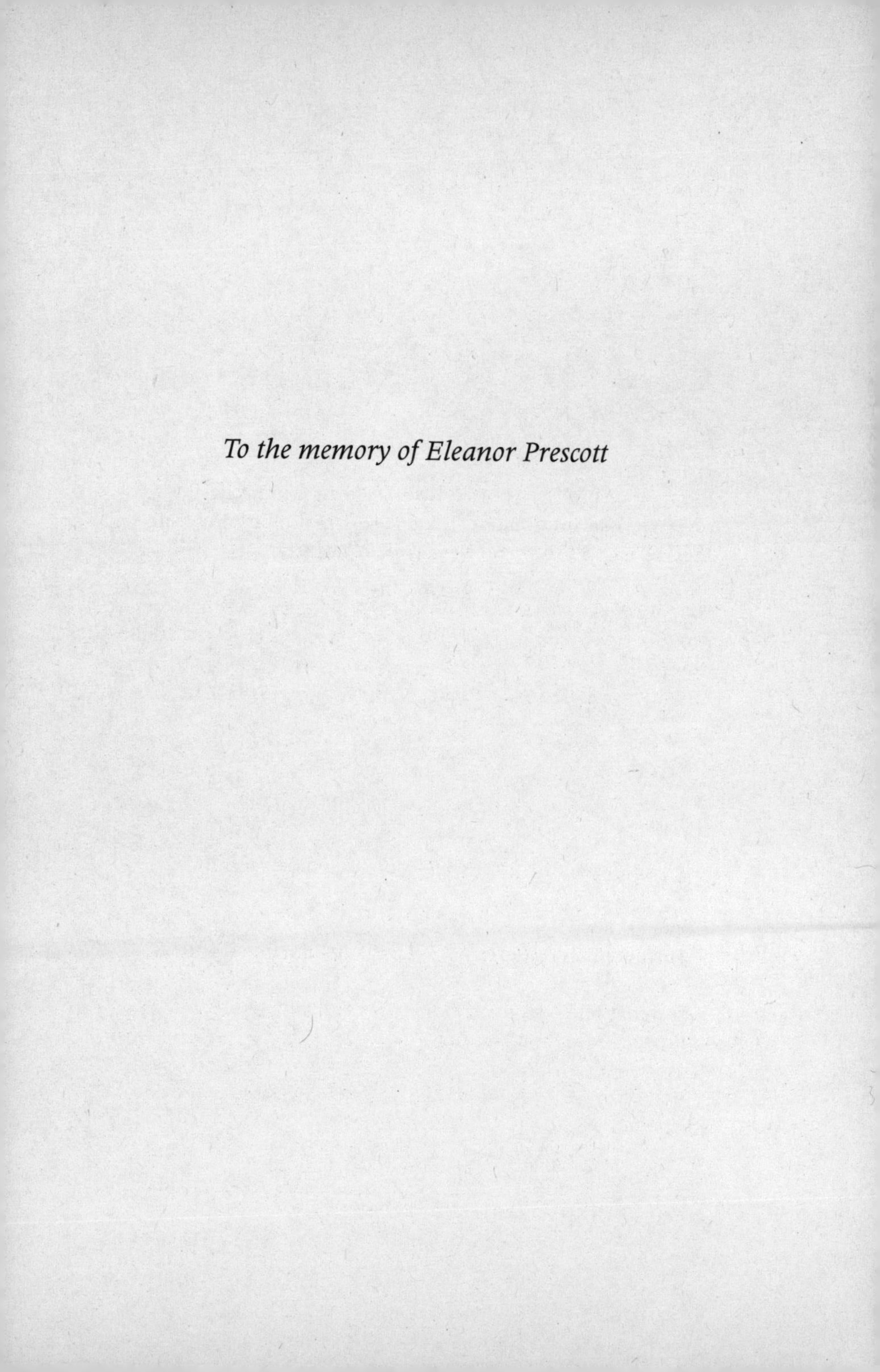

To the memory of Eleanor Prescott

CONTENTS

PREFACE

◆

On March 28, 1979, Americans were glued to their TV sets as they learned about the partial core meltdown at Three Mile Island, Pennsylvania. I, however, was otherwise engaged. I was in Santiago, Chile, holding my first child, an adorable seven-week-old baby boy. Those days were a jumble—a time of processing papers through immigration, visiting the American embassy for clearance, sitting in a dark Santiago movie theater watching *Grease* while yearning to be home with my new son and my husband Ernie. Little did I know that *The Adoption Resource Book* was also aborning in Santiago.

Why did I write a book about adoption? This question comes up again and again. Was I a social worker passing on her long experience in the field? Was I a psychologist who counsels children and parents and wants to promote family health? Was I a lawyer who had handled many a tricky adoption?

No. The answer is really very simple. I'm the mother of two children who are adopted. I am also a journalist and a professional researcher. From the time that I made my first inquiries about adoption in the seventies, I found myself putting my researching talents to work. As I made my calls and built up my own "adoption file," I wondered: What do others do? How do they get the information they need? When I looked at general books on adoption, I was surprised at how much was missing. I began to feel that there ought to be a clear, accurate guide that anticipates many of the questions and presents much of the information that I—a prospective adoptive parent—had to learn from others piece by piece. I feel that poor information (and sometimes misinformation) too often stands as a barrier between prospective parents and children who need homes. So I wrote *The Adoption Resource Book.*

The first edition of the book appeared in 1984. You are now reading the fourth edition. In the years gone by my children, Seth and Eve, have grown up. I've experienced the pleasures, and the pain, of parenthood. I've shared with Seth and Eve the joy of watching friends adopt. And I've tackled my children's questions about adoption: What is adoption? Why was I adopted? What do you know about my other parents?

As my children have aged, so has this book. Although I knew the time had come for another revision, the spirit was not there. For, in the past few years, I've weathered the transition to a new life—and more recently, to a new job. Seth and Eve have had their own struggles as they stood on the cusp of adulthood.

It is to the readers of *The Adoption Resource Book* that I say thank you. From time to time an unsolicited fan letter, often accompanied by a photo of a young child, would appear in my mailbox. How could I answer a note that proclaimed "I just wanted to *thank you* for writing *The Adoption Resource Book.* It was the first book on adoption that I read (and I have since read almost everything available!) and there was a period of several months where it was with me at all times. From the bottom of my heart I thank you for doing your work and continuing to write."

And so I revised *The Adoption Resource Book* once again. The directories and resource sections at the back of the book have been redone to try to reflect the current adoption scene more accurately. I have rewritten and updated extensively, and within chapters, I have included much new material. I have striven to create a fresh and current book that presents a picture of adoption in the late nineties.

My writing on adoption for magazines continues to influence the content and shape of the book. Ghostwriting the story of two teens' decision to pursue an open adoption for *YM*, interviewing adoptive parents on their far-flung experiences for *Cosmopolitan*, telling the story in *McCall's* of a Korean adoptee whose birth mother provided the bone marrow for a successful transplant in his battle against leukemia, describing the options available for financing an adoption in *Money*, all opened up new windows for me. In *The Adoption Resource Book* I offer you glimpses.

The Adoption Resource Book is just the beginning of your learning about adoption. It provides the necessary overview, as well as detailed, specific information. *The Adoption Resource Book* will have fulfilled its purpose if it makes your exploration of adoption just a little bit easier.

◆

Although writing a book ultimately comes down to the relationship between the author and the words used to convey the story, its creation depends on the help of many people. My thanks to them all.

Scores of adoptive parents have taken the time over the years to talk with me at length about their pre- and postadoption experiences. Their stories shaped the questions that I have tried to answer, and the scope of the book. Since their stories were frequently told in confidence, I have changed their names and avoided identifying details.

This book has profited from the activities of adoptive-parent groups around the country. I have relied on the expertise of staff and volunteers at the North American Council on

Adoptable Children, Adoptive Families of America, Families Adopting Children Everywhere, Families with Children from China, Families for Private Adoption, The Open Door Society of Massachusetts, Latin America Parents Association, Resolve, Adoptive Parents Committee, and New York Singles Adopting Children. I have also counted on national and local adoption conferences held by these groups and others, as well as information conveyed in newsletters to keep me current.

Many people have extended help when it was requested. Arline Tannenbaum and her staff at Work Family Directions (WFD) in Boston spent a day with me reviewing the book and offering suggestions for improvement. My friends forged through adoption have generously given of their time and expertise. Special thanks to Susan Freivalds, who read the entire manuscript and acted as a much-needed sounding board, and Mary Sullivan, director of the National Adoption Information Clearinghouse, who critiqued the manuscript and provided reams of updated information. Debra Smith and Lois Ruskai Melina also read portions of the revision. Adoptive parent and social worker Amy Rackear was always a phone call away, willing to listen to my latest turn of phrase. I would also like to thank Susan Caughman and Susan Soon-Keum Cox for their help.

Family and friends were there when I needed them. David Heim, Katherine Foran, Adrianne Navon, Megan Rutherford, Jeanne Lunin, Sherry Rodriguez, Blanche Gelber, Dan Carlinsky, and Bob Ross have cheered me on when the going got rough. Jennifer Bird Newton of *Fortune* has encouraged me to pursue my outside interests. Thanks also to Patricia Medved at HarperCollins for her patience. As for my family, Lotte Prager and Susan and Brian McCarthy, I know I can always count on them. And I thank Seth and Eve Gilman who, even on the worst of days, make life just a little bit brighter.

This book is dedicated to the memory of Eleanor Prescott. I met Eleanor when I was a freshman at Barnard College and we worked together on the Columbia *Daily Spectator.* Our lives have been intertwined since: through classes, jobs, marriages, adoptions, dinners at each other's tables. She first encouraged me to write some travel pieces for the *New York Times* and later passed my résumé on to a friend at Time-Life Books. She was the godmother of Seth and the loving Aunt Eleanor to both my children. For thirty years I was the privileged listener when I picked up the telephone and heard her say, "Hello, it's Eleanor."

Eleanor died last year, leaving behind many grief-stricken friends, including me. But the love she brought into our lives, and those of her father, husband, and children, lives on. This edition is dedicated to my friend, the journalist extraordinaire, Eleanor Prescott.

Lois Gilman
April 1998

1

LEARNING ABOUT ADOPTION

Once upon a time there lived a man and woman named James and Martha Brown. They had been married for a long time and were very happy together. Only one thing was missing in their lives. They had no babies of their own, and they had always wanted children to share their home.

So begins *The Chosen Baby,* Valentina P. Wasson's adoption classic for parents to read with their young children. James and Martha, so the story goes, meet with Mrs. White at the adoption agency. She asks them many questions and then visits their home to see where the child would sleep and play. A little baby named Peter is eventually placed in their home. When Mrs. White introduces them to Peter, she says: "Now go into the next room and see the baby. If you find that he is not *just the right baby for you,* tell me, and we will try to find another." But Peter is. An adoptive family is created.

The Chosen Baby, first published in 1939 and reissued over the years in updated versions, has been read by three generations of parents to their adopted children. Had Wasson written her story today, however, it might tell quite a different tale:

- James and Martha Brown contact Mrs. White at the adoption agency. She informs them that her agency places infants, but that it is the birth mother who selects the future parents of her child. Helen Doe looks at the autobiography that the Browns have prepared at Mrs. White's suggestion and Helen chooses them as Peter's adoptive parents. When Helen goes into labor, she calls to ask them to join her in the delivery room and witness their baby's birth. Afterwards, the Browns care for Peter at the hospital.
- James and Martha Brown have three children: two boys (ages ten and eight) and a girl (age fourteen). They have always wanted many children to share their home. They contact Mrs. White at the adoption agency to tell her that they would like to adopt two teenagers. They see a description and pictures of siblings John and Suzanne, twelve and eleven, in a photograph book distributed by their state that focuses on children needing permanent homes.
- James and Martha Brown have no babies of their own and they want children to share their home. So they place a classified advertisement in a newspaper in their state: "Adoption: Happily married couple wish to adopt newborn." Helen Doe calls them up about the baby she is expecting.
- James and Martha Brown contact Mrs. White at the adoption agency. Her agency places children from Russian orphanages. After she studies their home, she sends their application to Russia. A year later the Browns travel to Russia to pick up their nine-month-old son, Pëtr.
- James and Martha Brown have been nine-year-old Peter's foster parents for the past three years. They contact Mrs. White at the adoption agency to ask whether they might adopt him.

- Martha Brown has always wanted children. But she's forty and single. She contacts Mrs. White about the possibility of adoption. She learns that there are many infant girls living in orphanages in China and about the agency's adoption programs there. Martha travels to China to adopt eight-month-old Miao Miao.
- James Brown has always wanted children. But he's forty-five and single. He contacts Mrs. White about the possibility of adoption. He adopts eight-year-old Peter.
- James and Martha Brown contact Mrs. White at the adoption agency. She tells them that her agency will not take any applications but she will put their names on a waiting list. Five years later James and Martha Brown are still waiting.

The story of adoptive families has changed. Childless couples are still adopting, but so are couples with birth children, and so are singles. Agencies are still involved with the adoption of babies, but they are also placing older children, sibling groups, and children with physical and mental disabilities. Families still come to agencies for help in becoming parents, but they also pursue adoption on their own. They are also forming families by adopting children born abroad. And birth parents, once the unseen participants in the adoption story, are playing an active role in the formation of the adoptive family. The portrait of adoption today is a complex one, a composite of many different practices.

In fact the very definition of adoption is no longer as straightforward or as simple as it was once understood to be. Adoption traditionally was seen as an event that culminated when the new parents went to court and vowed, before a judge, to take a child, whose bonds with the birth parents have been legally terminated, as their new son or daughter. The child's past history—the documents that record how the child moved from his or her relationship with the birth family into the relationship with the adoptive parents—was sealed away. The adoptive parents then raised the child as their own, following the model of the family created by birth. To take a child as one's own often meant to cut him off from his genetic past.

Now that view has come under attack. The veil of secrecy that traditionally surrounded adoption is being lifted. Adults who were adopted as infants are telling us that growing up as an adopted child is different. They have come back to the agencies and the courts that hold their records and demanded the right to know about those other parents. They have challenged us to look at adoption as a lifelong event, with the court hearing marking the beginning rather than the end. They have told us that we can't obliterate their other parents. Birth parents, who released their children twenty, thirty, and forty years ago, are also returning to the agencies, telling us that the child they surrendered long ago has not been forgotten and that they need to know what happened to their child. And the birth parents of today are voicing the desire to play an active role in the adoption process and to maintain some contact with the child and the adoptive parents after the placement has been made. The story of the chosen baby is being rewritten. In its place we have the adoption triad—the birth parent, the adoptive parent, and the adoptee—all with needs and rights that must be acknowledged. We have a complex tangle of relationships.

In this new world of adoption no child is unadoptable. Adoption advocates have shown us that a family can be found for the twelve-year-old boy who's spent his life shuttling between foster homes as well as for the cute, cuddly newborn. The notion of who can be parents has expanded to include couples in their fifties, people with physical handicaps, single women and men, homosexuals, and lesbians.

Birth parents are encouraged to be the initial architects of the adoption plan for their children, and prospective adoptive parents are now spoken of as the resource for birth parents, not the other way around. As confidentiality gives way to openness, adoption is coming to be seen as a relationship between families, forged out of a mutual interest in a child, that extends for a lifetime.

New adoption practices have emerged. Among them: parent preparation for foster care and adoption in group meetings; the selection of adoptive parents by the birth parents; the encouragement of contact between birth and adoptive parents through meetings, telephone calls, or letters; the disclosure of full information about a child's background and family history to the adoptive parents; continued agency involvement with families after the finalization of an adoption; and the release of detailed information to adult adoptees about their past.

We are also coming to recognize the key roles that grief and loss play in the adoption experience. It is from loss—the birth parents' loss of the child born to them, the adoptees' loss of their birth parents, and the adoptive parents' loss of the child who might have been born to them—that adoption comes about. These losses and the ways they are mourned, the feelings such as shame and guilt that they generate, and the means by which they are resolved, must be confronted as they reverberate over the years. We are also analyzing the role that attachment plays in the development of the adopted child. What impact does shuttling through multiple foster care placements or lying, day in, day out, flat on one's back in an orphanage have on the growing child? While the questions themselves are not new, the recent experiences of adoptive families have brought them to the fore.

◆

The Adoption Resource Book tries to answer both the older and newer questions that adoptive parents have about starting and raising a family. Like many adoption handbooks, it begins with information about how to build a family. As chapters 2 to 6 make clear, however, there are many keys that will unlock the door to parenthood. Chapters 7 and 8 focus on the process of building an adoption dossier: what a home study involves and the paperwork that comes with adoption.

Chapters 9, 10, and 11 try to sketch out the needs of parents and children: the preparations parents should make; the weeks, months, and years that go into building a family; the issues involved in raising a family created through adoption. These chapters seek to point out what parents will need to consider rather than to provide definitive answers. Finally, there are state-by-state directories of U.S. and intercountry adoption agencies, a resource list, and a list of selected reference materials for further information.

Underlying this book are a few basic premises:

- Children have a right to grow up in permanent families. Adoption offers them this opportunity.
- Adoption is one way of building a family. It is no better or worse than any other way. It is different, however. That difference must be acknowledged and dealt with. Your parenting will be influenced by the experience of adoption.
- Prospective parents need good, basic, accurate information about adoption and the child they plan on adopting.
- Adoptive families need support from others, support that begins when parents first think about adoption and continues throughout the life of the family.

- Adoptive parents must focus on the needs of their children as well as their own needs. Communication and openness are important.
- Adoption is a lifelong experience.

APPROACHING ADOPTIVE PARENTHOOD

Adopting a child will involve making many decisions. What kind of child do you see yourself adopting? Do you want to adopt through an agency? If not, what other means will you use to make the adoption happen? First, though, you should look at yourself. Is adoptive parenthood, or even parenthood itself, what you really want? Your feelings will influence the type of child that you seek to adopt and have a direct impact on the child that you raise. Since adoption involves deliberate family planning, as you get started, ask yourself these basic questions:

- How important is it for you to be a parent?
- How important is it for you to have a baby?
- How important is it for you to experience a pregnancy?
- Are you satisfied that you can provide a healthy family life for a child?
- Have you explored adequately other avenues than adoption for parenting?
- If you have a fertility problem, how have you dealt with it? Are you still grieving?
- How do you feel about parenting a child who is not biologically related to you?
- Can you love a child for what he is, rather than what you hoped he would be?
- Do you have a fantasy child? How does adoption fit with this image?

- Do you have the ability to accept a child different from yourself?
- There are risks in adoption, as there are in all life experiences. How willing are you to accept risks?
- What types of risks are you willing to take? How would you feel—and what would you imagine yourself doing—if the child you adopted turned out to have special needs that you hadn't been looking for?
- Your child is going to think about his genetic history and relinquishment. Are you prepared to deal with these realities of adoption? How willing are you going to be to explore for answers for your child?
- What are your fears about adoption? Are you worried that you will never be seen as your child's real parent? What else concerns you?
- Where is your spouse/significant other on this? How do other members of your family feel?
- Do you have the perseverance to adopt?

Observes adoption consultant Kay Donley Zigler: "Families have to understand that with adoption, as with birthing, there is an element of risk that cannot be controlled. You prepare yourself for what is known and what is expected. Then you proceed. That is the way life is lived. People who come to the adoption agency expecting the Good Housekeeping seal of approval on the forehead of a child should think of something else."

THE DECISION TO ADOPT

Have you ever wanted to ask someone what went into their adoption decision? Here's what some adoptive parents and birth parents have said about the decisions they made.[1]

Ellen Lyons, who with her husband Nick adopted a newborn:

"As we got closer and closer to understanding what our fertility options were—whether we were going to move into in vitro fertilization or not, as we got to the point of making the decision of stopping the cycle of Pergonal—I had to open another door. That way I was able to close slowly the infertility door and to open slowly the adoption door. We spent about six months going back and forth. At some point we made the decision we were not going to do in vitro. And my husband said to me: "Do you really want to be pregnant or have a baby?"

Abby Elkins, a single woman in her forties who adopted a one-month-old special-needs infant:

"I was getting to be a certain age, and I knew that I really wanted a family. I never thought that I wouldn't have one. It surprised me that I felt a lack of being a parent. My mother's dying made me realize what she had been to me and that I had always expected to be that to someone. I looked at my life. I had been assuming that I had forever. I realized that I wanted to adopt. And I just said that there are children out there who are already made. It didn't seem logical to me to have a biological child. I have this really strong sense that where the child comes from is not important, it's the spirit inside. If this child is put into your care—whether you give birth or adopt—it's your child."

Johanna Williams, a single lesbian mother in her forties who adopted two four-year-old girls from two different countries in Latin America:

"I decided years before I came out that I wanted to adopt. Then I had to deal with coming out, so it had to be postponed. I thought about adopting for a good ten to fifteen years before I ever did it. Adoption seemed like what I wanted to do; artificial insemination did not.

"I hadn't considered international adoption until I ran into an acquaintance at a gas station who had a child who was clearly Hispanic. So I said 'My goodness, tell me about this.' And I adopted older children because that's who I wanted to adopt."

THE DECISION TO PLACE

Margaret Alcott, birth mother who placed her infant daughter:

"I'd had two abortions and went through very bad feelings afterwards. It was terrible.

"When I became pregnant with my daughter, I didn't go to a doctor or anything for six months because I didn't not want to be offered the option of an abortion. I thought about keeping the baby, but I knew that the father wasn't going to marry me. I just couldn't see raising the child on my own. It just wouldn't have been fair to the child. I couldn't give a child what a child needed. When the option of a private, open adoption came along, I felt that this was something I could go with. Now I see her getting fully what she needs."

Sara Charles, birth mother who placed her infant daughter:

"My boyfriend Matt and I had been dating for four months when I became pregnant the summer after high school graduation. Right from the start, I decided I couldn't have an abortion. I'm Catholic and I knew that I couldn't face myself if I chose that route. I also felt that getting married and raising the baby would create more problems for Matt and me. He was twenty, on leave from college, working and living at home. And college was still in my future. What kind of life could we offer our child? We needed another solution.

"My mom and dad took me to an adoption agency and the people there told me about the difference between traditional and open adoption. It was several months before I finally made up my mind to have an open adoption.

"Picking the family was very important, but it was also very hard and I cried all the timc. I loved my baby so much, yet I was going to give her away. But if I kept her, I knew that life would be a struggle. I loved her enough to let her go."

Matt Thomas, birth father of Sara Charles's infant daughter:

"When Sara told me she was pregnant and that she wouldn't have an abortion, I was startled. Right then I knew that we had to deal with this and that I wouldn't walk away from her.

"Fathering this baby is the toughest problem that I have ever had. As I watched Sara with our daughter in the hospital, I wondered if we should change our minds and keep her. And when the adoptive parents took Danielle home, that was really rough.

"But the worst day was when we signed the rights over and had no more control over our daughter's life.

"I'm convinced that adoption was the right thing for us. We both felt that we couldn't drop everything and raise a child the way we wished."

COMING TO TERMS WITH YOUR INFERTILITY

In 1995 the number of women of childbearing age who experienced difficulty conceiving or carrying a baby to term reached 6.1 million.[2] The number of childless women has risen (from 4.9 million in 1988) because of women's decisions to delay childbearing and because of the aging of the Baby Boom generation. If your inability to produce a child biologically has led you to think about adoption, you will want to be sure that you have resolved your infertility before you adopt a child.

What Do You Know about Infertility?

Contrary to what you may have heard, infertility—a disease or condition of the reproductive system—affects men and women with equal frequency. Experts estimate that perhaps half of the couples who seek treatment for infertility will achieve a pregnancy after intervention. The past two decades have witnessed countless breakthroughs in the treatment of infertility. The arsenal in the array of fertility treatments includes microsurgery, the use of powerful infertility drugs, donor eggs and frozen embryos, and a variety of assisted reproductive technologies, including in vitro fertilization (IVF), gamete intrafallopian transfer (GIFT), and intracytoplasmic sperm injection.

We've come a long way from that day in 1978 when the first "test-tube baby," Louise Brown, was born in Britain. We marveled in 1984 at the first baby created from a donor egg and the first baby from a frozen embryo. By 1994 the menopausal barrier was breached with the birth of a baby to a sixty-two-year-old Italian woman. And in 1997 we gasped following the birth of the world's first living septuplets, conceived after their mother took a fertility drug. More than thirty-three thousand IVF babies have been born in the U.S. alone (nearly seven thousand in 1994).[3] Other babies are conceived through donor insemination (AID), a simple procedure performed at a doctor's office in which the sperm of an anonymous donor is inserted into a woman's vagina near the cervix. For others the choice has been to find a surrogate mother who agrees to be artificially inseminated with the man's sperm, to carry the pregnancy, and after delivery to relinquish all parental rights to the baby. The permutations and combinations of these new conceptions—whether they be donor insemination, IVF, embryo transfer, freezing embryos, or surrogate mothers—are many, and the legal and ethical questions that they have raised are heatedly debated.

You'll want to do some basic reading about infertility and the new medical technologies. As Dr. Sherman Silber states, "Even for those who have no hope of pregnancy, at least a clear understanding of how their bodies work can prevent needless anxiety about whether or not they have gone far enough in their search."[4] There are many excellent books (see appendix C) that you can consult. Understanding human reproduction and infertility enables you to ask the appropriate questions and to find the realistic answers that you will need to come to terms with your medical condition.

If You Adopt a Child, Will You Get Pregnant?

Perhaps you've wistfully thought—or a relative has suggested—that as soon as you adopt, you're bound to achieve a pregnancy. After all, Cousin Irma did. Pregnancy following adoption is one of those adoption myths that refuses to die. Reports Linda Salzer in *Surviving Infertility*: "A number of well-designed, controlled studies have investigated this idea and found no difference in pregnancy rates between those couples who had previously adopted and those who had not."[5]

What Medical Advice Have You Sought?

Both of you will need a full medical workup by a specialist. Fertility problems are equally common in men and women. For the man, that means a physical examination as well as a semen analysis. Sometimes both the man and the woman contribute to the problem. Small changes in both may result in a pregnancy.

Your regular family physician or your gynecologist may be a fine doctor, but he or she is not necessarily the person most qualified to analyze a fertility problem. Some gynecologists, urologists, or reproductive endocrinologists have developed specialties in infertility. The **American Society for Reproductive Medicine** (see appendix A) can refer you to qualified specialists in your area. The national self-help organization **Resolve** (see appendix A), which has local chapters throughout the United States, also provides infertility counseling and referral services. Support groups will make referrals to local physicians, offer lectures and workshops about fertility issues, and give you a chance to talk about your feelings.

If you have a choice of several specialists, try to learn a little about them before you make your decision. Does the doctor have a subspecialty within the field? Does the physician work in a team with other specialists? Is there an infertility counselor (a therapist who will talk with you) on the support staff? Be sure that you find a doctor with whom you feel comfortable and who will permit you to ask questions. Your physician has many infertile patients to consider; you have only one—yourself.

Even after you have found your doctor, you may want to talk with another specialist to confirm a recommended course of treatment, to get a second opinion before surgery, or to help you decide whether it might be time to give up altogether. Before your visit, check with the specialist to be sure that your own physician has forwarded your medical records. It can also be helpful for you to prepare your own medical résumé for the consultant, a summary of your past history, surgery, and drug therapy. Preparing this résumé will force you to evaluate where you are.

What Have You Asked Your Doctor?

Ask all the questions that you want answers for, and don't be shy about bringing in a list. You'll want a full explanation of any procedures your doctor is advocating, including their risks and success rate. The success rates of IVF clinics vary significantly; you can get information on individual clinics from a national study by contacting Resolve or checking the website of the federal agency, the **Centers for Disease Control** (see appendix A). Pin the doctor down as to the expected length of any course of treatment. You have a right to know the game plan. If possible, have your spouse or a significant other present, to give you moral support and to be sure that all issues that concern you are raised.

Have You Acknowledged Your Feelings?

If you have been struggling to become pregnant, you've probably felt overwhelmed, guilty, and cheated. There may be tension in your marriage. You may have harbored thoughts of divorce so that your spouse can find a more fertile partner. You've probably found it painful to be around friends with children. You may find that your sleep is disturbed, that you have nightmares, that you awaken feeling distressed. Says infertility counselor Roselle Schubin: "As a medical problem, infertility is rather unique. You can't get adjusted to it. Every month the question arises—will ovulation occur and will the husband perform sexually? Infertile couples are in an almost constant state of crisis."[6]

Coming to terms emotionally with an inability to conceive is difficult enough; often, it is compounded by depression. In *An Empty Lap: One Couple's Journey to Parenthood,* Jill Smolowe captures the painful sense of splintering that can attend depression and make it so difficult to move on. "But who is this Jill?" she asks at one point:

And how is she to make a sensible decision whether to discontinue fertility treatments or persist? The person who now inhabits my body and mind is eerily unfamiliar. Unreasonable. Unreliable. She's a woman who sees only the gallows, never the humor. . . . I detest this fragile, morose person I've become. Even as I inhabit the skin of this humorless woman, I never lose sight of the fact that this is not a person I want to be around. I resent her unfailingly dark mood. Her brooding. Her tentativeness, indecisiveness, her lack of resilience. I not only find her self-absorption exhausting, but feel no sympathy for her, with her constant thoughts of me, me, me.

Even more intolerable than the presence of this loathsome stranger is the absence of the person who's always been my steadiest and most reliable companion.

'I don't know this person I've become,' I say to Joe repeatedly. 'She's not the real me.'[7]

To work through your infertility you must face it openly. Talk to your spouse and others and express your feelings. Support groups like Resolve can help you. There are several excellent books (see appendix C), including Paulette Bates Alden's, *Crossing the Moon,* Anne Taylor Fleming's *Motherhood Deferred: A Woman's Journey,* Debby Peoples and Harriette Rovner Ferguson's *What To Expect When You're Experiencing Infertility: How to Cope with the Emotional Crisis and Survive,* Salzer's *Surviving Infertility,* and Smolowe's *An Empty Lap,* that focus on the emotional challenges infertility poses.

Since infertility involves loss, you must grieve for the child you never had, for the child who might have been, for your inability to create or sustain life. You'll feel angry, upset, guilty, and, finally, you'll be able to let go. Coming to grips with your infertility may mean giving up the quest and accepting yourself and your family as you are.

How Do You Know That You're Ready to Think about Adoption or Child-Free Living?

There comes a time when people with impaired fertility begin to question whether they should move beyond the medical tests and procedures. Some will decide for child-free living; others will choose to pursue adoption. Each family's timetable is different, and it's not uncommon for one partner to be ready long before the other is. That may be upsetting, but it is quite natural for spouses to reach the decision to adopt at different points in time. Smolowe gives us a glimpse at how wide this gulf can be:

> *During the last ten days, I've silently visited and revisited Joe's four inconsistent comments about adoption, each of them squeezed from him under the strain of my anguish and anxiety, sometimes to soothe, sometimes to get me off his back. 'Why would I want to raise someone else's kid?' 'Maybe I should see a therapist to deal with my resistance.' 'It will be at least a year before I can even begin to consider adoption.' 'It's not going to happen.'*
>
> *. . . Years later Joe will tell me, 'I don't remember any of that.'*
>
> *. . . It will sadden me anew to think how alone I was, how far apart two people who love each other can be. How at the very moment when I was clutching at adoption as the only remaining line that could reel me back to shore, my only potential rescuer wasn't even aware that I was drowning.*[8]

After several years of struggle, Jill and Joe traveled to China to adopt their daughter Becky.

"The process of coming to grips with adoption is time-consuming and very emotional," says Linda Salzer. "It can start at a point where people say 'I will never adopt' or 'I don't want anything to do with it.' There are a lot of people who ultimately adopt who had that kind of viewpoint."

How then do people get from point A to point B? Salzer offers the following questions as guideposts:[9]

- Have you exhausted all the medical possibilities that you feel comfortable with or can afford to pursue? You should do as much as you feel physically, emotionally, and financially able to do. That varies by the individual. Some people will try in vitro fertilization six times before they say enough; others will say they don't even want to consider hormone treatments.
- Are you feeling now that parenthood is more important, or is pregnancy still a major concern for you?
- Are you upset that infertility seems to have taken over your life? Have you gotten to the point where you are wanting to put this chapter behind you?
- Are you feeling that your present efforts and treatments are hopeless? Observes Salzer: "Many people are able to say that there was a point in their treatment when they moved from hope about each coming cycle to where they said 'I'm starting another cycle, but I know that it's not going to work.'"
- Are you upset with the kind of person you've become? Are you tired of having to avoid your friends with children because of the emotional pain it causes you? Are you tired of being depressed and dragged out?
- Are you looking forward to the time when you can stop taking your temperature and can forget about fertility drugs, visits to the doctor, and what the latest infertility research shows?

- Are you feeling the need for some form of closure? Are you thinking to yourself, "I'll try two more cycles of donor insemination and that's it"?
- Are you finding yourself wanting to talk about alternative means of achieving parenthood?

If you answered yes to many of these questions, chances are that you should evaluate your alternatives. Getting to the next step, says Salzer, "is answering those questions and being able to talk about adoption without bursting into tears. You're starting to feel excited that you will have a family in the not-so-distant future." Observes Amy Rackear, an adoption social worker in the New York metropolitan area and past president of Resolve of New York City: "Adoption slowly walks us through our future, encouraging us to evaluate the dynamics that propelled our journey through treatment. You must now examine your goals and priorities in a new light. How you resolve those concerns intercepts the juncture between adoptive parenting and child-free living."

What happens as you take this next step? Rackear eloquently chronicled the change in her writing about her son's adoption:[10]

On tiptoes and with unprecedented trepidation, I approached the threshold of adoption. I searched within myself for any predisposition or bias that might curtail my ability to effectively parent a child to whom I was not genetically linked. I asked myself that most chilling of questions: 'Could I love him?' He whose face mirrored neither my hazel eyes nor my husband's gentle aquiline nose. 'Would I love him?' A baby whose heartbeat did not result from my husband's embrace. 'Will I love him?'

One night, when his delivery was imminent, the years of trying—and changing—culminated in a single thought. His homecoming would be a real product of our love. It was our courage, tears, patience and understanding; it was our commitment to each other and prayer for a child with whom to share our gifts; it was love that finally allowed this moment. Together we would bring our baby home. And therefore, our family grew not from one, but a thousand embraces. 'Do I love him?' My son has forever altered my concept of that word and the world. He has taught me mother love.

GETTING INFORMATION ABOUT ADOPTION

As you contemplate adoption, you will need to explore resources that will help you build your family and resources that you can turn to for continuing information and support in the years ahead following the adoption. The **National Adoption Information Clearinghouse** (see appendix A) is a good place to begin as you can obtain referrals to local agencies and support groups as well as numerous free information sheets.

If you have access to a computer and subscribe to a commercial online service or can reach the Internet directly, there's a gold mine of information at your fingertips (see appendix A). In commercial online services there are special bulletin boards where members communicate and even hold online town meetings. On the Internet there are usenet newsgroups, such as **alt.adoption.agency, alt.support.foster-parents,** in which participants post messages. There are innumerable websites on the World Wide Web, from the wide-ranging **Adopting.com (http://www.adopting.com)** and **AdoptioNetwork (http://www.adoption.org)** to more specialized sites featuring open adoption **(http://openadoption.org),** support groups for families pursuing intercountry adoption (**http://www.fwcc.org** for Families with Children from China), infertility (**http://www.resolve.org/** for Resolve), single motherhood (**http://parentsplace.com/readroom/smc** for Single Mothers by Choice), or an agency (**http://www.holtintl.org/** for Holt International Children's Services). These sites also provide hyptertext links to other resources. To cast your net even wider, you can use one of the search engines (Yahoo! AltaVista, and Infoseek, among others) type in keywords such as adoption, intercountry+adoption, foster+care, or open+adoption, and glean hundreds of websites touching on your subject. For a printed source of information, that includes government sites as well as support groups and agencies, you can turn to *Adoption Guide to the Internet,* which is compiled by the National Adoption Information Clearinghouse.

Using computer links you can send messages to an adoption e-mail pal, request further information, download applications, fill out forms, and do a variety of other tasks that you might accomplish through telephone, letter, or fax communication. Keep in mind, however, that *privacy is not guaranteed on the Internet.* When you provide your name, address, and other details about yourself, there is no guarantee that the information will not be shared with others. L. Anne Babb, webmaster for Prodigy's Adoption Community, the American Adoption Congress, and AdoptioNetwork Cleveland, offers excellent cautionary advice in *Adoptive Families* magazine:[11]

- Whether adoptive parents choose to participate in newsgroups, e-mail lists, chats or BBS, they should know that cyberspace is open to anyone who owns a computer and has an online connection. Just as in face-to-face dealings, people encountered online can be deceptive, have personal agendas, and even be a little (or a lot) unbalanced.

- A good rule of thumb is that if it sounds too good to be true, it probably is. . . . No matter how cute the photos of the children splashed across a Web page, chances are that the quick, easy and inexpensive placement of a healthy baby into any adoptive parent's arms is highly unlikely.

Mary Sullivan, director of the National Adoption Information Clearinghouse, cautions that all information gathered via chat rooms or bulletin boards should be treated as "personal opinion, second- and third-hand information" and that you should be sure to cross-check with parent support groups, social service organizations, and books.

Your initial steps will take you in several directions: (1) making contact with adoptive families and parent groups; (2) checking with social service agencies for general information as well as for details about specific adoption programs; and (3) reading.

Making Contact with Adoptive Families and Parent Groups

Getting to know other adoptive families is a first step in adoption and one you should continue to take as the years pass by. You may know people who have adopted and who will share their experiences with you. Spend time with their families and observe their children. If you are thinking about an intercountry adoption, talk to people about their experiences and observe their children. If you are contemplating an older-child adoption, spend some time around older children. Ask parents what it's like to start a family with a ten-year-old. If you are interested in adopting a child who has a special need, such as a physical, mental, or emotional disability, try to observe a child with this problem.

There are several hundred parent groups in the United States. You can learn about groups in your community by contacting the National Adoption Information Clearinghouse.

Adoptive Families of America (see appendix A) also serves as a clearinghouse and provides "problem-solving assistance and information about the challenges of adoption to members of adoptive and prospective adoptive families." Membership includes a subscription to the informative bimonthly magazine *Adoptive Families*. Adoptive Families of America also stocks an extensive collection of adoption-related books, audiotapes, dolls, and other products that it sells by mail order. Sometimes, however, it's as simple as checking in your local telephone book under "Adoption."

Local groups can give you basic information about adoption. The Open Door Society of Massachusetts (1750 Washington Street, Holliston, MA 01746; 800–932–3678), for example, is a state-wide organization with a membership of more than one thousand families and chapters throughout the state. It publishes a newsletter, maintains a library of audio- and videotapes on adoption that members can borrow, sells adoption-related books, organizes discussion groups, and holds an annual New England Adoption Conference. Some parent groups have developed adoption information courses. Families Adopting Children Everywhere (FACE; P.O. Box 28058, Northwood Station; Baltimore, MD 21239; 410–488–2656) offers a course on family-building through adoption at various locations throughout Maryland and Virginia. The course, which extends over several weeks, uses parents and experts to provide an overview of what's happening in domestic and intercountry adoption. Says Clyde Tolley of FACE: "The course covers the waterfront and provides a general introduction for folks unfamiliar with adoption. It gives them the chance to make decisions about whether they want to adopt, and if they do, which alternatives are going to meet their needs. While there may be books that give an introduction, the experience is not the same as going to a class and participating with adoptive parents, agency people, birth parents, and adult adoptees." The FACE course has served as the prototype for many adoption information courses around the country. If you've got doubts and concerns about adoption, sitting in a class may help clear them up. Observes Peggy Phillips, an adoptive parent who developed a Pennsylvania community college course: "It is much easier to walk out of a class than an adoption agency to which you might be financially committed. This way, you can learn the pros and cons and ask questions you might feel hesitant to broach at an agency for fear you might say something out of line."

The **North American Council on Adoptable Children** (NACAC; see appendix A) is a nonprofit coalition of individuals and organizations working for the rights of children in the areas of foster care and adoption, with a particular interest in waiting children. As a major national adoption organization, it functions as a clearinghouse for adoptive-parent support groups around the country. Its state representatives will inform you about local parent groups and agencies. They'll be glad to answer many of your basic questions about your state's adoption practices. As an adoption advocacy group, NACAC also monitors federal child welfare legislation, pushes for better access to adoption services, and holds an annual national conference.

The **National Council for Single Adoptive Parents** (see appendix A) serves as a clearinghouse for singles seeking information. Membership entitles you to a list of agencies and other contacts (with updates) that singles will want to approach about adoption. This organization can also provide you with the names of single-parent groups as well as single parents to talk to. *The Handbook for Single Adoptive Parents* (available by mail order) is an excellent introductory guide to single parenthood offering help on such topics as the mechanics of adoption, managing once you've adopted, and handling challenges. Another specialized support organization is **Stars of David** (3175 Commercial Avenue, Northbrook, IL 60062; http://www.starsofdavid.org), which is a support network for Jewish and partly-Jewish adoptive families. Gay and lesbians can receive help from the **Gay and Lesbian Parents Coalition International** (GLPCI; P.O. Box 50360, Washington, D.C. 20091; 202–583–8029; http://www.glpci.org). If you are considering intercountry adoption, you'll get a wealth of information from a support group such as **Families with Children from China** (P.O. Box 865, Ansonia Station, NY, NY 10023; 212–579–0115; http://www.fwcc.org/).

An excellent way to obtain a quick, general overview is to attend an adoption conference or daylong workshop. The Adoptive Parents Committee (P.O. Box 3525, Church Street Station, New York, NY 10008–3525; 718–259–7921) is one of many support groups holding annual conferences, while Single Parents for the Adoption of Children Everywhere (SPACE; 6 Sunshine Avenue, Natick, Massachusetts; 508–655–5426) devotes a biennial conference to the concerns of single adoptive parents. Check with the National Adoption Information Clearinghouse or Adoptive Families of America to find out when an adoption conference or workshop is being held in your state.

Checking with Social Service Agencies

Seeking out a parent group is a beginning; so is contacting your public agencies. Your state department of public welfare may be able to supply you with useful information: brochures detailing state adoption programs, subsidy programs, factsheets describing intercountry adoption procedures. Some states now have toll-free telephone numbers that you can call to request information about adoption.

You'll also want to start by getting in touch with local agencies, both public and private, to learn about their specific programs. Chapter 2, "Exploring Adoption through an Agency," provides a basic orientation to agencies and how they work. Appendix B lists agencies state by state. Whatever type of adoption you choose to pursue, there's a good chance that you will need an agency's involvement to bring it to fruition. Touching base initially with agencies gives you a better grasp of adoption in the U.S. and in your community today.

Reading

Parents read books that focus on child care and child development. As an adoptive parent, you will also want to read books that touch on some specialized topics related to adoption. References to some of these works are placed at the appropriate points in the text.

Appendix C, entitled "For Further Reference," surveys current books about adoption. You may want to read some of these now; others may be more relevant in the years ahead. As you start making your adoption plans, you may want to mix your general reading with some personal accounts. Books like Maggie Francis Conroy's *A World of Love,* Patty Dann's *The Baby Boat,* Michael Dorris's *The Broken Cord,* Dion Howells's *The Story of David,* Jill Krementz's *How It Feels to Be Adopted,* Jill Smolowe's *An Empty Lap,* Susan Wadia-Ellis's *The Adoption Reader,* Jan Waldron's *Giving Away Simone,* and Jana Wolff's *Secret Thoughts of an Adoptive Mother* bring the adoption experience up close. Each captures family life and feelings.

THE CHILDREN NEEDING PLACEMENT IN THE U.S.

Despite rumors you may have heard on television or from a neighbor about the lack of infants needing adoption, you'll find that infants are still placed for adoption. Since many people want to adopt healthy infants, some agencies will inform families that they can expect to wait for months or occasionally years. At agencies where the birth parents choose the adoptive parents, however, you may not be asked to wait since the agency needs to offer a sizable pool of prospective adoptive parents to birth parents. (Once you are involved in an agency program, you might still wait for a birth mother to choose you.) Chapter 2 explains agency adoption programs, while chapter 4 focuses on how open adoptions work.

There is another way that infants enter adoptive families, however. In the majority of states birth parents may bypass agencies and choose to place their babies directly with adoptive parents. Chapter 3 provides a full discussion of independent adoption, while chapter 2 (see pages 60–64) discusses a hybrid known as identified adoption.

When you inquire at an agency about adoption, you may be told that the children currently waiting for homes are older, or black, or of other minority-group parentage. They may be part of a sibling group. Some may have physical handicaps such as cerebral palsy, hydrocephalus, spina bifida, or Down syndrome. Others have emotional handicaps or are developmentally delayed. Some of the older children are physically healthy (though they may have emotional problems) but wait, nonetheless, because of their ages. There are also younger children, including babies and toddlers, needing adoptive homes; most often their mothers were known to have used alcohol or drugs during their pregnancy, and the children have been deemed "at risk" for future problems. Some infants have also tested positive for the HIV antibody. Most agencies occasionally place healthy white toddlers and young school-aged children, but they will have waiting lists for these children. The profile of the black children waiting for adoption, however, is different. There are black children of all ages waiting for homes. Black sibling groups are particularly common.

Children who have been waiting for adoptive families for a period of time are often referred to as "waiting children." Children who have disabilities are often referred to as "special-needs" children. The definition of a special-needs or a waiting child varies state by state. In some states and at some agencies you may find that children who are members of a minority group or who are older are referred to as special-needs children. Chapter 5 discusses waiting children in the United States.

Chapter 6 discusses the children in other countries who wait for homes and who have been placed in American adoptive families.

MAKING YOUR ADOPTION PLAN

The chapters that follow survey how you can go about building your adoptive family: working through an agency; working independently; searching for an infant or an older child in the United States; searching for an infant or an older child abroad.

Your homework begins now. To make your adoption plan you must:

- Pull together as much information as you can, from a variety of sources, sift through it, and evaluate it.
- Think about your own and your significant other's comfort levels with adoption.
- Determine the kind of child you hope to adopt. Do you imagine yourself the instant parent of an infant, of twins, of a three-year-old and a six-year-old? What feels comfortable? Do you think that a child of a different racial or ethnic heritage will be accepted in your family and community?

- Find a parent group that you can turn to for support and join it.
- Understand the ins and outs of the adoption process.
- Learn what the various adoption options are in relation to the child you imagine adopting.
- Decide what's of primary importance to you. You'll need to think about waiting times and risks, for example.
- Evaluate your financial resources. What is the state of your finances? What costs can you assume? What potential benefits, such as an employer adoption-assistance program or a state subsidy program, can you tap?
- Assess your flexibility on various adoption issues such as your need for confidentiality.

As the next chapter on agencies makes clear, not all agencies are alike. Their philosophies may differ radically. How they approach adoption may directly influence how you view adoption and how you create your family. Sometimes it is possible for you to make choices; sometimes not.

Your basic goal now, as you ferret out information, is to seek out supports and build your own adoption network. The friends that you make, the groups that you join, the services that you uncover will stay with you in the years ahead.

You're beginning a journey that has no end.

2

EXPLORING ADOPTION THROUGH AN AGENCY

◆

As Deborah Williams turned forty, she realized that something was missing in her life. 'My biological clock seemed like a time bomb, and something went off in my head,' she recalls. 'I knew single people could adopt, but the challenge was figuring out the agency to use.' So she went to her local library to do research. Money was an issue so Williams decided to list all the adoption agencies in New York City, ranking them according to the population they served and the fees they charged. 'The agency I chose,' she emphasizes, 'came to the top of the list because it had a sliding scale for fees.'

Whatever kind of adoption you're thinking about, your road to parenthood will probably take you through, or at least past, an agency. There are different types of agencies that you can contact. Each state has a public agency charged with the care of children in that state. The state agency—frequently identified as the Bureau of Family and Children's Services, the Division of Social Services, the Department of Human Services, or the Department of Public Welfare—oversees the provision of services to children, including foster care and adoption. The state agency usually has local—often county—branches around the state. In addition, cities may have their own departments of social services for children in their care.

Although public agencies are supposed to serve the people in the state, yours may not be able to work with you. State agencies today focus on placing waiting children and often will not accept applications for non-hard-to-place children. You may be told that you will have to wait several months or years before the agency is ready to take a formal application. A public agency may also be so understaffed that you will need to wait for months or even years before it can work with you. If you wish to adopt a child from overseas, many state agencies will decline to study your family, since their main priority is to help find permanent homes for children currently in their care. Check with your local public agency or your state adoption unit about adoption policies in your state.

States also license private child-placing agencies, which may be nonprofit or for-profit. These agencies have as their clients birth parents considering adoption for their child, prospective adoptive parents, and older children needing adoptive homes. Many have also developed extensive intercountry adoption programs. You will also discover that some agencies, while not placing children themselves, counsel families pursuing an independent adoption, an intercountry adoption, or the adoption of a waiting child in another agency's care. Some agencies serve members of particular religious denominations; others have no such restrictions. Some private agencies are branches of a national religious or church-sponsored organization. A private agency with a name like Presbyterian Children's Home and Service Agency does not necessarily limit its services to Presbyterians or place only Presbyterian children. The name may simply reflect past, rather than current, practice. (Some agencies have been placing children for fifty years or more.) Some agencies do have a religious standard for service, but it may be broader than a particular denomination. You may find agencies that only work with Christian families, with "evangelical Christians," "dedicated Christians," or those "actively involved in a pro-life, Bible-teaching church." Other agencies are strictly nondenominational. Don't eliminate any agency from consideration on the basis of its name.

Some agencies will take applications from families throughout the United States. They may have a representative or a branch office in various states, may coordinate service with a local "networking" agency, or even accept the paperwork prepared by your local licensed agency or social worker. Many agencies, however, do impose geographical restrictions. Their area of service, often determined by the licensing authorities of a state, will be limited, and you'll need to determine that fact at the outset. You may also discover that your local agency, while it may not have adoptable children to place with you, may be able to do the paperwork, such as a home study, that another agency requires.

Certain agencies have also developed specialties. The Family Builder agencies, such as Spaulding for Children in Houston, Texas, Children Unlimited in Columbia, South Carolina, and Project STAR in Pittsburgh, Pennsylvania, are part of a network of nonprofit adoption agencies located around the United States that focus on older, handicapped, and minority children. Since these agencies serve waiting children, they charge no fees to adoptive parents and collaborate with other agencies in accepting referrals of children needing families. Other agencies, such as Holt International Children's Services in Eugene, Oregon, focus on finding homes for children through intercountry adoption.

The Institute for Black Parenting in Los Angeles serves minority children and families. There are no fees for services, and the staff work evenings and weekends so that prospective adopters don't have to take time off from work. "We follow the philosophy of empowering black families. We guarantee our families a culturally sensitive social worker," says executive director Zena Oglesby. "We help them complete their paperwork. We make sure that they're getting good treatment on the front end, so that they're available for the thousands of black children who are available."

REQUIREMENTS

Regulations in every state are made "in the best interests of the child" and seek to protect everyone's rights. Each state has its own laws and requirements.

All agencies have some requirements for prospective adopters. Some have just the minimum mandated by state law, while others have added criteria of their own. While rare, you may find that an agency restricts its clientele to nonsmokers or bars overweight adults. It's not uncommon for an agency to have more stringent requirements for families seeking to adopt healthy infants than for families interested in adopting older or special-needs children.

SOME COMMON REQUIREMENTS

AGE

- You may be between twenty-one and sixty years old.
- An agency may be concerned that you be young enough that you can see your child grow to maturity.
- An agency may specify a minimum number of years or a maximum number of years that can separate parents and children.

MARITAL STATUS

- Couples may have to be married a certain number of years before they can apply. Some agencies will consider the length of the relationship rather than the marriage.
- Previous divorce is usually acceptable. Some agencies may limit the number of prior divorces the couple may have had. Some agencies also will establish a longer minimum length of marriage time for couples who have a divorce history.
- Singles may be acceptable.

INCOME

- For infant adoptions, some agencies may require that you meet a specific financial standard.
- Most agencies will ask that you show that you can manage effectively on your income.

HEALTH

- Agencies usually require medical exams and may ask for evidence that you are in reasonably good health.
- Some agencies will require that you provide a fertility report and that you not be actively involved with infertility treatments.
- If the preadoptive mother becomes pregnant during the adoption process, the agency may ask that it be notified. Some agencies will put a current application on hold until after the birth. There may be a waiting period after the birth.
- If you are significantly overweight, an agency may question your health and life expectancy.
- If you have a history of alcohol or substance abuse, an agency may ask for further explanation.
- You may be asked about psychiatric or psychological counseling that you received.

RELIGION

- Some agencies may require that the child be placed in a home of the same religious background as the birth parents.
- Some agencies may require that you have a religious affiliation and may ask for a recommendation from a pastor.

FAMILY SIZE

- When placing a healthy infant, some agencies may state that only childless couples or those with no more than one other child in the home will be considered for healthy infants. If birth parents control the selection of adoptive parents, individual criteria may be set by them.

- Some agencies will not accept applications from singles for infant adoptions.
- Some agencies may discriminate against large families.
- If you have previously adopted, you may be asked to show evidence that the adoption has been finalized before starting on another adoption.

EMPLOYMENT

- Some agencies will ask that one parent take a couple of weeks—or months—off from work to help the new child settle in.

PERSONAL HISTORY

- Many agencies will require a criminal history background check by the local, state, or federal authorities. This may be mandated by the state.
- Many agencies will require a child abuse background check by local or state authorities. This may be mandated by the state.

RESIDENCY

- Some agencies may serve only a specific geographical region.

CITIZENSHIP

- If you are adopting internationally, one parent must be a U.S. citizen.

Agencies that feature a variety of programs may have different requirements for each of them. You may discover that an agency, when placing its own infants or working with a pool of birth mothers, will set an age limit, often specifying that the applicants, or one of the applicants, be no more than thirty-five to fifty years old. (Others will stretch the age limits but indicate that the birth parents, who are doing the selection, will have their own criteria.) Or the requirements may state that the combined ages of the couple cannot exceed eighty, eighty-five, or ninety years old. They may also ask that the applicants show medical evidence of infertility or of a medical or genetic problem that would make pregnancy inadvisable. Some agencies will require that child care during the first few months after a baby's arrival be provided by one of the adopting parents or that it is shared by the adopting parents. Where the child is school-aged, an agency may ask that one of the parents be at home when the child leaves for school and returns.

Agencies serving minority, handicapped, or older children often are much more flexible. Consider the message to adoptive parents of the Institute for Black Parenting in a brochure:

> *Age requirements are flexible. Married and/or single men and women can adopt. You can be divorced. You don't have to be rich. You don't need money in the bank. The size of your home doesn't matter. You can live in an apartment, and children can share bedrooms. Mothers can work. Arrangements can be made for the care of children. You can have your own children and adopt. The amount of education and kind of job you have makes no difference. You can be of any religious faith.*

"We're processing many of the families who were kicked out of the public sector," observed Oglesby. "When agencies say 'you're too old,' or 'you're a forty-five-year-old grandmother so you can't raise an infant,' they're screening out much of the black culture. Why wouldn't single parents be considered a major resource when 50 percent of black families are headed by single parents?"

For this agency singles are the "placement of choice" for many children. But other agencies are still wary of singles, who must be prepared to overcome barriers thrown up in their path. Singles may encounter agencies that will not allow them to apply to adopt healthy infants and younger children. "Singles should not be asked to settle for a child they are not going to be comfortable with," says social worker and single adoptive parent Ann Feldman. "They should hold out for the child they want to parent."

People with chronic medical problems or physical handicaps must also be prepared to convince an agency that their condition will not affect their ability to raise a child. If you have a serious medical problem that is controlled by medication, have had major surgery, or have an illness that is in remission, don't be surprised if the agency asks for a detailed statement, including a prognosis, from your physician. "We had a very hard time getting our foot in the door of an agency," recalls Alice, who had suffered from Hodgkin's disease and was left sterile by the chemotherapy used to combat it. Five agencies turned her and her husband Ned away despite a doctor's clear explanation of her good medical prognosis. "Hodgkin's has a 95 percent cure rate, and I had been disease-free for three years," Alice recalls. "All we got was the standard answer of 'wait five years,'" Alice is also upset that the agencies were unable to view her illness with a more positive attitude. "We felt that the battle against Hodgkin's had strengthened our marriage," says Alice. "We'd been through this, and we knew we could do much for a baby. Yet the agencies treated my history as a turnoff."

As Alice and Ned struggled to find an agency to work with them, their adoption plans changed. "In the process of the search," she says, "we wondered what we were searching for." They saw that their own brush with death, their experience working with the medical establishment, and the strength they drew from each other made them comfortable with the thought of adopting a baby with serious medical problems. Says Alice: "If a child needed parents who could understand her problem and not treat her as if she were different or handicapped, we could do that. We were asking people to take a risk with us, so we decided to take risks too."

With the help of a sixth agency, one that catered to nontraditional clients, Alice and Ned adopted a newborn girl with a major congenital heart defect. Their daughter had one heart operation as an infant and faces another at her third birthday. For Alice and Ned the adoption has brought only joy. "We feel so blessed and enriched by our daughter's first year," says Alice. "We're scared about the next operation, but we know that we've been in that place before."

If you already have several children, don't be surprised if an agency tries to discourage you from adopting or turns you down. Again you may even be told that you are eligible to apply only for specific children. "After three boys, I wanted a baby girl," says Cynthia. She was still of childbearing age and could try again. But she wanted to adopt. "My husband and I went to many agency orientations, but they said 'Don't waste your time, we won't even look at you because you have children.' Finally our local public agency gave us a chance after we said we were willing to take many risks." Two years later, Cynthia became the foster mother of a baby girl, a newborn who had been abandoned on a New York City stoop on a cold winter day. She accepted the "legal risk" that a member of the birth family might come forward and was willing to wait several years after her daughter's placement for the requisite adoption paperwork to be completed.

Prospective adoptive parents who are gay and lesbian may have a tougher time adopting a child. The laws and policies of each agency and state (there are states that block adoptions) will vary, so that using the "grapevine" and getting to know other gay and lesbian adoptive parents is critical. They may steer you to social workers and agencies who, while not publicizing the fact, are friendly to gay and lesbian adoption, and can advise you on what to disclose about your sexual orientation. Whatever you do, counsels April Martin in *The Lesbian and Gay Parenting Handbook,* "Do not lie at any time in the adoption process. Though it is legal to omit any mention of your sexuality, it is illegal to lie about it when directly confronted. If you are asked a direct question, you must tell the truth."[1] To explore the possibilities of adoption, Martin's book is an excellent starting point, as is the **Gay and Lesbian Parents Coalition International** (see appendix A).

Don't be discouraged if you're told that one agency will not consider an application from someone with your particular background. Another agency may be happy to take you on as a client. "It sounds crazy, but we really feel more comfortable with people who have something to draw on—the recovering alcoholic, people who have been through divorce or the death of a child, even people with a criminal history in the past," says Barbara Holtan of Tressler-Lutheran Services in Pennsylvania. Her agency, which has focused on special-needs adoption, placed three siblings with Sam, who's a quadriplegic, and his wife Sarah. Observes Holtan: "If anybody knows how to get community resources, they do. They know what patience is and what long-term commitment is. We take each person as he comes."

MILITARY FAMILIES AND AGENCIES

For military families the biggest adoption hurdle often comes from the transiency of their military life. A couple may apply to an agency for a child, only to find themselves put on hold for an orientation or home study because the military spouse is away from home. Or a couple may wait on a list for service, get near the top, and then find that orders for a change of assignment have come through. At the next stop they have to start from scratch.

Moving around makes it tough to find an agency to perform even the basics. You'll want to do some serious shopping, exploring how each agency's process works. Your goal is to find an agency with a broad search capability that is willing to expedite or tailor its process to meet your particular needs.

Here are some strategies that may help:

- Tell your commanding officer that you are adopting and address your need to stay in place longer than usual.
- Explore the possibility of tapping into an agency that places in several states or networks with other agencies around the country.
- Try to find an agency that has a good reputation for placing children quickly.
- See if the adoption agency will process you in stages without penalizing you. At Catholic Charities in Richmond, observed adoption coordinator Barbara Smith, "our big problem with naval families is that the husband will go out to sea. So we start the home study and then pick it up as soon as the husband comes back."

- Be sure that the agency understands how the interstate compact on the placement of children works. Even if you're overseas, families living on military installations can adopt children from the U.S. because U.S. military bases are considered American soil. The interstate compact will be arranged through the state where your child resides and the state of your legal residence.
- Even when your spouse is away from home, keep him or her involved in the adoption process. Are there forms that can be completed while at sea or an autobiography that can be written? Is there other paperwork, such as fingerprinting, that can be accomplished?
- If orders to move do come through and an adoption seems likely, apply for a compassionate stay. *Air Force Times* reports that "every service allows for a delay or change of orders on compassionate grounds in adoption cases."[2]
- If you are interested in a special needs child, identify yourself to a nearby adoption exchange. Some exchanges recruit families on military bases.
- If you know that you're moving, find out about the adoption resources in the area you are relocating to *before you even get there.* Perhaps an agency, if it understands your particular circumstances, will permit you to make an application before you arrive. If not, file your application as you unpack.
- If you are contemplating a foreign adoption, present your situation to the foreign source or agency at the outset and see what arrangements can be worked out with them.

- If you are seeking to adopt an infant, look into the possibility of independent adoption (see chapter 3)

For an excellent overview, consult the booklet *You Can Adopt: A Guide for Military Families* (available from the **Adoption Exchange Association**; see appendix A). In addition to the national adoption support organizations, the Military Family Resource Center in Arlington, Virginia, and the National Military Family Association in Alexandria, Virginia, can help.

FEES

Most public agencies charge no fee for adoption services. Private agencies usually do, although they may reduce or waive their fees when families adopt waiting children. Fees for different programs within an agency often vary.

Some private agencies have a set fee, which might range from ten thousand to upwards of twenty thousand dollars for the adoption of a Caucasian infant. Other agencies have separate charges for various services: application, home study, agency or placement fee, staff travel, foster care, and post-placement supervision, for example.

Some agencies determine their fee on a sliding scale, based on a family's income. Sliding-scale fees often have a set minimum and maximum. You will find that fees vary widely around the country. While some states set ceilings on the fees that agencies can charge, others do not. At some agencies, when you are adopting a healthy infant, you may be asked to pay the birth mother's medical and living expenses in addition to various agency fees for its services. If you are adopting from abroad, you will be paying the fees of the agency in the

U.S. whose program you sign on with and, most likely, those of its counterpart abroad. If there is a local or networking agency, there will be additional expenses. (For a full discussion, see chapter 6.)

Be sure that you get a careful written breakdown of an agency's fees, establishing what is—and is not—included. You'll also want to know what additional expenses you could incur if a placement should fall through. Some agencies also offer prospective adoptive parents the opportunity to purchase adoption insurance that reimburses them for expenses incurred if an adoptive placement falls through.

The legal fees for the finalization of the adoption in court are usually separate.

CONTACTING AN AGENCY ABOUT A U.S. ADOPTION

Learning about agencies involves evaluating them and exploring the types of programs they offer. Ideally you should be able to find several local agencies that provide different kinds of services, and then select the one that most closely fits your needs. But that is not the reality of adoption. The type of child that you seek to parent may involve your waiting for a period of time with a local agency. Finding an agency that meets your needs and is able to work with you may take some searching. If you live in a state like Alaska, your choice of *local* agencies to contact will be limited to the public agency and a handful of private agencies. If you live in a state like New York, your choices are much greater. Whichever state you reside in, however, you can, if you wish, range beyond your local area to find an agency to work with. The state-by-state listing of agencies in appendix B can help you get started. **Adoptive Families of America** and the state representatives of the **North American Council on Adoptable Children (NACAC)**, in addition to the state directory, can give you up-to-date information. You can also check with the

National Adoption Information Clearinghouse. If you can access the Internet or an online computer service, check out postings on the World Wide Web or adoption message boards.

What happens when you get started? It's possible that your first telephone call to an agency could start and end with disappointment when you're told: "Sorry, we're not taking any applications right now"; "Sorry, our next intake meeting is two months away"; or even "Sorry, we don't place children." There are children who need homes, so persevere. Don't be put off by an agency's perfunctory first responses. Observes adoption advocate Susan Freivalds: "It sometimes feels as if these first put-offs are part of the screening process." Don't give up. Ask questions. When will the agency be taking applications again? Can you put your name down now for that far-off orientation meeting? Any chance that they'd move up the date? Recalled one adoptive parent who successfully adopted an infant through an agency: "You can't be frightened by the agencies. You have to be persistent to become an adoptive parent."

If you are interested in adopting an infant, particularly a white infant, find out what types of infant-placement programs the agency has. While there are still some traditional agencies that select the adoptive parents for infants, the overwhelming majority now allow the birth parents to select their child's parents from a pool of waiting adoptive parents. With a direct placement the agency is therefore always working with a number of prospective adoptive parents but may "open or close the intake" of them depending upon how many birth parents it is currently serving. Other agencies have parent-initiated programs: the agency provides counseling to adoptive parents but then asks them to search directly—through the circulating of résumés or advertising in newspapers—for birth parents. And many today have both.

Surprising as it may seem, some agencies have discouraged people who are considering an older child. One hotline for an adoptive parents' group received calls from people who had been told by a local pubic agency that there were no older children needing adoption. This agency did not refer callers to the state photolisting book, which included descriptions and photos of waiting children. If you are interested in an older child, insist on coming into the agency, talking with them, and looking at the state's, not just the agency's, listing of waiting children. If you are getting the brush-off from a worker, insist on talking with the adoption supervisor. If the agency informs you that it doesn't serve families seeking waiting children, ask for a referral to an agency that does. *Don't let an agency simply tell you that there are no children.*

Be sure that you pin down the workers at an agency about its waiting list. How does the agency determine who may file an application? Is the waiting list for a child placement or for a home study? As will become clear in later chapters, having a completed home study opens doors to finding children. Unless you are specifically waiting for one of this agency's children, make it clear that you have a strong interest in a home study. It may serve as your passport.

From your telephone inquiries and from the brochures that the adoption agencies provide, you can also get a sense of an agency's "style." Some agencies handle the whole adoption process—walking you through it step by step, prescribing what's to be done when. Others are much more casual, expecting you to take the initiative and to inform yourself about procedures and deadlines, but offering help when called upon. You'll need to screen the agencies just as much as they do you.

GETTING ORIENTED

Most agencies begin the adoption process with an orientation meeting. An agency may hold orientations once a year, once a month, when it has several interested applicants, or when it has social workers free to do home studies. Orientation meetings offer a chance for the agency to provide you with information about adoption, about its policies, and the whole process.

Typically you'll be asked to come to the agency's office for a group meeting, where you'll be apprised in a few hours of the adoption basics. But there are variants: one Vermont agency, which places newborns and babies, starts prospective adopters off with a weekend retreat at a bed-and-breakfast where they are immersed in the ins and outs of infant adoptions. Agencies accepting applications nationwide from families for infant-placement programs often ask them to fly in for an intensive orientation. Still others will teleconference with interested families in lieu of attending an adoption meeting. And some will take their orientation program on the road, reaching out to families by offering informational meetings at various sites around the country.

The orientation meeting is also a notorious part of the self-selection process in adoption. People may attend a meeting, walk away discouraged, and decide that they can't adopt or that the process is too cumbersome.

Consider the very different experiences that one prospective adoptive parent had at two New York City agencies. The group that met at one agency was rather diverse—a few white couples, some Hispanic women, some older black women, and some young black couples. Two social workers from the agency welcomed the group and began listing the agency's requirements. Although New York State had very few requirements for adoption, this agency had many. It had rules about the age gap between parents and children. It had rules that "you cannot share a room with the child if it is over a year old" and a rule that "children of opposite sexes may not share a room," whatever their ages. The social worker did not make clear to the group that these were her agency's rules only—that the same restrictions might not exist at another agency. She then talked about the children served by the agency and made clear that infants were a "rare breed." Although New York State expects the agency to show prospective adopters a copy of the New York State photolisting books, this worker announced: "I didn't bring the New York State books because it becomes very confusing. I brought a sampling of the children listed. These children happen to be ours." So the group saw photos of perhaps thirty children, not the several hundred typically featured in the state's book.

After the meeting the group examined the photographs and profiles of the children for whom the agency was currently seeking adoptive parents. A young black couple was dismayed to hear "no infants." An Hispanic woman, who wanted a school-aged girl, was concerned that most of the children pictured were boys. If these were all the children needing adoption, she was out of luck. Another woman commented that there were only photographs of thirty children and there were at least thirty people in the room. There clearly were not enough children to go around. A single black woman in her fifties who had a grown son concluded that adopting an eight-year-old was impossible since the worker had asserted that there could be no more than a forty-year age span between parent and child. So most of the group left, convinced that the kind of adoption they wanted was out of the question.

Sound familiar? Perhaps you've had the same experience. What would have happened if you stepped into the orientation session of another local agency, which prides itself on its outreach program? This agency's social worker, herself an adoptive parent, informed the group that the agency had a small number of children to place but she considered all of the state's waiting children hers. To prove her point, she had circulated the New York State photolisting books before the meeting began. She told the group: "You go through the books and ask to have your home study sent out." She promised that every time families pursuing an adoption met with their social worker, they'd look at the photo books because "every two weeks there are thirty new kids" in the state's photolisting book. There might be six hundred new kids featured in the next year."

She tackled the question of infants head-on: "What does it mean that you want a baby? Do you want a newborn? A child in diapers?" By her second definition, a two-year-old could still be a baby. She asked another caseworker, the mother of a recently adopted teenager, to talk. The mother said: "My son needs to be the baby. This is a fifteen-year-old who needs to be cuddled and who likes to sit on my lap. He's Swiss cheese, all full of holes that need to be filled up." So much for babyhood and diapers. "Expand your horizons," both workers urged.

During this orientation prospective parents learned about adoption today. But they also learned much more about the spirit they would need to go on, whether with this agency or elsewhere. "If you definitely want to adopt," the agency worker told them, "you'll find the way. There's a push. If you want it, you'll do it." Many of the people who attended this meeting would not work with this agency—some wanted infants (and would probably pursue an independent adoption); some wanted to consider an intercountry adoption (and were referred to other local agencies with special programs); others were not ready. All left with a much clearer understanding of the adoption process.

Agencies are not all alike. You must choose with great care. The agency that promises to do your home study the soonest may not be the best choice for you. Examine the agency and its practices carefully before you commit yourself. What is its philosophy towards adoptive parents, adoptees, and birth parents? Is it contemporary in its thinking? Is its recommended reading list current? What's the last adoption-related book the caseworker read? What national organizations is it affiliated with? Be sure you understand how the agency—or a specific program—works: will there be a direct placement, where the agency draws upon its own pool of adoptable children or birth parents, or is there a networking process in which the agency turns to others to facilitate the placement?

Can you talk with people who've adopted through the agency? Advises Ernesto Loperena of the New York Council on Adoptable Children: "You should always look for other adoptive parents who have been through the experience to find out whether they were able to get good, decent service. Don't just rely on what the agency says." Singles will want to be especially clear on how amenable the agency is to working with them. Be sure to ask other singles who used the agency how long their adoption process took.

If you are hoping to accomplish the adoption of an infant born in the United States, examine the agency's programs carefully. How are birth parents located? Does the agency or the prospective adoptive parents find them? If the agency assists the birth mother in selecting an adoptive family by presenting to her profiles of applicants, how extensive is the pool they proffer? If the agency asks you to seek out birth parents, will its staff assist in résumé preparation or screen birth parents? What counseling services does the agency provide to its clients? If a birth parent needs financial assistance or housing during the pregnancy, what assistance—if any—will the agency offer?

You also need to explore the agency's policies toward birth parents and confidentiality. Most agencies now foster some contact among birth families, adoptive parents, and adoptees. At some agencies birth parents select the adoptive parents, meet with them before the birth, and exchange full identifying information (last names, first names, addresses). They are encouraged to share the birth experience together and to think about the ongoing relationship—communicating through letters and photos, talking by telephone, and visiting during the year. At other agencies, however, birth parents pick the adoptive parents through the review of non-identifying information, meet with them on a first-name basis only, and communicate with them indirectly after the birth, with the agency typically serving as the intermediary. You'll want to do some reading about open adoption at the outset (see chapter 4 for a fuller discussion) and ask basic questions: What do you mean by open adoption? How many open adoptions have you done? What kind of information is shared between birth parents and adoptive parents? What do the birth parents decide? What do the adoptive parents decide?

Find out the details about the selection process itself. Do the birth parents choose adoptive parents from *all* adoptive parents working with the agency, or does the agency preselect a handful? Even the most progressive agencies sometimes exercise control in this area of the process. In the agency's experience, are there any families who tend to wait longer? Why?

If you choose an agency that practices semi-open adoptions, be sure that you inquire about the agency's policy towards opening up an adoption further in the years ahead. Kathleen Silber, coauthor of *Children of Open Adoption*, reports that at one agency "if a letter came through with identifying information, the worker would black it out so that the people could not open up the adoption." You don't want to be caught in a situation where the agency will not allow direct contact between families even if both of you are interested.

Try to attend the orientations of several agencies. "It drives me crazy that people will shop for days for a color television, but when it comes to adoption, they just wander into the first door or pick the first name in the phone book," says James L. Gritter, author of *The Spirit of Open Adoption*. He recommends exploring the workers' own attitudes toward adoption. What would the worker do, for example, if she were pregnant and eighteen? What would the worker do if she were thirty and infertile? Says Gritter: "You're going to have to ask yourself—Is this person square with me? Can I trust this person to join me in designing this life-altering event? There are going to be some hair-raising times along the way, and I need a rock." Observes Dawn Smith-Pliner of Friends in Adoption: "People are paying someone for their services. Yet they feel so vulnerable, they become namby-pamby. I say, 'Wait a minute, where is your backbone?' If you don't like the social worker who does your home study, ask for another. Know your rights. Be steadfast in what you want. Adoption is not a compromising endeavor."[3]

The time you take at the outset will not only help you determine whether the agency is right for you, but may help the home study process that follows go more smoothly.

BASIC QUESTIONS TO ASK AN AGENCY

Agencies will ask you many questions during the adoption process. Before you commit yourself to any agency, however, you'll want to pose some basic questions as well.

Tell me about your requirements for adoptive parents.

- Are there age, income, or other criteria?
- What are your medical requirements for applicants? If a family is applying for an infant, must they present evidence of a fertility problem?
- Do you have religious restrictions?
- Do you have residency restrictions?
- Can you place out of state?
- Do you have a minimum income requirement?
- What is your policy on divorce?
- What is your policy on single parents? Have you placed children with singles? What type of children have you placed with singles?

Tell me about the guidelines you use if the prospective adoptive parents already have children.

- Is there a maximum number of children a family may already have prior to adoption?
- Will you place a child older than the oldest in the family? Same age as another in the family?
- Do you place infants in homes where there are already children?

Tell me about your agency.

- What are your fees? Any reductions for sibling groups?
- How many adoptive parents are waiting at this time for a placement?
- How many, and what kinds of, legally free children are in your agency's caseload?
- How many children did your agency place in adoptive homes last year?
- What were the characteristics of the children placed?
- Does the agency place children in prospective adoptive homes as foster children?
- How do you feel about working in a partnership with another agency to bring about an adoption?
- How many children from outside the agency, the county, or the state were placed with families studied by your agency?
- What professionals will be available to me, such as social workers, counselors, or attorneys for help with the adoption process?
- What are the services you provide to families for the *lifetime* of an adoption? Do you offer any services to your clients after the adoption has been finalized?
- What types of counseling services and support groups are made available to adoptive parents? To birth parents? To adoptees?
- What is your grievance process if I feel that I am not treated fairly? What kind of recourse do I have?

Tell me about the adoption process at your agency for adopting healthy infants.

- Who can adopt infants at your agency?
- In infant adoptions, what role do birth parents play in the selection of the adoptive parents? What role does the agency worker play?

Tell me about your agency's home study process.

- Could you briefly describe your home study? Do you offer group home studies? (See chapter 7 for a full discussion of home studies.)
- What is the estimated wait between application and start of home study for the waiting child? for the healthy infant?
- How long will it probably take to complete a home study?
- Will you do a home study for an intercountry adoption?
- Will you do a home study for an independent adoption? Will you provide counseling to me or to birth parents?
- Will you do a home study for single applicants?
- What paperwork do adoptive parents do in the preparation of the home study?
- Can I see a copy of the home study after it is complete?
- Will you forward copies of a home study to another agency? How often? Do you restrict the number of times you'll send out the home study? If I choose to work with another agency after the home study has been completed, can I take the home study with me?
- How long will it probably take your agency to assign a child after a home study is approved? (Ask

this question if the agency expects to place *its* children with you.)

Tell me about your agency's practices and policies.

- What type of background information do you share about individual children? Do you practice "full disclosure"? If so, what does it mean? What do you *not* disclose?
- If the child is in foster care, can the adoptive parents correspond, talk or meet with the foster parents? Can adoptive parents visit a child in its foster home? How do you feel about ongoing contact?
- How involved is your agency in exploring adoption subsidies that are offered by the local, state, or federal government? Do you help families to apply for them? Can families apply for them for their children after the adoption?
- What happens if I turn down a child who's offered to me? What's the agency's policy about future placements?

Tell me about your agency's guidelines for an open adoption.

- What type of contact does your agency encourage between birth parents, adoptive parents, and adoptees?
- Have you opened up any closed adoptions? Would the agency initiate contact and follow through if one of the parties had a specific reason for it to take place? What would be your policy, for example, if we decided we wanted to exchange letters with the birth parents? If we later decided to share full identifying information, would we be allowed to do that? What restrictions do you place?

INQUIRING ABOUT AN AGENCY'S REPUTATION

When Hannah and Joe Scapiti picked up their newborn son at the adoption agency, they also paid the agency seven thousand dollars to cover various fees and medical expenses. They knew that during the time after placement they would be uneasy that the birth parents could legally change their minds. But that, it turned out, was the easy part of this adoption. Over the next year, their relationship with the agency rapidly soured as they were asked to pay an additional four thousand dollars for medical bills, but were given no opportunity to examine them or see an itemized listing of expenses. They discovered that basic adoption paperwork had never been completed and were threatened by the agency director. ("I would hate to get the birth mother involved." "Are you refusing to meet with me? After all, I do have custody of your son.") With the help of an attorney they hired to represent their interests, Hannah and Joe eventually completed their son's adoption, but the bitter aftertaste remains. "We put our family's lives in the agency's hands," says Hannah. "Where are the authorities responsible for overseeing agencies?"

Hopefully, your child's adoption will proceed without a hitch, but what happens if it doesn't? Where can you turn? And how can you avoid potential problems by checking into an agency's reputation before you ever sign on?

Start with the licensing agency, sometimes referred to as the regulatory or certification agency, of your state. Find out if the agency has a license (you can ask to see a copy) and for what services the agency is licensed. Advises a Wisconsin licensing supervisor: "You can call and ask for information about an agency's track record, whether the agency's been cited for any licensing violations, and whether the licensing office has had any complaints. There is a tremendous volume of information available at the licensing agency that adoptive parents never ask for." (Some states will post adoption licensing information on a website.) Request also a copy of the state's rules governing agencies so that you understand what practices violate your state's laws.

You should also speak with the adoption specialist in your state's department of social services (see the state-by-state directory in appendix B). "A lot of the calls and complaints about agencies really don't have anything to do with whether an agency is violating a statute," observed Robert DeNardo of the Minnesota Department of Human Services. "But they have a lot to do with poor agency practice—all the way from poor customer relations, instances of staff rudeness, and high-handed behavior." While the department may not have done anything about a particular complaint, staff members will probably share the information they have with you. Inquiries and complaints can also be filed with your state's Attorney General's office, although these are sometimes referred back to the licensing or adoption unit for investigation. If your state or metropolitan area has a Department of Consumer Affairs, you might check whether they handle complaints.

If you're planning an interstate or intercountry adoption, you can contact the interstate compact administrator in your state's department of public welfare. The compact administrator oversees interstate placements (see chapter 8) and may have worked with your agency. You can also try speaking with the staff person who handles adoptions at the nearest office of the Immigration and Naturalization Service. Be sure to check also with national and local adoptive-parent support organizations about the reputations of agencies. **Adoptive Families of America,** for example, has published articles in its magazine about agencies that have gotten into trouble with their states. "We shared with prospective adopters information about a local agency that started charging all the people on its waiting list for telephone calls made by the agency to Colombia each month," recalls Cheryl Simons of the Latin America Parents Association in New York.

If you plan to use an agency as a springboard to working with another agency elsewhere, you'll want to know about its reputation for networking. Observes Ernesto Loperena of COAC: "Some agencies are good at internal or state stuff, but not at interstate. If that's what you're contemplating, you need to find that out up front."

IDENTIFIED OR DESIGNATED ADOPTION

Ellen and Nick Lyons live in Connecticut. When they decided to adopt a baby, several agencies encouraged them to consider a special service they provided: identified adoption.

In identified adoption, which is also referred to as "designated adoption," "parent-initiated adoption," or "networking" adoption, prospective adoptive parents who have "identified" a particular birth parent approach an agency for counseling and home study services. (*Identified adoption* is a misnomer since adoptive parents and birth parents may not know full identifying information about each other and may even work through an intermediary. Rather it describes the link between a particular set of birth parents and prospective adoptive parents.)

In identified adoption the prospective adoptive parents, not the agency, "find" the birth parents and put the adoption together with the birth parents. It is a hybrid, combining features characteristic of independent placements with those of more traditional agency adoptions. Prospective adoptive parents have the chance to begin the adoption process immediately—rather than wait on an agency list for a placement or be part of an agency pool of waiting adoptive parents that birth parents consider when they make their adoption plans—and exercise greater control over what happens. Agency programs often provide that the birth mother will be offered counseling and that its staff will arrange for prenatal care and delivery, housing, or other needed services.

Identified adoption can play a critical role in states that ban independent adoptions or third-party non-agency involvement, or require a home study by a licensed agency prior to an independent placement. It's also attractive to adoptive parents in states where the law allows the birth parents to change their minds for several weeks or even months after the placement in an independent adoption, but permits a shorter revocation period if an agency handles the adoption. For birth parents, identified adoption often gives them greater control over the adoption process than might be offered by their local agencies. They have the assurance as well that a licensed agency is involved and that counseling services are available to them.

While identified adoption is most commonly associated with newborn placements, it can happen in older child adoptions if the agency agrees to the plan. "The agency becomes more of a facilitator in identified adoption," points out adoption specialist Kristina A. Backhaus. "I'm the person who makes sure that all requirements and regulations are met, while the birth parents and adoptive family make sure the placement fits their needs." If the birth mother resides elsewhere in the state, or another state, the agency working with the couple may help arrange for the birth mother to receive counseling from another agency and may be involved in coordinating the paperwork of the people at the other end.

In Ellen and Nick's case they attended orientations about identified adoption at several agencies. "It's really important that you have a good fit," says Ellen. "If you choose well, your agency will not only do your home study but will guide you through the morass of state regulations. But you also have to understand the rules, and you've got to handle the negotiations with the birth mother yourself." She and Nick prepared a letter describing their adoption hopes, printed one hundred and fifty copies, and duplicated photos of themselves with their son Jonathan. But their plans to send the letter out to friends and colleagues around the country never got off the ground. "It was just magic," recalls Ellen. A friend who worked for Planned Parenthood in another state called to say that a very pregnant young woman had come into the office to discuss adoption. A description of Ellen and Nick was hurriedly faxed to her, they talked by phone, then met her and her mother (but without exchanging last names), and two weeks later the baby was born. "The agency provided comfort," says Ellen. "It was tremendously valuable hearing the social worker say 'I've done three like this.'"

That's not to say there weren't any hassles. The hospital where the baby was born did not permit either the birth mother or the adoptive parents to visit the infant, and a third party had to carry the baby out of the hospital. For Ellen and Nick the wait was mercifully short, but that's often not the case. Families may be aware of a potential child several months in advance and experience an agonizing wait. Recalls one adoptive parent: "It was torturous. It was like a pregnancy of sorts and the bonding began before birth."

There are other drawbacks to the identified adoption approach. Although every case is different, the costs can be high. Identified adoption also has the risks—both financial and emotional—that independent placement adoption incurs. Says Backhaus: "We had one family that had three placements that didn't go through. All three birth mothers initially said that they wanted to go ahead with the adoption, and all three birth mothers changed their minds within forty-eight hours of the birth." Backhaus estimates that as many as half of the families who've worked with her agency on an identified adoption had a potential adoptive placement that didn't work out. And she's clear about families' financial vulnerability: "We have no way to get the money back. We can't act like a bill collector."

Since many agencies now offer identified, designated, parent-initiated, or networking adoption as one of their adoption services, you'll want to ask some questions before you sign on.

- How long has the program existed?
- How many intrastate and interstate identified adoptions has the agency done? (To get a sense, you can also ask your state's interstate compact administrator which agencies' paperwork are handled most often and if there have been any problems.)
- What services does the agency provide?
- What are the possible expenses for this type of adoption?
- Can the agency break down its fees for you? (For a full breakdown of potential expenses in an independent adoption, see chapter 3.) If an identified adoption is interstate, potential expenses include two agency fees, attorneys' fees, medical expenses, living expenses, and transportation costs.
- If a prospective adoption falls through, is there an additional fee for the next potential placement?
- How does the agency handle the birth mother's expenses?
- Is there an escrow account set up?
- Will the baby need to be in foster care prior to placement?

- If it is your preference, will the agency permit direct-from-hospital placement?
- What happens if the adoptive parents decide not to go through with the placement because the baby is born with a medical problem?

It's critical that both you and the agency understand state law. In some states, for example, it's illegal for any money to go directly from the adoptive family to the birth family or to their representative. Everything has to go through the agency, and the agency in turn has to provide an accounting to the court. There are also regulations governing termination of parental rights. Observes Backhaus: "I spend the majority of my time trying to figure out whether certain situations will meet state regulations and making sure that we're not going to cause a problem for the birth mother in another state."

LEGAL RISK ADOPTION

To move children more quickly into permanent homes, agencies employ another kind of placement: legal risk adoption, sometimes called foster/adoption. A family agrees to take a child—one whose permanent plan is expected to be adoption—into their home as a foster child, while the sometimes lengthy legal process goes on.

Hillary was placed with her adoptive parents at two months, but her adoption was not finalized until she was nearly four years old. Explains her adoptive mother:

Hillary's mother was a patient in a mental institution. The mother's condition had been caused by a childhood fall and she had been admitted to the institution by her mother, who had many children and who couldn't handle her daughter's injury. She'd been there for eighteen years and had become pregnant. The agency did not know who the father was. They had to track down the mother's relatives to notify them about the grandchild and to get their release. Even if the agency failed to find the relatives (they had not visited her in the eighteen years), it would still take time.

There was a lot of red tape involved in Hillary's adoption. The agency went through a long search for the mother's family, and over the years there was also a switch in social workers. Although Hillary's mother knew from the day that Hillary arrived that she was likely to stay, "every once in a while we'd see a report on television where a family had to give a child back. And we'd get very nervous."

Legal risk adoptions often involve the placement of younger children, even infants and toddlers, in adoptive families. Children have the chance to get into their permanent homes faster; parents have the chance to raise their children from infancy or toddlerhood. But legal risk adoption brings with it emotional strain. Said one parent about the legal risk experience: "It's living on an emotional roller coaster. One day you're high—she's ours. The next day, reality—another court delay. How do you cope with that reality?"

Since legal risk placements begin as foster care arrangements, birth parents have the right to visit with their children in their new homes or at the agency. There is a real risk that the birth parents will decide not to relinquish the child. It can and does happen. Bonnie O'Connor became the mother of a two-year-old boy through a legal risk placement. His mother had brought him to the agency saying that she wanted to relinquish her parental rights voluntarily since she had been separated from his father and the father had recently been killed in an auto accident. Recalls Bonnie: "He fit right into our lives. Days and weeks passed. His birth mother never asked to visit him and she remained firm in her decision." After four months of counseling, his mother set a date with the agency to sign the relinquishment papers. That day arrived, but his mother didn't keep her appointment. "A little later in the day," Bonnie remembers, "she called the social worker and said that she wanted to see her son. She was beginning to doubt whether she could follow through on her decision to surrender him." The visits began, and over the next few weeks she visited frequently. Finally his birth mother took him home. "Having him leave was devastating for us and we missed him tremendously," says Bonnie. "I think about him often and wonder how they are doing." Bonnie and her husband went on to adopt four other children but the pain of forming an attachment to, and then losing, one child is still there.

Abby Elkins is a single parent who's been raising Jason, now two, since he was a month old. The agency that placed Jason, a premature infant who had been exposed prenatally to cocaine, felt there was little risk involved in the adoption because his mother had disappeared from the hospital shortly after his cesarean birth and hadn't returned for any medical follow-up. But when Jason was seven weeks old, his mother returned to the hospital to challenge the adoption and claim him. Although the court has never granted the birth mother custody, her parental rights have also not been terminated and the battle drags on. Says Abby: "The longer it goes on, the more crazy it is. I can't believe that this child would be better off with this mother after two years. At the last court hearing she couldn't remember the address of her home." Adds Abby, "What scares me most is the thought 'what if she gets custody and he's neglected and beaten when he's with her?'"

If your agency offers you a legal risk placement, be sure to elicit as much information as possible. What were the circumstances of the child's abandonment? What kind of risk are you talking about? Risks can be of varying degrees, and some agencies will rank them low to high. What is known of the birth parents or the immediate family? What type of involvement and contact have there been? How many releases have been signed? When is the legal case likely to be presented to the court? Ernesto Loperena warns that "agencies sometimes use the prospective adoptive parents as leverage in court" to force the birth parents or judge to make a decision. In situations where the birth mother is involved, says Loperena, "the court tends to lean over backwards to make sure that the mother has been given every chance."

How much risk do you feel you can handle? Even with a low-risk situation the court case can drag on, or something unexpected can happen. Are you willing to live in a state of limbo? Says Loperena: "I caution people about legal risk adoptions. I have seen the emotional ups and downs, the peaks and valleys, that families go through. Although the odds with legal risk adoption may be in your favor, somebody has to be in that percentage of families where the child is reunited with the biological mom."

FOSTER PARENT ADOPTION

The majority of children who enter foster care will return to their families or relatives after a period of time. Yet many children begin their lives in their adoptive homes as foster children. "There is no longer a hard-and-fast distinction between foster parents and adoptive parents," says New York social worker Mary Helen Evans, who worked for many years in foster care. "Every foster parent is a potential adoptive parent, and foster parents need to think about adoption before the agency comes to them to discuss adoption." In fact some agencies process prospective adoptive parents and foster parents together. But foster parents must also be prepared to see children go home to their first family and provide them with the necessary emotional support.

Foster parents are often given the opportunity to adopt a foster child, particularly if the child has been living in their home for an extended period of time. Agencies will ask the foster parents if they would like to adopt their foster child when he is freed for adoption. But foster parents may have to push the agency to make a permanent plan for their foster child or to let them adopt that particular child.

If you are interested in adopting a foster child in your care, adoption social worker Debra Smith counsels:

> *The central issue in changing from the role of foster parent to that of an adoptive parent is that of redefining your* attachment *to the child that came about through daily living as a full lifetime* commitment. *Are you ready, willing, and able to see this child through to adulthood and to afford him or her all of the opportunities—and burdens—that being a member of your family entails? Can you see this child being a part of your life long into the future?*[4]

Talk first with the agency responsible for your child. You should be asking questions right along about the status of the child and the long-range plan for his future. Under federal law you must receive notice of—and the opportunities to be heard at—hearings or reviews regarding your foster child's status. Find out also what rights you have under county or state law. Under your state's laws, you may have the right as a foster parent to be considered as the first adoptive parent if the child has been in your home for a specific period of time. You might have standing in court, and the right to initiate petitions for termination of parental rights, guardianship, or other needs of the child as you perceive them.

When your caseworker indicates that the agency is thinking of terminating parenting rights, be sure to indicate your interest immediately, both verbally *and in writing* in becoming an adoptive parent. Don't be afraid to be assertive in your request. If you feel that your interest is not being given proper consideration, go up the line beyond your particular agency worker, to the supervisor and even the administrator of the agency. If you wish to be included in the court hearings regarding this child, ask whether you have the right. If so, find out if you can be represented by an attorney if you wish.

You'll want to inquire about subsidies for your child and your ability to get them. Sometimes agency workers will try to dissuade foster families from applying for subsidies, suggesting that there are other prospective adopters interested in the child who don't need them. If you feel that your child may be eligible for a subsidy, don't hesitate to ask for it. You'll also want to push for a full disclosure to you of your child's medical and background history. Even though you've had the child living with you for a period of time and know him well, there may be aspects of his family history that were not shared with you at the time he came into your care.

You'll probably want to link up with a local adoptive-parent or foster-parent support group. Another resource is the **National Foster Parent Association** (see appendix A). Finally, if you don't want to be considered as the adoptive parent of your foster child, speak up. This needs to be known by your worker in planning for the child.

CONTACTING U.S. AGENCIES ABOUT INTERCOUNTRY ADOPTION

Some agencies in the United States have developed intercountry adoption programs. Of these agencies, some place children only with families who reside within a certain geographic area, while others accept applicants from throughout the United States (for a full discussion, see chapter 6).

An agency may have intercountry adoption programs for several different countries. Each program may have different requirements. South Korea, for example, required that the agency placing the child do both the pre- and postplacement supervision. While an agency like Holt International Children's Services in Eugene, Oregon, might place children from Thailand in many states by accepting referrals from a local agency, it has placed South Korean children only in states where it is licensed.

As you learn about agency programs, you are likely to discover that you are ineligible for some agency programs but not others. It sometimes takes singles and older couples more time to find the right program. If you don't meet the requirements of your local agency's intercountry program, it just means that you will need to contact an agency outside your immediate area that is able to make a referral through a local agency.

The National Adoption Information Clearinghouse, Adoptive Families of America and the **Joint Council on International Children's Services** (see appendix A) can direct you to agencies and the most current information. The *Report on Intercountry Adoption*, produced by the **International Concerns for Children** (see appendix A) is a compendium of intercountry adoption information; it lists adoption programs country by country and tries to keep people informed through its annual volume and updates.

In most states, whether or not you choose to work with an agency that has an intercountry adoption program, you will need to work with an adoption agency in order to complete an intercountry adoption. The United States Immigration and Naturalization Service requires that all individuals who bring a child into the country for the purpose of adoption submit a home study. In some states you may be able to have a certified social worker do your study, but in most you will need to have an agency undertake it. When you approach an agency, explain that you are seeking an intercountry adoption. Often an agency that has a religious requirement for placing its own children can waive this requirement if you make it clear that you need their help in completing an intercountry adoption. Some agencies may have restrictions, however, about the types of foreign sources they will work with, or may require that the agency that will be placing the child make a formal request for their assistance.

TAKING YOUR BEARINGS

As you think about the type of child you hope to parent, you will begin the process of getting to know agencies and how they work. As you learn about various adoption options, you will discover that adoption involves linkages, communication, and coordination between people and organizations. Let's sum up what you can expect as you interface with one or several agencies:

1. Your phone calls, letters, web-searching, or speaking with people leads to
2. Your contacting one or several agencies and attending a general information meeting or participating in a teleconference
3. You learn about options at the agency that may include:
   - infant adoption programs for domestic-born children
   - special-needs, waiting-child or minority programs
   - foster/adopt, legal risk or foster parenting programs
   - intercountry adoption programs
   - open adoption programs
4. As a result of your orientation, you receive an application packet

5. Your contact with the agency continues and you submit paperwork that may include medical data, letters of reference, and other descriptive material about yourself
6. The agency's home study process begins
7. Eventually you are offered the opportunity to parent a child. How the child referral and placement process works will be determined by the type of child you choose to parent.

After your child enters your home, the agency is likely to follow up on the placement to see how your child is doing.

3

SEARCHING FOR A BABY INDEPENDENTLY

◆

Pat and Gary Pawling contemplated adoption for several months before attending an adoption-orientation class run by a local parent group. When the discussion got around to independent-placement adoption, another couple mentioned that they were running classified advertisements expressing their interest in adopting a newborn in newspapers around the state. The two couples chatted about possibly pooling their resources. Nothing more was said. Pat went home and started compiling a list of newspapers in which she might run such a personal advertisement. A month later the other couple called her. They'd had two responses from birth mothers to their classified ads and both women had already given birth. Were Pat and Gary interested in talking with the birth mother of a day-old boy? They were, and a week later, after contacting an attorney and completing the necessary paperwork, they picked up their new son.

Not all nonrelative independent (non-agency) placements happen like this, but some do. Most independent placements, in fact, involve a stepparent adopting the child of a spouse, or a relative adopting, for example, a niece or nephew. But private infant adoptions, or "direct adoptions," as nonfamilial independent placements are often called, are also common.

THE LEGALITY OF INDEPENDENT ADOPTION

Independent placement is legal in most states, although the laws governing it will vary. Some states impose few or no restrictions on independent placements. Others mandate that a child must be placed for adoption directly by the birth parent with an adoptive parent; intermediaries are forbidden.

Your state department of social services can tell you what is legal in your state. The state-by-state directory in appendix B provides a brief summary. You can also obtain a summary of your state's adoption law from the **National Adoption Information Clearinghouse** (see appendix A). If you live in a state where independent adoption is not permitted or is restricted, find out whether an "identified adoption," a hybrid that mixes features of agency and private adoption (see chapter 2) is possible. If you are considering an independent placement across state lines, you will need to ascertain what is legal in both states and how the interstate compact, which establishes procedures for the transfer of children from one state to another, will be involved. In most states you'll find that birth parents cannot relinquish a child to you before birth and, typically, have the right, for a prescribed period of time, to change their minds.

No doubt as you ponder independent placement you'll be warned about "gray market" adoptions, "black market" adoptions, and baby brokering. These are terms that people have used from time to time in reference to independent adoptions. What do these terms imply? A gray market, as the dictionary defines it, is a market using irregular channels of trade or undercover methods not actually or explicitly illicit and dealing chiefly in scarce materials at excessive prices. The implication drawn by some is that non-agency adoptions are gray market in that they use irregular—that is, non-agency—channels. A black market adoption, technically speaking, involves an illegal market in which goods are sold in violation of price controls or other restrictions. Huge amounts of money are reportedly passed along in trade for babies. Using an intermediary when one is forbidden by state law would also be a black market adoption. Baby brokering also suggests schemes and trading in babies.

As adoption practices evolve, it becomes hard to use these terms meaningfully. How do you refer to an agency placement that charges a very high fee or advertises for birth parents in the classified section of a newspaper? Agency adoption, like independent adoption, can also involve "brokering" if one recognizes that the agency can "act as an agent for others in negotiating contracts for a fee." Independent placement adoption is just what it says: a non-agency placement that results in an adoption whose circumstances adhere to the rules of the state. Some practices smell fishy and may be illegal whether they are handled by individuals or agencies.

DECIDING FOR INDEPENDENT ADOPTION

At age twenty Heather Byrd had tubal surgery and was informed by her gynecologist that birth control was unnecessary because she had medical problems that would not allow her to achieve a pregnancy. Her doctor's assessment was wrong, however, and she became pregnant. "I was very scared as soon as I missed my period, because I knew that I couldn't afford a child and wasn't ready to get married," says Heather.

After deciding against an abortion, Heather called local adoption agencies. "I wanted to know the environment my baby was going to, I wanted to know the people, and I wanted them to know me as a human being," says Heather. "I didn't ever want her to think that she came from bad birth parents. I'm not a druggie, I'm not an alcoholic, I'm going to do my best to get by. I wanted her to feel proud of me and I wanted her to feel proud of her father."

At the agencies she contacted, however, the files were closed and there were rules that birth parents could not meet adoptive parents. So Heather spoke with her gynecologist about her dilemma and learned that he'd recently received a letter from a couple hoping to adopt. "Everything in the letter appealed to me about them," recalls Heather, "except their age—Mike was fifty-seven and Cindy forty-five." She called them up, however, and "as we started talking, it turned out that Cindy had been brought up the way I was and we had similar values. Mike and Cindy were clearly honest, trustworthy, loving people." The couple invited her to their house and while there, Heather asked them the questions she needed answered: What's your background? Any alcoholism? How were you raised? How would you handle my child as a teenager? Are you going to buy your child a car when she's sixteen? How will you discipline? Says Heather: "I wanted to pick a family who would give a child choices, a family where a child could make her decisions right or wrong." Despite Mike and Cindy's age, and the fact that they already had grown children, Heather decided these were the right parents for her child.

For Carrie Sullivan, seventeen, unmarried, and living at home with her parents in a small town, the road to independent adoption was different. Just a few months before, Carrie had given birth to a child. She was struggling to raise that child while attending high school. She had thought that she was practicing birth control, but with the method she chose, she found herself pregnant again. First she delayed telling anyone because she was embarrassed. Then she decided that, for her, abortion was out of the question. So, when she was several months pregnant with the second baby, she told her minister's wife of her problem. She wanted to release the child for adoption, but was adamant that she did not want to approach the local agency; she did not feel comfortable talking about her situation with strangers, particularly when she felt that they might question how she could become pregnant twice in little more than a year.

Said the minister's wife: "Carrie had a fear of interrogation by adults, a fear of sexual questions, a fear that she would have to tell her story to many people. She wanted one person who would be her advocate, whom she could tell what she wanted and when." The minister's wife became that advocate and her intermediary.

Meanwhile, Earl and Alice Addams, a couple who wanted to adopt, had approached a local agency and placed their name on a waiting list for a home study. Through mutual friends, the minister's wife heard that they had been making inquiries about adoption and had been thinking about the possibility of an independent adoption. She contacted them on Carrie's behalf. After Carrie's son was born, Earl and Alice became his parents.

Birth parents may decide to place their children for adoption independently because they want more control over the process. They may feel it is important to select the adoptive parents, to talk with them, and to meet with them, to exchange names and addresses. They may want to know how their children fare after birth and discover that a local agency's policy will not permit contact over the child's lifetime. Many agencies now permit these practices, but others don't. Financial need may also play a role in birth mothers' seeking out independent placement. Some agencies cannot pay medical bills or other expenses, although they may direct a woman to public assistance and other forms of aid. Many states, however, will permit adoptive parents to pay for reasonable expenses in an independent placement. A birth mother may also be reluctant to approach an agency for counseling, fearing that the questions will be intrusive and the social worker will be passing judgment on her. Or the birth mother may have gone for an interview at one agency and been turned off by the person she met.

Adoptive parents may seek out an independent placement because there are waiting lists with local agencies for their varied programs or too many agency restrictions (age, fertility history, length of marriage, and religion are common barriers). Or there may be no suitable agencies in their area. Some adopters may feel strongly that they want to have more information about their child and the birth parents than their local agencies have been willing to provide. Others may desire a more closed—or open—adoption than their local agencies permit. It's even possible that adoptive parents have been planning on an agency adoption, doing all the necessary paperwork, when the opportunity for an independent placement falls into their lap. Ron and Dorothy Sanders chose an independent placement adoption because they wanted to adopt a newborn directly from the hospital, while their local agencies insisted on a period of foster care. Jack and Wendy Wilson adopted their first child through an agency and had planned to put their name on the waiting list for a second, but pursued an independent opportunity instead after a colleague of Jack's happened to hear about a pregnant teen interested in a private adoption. Despite what you may read in the press or hear bandied about, most people who adopt independently are not forced to do so because of their rejection by an agency, but rather choose to because they believe it is most appropriate for them.

Finally, if you want to have direct contact with a birth mother, such an arrangement is quite common in independent adoptions. In fact, some states have laws requiring face-to-face contact between birth and adoptive parents in an independent adoption. For a more complete sense of open adoption's potential in independent placement, see chapter 4.

GETTING PREPARED

If independent placement interests you, your first step will be to understand what is permitted. Here are some basic questions to ask the state social service department or other knowledgeable resource:

- Who can legally place children for adoption in your state or the state where you plan to seek a placement?
- Must you meet directly with the birth parents?
- Can you use an intermediary if you don't wish to have face-to-face contact with the birth parents?
- Can you pay an intermediary, such as an attorney, to locate a child for you?
- Can you advertise your interest in adopting a child in a newspaper?
- What type of parental releases and/or consents must you obtain? How long must the birth parent wait to sign the consent to release after the child's birth?
- What are the waiting periods required for the releases?
- What are the rights of the putative father? (Once you identify a particular child, be sure to ask who the putative father is, where he is now, and whether he's agreed to the adoption plan.)
- Does the state require that adoptive parents and birth parents be of the same religion? Can religious restrictions be waived?

- Does the state require a home study before placement? If so, who can do it?
- Does the state require a fingerprint check or a criminal background check before placement?
- Does the state have a residency requirement?
- What expenses related to the adoption can you legally pay for?

If you are adopting in another state, you will need to find out what is legal there. You must consider the standards of the interstate compact. And if you are considering adopting a child of Native American ancestry, be sure that you understand the regulations of the Indian Child Welfare Act of 1978. This federal law protects the rights of Indian children, families, and tribes. It stipulates that in all foster care, preadoptive and adoptive placements, preference is given, unless there is good cause to the contrary, to placing a child with a member of the child's extended family, other members of the child's tribe, an Indian foster or adoptive family, and an Indian-operated institution. Placements with non-Indian families are considered a last resort. Even if the birth parents are not living on the reservation, and even if they have said that they want you to become the parents, the tribe has the right to intervene in court proceedings and make its own decision. There have been major custody battles around this issue; when the tribes have opposed the placements, the courts have made adoptive parents relinquish their children.

You may also want to explore whether an independent adoption or an identified adoption through an agency (see chapter 2) best suits your situation. Some states permit birth mothers several weeks or months to change their minds when they place a child independently but have a much shorter revocation period when an agency is involved.

As you gather information, you'll want to connect with an adoptive-parent support group. **Families for Private Adoption** (see appendix A) is one group whose members have successfully adopted independently and which has produced an excellent, comprehensive workbook, *Successful Private Adoption!* Although some of the information is geared specifically for Maryland-Virginia-District of Columbia residents, much is of general interest. Check also with the infertility support group **Resolve** (see appendix A). It's also helpful to do some reading about independent adoption. See the reference list in appendix C for suggestions.

Meanwhile, you still have more questions to ask and answer for yourself:

- Do you want to have contact with the birth parents?
- What do you mean by contact? Face to face? Letters? Photographs? Telephone calls?
- Do you want to use an intermediary?
- How much anonymity do you want?
- What questions do you want to ask the birth parents?
- Are there aspects of the birth parents' medical history that concern you such as smoking, drinking, possible drug use?
- What type of counseling have you had? Do you want the birth parents to have had counseling?
- What medical risks are you willing to assume?
- Will you accept a child born with a birth defect?
- What is the state of your savings?
- Can you afford to pay the legitimate pregnancy-related expenses?
- Can you afford the expenses of a cesarean section if it occurs?
- Are you willing to travel to pick up your child?

- Are you willing to live for several weeks in another state if that is necessary?
- Are you willing to bring the birth mother to your state to give birth to her child?
- If you bring a birth mother to your state, what facilities and costs are involved in providing shelter and maintenance for her?
- Whom will you turn to for legal advice?
- Whom will you turn to for both obstetrical and pediatric medical advice?
- How much risk and uncertainty are you willing to live with?

THE RISKS OF INDEPENDENT ADOPTION

"Hope wants the baby back!"

On a sultry summer evening Jeanne and Harvey Hammer got the telephone call every adoptive parent dreads. The sixteen-year-old birth mother of their seven-week-old daughter Rebecca had changed her mind about the placement. "I was hysterical, I was sobbing, I couldn't believe it," says Jeanne, her voice breaking as she remembers the events of a year past. "I was Rebecca's mother," she says softly. For seven weeks she'd loved and cuddled Rebecca, but her state's adoption statutes give birth mothers ninety days to revoke their consent. Jeanne and Harvey had known the risk when they'd brought Rebecca home but they'd made the decision for independent adoption. They tried to fight to keep Rebecca—the local court held a hearing—but the judge told them that the birth mother had an ironclad right to her child. "It was over. I packed a diaper bag full of clothes and formula and put Rebecca's baptismal cap in there with a note," recalls Jeanne. At their attorney's house they returned the baby to Hope.

"This was so horrible to go through," says Jeanne. "I was devastated. I would wake up in the night crying. I knew that I had to grieve, to experience the despair and sorrow." Then there was the anger: "We had this feeling that we were stiffed, that we'd spent thousands of dollars and didn't have a child." Jeanne and Harvey worried how they would ever adopt again when they had just spent so much of their savings. "And we had to grapple with this angry feeling that Hope had used us."

It took months before Jeanne and Harvey felt strong enough to consider adoption again. When her sister met a young woman interested in adoption, Jeanne insisted that the birth mother go for counseling, that the adoption be handled by an agency as an identified adoption, and that the young woman also be represented by an attorney. "I believe in private adoption, but for my own peace of mind the second time around," says Jeanne, "I insisted on an identified adoption with the birth mother receiving counseling at the agency. I couldn't go through ninety days of wondering whether we'd get a phone call demanding the baby back." This time the adoption went without a hitch, and Jeanne was even present for their baby's birth. Still there are the strong memories of Rebecca. "We lost our first daughter," she says. "I wonder and worry about her. We had two children; now we only have one."

Independent placements sometimes unravel. The possibility of disappointment with independent adoption begins early. You may hear of a woman in her third month of pregnancy who is thinking about surrendering a child for adoption. Recalls one adoptive mother: "Before Sarah's adoption came through, we had other leads; they always seemed like sure things, and then they would fall apart." You will have to wait out the pregnancy realizing that the birth parents may indeed change their minds either before or after the child is born. Recalls Audrey: "The baby was born. We had the crib sitting by the bed. We gave her a name, Caroline. We had a baby shower." All that remained was for Audrey and her husband to travel to the distant city to pick their daughter up. On the day that the baby was to be released from the hospital, they flew into town. "When we got into the lawyer's office, we knew by his face that the mother had changed her mind. It was like a miscarriage—very painful." Remembers another woman about the failed placement of an infant boy: "It was devastating. He was ours. He was ripped out of our arms even though we didn't get him."[1]

Even after your child is placed in your home, depending upon your state's law, the birth parents may have the right to change their minds for a specified period of time. If the birth parents have received proper counseling and their decision was made without duress, this is unlikely to happen. But, as Jeanne and Harvey discovered, it can—and does. Can you live with that uncertainty?

There is also a financial risk. You may pay for medical care, counseling, or other legally permissible services, but you won't necessarily get your money back if the adoption fails to go through. Bob and Adrienne Bauer had an adoption crumble after they had flown cross-country to pick up the baby. By that time their out-of-pocket expenses exceeded $4,500, including the $2,000 they spent for their airfare and hotel bill, $1,200 for legal fees, and $1,300 on the birth mother's expenses for rent and food prior to the birth. Sometimes you can ask the birth mother for repayment of her costs, but the chances of reimbursement are mighty slim.

Just how much risk and uncertainty you are comfortable with should be weighed carefully.

ASSESSING RISKS

How can you minimize the risks you will be exposed to? The editors of *Successful Private Adoption!*, in a worksheet entitled Choosing Birthparents, identify some "red flags" that can be seen as "warning signs of potential problems. The purpose of identifying the red flags is to assess the risks involved with a particular set of birthparents before becoming emotionally and financially involved." In assessing red flags, you'll want to be sure that you analyze how they apply to both birthparents.

Using the "red flags" offered by Families for Private Adoption in *Successful Private Adoption!* as a starting point, let's take a look at some of the markers you, and the people helping you bring the adoption to fruition, should consider:[2]

- *Economics.* If the birth parents have few financial resources available to them, there is a greater likelihood they will place the baby.
- *Relationship between the Birth Parents.* If the birth parents' relationship is stable, there is a greater possibility that they will choose to parent the child. Married couples, even if they are separated or experiencing problems in their relationship, will be pressured by family and friends to keep the baby. An unmarried couple living together or involved in a long-term relationship will also feel pressure.

Be forewarned also if the birth mother says that she doesn't know the identity of the birth father. "It is *rare* that the identity of a birthfather is unknown. If a birthmother is reluctant (or refuses) to identify the birthfather, a major red flag exists in the potential adoption."

- *The Extended Family's Feelings.* Although the parents of the child (even if they are underage) must consent to the adoption, the feelings of their extended families—particularly their parents—will impact on their decision. When family members oppose an adoption, birth parents are likely to have difficulty deciding for an adoption plan.
- *Failure to Keep Appointments.* If a birth mother consistently misses legal and medical appointments or counseling sessions, this may be a sign that she is ambivalent about her decision.
- *The Birth Parents' Future Life Plans.* The presence of plans—such as the commitment to stay in school or attend college—may influence the adoption decision, says Washington attorney Mark McDermott. In the absence of plans, parenting a child may become a more attractive option to a birth parent.
- *The Newborn Has "Minor" Health Problems.* An easily correctable medical problem that crops up when the baby is born may be used by the birth mother as the excuse for not making the placement. The birth mother may even see this as divine intervention telling her not to make an adoption plan. A scenario such as this can't be anticipated in advance but occasionally happens.
- *Birth Parents' "Loss" History.* Just as you have experienced losses that influence your feelings, so have birth parents and you need to find out about theirs. Among potential losses: miscarriage, abortion, a

child lost through a custody battle or divorce, and a previous adoptive placement. Could this next loss be one too many for either one of them?

- *Reasons for Choosing Adoption.* Even the youngest of birth parents should be able to articulate why they are making an adoption plan. Is there perhaps a "hidden agenda" that you need to know about?

SEEKING LEGAL ADVICE

As you pursue an independent placement adoption, you will need to consult with an attorney. Chapter 8 provides general information about interviewing attorneys. To find attorneys with an expertise in independent adoptions, check with adoptive parents, with adoptive-parent groups, your local and state bar associations, and the **American Academy of Adoption Attorneys** (see appendix A). Be sure that you find out what role the attorney is allowed to play in the adoption. Remember: an attorney's role is to have a legal strategy that makes it possible for you to accomplish an adoption. In some states lawyers are permitted to handle all aspects of the adoption; in others, they are limited to drafting legal documents and representing their clients in court.

Explore how active the attorney will be in the independent placement process. Following are some questions to ask:

- What matchmaking role—if any—does the attorney play?
- Who will interview the birth parents on your behalf? If the attorney is not available to talk to birth parents, who in the office does?
- Who provides counseling of the birth parents? When does it take place? Is this something that might be ongoing or does it stop once the baby is placed?

- Will the attorney take charge of the medical arrangements?
- Will the attorney represent you in court?
- Who will represent the birth parents in court? (Many courts do not permit one lawyer to represent both you and the birth parents, since there may be a conflict of interest.)
- Who will handle the rights of the putative (supposed) father?
- How many independent adoptions and agency adoptions has the attorney handled? How recently? How many interstate adoptions has the lawyer handled and how recently?
- What are the attorney's fees and what do they cover? Is there a retainer? How is billing handled?
- How will funds be disbursed to the birth parents? Will an escrow account be set up?
- If you want to, can you participate actively in the process and reduce the lawyer's time and fees? What would you do?
- Should there be a written agreement with the attorney, before the child arrives, as to what services the attorney will provide?
- What does the attorney know about open adoption? Has the attorney attended any workshops or conferences that focused on open adoption? What are the attorney's views? How current and well-read does the attorney's thinking seem?
- How does the lawyer feel about contact between adoptive parents and birth parents? Is contact between adoptive parents and birth parents encouraged before the birth? After? How does the attorney feel, for example, about letter-writing? About meetings? What role is the attorney willing to play before and after?

- If there is no direct contact between the adoptive parents and the birth parents, who might handle a question that arises in five years? Is the attorney staffed for this? How are requests handled now?
- What kind of records does the lawyer maintain? What happens if the practice closes? Where will the information go?
- How accessible is the attorney? Who returns your phone calls? How much time elapses between the time of your call and the response? (You can ask other adoptive parents about their experiences.) Are your questions answered satisfactorily?
- Are you kept up to date and do you receive relevant correspondence and documents? What are the arrangements for weekends and other times when the attorney is not in the office?
- Do *you* feel comfortable with the lawyer who is about to share the intimate procedure of family-building? Do you trust this person?

Be sure that you check the lawyer's reputation among colleagues and other adoptive parents. Has the court ever questioned the independent adoptions the attorney has handled?

If so, why? You can also check with your interstate compact administrator and attorney general's office. If you have any doubts at any point, get other legal opinions.

While it's tempting to use as legal counsel a sympathetic friend, relative, or the attorney who handled your latest real estate deal, beware. One couple lost their baby in part because of their lawyer-friend's inexperience. The father of their just-arrived baby learned after the fact of the placement of the infant and insisted on his right to the child. Their attorney had not demanded that the father be located and his feelings

THE RIGHTS OF BIRTH FATHERS

The spectacle of an inconsolably wailing, two-and-a-half-year-old named Jessica being carried out of the home of her adoptive parents, Jan and Roberta DeBoer, to go to the home of her birth parents, Dan and Cara Schmidt, riveted Americans' attention in 1993 and raised questions about the conflicting interests of parents and children. In Jessica's case, the true identity of her birth father had not been revealed at the time of her placement so her birth father had not given his assent to the adoption; in addition, her birth mother's consent to the adoption had been signed too early. So when the birth parents decided to contest the adoption, they had legal grounds. For two years the case made its way through the court systems of Iowa and Michigan until that fateful day in August when Jessica rejoined her original parents.

A second case grabbed America's attention in 1995 in the "Baby Richard" saga when it learned that a birth father, having been told by the birth mother that the boy was dead, contested the placement of his son upon learning the truth. (He had terminated his rights to the baby.) Once again, after a protracted court battle between the adoptive parents and the birth parents, the child, now four years old, was returned to the birth parents, who had subsequently married.

"Address the birth father issue at the very beginnings of your discussions with any birth mother," urges attorney McDermott. "Failure to properly address the birth father issue is the primary cause of problematic adoptions. Most of the time, the birth father will not assert an interest in parenting the child and the law of your state will provide a legally sufficient way to protect yourself by terminating the birth father's rights."[3] If the birth mother says she doesn't know who the birth father is, experts urge that you:

- Know your state's laws and court decisions in regard to birth father rights. Many states are now establishing putative-father's registries by which the "presumed" or "reputed" father can indicate his interest in a child. The state is then required to inform the father of legal proceedings.
- Follow state law to protect the birth father's rights.
- Think carefully about whether you should pursue the adoption of a child whose birth father is not known, since a birth father could appear later.[4]

The National Adoption Information Clearinghouse and the American Bar Association Center on Children and the Law in Washington, D.C., can provide you with helpful information.

about relinquishment obtained before the baby entered their home. "An adoption is something you want to do absolutely right," observed one attorney with an expertise in private adoptions, "because it's not the sort of case you want to have to win before the court of appeals."

SPREADING THE WORD

In her Christmas cards, Fay Alfred wrote: "We're trying desperately to adopt and if you hear of anything, let me know." Shortly after Christmas, she got a call from a physician for whom she had once worked who had moved out of state. He had a patient who had just given birth to a baby boy. Were they still interested in adopting? She was, and she did the necessary paperwork to travel across the country to pick up her son. Five months later, Fay got a call from her obstetrician, who told her he knew of a baby. Not right now, Fay said, but thanks and keep me in mind for the future. And two years after those cards went out, Fay's sister's obstetrician called from another state to ask whether they were still interested in an independent adoption.

Sherry and Paul Landau have a similar story to tell. In their New Year's greetings, they expressed their wish to adopt a newborn. A former neighbor in another state gave their letter to her rabbi, who forwarded it to a pregnancy counselor he knew in still another state, who showed it to a teen client who came into her office a few days later. The adoption of their second child was equally serendipitous: a friend's friend, who was an adoptive parent, was in contact with her child's birth grandparents. And this birth grandmother had a step daughter who was pregnant and interested in placing her child for adoption. A few telephone calls got the process started, and Sherry, who happened to be visiting her friend the following week, stopped en route to meet the young woman.

Spreading the word—telling others that you are interested in adopting a child and are willing to adopt independently—is a crucial first step—and possibly the only step you may have to take in pursuing an independent placement. If you want to adopt, you must talk about it. That means telling your parents, your aunts and uncles, your cousins, your neighbors, your friends, and whomever else you can think of. "I called everybody that I knew," recalled Roberta Rolfe, whose daughter arrived several months after her inquiries began. "I promised myself that I'd make one telephone call a day. At parties I'd walk up to people, complete strangers sometimes, and say 'Hello, my name is Roberta Rolfe and my husband and I want to adopt a baby. Do you know of anyone who wants to put up a baby for adoption?" (She'd hand them her business card with the handwritten message "Hoping to Adopt.") When Roberta accompanied her husband on a business trip to Louisiana, she picked up the telephone and called the local department of social services to inquire about adoption. "It was an obsession. There was nothing more important than this," says Roberta. "I was monomaniacal."

Was Roberta crazy? No, the more people that she told, the greater the likelihood that someone might know someone. Beyond family, friends, neighbors, and colleagues at work, reach out to other people within your community. Go through your address book, your parents' address books, your sister's address book. Are there some old college chums who might help? Adoption counselors particularly recommend that you contact nurse-midwives, physicians, social workers, birth control counselors and other health professionals, clergymen, teachers and high school principals, and even beauticians. These are often the people who might come into contact with pregnant women. Establish as extensive a network as you can; indeed, if state laws and finances permit, explore the possibility of contacting people in another state.

How should you go about letting people know? Some adoptive parents use the telephone; others send out letters; while still others try to talk to people in person. Encourage the people you contact to talk with others about your desire to adopt.

Keep track of all your contacts. Get a notebook and record details about everyone you approached and exactly what they were told and what they told you. Follow up on as many leads as possible—and be prepared to retrace your steps at a later point.

There are also more formal ways to alert others to your needs. Some prospective adopters have done mass mailings of letters to obstetricians, pediatricians, and family practitioners whose names have been taken from phone books and medical directories (including the membership directory of the American College of Obstetricians and Gynecologists). There are even adoption services around the country that sell preaddressed mailing labels or will do the mailing for you. Other counselors have suggested contacting abortion clinics, right-to-life groups, planned parenthood centers, and free health clinics.

Some people have tried sending out detailed autobiographies or résumés along with their letters. The autobiography or résumé should include a phone number where you can be reached—collect! You might also give the names of other contacts (for example, your attorney). Round out your profile with a snapshot of yourself.

You might also want to print business cards (e.g. "Adoption—a gift of love. Call us Collect Anytime. We can offer you a choice.") that you hand out and post on bulletin boards in supermarkets, laundromats, restaurants, and other public places. Some families have gone one step further, creating adoption signboards that sit atop their cars as they drive around!

Placing advertisements in newspapers is one technique that adoptive parents use frequently. Just as agencies have found that newspaper features about a particular waiting child will elicit a response from potential adopters, prospective adoptive parents have found that placing an advertisement in the personal section of the classifieds alerts birth parents to their desire to parent a child. The ads convey their concerns:

> ADOPTION, NOT ABORTION: Let us adopt your baby. We are a young, happily married couple who wish to adopt an infant into our home. If you can help us, our gratitude goes to you. Expenses paid.
>
> ADOPT: Childless couple will be wonderful parents and give terrific life to newborn. Answer our prayers.
>
> ADOPT: Happily married couple, will provide love, finest education, country home for baby, confidential, expenses paid.
>
> ADOPTION: If you are considering adoption, I am a single man, financially secure, who will be a caring and devoted parent. You will always have a place in this child's life. Please call collect so we can talk. Confidential. Expenses paid as legal.

In states where newspaper advertising is legal, the ads have become so widespread that birth parents seeking an independent placement will often start there. "I had seen the personals for a long time," says one birth mother who interviewed fourteen couples before making her decision. "There were always a lot of ads in the newspaper, and they caught my eye. I felt awkward with the first couple I spoke with, but then I felt better." She found the couple she wanted: married with other children. "I feel like I had more control in selecting my baby's parents by being able to call the adoptive parents directly," observed another.[5]

How does the advertising process work? You begin by locating newspapers that accept this type of classified ad—the *Gale Directory of Publications* and *The Editor and Publisher Yearbook* are two directories found in library reference rooms that describe publications nationwide. Do you want to use a national newspaper, such as *USA Today,* daily newspapers, which can cost more than $100 a week, or smaller weekly and monthly papers? Consider also college newspapers, limited circulation papers such as *The Pennysaver* or the *Thrifty Nickel,* or free newspapers that are distributed within communities. It may be possible to advertise simultaneously in a group of newspapers at a discount price through a newspaper chain or a regional or statewide newspaper association. Consider also niche magazines: one couple, who are committed vegetarians, got responses from a classified they placed in *Vegetarian Times*!

Be sure to ask for a copy of your ad to make sure that it runs and that it contains correct information. You may also need the ad for legal purposes: some states require that you attach a copy of the ad that found your birth mother to the court adoption petition. Since you can't predict in advance which ad will ultimately lead to success, you'll need to keep all the ads you run along with other important documents.

While you could list your home telephone in the advertisement, many would-be adopters install a second telephone line—the so-called babyphone—and arrange to have an unlisted telephone number specifically for adoption inquiries. You'll want to consider if you should use an answering machine with it: some birth parents are put off if they get a recording instead of a friendly voice, but if you're at work all day you may need to think seriously about this method and create a welcoming message. If you use a machine, your message should state a time for a callback and allow the caller several minutes in which to leave a message for you before the telephone cuts off. (With the new telephone technology, you may want to explore the variety of other personalized options such as Call Forwarding.)

As part of your preparation process, you'll also want to work up a brief questionnaire covering the birth parents' ages, due date, ethnic background, marital status, medical history, religion, financial situation, and reasons for choosing an adoptive placement, which you can keep by the telephone and fill in as you talk. (And you'd better be prepared to answer questions about yourself.) You'll want to talk with your attorney in advance to discuss the legal requirements.

When the ads appear, you'll receive responses either directly from the birth mother or from an intermediary, such as her sister or a friend, speaking for her. Remember that the caller will be as anxious as you are. Be sure that this is not an interrogation session but a time that you exchange some information about each of you. You may talk several times and may then refer her to your attorney, if state law permits, to make the arrangements. It's quite possible that you'll meet or maintain a telephone relationship for several months.

Don't be surprised if your ad is not the only one appearing in a particular newspaper. Make your ad as personal as possible and don't be hesitant about using some key words—loving, financially secure, family values, stable home—that might draw a birth parent's attention to you. Try to put yourself in the place of the birth parent who will be reading the newspaper. Don't pinch pennies—or words—when writing these ads. They speak for you. Be aware also that you may need to run ads for several months in several newspapers. (You may want to create several different ads of varying lengths.) The costs can mount into the hundreds or thousands of dollars if you spread your net wide over an extended period of time. "The advertising became addictive," recalled Bob Bauer, whose expenses rose into the thousands. "My wife and I felt uncomfortable if a week or two went by and we hadn't run an ad." Naomi and Nicholas Adler placed ads in weeklies that covered an entire county in several states and changed the ads and newspapers frequently. They limited their advertising expenses to two hundred dollars a month. Recalls Naomi: "It was absolutely horrible to sit by the telephone. It was horrible when it didn't ring and when it did." Finally, four months after they placed their first ad, the call they were dreaming about came, and two months later they were parents of a little girl. Says Naomi: "We'd tried word of mouth and didn't come up with anything. Advertising gave us the chance to reach pregnant women directly and also gave us the chance to weed out situations that we didn't think were legitimate." Naomi now looks back with enthusiasm: "The whole experience was so exciting. It's hard to believe that it really happens all the time."

It may happen all the time but, as Naomi noted, it's emotionally draining. "Nobody prepared us for this drama that thrusts total strangers into instant and painful intimacy," observed Dorothy Kalins in an article in *New York* magazine. "You get in fast and deep, and then it's over. Forever." Describing her reactions to the babyphone she notes: "We are no longer freaked every time the phone rings. But it still feels like we're involved in some secret cabal, racing home each night to participate in seances where disembodied and unknown voices are channeled in (collect) over an unlisted phone that lives in a closet."[6] You may receive many calls and talk with many people who never follow up. You may get crank calls and offers from people to "sell" you their baby. Recalls Laura Stanton: "One lady called who had a six-month-old girl and she wanted fifteen thousand dollars just for herself. I had a truck driver who called me and said that his route was through New York and he wanted to drop the baby on my doorstep. It just went on and on."

Find out whether it is legal to place an ad for an adoption in a state. Check also with the state department of social services, a knowledgeable adoption attorney, and parent groups. You may have to search around for newspapers to take your ad. Also you may want to consider the various newspaper advertising services that have sprung up around the country, but be sure to check out their reputations. For a fuller description of the process, giving step-by-step instructions, take a look at some of the resources listed in appendix C. For a sense of the roller-coaster ride, try Barbara Shulgold and Lynne Sipiora's *Dear Barbara, Dear Lynne: The True Story of Two Women in Search of Motherhood.*

SPREADING THE WORD AND COMMUNICATING VIA THE INTERNET

As the use of the home computer expands—and access to the Internet increases—more birth parents and prospective adoptive parents are likely to make the links electronically. You might create a home page that includes a Dear Birth Mother letter, your photo, descriptions of yourself, a favorite poem, your e-mail address or Uniform Resource Locator (URL), and other pertinent information.

The search engine Yahoo! can lead you to adoption classified advertisements. There are several Internet services that you can use for a fee. You may want to check with the National Adoption Information Clearinghouse about them to find out about their reputation.

What can you expect if you create a web page? Liz Bear says that she would get e-mail from birth mothers who wanted to ask advice or communicate with someone as they wrestled with their placement decision. Adoptive parents would e-mail encouragement, while she also heard from "listing agencies" that offered her their services. "It's a rather passive process," she says. "You don't find the birth mother; the birth mother finds you."

Even if you spread the word the old-fashioned way—through talking, letters, the classifieds, or business cards, be sure that you give your e-mail address if you have one. Who knows what's in your electronic future!

You'll find a good introduction to the possibilities for independent adoption in cyberspace in Jana Apergis's "Seeking to Adopt: Creating a Website to Spread the Word," *Adoptive Families* (May/June 1997). The National Adoption Information Clearinghouse publishes a guidebook to the use of the Internet that it updates periodically.

THE COSTS OF AN INDEPENDENT ADOPTION

Costs for independent adoptions can soar beyond twenty-five thousand dollars. It's difficult to come up with exact or typical figures because each adoption is different. If the birth mother is living at home and has health-insurance coverage under her parents' policy, then the expenses of the adoption will be much less than if the birth mother has no health insurance and delivers the child by cesarean section. If the birth mother travels to your state to give birth and resides there before delivery for a month or more, the cost will be higher. (Or if you travel to her state and she misestimated her due date by several weeks, consider what bills you will incur during the wait.) The difference to you can be as much as five thousand dollars.

Consider the cases of four Maryland couples, all of whom adopted infants born in the state.[7]

FAMILY ONE

- Total Expenses $6,496, including
- Advertising: $412. For five weeks in three in-state newspapers.
- Legal fees: $2,668. For their attorney and the birth mother's.
- Medical expenses: $3,094.

FAMILY TWO

- Total Expenses $9,140, including
- Newspaper Advertising: $228
- Legal fees: $2,968
- Medical expenses: $3,305
- Telephone installation: $130
- Pregnancy-related expenses: $2,384. Included lodging the birth mother for twenty-two days in a hotel prior to the birth.

FAMILY THREE

- Total Expenses $12,300, including
- Newspaper advertising: $524
- Legal fees: $8,641. For their attorney, the birth mother's, and the birth father's.

- Medical expenses: $2,155
- Travel: $423
- Home study: $400

FAMILY FOUR

- Total Expenses $15,319, including
- Failed first adoption: $3959. Birth mother revoked her consent after the baby was in their home. (There were no medical expenses as the birth mother and baby were covered by Medicaid.)
- Failed placement: $1,045. Birth mother changed her mind before the birth.
- Successful third adoption: $10,319

What do you imagine the expenses would have been for any of these couples if the birth mother, who had no medical insurance, needed to be hospitalized for ten days and the adoptive parents were expected to pay her bills? Recalls an attorney about one such adoption: "The birth mother became ill after delivery with an infection. There were bills for ambulance services, the hospitalization, the obstetrical fee, surgery, and psychological counseling. We had bills for absolutely everything. We had affidavits explaining the bills." One way that you can trim costs is to limit your search to birth mothers who have medical coverage through themselves or their parents or who will qualify for public assistance.

Given the variables, a cardinal rule for assessing costs in an independent placement must be that all expenses be reasonably documented—there should be receipts for all expenditures. Attorneys should be paid for the professional legal services they perform. Avoid using the lawyer for routine hand-holding, since those intimate chats on the telephone are typically billed. Physicians should be paid for the professional medical services they render. Social workers or clergy should be compensated for any professional counseling services they perform. You should not be paying an attorney or anyone else a "finder's fee."

Warning: You should not be paying for the birth mother's college tuition, the down payment for her house (or her parents' house), a vacation in Europe, or "designer" maternity clothes. You may be asked to cover such expenses, but these expenses are not considered reasonable expenses. When you finalize the adoption in court, you may be asked to submit a sworn accounting of all payments made, or your actual receipts, and the judge may look very carefully at all expenses incurred.

GETTING BACKGROUND AND MEDICAL INFORMATION

Adopted children have many questions about their birth parents. To help you get the information your child will need, you'll want to create some forms (much as an agency does) that you can have your child's birth parents and their families fill out. (You might also use *A Birthmother's Book of Memories,* available from R-Squared Press, 721 Hawthorne Street, Royal Oak, MI 48967; 810–543–0997.) Explain that you will keep this information confidential, but will share it with your child in the future. Let the birth parents know you will also provide pertinent medical details to your child's future physicians. Request some photographs as well. Here are some of the topics you'll want to cover:[8]

- General description: age, height, weight, bone structure, eye and hair color, blood type, birth date and place
- General medical: vision, dental history including orthodontia, medical problems corrected as a child. Create a checklist that includes medical conditions such as arthritis, cancer,

INDEPENDENT ADOPTION EXPENSES

YOUR GENERAL ADOPTION EXPENSES

- Home-study fee (home study usually required before placement)
- Medical Exams
- Fees for documents (e.g., birth certificates)
- Photocopying fees
- Court costs for completion of the adoption
- Long-distance telephone calls (these mount rapidly if the adoption is interstate)
- Your attorney's fees

BIRTH PARENTS' AND INFANT'S EXPENSES

- Birth mother's hospital and doctor bills
- Birth mother's lab fees, vitamins, tests, drug bills
- Counseling for the birth parents
- Birth parents' attorneys' fees
- Infant's hospital-nursery and pediatric bills
- Infant's drug bills

OTHER POSSIBLE EXPENSES

- Birth mother's lodging and maintenance expenses for one or several months (if permitted by state law)
- Birth mother's or birth father's travel expenses for the surrender of the child (if permitted by state law)
- Putative father's pregnancy-related expenses
- Your travel, including air fare and car rental, and accommodation costs to meet birth parents or to bring baby home
- Postage for mailing out your résumé
- Classified advertising expenses for several months
- Installation of a separate phone for your search

high blood pressure, heart disease, diabetes, birth defects, acne, overweight, allergies, anemia, epilepsy, alcoholism—even trick knees. Ask the family to indicate if anyone has suffered from the condition and if so, to give some details. Did the birth mother use drugs or alcohol during the pregnancy? What about the birth father?

- Education: school history, learning disabilities, particular problems, particular talents.
- Family: parents, siblings, grandparents. Get general descriptions of them and details about their medical histories, their schooling. Has anyone in the family died prematurely? If so, why? Is there any family history of chronic disease? Is there any history in the family of substance abuse? Would the birth families be willing to fill out family trees for you?
- Talents, interests, hobbies, sports abilities: the birth parents and their families.
- Ethnic background.
- Personality of birth parents and their families.
- Why the birth parents have chosen adoption and what they wish you to share about themselves with their child.

TAKING YOUR BEARINGS

I wanted a baby. After years of marriage and wanting to have a child, you're willing to do anything. That puts many couples into dangerous situations. You're afraid to turn away any situation whether it's legal or black market or anything in between. It takes a tremendous amount of courage to say no when your gut feeling says that this is the wrong thing to do. I want to warn other couples who are desperate to have children to go very cautiously in their pursuit. There are a lot of people out there who are playing on your desperation. Never become that desperate to fall into the hands of those characters. There's a baby out there.

Those words were spoken by a woman who thought that an adoption service, which promised to find her a baby, was the solution. She sent the man running the service thousands of dollars to advertise for a child for her. Nothing ever happened, and the service eventually was closed down for violating state law.

If you decide to pursue an independent placement adoption, you should proceed cautiously at all times. "Be willing to walk away if it's not going right," urges attorney Mark McDermott. "People who are hoping to adopt are so anxious to do so that they are vulnerable to scams or high prices."

Be on the alert for:

- *Parental Consent.* No one should be pressured into releasing a child for adoption. Be sure that the parent has made the decision without duress. Be sure that you obtain the father's release. If there is no father's release, you may be asked to locate him. The rights of unwed fathers vary state by state, but the courts have increasingly recognized their claims and so must you.
- *Attorney Expertise.* Be sure that your attorney is experienced in adoption law, particularly for independent adoption and for the county where you will be adopting your child.
- *Pressure from Intermediaries.* Don't let anyone tell you that this is a "once in a lifetime situation." Independent adoptions happen all the time.
- *Costs.* Examine these carefully. Are you being asked to put down money to place your name on an intermediary's waiting list? Are you being asked to advance large sums to a birth parent prior to placement? If you are being asked to put money

into escrow, what is it for? Are you receiving an itemized bill for expenses?

- *Health.* Get as extensive a set of medical records about the birth parents and the child as you can. Don't hesitate to ask questions and to have the basic medical tests performed. Arrange to have the infant assessed by your pediatrician or by another physician of your choice. Don't assume that "routine newborn care" has been complete unless you have the records that document it.
- *Counseling.* Be sure that the birth parents have adequate counseling and, again, that their decision is not made under pressure from you or anyone else.

Remember, in an independent adoption, you are relying on yourself, rather than an adoption agency, to insure that your child's placement proceeds legally and successfully.

4

UNDERSTANDING OPEN ADOPTION

As the guests milled around at her wedding, Joan Smith beckoned young Michael Blair to her side and asked the photographer to snap a picture of her and the child. "This is the little guy I had six years ago," she said. "And this—pointing to a smiling couple standing nearby—is his mother, Sharon, and his father, Ralph."

For Joan, Michael, Ralph, and Sharon the wedding was just another chapter in the story that began when Joan, eighteen years old, unmarried, and living at home with her parents, released her infant son, Michael, at birth for adoption. She had selected Ralph and Sharon Blair as the family that she felt matched her own after reading applicants' autobiographies shared with her by the agency's social worker. She saw her son at the foster home prior to his placement and also met with Ralph and Sharon. Joan was determined to do an open adoption because she feared that "I would be wondering every time that I saw a child on the street whether he was my son. I told my counselor that I wouldn't give up my child without knowing the parents. I wanted to know who he was throughout his life."

Joan hasn't had to wonder. The families, who live several hundred miles apart, typically get together in the summer and around Christmas, with Sharon sending photographs in between. Joan's known by her first name, while Michael and his brother call Joan's parents Grandma and Grandpa. "In this family," says Sharon, "several older couples have that title, but the kids know that they're Joan's parents." The kids also know who Joan is. Sharon's overheard Michael telling a friend "about Joan who carried me in her belly," and laughs remembering how Michael informed Joan at the wedding that, "that man who put me in your belly came to visit me this year." While Joan has lost contact with her son's birth father, the Blairs have spent some time with him.

Both Joan and the Blairs are pleased with how the open adoption has worked out. "If I don't talk to Joan or see her in a year's time," says Sharon, "I miss it. It's really a loss. And Michael will say 'we haven't seen Joan for a long time.' The need is there." Says Joan: "I'm happy with what I have, but the adoption is not going to be forgotten. I'm glad to get pictures of Michael, to see him, to talk to him, to know he chipped his teeth, and that he likes sweets like I do. I think it would have driven me wild not knowing."

Yet this is not shared parenting. For Joan, "Michael's like a friend's child whom I really care for. I don't look at him as though he's my son, although I will identify him as my son. I catch my breath sometimes just watching him—realizing that I have a school-aged child now." Sharon is equally clear about the relationship between the two families: "Joan has nothing to say about the way we raise him. She doesn't know every time Michael falls and hurts himself." Open adoption is "like sharing your life with a friend," says Sharon. "I wouldn't ask my friend where she'd send my kids to school, and I wouldn't think of asking Joan. But if there's something special that happens, our friends would know—and Joan's a friend—so she would know."

In open adoptions birth parents and adoptive parents meet one another, share identifying information, and communicate directly over the years. They may get together often, occasionally, or not at all as the individuals determine what is best for them.[1] With two daughters adopted eight and four years ago, Donna and Bill King have met members of their daughters' birth families at the time of their placement, exchanged names and addresses, and have corresponded faithfully with them since. But as far as Donna's concerned that's as far as she wants the relationship to go right now. "I don't think we've even talked about getting together," says Donna. "I don't know if I'd be in favor of it at the age my daughters are now. That would blow their minds. My husband and I aren't comfortable with either of them meeting their birth parents until they're seventeen or eighteen."

Claudia and Bob Bender feel similarly. They met with the birth mother and her family a week before their son Joel was born. They paced the floor of the hospital waiting room with Joel's birth grandmother and ate dinner at her house afterwards. Since then they have written and talked by telephone. "At this point everybody agrees that face-to-face contact is something we're not going to be doing for a while," says Bob. "I think there are a lot of unanswered issues. Maybe that's being a little conservative, but I think there are some risks for Joel. I know a lot of people don't feel that way, but I'm not altogether persuaded. At this point I'm not willing to take the risk."

Open adoption is based on the assumption that people are capable of choosing each other and staying in touch directly, trusting each other enough to sustain a relationship and work together cooperatively to advance the best interests of the child. It assumes that adoptees are entitled to a full knowledge of their birth heritage and that birth parents have much to offer their children. As a corollary, open adoption advocates say that birth and adoptive families must view each other as members of an extended family. Observes James Gritter, author of *The Spirit of Open Adoption* and a pioneer in developing open adoption: "Early on we viewed open adoption as connections, as people having a natural interest in one another. It has evolved to a very interesting relationship—really like relatives."

There are many "open" adoptions in the United States that stop far short of the criteria some advocates propose. These adoptions might best be described as "semi-open" adoptions or even just "open placements." In many instances, while the birth parents and adoptive parents do meet, their first names may be revealed but no other identifying information. Any subsequent communication is carried on through an intermediary. Sometimes there will be no contact between the parents after the baby's birth. When you talk with adoption agencies about their "open adoption" program, find out what their expectations are. An agency that proclaims it has "newborn infants available by open adoption placement" but then notes "no identifying information revealed" is serving up something other than an open adoption in the full sense of the word. If you are arranging a private adoption, be sure to clarify with the birth parents their ideas and expectations of open adoption. If there are intermediaries involved, you'll need to explore their opinions about open adoption and make sure that they are clear about what you and the birth parents have in mind.

Keep in mind that open adoption is not just for infant placements. Older children may stay in touch with their birth families, and this can be important for their adjustment and growth. "Now that David sees his birth mother on a regular basis," reported one adoptive parent, "he sees that she is very different from the person he remembered. He has stated many times that he is no longer afraid for her because she can now take care of herself." This birth mother has also let her son know that she is happy with the adoption: "David's birth mother gave him a very clear message that we are his parents and this was the plan she had made for him. Her role has been that of an interested person who cares about him very much, but who is not and never again will be his parent."[2]

As you explore the world of open adoption, you will find yourself entering into recently charted territory. There are ever growing numbers of birth parents, adoptive parents, and adoptees creating new family relationships. And there is an ever expanding literature—*The Spirit of Open Adoption, Giving Away Simone, The Open Adoption Experience, The Story of David*—to point the way. (See appendix C for details and discussion of these and other works.) But questions remain. As Becky Miller, a committed adoptive parent who's appeared on open adoption panels, put it: "We all wonder how the kids will view the situation in ten or fifteen years. Will they think that this is strange? Whether you are the adoptive parent or the birth parent, you hope that your child understands and accepts how this all came about."

This chapter, drawing on interviews with birth and adoptive parents who have chosen open adoption, the experts who have developed pioneering programs, and the literature that describes open adoption, seeks to help you understand the process. While the following pages explore basic questions and answers, they can only provide a brief distillation of a complicated, and evolving, subject. You will want to dip into the readings and other materials cited and find adoptive parent and expert support in the larger community.

THE ADVANTAGES AND DRAWBACKS OF OPEN ADOPTION

> *When Katherine was six years old, she wanted to know how long her birth mother was in labor. Her questions regarding this matter became a point of intense fixation. This had to do with the building frustration of not receiving an answer since her mom did not have the information. In an effort to dissipate the mounting feeling, it was decided that Katherine could write to her birth mother and ask for the missing information. . . .*
>
> *When the answer arrived it was dramatic to witness how the information was absorbed and the whole matter became 'no big deal.' It is amazing to behold such a transformation of emotional energy when an answer becomes available.*[3]

"For the adoptee, open adoption provides answers to his normal questions," observe Kathleen Silber and Patricia Martinez Dorner in *Children of Open Adoption*. "He can get immediate answers when questions arise and can go on with other developmental tasks without getting stuck on adoption issues."[4] When communication lines are open, the adoptee is also guaranteed continued access to genetic information. "In addition, with open communication within the family, the adoptee does not have to feel that he is being disloyal to his adoptive parents by being curious or asking questions about the birth parents," write Silber and Dorner. "He is allowed to care about both sets of parents without feeling guilty."[5] With the birth parent only a letter or a telephone call away, there's also less reason to fantasize about his other parents. They are real people whose likes and dislikes he knows. As for his adoptive parents, he has a "sense of belonging" since he is aware that his birth parents chose them for him.

For the adoptive parent, open adoption starts with a feeling of empowerment. Consider this adoptive mother's account:

There were about 15 people in my sister's house—Erin's [the birth mother's] friends, our friends. It was an incredible experience. Each person held Heather [the baby] while she or he talked about what this situation meant to them. . . . Bernardo [the birth father] was the last one to talk. Then he and Erin brought Heather over to us. He said 'Aquí les entregamos nuestra hija.' [We bring you our daughter.] Erin said, as they handed Heather to us, 'We give you your daughter.'[6]

Observes Becky Miller: "There is an entitlement for the adoptive parents because the birth parents have given you permission to love this child. The birth parents wanted us at the hospital when our children were born. That's definitely real entitlement." Recalls an adoptive father of the birth experience: "It was amazing—one, two, three, and he was out. I was on Karen's right side and Barbara was on her left."

Knowing the birth parents also helps mitigate fears adoptive parents might have concerning the birth parents and makes it easier for adoptive parents to explain adoption issues to their children. Ruth McRoy, Harold Grotevant, and Susan Ayers Lopez reported in their study of changing adoption practices, which examined the experiences of families whose children were between the ages of four and twelve and whose children had been adopted through an agency as infants, that "the lowest degrees of fear of reclaiming were in the ongoing fully disclosed adoptions. In fact, 77.2 percent of adoptive mothers and 82.5 percent of adoptive fathers in fully disclosed adoptions indicated 'no fear' of reclaiming."[7] Says adoptive parent Donna King: "You've met a couple of very nice people who just happened to get into trouble like anybody could have. You can face your children a lot easier when they ask because you've met these people and you're comfortable with them. You don't have to make up any stories about who they were and how they are."

For birth parents, open adoption brings a greater sense of control. While they will still grieve for their loss, they will know that they have made a plan for their child and that they will not be cut off from direct knowledge of their child's well-being. As birth mother Sara Charles put it: "I feel good to see my baby with a happy smile, with people who have time for her and who are letting me share in that joy."[8]

Open adoption advocates talk about the "honesty" of this kind of adoption, with no secrets or sealed records involved. The unknown, say advocates, compounds children's fears that something wrong with them must have led their birth parents to abandon them. McRoy and her associates found that "virtually all of the children, no matter what type of adoption they had, wanted to know more about their birth parents."[9] They note that "young children seem to derive benefit from contact with their birth parents, reaffirming the birth parents' love and providing opportunities to explain the circumstances which led to the adoption plan." In the case of one eight-year-old, they note, she reported: "I asked if my birth mother still loved me and my mom goes, 'Of course she does.' My mom says she does and I believe her, 'cause every time my birth mother comes up to see us, she's always hugging me and stuff."[10] Maintains Kathleen Silber: "Open adoption makes adoption very concrete. It's much more understandable."

Yet open adoption is also complex and there is still plenty of pain. "I can't explain how much I hurt," recalls Sara Charles. "My whole heart broke. When the adoptive parents walked out of my hospital room with Danielle, I started bawling. It was a big loss." Two years later, talking about the adoption can still bring tears to Sara's eyes and a lump in her throat. With an open adoption, this pain is witnessed up close by the adoptive parents. "We've seen what a tremendous sacrifice giving up a baby is for a birth parent and how tough the decision is," observes Becky Miller, the adoptive mother of Sara's child. "Both joy and grief comes out of this type of situation. We have tremendous joy over being able to parent, but we also experience and feel the pain that birth parents go through."

There may be strains after the placement as adoptive parents and birth parents discover the differences between their expectations and reality. "Everybody's feelings change a little bit after the baby is born," says Silber. "The birth mother may have thought she didn't want a lot of contact while she was pregnant but once the baby is born, she will want more contact than she thought. Everybody makes this agreement not knowing how it feels to give up a baby, or how it feels to parent a baby." To ameliorate this strain birth and adoptive parents may need to meet with a mediator, such as an adoption agency social worker, after the placement to express their feelings and discuss, once again, how they see the relationship developing over time.

There may be additional strains if family and friends do not understand or are not supportive. It's possible that a relationship develops between the birth grandparents, rather than the birth parents, and the adoptive family. While this may bring great joy to them, some adoptive grandparents may resent these other grandparents. Observes adoption specialist

Marlene Piasecki: "In some families who've waited a long time to have a child, the two grandmothers want to be supreme. They don't want another grandmother in the picture."

Some adoptive grandparents may also be plagued by doubts and insecurities. At the time of their son Jonathan's adoption, Marlene and Eric Wilson were sure that his parents, Gregory and Dorothy, were enthusiastic supporters of the open adoption. After all, the special adoption babyphone that birth mothers called in to had been installed in the senior Wilsons' home (Marlene worked long hours, while Dorothy was at home). Dorothy had talked with several birth mothers. The two families had discussed adoption frequently—even watching some TV broadcasts about open adoption together—and Eric's parents knew that they had met Jonathan's birth mother at the time of the placement and continued to hear from her. Three years later, however, when Marlene announced that Jonathan was going to see his birth mother on an upcoming vacation, Eric's parents were horrified. "You're not going to see her?" said a panicked Dorothy. "I have a lot invested in this child." Marlene's in-laws had revealed their secret fears: that the continued contact through telephone calls, letters, and occasional visits could lead to a situation where they might eventually lose him to his birth mother.

Other families will react differently. Recalls Donna King: "My parents were terrified when they first heard about open adoption. They didn't like it at all. They were concerned that the birth mothers would come back and take the babies since they knew where the babies were." Eight years later she says, "they understand open adoption a little better now and think it's kind of neat."

In the long term, there is also the possibility that, as the birth parents' lives take on new shape, they may request that contact be reduced, they will be inconsistent in their contact, or even drop out of their children's lives. This has led to emotional distress for the children as they wonder why their birth parents have chosen to stop communicating with them. (For a fuller discussion, see the section on The Children of Open Adoption.)

OPEN ADOPTION: YOUR FEARS AND THE FACTS

If you are contemplating an open adoption, you probably have many questions. Here are the questions that people frequently ask at the beginning and what the experts have to say:

How likely is it that the birth parents will change their minds after the baby is born and we have taken custody?

In any adoption where the baby goes directly from the hospital to the adoptive parents' home there is the potential risk that the birth parents will change their minds during the time before they legally terminate their parental rights. "That is the period of highest vulnerability for the adoptive family," admits Gritter. "Good counseling doesn't mean that somebody is fixed in an adoption decision."

Putting a child into temporary foster care until the birth parents' decision is legally irrevocable is an option that some agencies will offer to adoptive parents. Others feel that this denies adoptive parents the chance to build a relationship with the child from the outset and moves the child unnecessarily. And foster care also displeases birth parents.

So there's a risk that the adoption will unravel after the baby is born or in your home, and there's no blunting the pain when an open placement fails. When they brought three-day-old Joseph home, the Dredges knew that they would be in regular contact with his birth mother and that the birth mother could reclaim her baby for a period of time under their state's law. But when the birth mother called nine weeks later to inform them of her change of mind, they were shocked. "I didn't believe her," recalls Sue. "I was just floored. I pleaded with her." But the birth mother had made up her mind, and two days later, the Dredges bade farewell to their new son.

Sue's voice catches and tears well in her eyes as she recalls that day. Returning to the empty house, particularly the baby's freshly painted blue bedroom with its decorative border, was so very difficult. "It was almost like he had died," says Sue. On Joseph's first birthday Sue had the chance to see him again. Others might have declined, but she accepted the invitation to attend his birthday party. "I had kept focusing on Joseph in my mind as this little baby who wasn't growing," she says. "I needed to know that he was okay." He was, and "seeing Joseph," she says, "was like closing a chapter in a book."[11]

If you already have an adopted child in your home, you'll also need to think about the potential impact on your older child if the birth parent reclaims the baby. How will you explain to your child what has happened?

For basic advice, see "When the Birth Parent Decides to Raise the Child," in Lois Ruskai Melina and Sharon Kaplan Roszia's *The Open Adoption Experience*. As they note:

> *Adoptive parents take the risk of having a child reclaimed not when they become involved in an open adoption but when they become involved in an adoption system that places children with their adoptive parents before the children are legally free for adoption—a process that includes confidential adoptions as well as open adoptions."*[12]

Will the birth parents show up at our door uninvited if we share our name and address?

"I've never known a birth mother to show up uninvited," says Silber. "Birth parents have spent considerable time and effort to arrange for their children to have a stable, loving environment and do not want to jeopardize this." In fact, birth parents and their families are likely to be very concerned not to intrude into the adoptive family's life. "I still feel stupid if I call the adoptive parents," one birth mother confided to a group of prospective adoptive parents at an agency orientation. "I don't want to seem like I'm barging into their lives." Sara Charles is equally clear about her respect for the adoptive parents' privacy: "I'd love to see Danielle all the time, but I don't want to be a problem. Every family needs time alone."

Do adoptive parents have any control over the experience? What if you're chosen by a birth parent that you don't like?

Typically, with an agency or private placement, it's a mutual choosing. If you feel uncomfortable, you should be able to say no. The birth parents may select a particular family, but then there should be a meeting where you get acquainted. The placement should not proceed unless both sides agree to it and are satisfied with the plan.

Sara Charles describes their interviewing process: "We selected four couples to interview. They were all very nice, but something just didn't click with the first two. The third couple was Becky and Bill. We sat around for hours talking and drinking pop. As we left, Matt said, 'They're it!' and I knew he was right."

Just as birth parents take their time and often interview several adoptive parents before making their decision, you should also feel free to meet with several birth parents. If your initial talks or meeting with a birth parent leave you feeling uncomfortable, take the risk and say no. After all, you are making a commitment for a lifetime.

Is this shared parenting? Aren't the adoptive parents really just glorified babysitters?

No matter how open the adoption is, it isn't shared parenting. If a birth mother envisions coparenting, then adoption isn't the choice for her, and the social workers who are counseling her should be helping her find a way to raise the baby. The birth parents are not parenting their child or participating in childrearing decisions. As in other adoptions, there is a complete and irrevocable legal transfer of parental rights and responsibilities by the birth parents.

"Open adoption isn't shared parenting," says Becky Miller. "Danielle is with us round the clock. She has bonded to us and knows us as Mommy and Daddy. But there's nothing wrong with having more people—Sara, her birth father Matt, and their families—love Danielle."

If children have an open relationship with their birth parents, will they be confused as to who their parents are? Won't they see their birth parents as their "real" parents? Could adoptive parents lose their parental relationship with their children?

Silber maintains that "it's the adults who are confused and freak out about the concept of open adoption, not the kids. Children know who mommy is: she's the woman who's there every day. When children need mothering, when they fall down and skin their knee, they run to Mommy. They can clearly understand who's Mom and who's the birth mother. No matter how open the adoption is, from the child's point of view he doesn't have two mothers."

Your child will acknowledge his birth mother or birth father just as he will other adult relatives or close family friends who visit during the year. Think of it this way: he doesn't become confused as to their roles in the family just because they say they love him and shower him with kisses and gifts. Even when birth parents or birth grandparents visit regularly, children see them as their parents present them—as other caring relatives or friends.

It's important, however, to tell your child that this is the birth mother and that he grew in her womb. From the time you first start talking about adoption, you'll want to present your child with the truth. You'll also want to refer to the birth parents by their first names. (They are not "aunts" or "uncles.") And, as your child grows, you'll need to further explain the relationship, filling in the details and discussing it more than once. (For a general discussion about talking with children about adoption, see chapter 11; Melina and Roszia provide specific guidance in *The Open Adoption Experience*.)

Does having an open adoption automatically mean that you're going to have a visiting relationship?

Silber maintains that "people meet initially, but then decide how much contact they want on an ongoing basis. A lot of open adoptions include visits, but a lot don't. Some families keep in touch through letters and pictures." Sharon Kaplan Roszia, co-author of *The Open Adoption Experience*, emphasizes that "open adoption was created for children. They should have the opportunity to have their heritage and their linkages preserved. The adults involved don't have a right to say that they don't want to stay in touch. It's the right of the child to have that preserved."

As your child grows, he will better be able to express his own feelings about open adoption and how contact is maintained. He may be content knowing that you write or talk with his birth parents from time to time. Or he may ask that he have the chance to see them.

If you set up an arrangement one way, does that mean it will stay that way over time?

No relationship is static. Open adoptions evolve as people change. Often the contact is most frequent during the first year after the baby's birth. As the birth mother gets on with her life, perhaps finishing school, getting married, and having other children, the frequency of contact might be less than it was at the beginning.

But it can work the other way. In the McRoy and Grotevant study, they found that "almost two-thirds of the fully disclosed adoptions did not start that way."[13] They observe that:

> *Our many discussions with birth mothers, adoptive parents, adopted children, and agency professionals have shown us that openness in adoption is an ongoing process rather than a final state. Relationships that work the best seem to be those that can evolve mutually over time. Initially, they appear to fall well within the participants' limits of acceptability, and the relationship process toward greater openness is interactively determined by all those involved.*[14]

Is an open adoption legally binding?

Laws regulating open adoption are different in each state. While a handful of states have enacted laws allowing birth parents to bring a civil action to enforce an openness agreement, the majority relegate enforcement to the realm of goodwill, treating the agreements as voluntary gentlemen's agreements. Observed attorney Amy Silverberg in an article in *Adoptive Families* magazine: "If a dispute over openness is challenged, the Courts usually do one of two things: rule that no agreement existed or that unless a specific law exists to the contrary, the agreement is not enforceable and that the adoptive parents are free to honor it or not, if they wish."[15] Silverberg says that even in states where there are statutes sanctioning enforceability, "the courts will not allow the adoption to be jeopardized." As open adoptions become increasingly common, however, individual courts may interpret this differently and could even overturn an adoption.

If you already have an adopted child whom you adopted through a closed adoption, is it going to be difficult to explain to your first child what's happening with your second child?

If you adopt two children, even in a closed adoption, each one is going to be different and there will be different explanations for each child. So it will be with your open adoption. Silber reports that in the situations she's observed where one adoption is closed and the other is open, the birth mother in the open adoption often becomes the "family" birth mother, acknowledging both children and bringing presents to both of them.

Since the literature on raising children in open adoptions is scanty, we must depend in part on what birth and adoptive families report. Sharon Blair says that "whenever we see Joan, she treats Michael and his brother Mark just the same. It's nice because Mark isn't the outcast." Remarks one birth mother about the other adopted child in her child's family: "I love him too. He's just as special as the rest of them are."

Is an intercountry adoption automatically a closed adoption?

Contrary to popular opinion some open intercountry adoptions do occur. Just as adult adoptees have returned to their birth country to seek out further information about themselves, adoptive parents have found that in some circumstances they can meet their child's birth family. Elyse met her daughter's birth mother Maria at a brief meeting in the Lima office of her Peruvian adoption attorney. "Tears ran down her face," recalls Elyse. "I made a move to comfort Maria. It seemed she was going to embrace me. But we didn't." Another adoptive parent met his son's birth father in Romania at the time of relinquishment. "He took me back to his flat to meet his three older daughters. We had coffee, sat on the floor, and cried. It was very emotional. I took photos of Michael's father and sisters, and they're now in a scrapbook."

IS OPEN ADOPTION FOR YOU?

"There's just not one way to do an open adoption," observes Harold Grotevant. "This is not an all-or-nothing situation." At the outset of the process, you're likely to be uncertain and even uncomfortable with parts of the process. As you come to understand the philosophy of open adoption, you've got to assess your own readiness and comfort level. You'll want to read some of the basic literature (see the synopses in the reference section in appendix C). It's helpful to hear adoptive parents talk about their ongoing experiences. Check whether a local parent group holds an adoption conference or workshop featuring panels on open adoption or discussion groups with birth parents. Attend the general orientations of local agencies or organizations advocating open adoption and listen to what they have to say. Take the time to educate yourself about the process.

Then ask yourself some basic questions. You may discover that you're comfortable with the idea of an open placement but not with a fully open adoption.

If you came to adoption through experiencing infertility, how have you resolved your feelings about infertility?

Having a relationship with birth parents and their families openly acknowledges that somebody else gave birth to your child. If acknowledging the difference between parenting a child who was born to you and parenting a child by adoption makes you uncomfortable, then you are going to have trouble with openness. Observes one adoptive parent: "Open adoption touches upon that matrix of feelings that adoptive parents have toward their children and towards birth parents. It really puts everybody on the line. Are you going to admit that you are an adoptive parent? It's the attitudes towards birth parents and towards adoption that are the real issue in open adoption—not the mechanics."

How do you define your family? Who can be in your family? Can you perceive the birth family as part of your family?

This is a question that Sharon Kaplan Roszia likes to pose to families. She asks them to think about their relationship to their spouse's family when they married. While you may not have been enamored of your in-laws, you probably worked at integrating them and their extended family into your new family. Chances are that you and your spouse didn't flip a coin at the wedding, says Roszia, to decide which family could stay and which had to go. You found a way to link up both families for the sake of your spouse and later, your children. Are you prepared to find a way to bring the birth parents into your family?

Can you make space in your life, in terms of time and energy, for other people?

"Some people are very private and focused on their own small nuclear families," says Roszia. "They are not going to be comfortable with an open adoption. The families I see moving into open adoption expect to share their kids with a lot of people and feel that the more love, and the more relatives, the better." Families involved with open adoption often say that their children are on loan to them and that their job is to be the best possible parents as their kids are growing up.

Even if these are your feelings, keep in mind that you're going to have to put time and energy into the relationship. Observed one mother: "Several adoptive mothers in my group noted that they barely have time to write and send pictures to members of *their* families, much less their children's birth families. For one mom with four children, sending letters and pictures was almost a full time job!"[16]

Do you secretly believe that if you do the open adoption or open placement "right" at the beginning, then the birth parents will go away and leave your family alone?

"That's a question I often ask people," says Roszia, "and they often say to me 'you're right. My secret thought is that if I'm very open and loving and show the birth parents what a good parent I'm going to be, when they're comfortable with me, they'll go away.'"

Families should not agree to any form of openness just to have a placement. The worst thing is for adopting parents to say "yes, I would do anything," and then after finalization to say "no." Emphasizes Gritter: "Don't do something for the sake of expediency that really works against your grain."

What about the members of your extended family? How are they going to feel about open adoption?

Maybe you've decided that you are comfortable meeting and communicating over the years. But you're not so sure you want your parents or other relatives to know the details of the arrangement. If so, you're perpetuating the secrecy that open adoption seeks to avert, and you're putting yourself and your child in a very uncomfortable situation.

It's not uncommon, however, for family members to be wary of open adoption and to have all the questions and concerns you initially had. Educating them about open adoption, and encouraging them to express their feelings, is important.

How flexible are you?

Open adoption experts believe that adoptive parents must be able to improvise. Think about what you imagine an open adoption will be like and what your comfort level will be. Then keep in mind that whatever you decide, it may change. You may decide you want to be relatively closed and that's what the birth parents want but five years later you or the birth parents may try to initiate some contact with each other. Or your child will express an interest in meeting his birth parents. While you may make important decisions and commitments now, this relationship will *not* be static.

CREATING AN OPEN ADOPTION

If you participate in an agency's open program, its counselors should help you define the issues that need to be discussed, provide guidance in communicating with birth parents, and be present at the meeting or meetings you initially have with each other. If you are pursuing an independent adoption, a counselor of your mutual choosing can provide similar assistance. Oregon open adoption specialist Jeanne Etter has created excellent parent empowerment workbooks—which you can obtain through the **Child Welfare League of America** (see appendix A)—that can help you plan an open adoption. You can obtain referrals to counselors and agencies with expertise in open adoption from the **National Adoption Information Clearinghouse** and the **National Federation for Open Adoption Education** (see appendix A). Says Kathleen Silber: "It really helps to have an objective third party. It's important to have somebody facilitate discussion and help both sides." Keep in mind that the first meeting or telephone call between you and a birth parent is like a blind date: you don't know what to expect and you're all very nervous. Emphasizes one birth mother: "We are scared of being rejected too."

How Does the Process Unfold?

At one adoption agency, the birth parents select the adoptive parents by examining portfolios containing everything from autobiographies and photographs to the family's financial profile. After the birth parents choose the prospective adoptive parents who interest them, there's a meeting to make sure that the families feel compatible. Finally the agency holds what's referred to as a "vision merging session" where the families focus on their visions of adoption and how they foresee it working out over time. ("Vision merging" sessions are common at many of the agencies and organizations encouraging open adoptions.) The intention is to tap into the families' mutual value systems and to get down to specifics. The families discuss what will be happening around the time of the baby's birth, and what they envision in the days, weeks, and months afterwards. "All the things that are predictable will be ironed out in advance," says open adoption specialist Gritter. "What is crucial is that the families have a sense that they're working together and that they have problem solving skills to figure things out on their own." You may even talk about who's going to call whom first after the baby goes to the adoptive parents' home. Emphasizes Silber: "This way everybody knows what to expect."

Whether or not you're involved in a formal open adoption program with prescribed steps and procedures, there are many issues that need to be discussed by you and the birth family. You'll need to explore the type and frequency of communication and visitation that you'll have, both pre- and postbirth, and its frequency, what information will be exchanged and what your child will be told, how birthdays and other occasions will be celebrated, how your agreement can be modified or adapted over the years, and how possible conflicts will be mediated. Open adoption experts, including

Melina and Roszia in their book *The Open Adoption Experience,* suggest that among the subjects you'll want to explore are:[17]

- What's the relationship going to be like during the rest of the pregnancy? Will you be in touch before the birth? Will you get together?
- Will you be called when the birth mother goes into labor?
- Where will you be during the birth? In the delivery room? In the waiting room? Not in the hospital at all?
- If you're in the delivery room, who's going to hold the baby first?
- What happens if there's a problem at the birth?
- How much contact will there be in the hospital? What type of visitation rights will you have? (You'll need to be sure that the hospital is willing to allow you to visit.)
- Who's going to feed the baby?
- Where is the baby going to be in the hospital? In the nursery? In the birth mother's room?
- Who's going to name the baby? Are you going to name the child? Does the birth mother want to participate in that? How do you feel about it?
- If the baby's a male, will there be a circumcision?
- Where is the baby going after release from the hospital? To your home? To foster care? (At some agencies this is referred to as "cradle" care.)
- What's going to be the pattern of contact? Are you going to be in touch by letter? By telephone? By visiting? Will the contact go through the agency or will you communicate directly? How frequent will this be? If there is visitation, where will the meetings take place?
- What's going to be the pattern of visiting? If the birth parents must travel to visit your child, who will pay for their expenses?

- What's going to be the relationship with other members of the birth family? Will you be in touch with them?
- If one of the birth parents changes their mind about the adoption, how is that going to be handled? Who will contact whom?
- What about your will? Who will be the child's guardian? Who else in the adoptive family is convinced that this open adoption is a good one?
- If something needs to be discussed in the future, how will this be handled? Who's going to be there to help you negotiate any major disputes? What happens if some serious problem develops, for example, if the birth parent or a member of the extended family tries to intrude or one of you doesn't keep up your part of the bargain? Who will negotiate a solution? Where will you turn for help? And who will pay for the counseling?

It's important to talk about these details in advance so that you minimize the number of potentially awkward moments later on. You want to avoid creating situations where someone feels hurt or disappointed. One birth mother recalls the discomfort she felt at the hospital when "everybody in the room was crying except for the adoptive parents who had the biggest smile on their faces." Another birth mother says she was unsettled by the adoptive parents' taking video pictures of the new baby in her hospital room. Says Silber: "All these kinds of details are important to talk about first, before you get into the emotional experience of the hospital."

You'll also want to consider the possibility of formally getting together for another planning session with the birth family and an uninvolved third party a few weeks or months after your child's placement. Involving a third party, who might even be a divorce or mediation counselor in your community rather than an adoption worker, makes it easier for people to express their feelings at a time when everyone is concerned about not upsetting the other. After the birth you'll be talking about how you see the relationship developing over time, how you feel about your ongoing contact, and what's happening with other family members. "We actually talk about all these things prebirth," observes Silber, "but postbirth it's for real, and families are able to look at it more clearly than when it was more abstract."

THE CHILDREN OF OPEN ADOPTION

"Kids are growing up with open adoption as a big ho-hum. They seem to be more relaxed and are not seeming to struggle with the issue of adoption in quite the same way. Everything is right there. They can touch it, talk about it, and ask questions about it." That's been the assessment of Sharon Kaplan Roszia, coauthor of *The Open Adoption Experience*. Her views are shared by Kathleen Silber: "The children of open adoption find the experience to be 'no big deal.'"[18]

That said, it's clear from talking to the advocates that the lives of the children of open adoption are not problem-free. One significant problem seems to be inconsistent contact or a drop-off in contact by birth mothers as the years pass. As they finish school, move, marry, and start raising their own families, birth mothers' contact with their children frequently lessens or even ceases. For the adopted child that's painful: accustomed to visits, telephone calls, or just letters, the kids feel hurt, sad, and mad when that abates. "We keep seeing more and more that kids are upset," says Silber. "They've been used to having a certain relationship with a birth mother, even if it's just hearing from her once a year. When the child stops hearing from her for two years, the child perceives this as a rejection—'I was given up once and now she's rejected me again.' It's a double whammy." As one seven-year-old involved in a fully open adoption told McRoy and her colleagues: "Couldn't we just stop talking about my birth mother? It's making me sad. Because she used to live real near us and now she doesn't, and I'd like to see her. The only things that bother me about Sara [her birth mother] is I never get to see her."[19]

It's therefore important for the adults choosing to create an open adoption to understand its long range emotional impact on the child. "Birth parents and adoptive parents have to be convinced that open adoption is for the child," asserts Lois Melina. "This is not something that is done primarily for the birth parents, although there certainly are benefits. For birth and adoptive parents to stay involved when it gets difficult, they need to understand how this will help the child and believe it is a moral responsibility to stay in contact." Even if your child's birth parents stop writing or calling you after four or five years, you've got to continue to be in contact with them—even if it's just a brief note—for your child's sake. At a later point your child will be able to make his own decisions about the nature of the ongoing relationship.

The issue of sibling relationships also seems to be causing children and parents some concern and bafflement. Birth parents who later have other children are faced with the task of explaining to these children why they chose not to parent their siblings or half siblings. After birth mother Joan Smith gave birth to a baby girl, she confessed: "I'm really apprehensive about my daughter growing up and having to tell her that she has an older brother, Michael. That seems weird to me. I'm worrying about the reaction: what's she going to say and how is she going to react to it? I just don't know how I'll bring it up to my daughter."

For the children, themselves, there's the need to find the language and the way to describe the siblings in their birth family and their adoptive family. Do they count the siblings in their birth family when they tick off the number of brothers and sisters they have? Do they share with their friends the fact that they have siblings who don't live with them? Observes Roszia: "Kids are trying to figure out how they all fit and what to call each other. It appears to be a question that kids are chewing on. Because of divorce and remarriage, however, lots of other school-aged children are also troubling over the fact of siblings in other homes. This is not an issue that's unique to families built by open adoption."

Like other adoptees, the children of open adoption must also answer the questions posed to them by their friends and the larger community. There will be a reaction when the children start talking about those significant others in their lives. Curiosity and expressions of amazement are to be expected. Your own initial questions will be voiced by others. So will some negative opinions. It's even possible, as some families discovered, that there will be instances where families of children with closed adoptions, fearful of opening up a Pandora's box, try to prevent their children associating with the children of open adoption.

WHAT WILL BE

"Open adoption is an exquisitely difficult form of family building," concludes Roszia. "It is not an easy answer." Open adoption is complex and has its own share of pain. It is by no means a magic elixir that cures all the ills of adoption. "There are all these new experiences that you couldn't prepare yourself for," observes adoptive parent Merilee Scilla, whose daughter's fully open adoption dates back to 1983. "If I sit here and worry—open, closed, knowing my daughter's birth mother, not knowing my son's—I could probably go crazy. There are probably so many in-depth issues that nobody's done research on. I can't deal with the future. I can only deal with today."

This chapter and the growing literature that describes open adoption seek to provide you with glimpses of what might be. As the children of open adoption become adults and start to tell their own stories, we will all know more.

5

SEARCHING FOR A WAITING CHILD IN THE UNITED STATES

◆

Ruprecht's first foster child, Joey, arrived when he was nine months old, already seriously delayed, with a cleft palate and a bad heart, the result, in large measure, of the cocaine and alcohol his mother had used throughout her pregnancy. "One evening, I had given him a bath, bundled him up in warm jammies and was sitting in a chair, holding him close and feeding him his bottle when he gave me an amazed look that said 'My God! Have I gone to heaven? I didn't know life could be like this!' I will always remember that night. It was like he was saying, 'Thank you, God.'"

That was an epiphany for Ruprecht, the moment when she made up her mind to adopt the child. Nothing anyone said or did could dissuade her once her mind was set. Not the doctors who warned her that Joey might not make it through the major heart surgery that he required. . . and especially, not Joey's biological father, who marched up to her in court one day and threatened, 'If this adoption goes through, I'm going to hunt you down and kill you.'

> *The court battle was long and grueling, but in the end Ruprecht prevailed. For the past eight years, she and Joey, now a rail-thin boy with pale blond hair [and formidable developmental delays] have been mother and son.*[1]

John Hubner and Jill Wolfson share the saga of Joey and Sharon Ruprecht in *Somebody Else's Children*. Like Joey, tens of thousands of American children wait each year for an adoptive family. As you'll discover, there *are* babies and younger children to adopt. The majority of these children are in the foster care system. A demographic snapshot of these kids reveals that of the five hundred thousand children in care in 1996, one hundred thousand (20 percent) were eligible for adoption:[2]

- 51 percent were male; 49 percent female
- 4 percent were under one year old; 29 percent were between the ages of one and five; 27 percent were ages six to ten; and 39 percent eleven to eighteen.
- 38 percent were white; 45 percent black; 14 percent Hispanic; 1 percent Asian/Pacific Islander; and 2 percent American Indian

While two-thirds of the children in the foster care system have traditionally returned to their birth families, the others will eventually be freed for adoption—after a wait. An estimated fifty thousand to one hundred thousand youngsters at any time are "waiting to be adopted." These "waiting children" are often referred to as "special-needs children."

Some of these children have potential health risks because of their perinatal exposure to drugs or alcohol. They are children like Joey or Michael, who was described in a photolisting book as an alert three-month-old infant who was on an apnea monitor to measure his breathing and heart rate due to his prenatal exposure to cocaine. There are also healthy minority children of all ages needing adoptive families. And there are siblings such as Jonathan, nine, and Carolyn, seven, whose mother abandoned them and whose father is in prison. Within five years the youngsters had been in four foster homes. Said the therapist working with them: "Jonathan is small for his age, loving, and cuddly. Although Carolyn is younger, she bosses her brother around, is demanding, and throws temper tantrums."

Adoption workers tend to identify youngsters as "waiting" or "special needs" if they are:

- White, school-aged, and especially if they are over the age of twelve
- African-American, school-aged, and especially if they are over the age of eight
- Hispanic, school-aged, and especially if they are over the age of eight
- Part of a sibling group, particularly if they are school-aged or in a group of three or more
- Known to have intellectual, physical, or emotional disabilities. The disabilities they present may include hyperactivity, dyslexia, autism, mental retardation, Down syndrome, hearing impairments, blindness, cerebral palsy, and spina bifida
- Known to have suffered physical or sexual abuse in their birth families
- Born to drug-involved mothers. Infants are considered "at risk" if the mother used drugs during her pregnancy or if traces of a drug such as cocaine are in the baby's urine or blood or in the mother's umbilical cord. Some infants will show residual effects from their mothers' prenatal use of drugs after their birth and will exhibit a range of developmental difficulties or delays as they mature.

- Born to alcohol-involved mothers. Children whose mothers drank during their pregnancy may have alcohol-related birth defects. A child who's identified as suffering from Fetal Alcohol Syndrome (FAS) is often small, has certain distinct facial characteristics, and some level of mental retardation. Children with Fetal Alcohol Effects (FAE) have some of the characteristics of FAS, tend to be very active, and have difficulty completing a task before moving to the next.
- Found to test positively during infancy for the HIV antibody. Keep in mind that the majority of the babies born to HIV-infected mothers are false-positive and will convert to negative before the age of two. As the prenatal treatment of women infected with HIV increases, the number of children who test positively is expected to decline.

IS SPECIAL-NEEDS ADOPTION FOR YOU?

"Our daughter Sharon started life as a twenty-six-week-old preemie hooked up to a respirator. She was severely damaged at birth, with all sorts of medical complications, and the doctors didn't think she'd ever walk. She's almost three now, and the specialists working with her say she can enter a regular nursery school."

Those are the words of Sharon's dad Charles Waters. He beams with pride at her accomplishments—"It's a lot of fun to see her do things we never thought she'd be able to do"—but he's also realistic about the time and commitment this adoption has demanded. For the first two years of Sharon's life, Charles and his wife took time off from work at least twice a week for the medical appointments and physical therapy Sharon required. Life at home was also trying. "Sharon was not an easy kid to live with," he admits. "With special-needs adoption you've got to be willing to put up with a lot."

When you approach an agency about special-needs adoption, you're going to be given extensive information and also asked to assess yourself—and your family—quite candidly. You'll need to look at how you deal with problems and problem-solving, at how the adoption will affect yourself and your family, and how comfortable you will be tapping into school and community resources. For there's no doubt that these children present special parenting challenges, and the agency worker will want you to think about how you will face them.

"Love is not enough," insists Peggy Soule, executive director of the national photolisting service *The CAP Book*. "You have to be open to accepting help and assistance." Observes adoption expert Kay Donley Zigler: "Special-needs adoption requires honest, caring people who work hard at understanding themselves, at how they relate to people, and how they relate to a child."

If you are considering adopting an infant or youngster who is known to have been drug-exposed in utero, you'll need to weigh your ability to deal with risks and unknowns. These infants, often smaller and lighter, may be irritable and jittery, have poor sucking abilities that hinder feeding, irregular sleeping habits, rigid muscle tone, and may be difficult to console. Adoptive parents report that some babies object to being held, refuse eye contact, and cry all the time. While studies are also showing that the cognitive development of a drug-exposed infant, who grows up within a nurturing environment where the effects of poverty are minimized, may be minimal, behavior problems can continue as some children grow. Children who were drug-exposed in utero may still in their elementary school years be easily distracted and aggressive, and have difficulty concentrating and staying on task. Of these children, Dr. Ira Chasnoff of the Chicago-based **National Association for Families and Addiction Research and Education** (see appendix A) says: "Biologically, the cognitive effect appears to be fairly minimal, but behaviorally, a problem appears by school-age."[3] At a 1997 conference exploring adoption and prenatal drug and alcohol exposure, Richard P. Barth of the University of California (Berkeley) reported, for example, that "the number of moves a child had prior to adoption was more significant in determining how well the child was functioning eight years later than whether or not the birth mother had used drugs during pregnancy."[4]

Life with a drug-exposed infant, however, can be rough on a day-to-day basis. The birth mother of Linda Seijo's daughter used both alcohol and cocaine throughout her pregnancy, leaving her baby with the effects of both. "It was not uncommon during infancy for my daughter to wake crying seven times a night, sometimes inconsolably," reported Linda. "I held her as she screamed and tried to push me away." Observed another mother: "Do you know what it's like to hold a child you love and have her bite you?"[5]

It's also important to realize that researchers do not fully understand the nature of the neurological damage these children may have suffered and cannot say what the long-term effects will be. Observes MaryAnne Clarke of the National Adoption Center: "You have children with the potential for significant problems and disabilities that haven't manifested themselves yet. Families have to be willing to accept the worst, even if it doesn't happen, to be realistic and honest as to what they can accept." If you want to learn more about the health and developmental concerns surrounding adopted children who are alcohol- or drug-exposed, contact the **Evan B. Donaldson Adoption Institute** (see appendix A) in New York City or the National Association for Families and Addiction Research and Education in Chicago.

If you are considering an infant who is at risk of developing AIDS, then you must be prepared for the possibility that your child could die. And you've got to handle the fears that others have of these children. Joy and Jim Jenkins decided to pursue the adoption of a local "AIDS baby" abandoned at their local hospital because, as Joy says, "everybody needs love. I couldn't bear the thought of any child being abandoned with no one to call 'Mom' or 'Dad.' I didn't give AIDS a second thought." But, as she and Jim discovered, others did. When they discussed their decision with their family physician, "he stepped back, glared at us and in a very strong voice, tinged with anger, shouted 'You two are crazy. Don't you know this Goddammed baby is going to die?'" After the Jenkinses brought their son home, they had trouble finding a medical practice comfortable with handling an AIDS baby. "The physician's nurse asked me to place the baby on the table to measure him, and she tossed me the tape to do it," recalls Joy, who is also a nurse. "This being done, she handed me the thermometer to take his temperature. Then she remarked that she needed his blood pressure and slid over the cuff and pump for me to perform this job." Joy, having had enough, dressed her son, and walked out of the office.[6] The Jenkinses went on to form the **Children with AIDS (CWA) Project of America** (see appendix A), which recruits families who want to adopt HIV-exposed infants and children and drug-addicted infants, and also locates HIV infants and children. The Children with AIDS Project also serves children who will be orphaned by AIDS throughout the United States and maintains a database of recruited families and children.

You should also understand that there is a likelihood that a child in foster care may have experienced sexual abuse (see chapter 10, page 331–334 for a fuller discussion). Some will have entered the foster care system because of sexual abuse, while others may have been victimized by a child or adult while in foster care.

As you learn more about waiting children, you'll see that many waiting for homes are members of a minority group. The placement of children across racial lines has been controversial and a pitched battled waged over its desirability. In the seventies and eighties many public and private agencies were opposed to interracial placement. But the pendulum has been swinging back: federal legislation enacted in the 1990s prohibited states and agencies from using discriminatory practices, including denial of placement solely on race, in adoption and foster care placements.

If you are white and are interested in a child of minority parentage, consider whether your family and your community can provide the appropriate resources for the particular child you hope to parent. Evaluate carefully how you will meet your child's special needs and how you will provide positive role models.

As to the adoption of Native American children, these fall under the jurisdiction of the Indian Child Welfare Act. This legislation requires that the extended family of an Indian child be given first priority for adoption, followed by a member of the child's tribe, and then a member of another tribe. An agency that seeks to place a Native American child in a non-Native American home may in fact be violating federal law.

ARE YOU READY FOR A SPECIAL-NEEDS ADOPTION?

Here are some questions to consider:

How do you problem-solve?

- What life experiences have you had that prove your ability to deal with problems and to survive crises?

How do you feel about unknowns?

- What have you experienced that you've been able to manage?
- What was hard? How will that be useful to you?
- Has there been a problematic member in the family? How do you feel about the way the family dealt with the person? What would you do?
- How do you handle rejection signals? Do they devastate you? You may need to override rejection signals.

What's your perspective?

- How do you measure success? (Is it in terms of steady progress or achieving a goal?) If your child had a problem with stealing, for example, what would you consider success: when he stops stealing or when he steals less? Can you accept a partial success?
- What's your time frame? (Can you tolerate delays and wait for things to happen?) The progress of developmentally delayed children may be measured in tiny increments over an extended period of time. So too with children who are emotionally disabled. Says therapist Claudia Jewett Jarratt: "If you've got a child who's had five years of instability in his life, you've got to give him 'equal time' to turn around. Think in terms of five years—not one year."
- How do you feel about challenges?

- Are you flexible enough to change your expectations if things don't improve?
- How persistent are you?

When awkward situations arise, how do you handle them?

- Do you have a sense of humor? Do you use humor to defuse situations? Can you step back from a situation? Can you use humor nondestructively?
- How would you feel if your child had a handicap and people stared at you? "When my adopted FAS daughter was an infant, I would get looks that told me 'What kind of mother are you? Look at that scrawny, pale, sickly baby,'" recalls one mother.
- How would you feel if your child acted out in public? What would be your reaction if your child's teacher called and said that your child had been stealing other children's lunch money?
- Are you comfortable with counseling and therapy? Would you be embarrassed to ask for it? How would you feel if the school suggested to you that your child needed help?

What do you find difficult to accept?

- Do certain physical attributes turn you off? (If you feel uncomfortable around people with facial deformities, for example, then a child with a cleft palate would not be ideal.)
- How would you feel if you learned that your child had been sexually abused in a previous home? "The majority of the kids in the foster care system today have been exposed to sexual abuse," maintains Joan McNamara, co-editor of *Adoption and the*

Sexually Abused Child. "These are hurt, traumatized children, and the work you do in a family is going to be more important than that of any therapist. It's going to be made real by the continuity, safety, and warmth of a family."

- How comfortable will you be talking about sexuality and sexual abuse? Is there a history of sexual abuse in your past? If so, how was the experience resolved?

Where can you turn for support?

- How does your family feel about this adoption? How do the children already in your family or other relatives feel? Will they be embarrassed, resentful, annoyed, ashamed?
- What's your support system and extended network like? How will your neighbors feel? How about your school? Is your family physician going to tell you that you're crazy if you adopt a physically, emotionally, or mentally handicapped child?
- What local services can support your child?

What's your lifestyle?

- What children best fit into your lifestyle? (If your family relishes skiing and hiking, you might find it hard to accommodate a physically handicapped child. If you're a very social or church-oriented family, you might find it tough to deal with a child who acts out publicly. What happens the first time your child swears in public?)
- How flexible is your work schedule? Can you find the time for doctors' appointments, therapy, even hospital stays?

What can you cope with and what can't you?

BEGINNING THE SPECIAL-NEEDS ADOPTION PROCESS

Your first—and last—step in pursuing the adoption of a waiting child might just be to contact your local public or private agencies. But what if nearby agencies say that they do not have any children needing adoption, or that they can't help you? People looking to adopt infants often spread their net beyond their local community and outside the agency system to try to locate a child. Families seeking to adopt older or special-needs children need not go outside of the agency system, but they may search—using local, state, and national programs created to serve waiting children.

There are local, state, regional, national, and cyber adoption exchanges that can act as "matching services," registering children, and sometimes prospective adoptive families, in order to make links. Many of these adoption exchanges create photographic listing books that describe waiting children. These images and books, resembling the multiple-listing service used by real estate brokers, provide capsule portraits of children. Some exchanges also bring children to life through videotapes. "The families see a child's personality," observed Marilyn Panichi of the Adoption Information Center of Illinois. "They get an alive, complete, vibrant picture of a child." To get the word out about their waiting families, some exchanges post information on the Internet and circulate "family albums" with photos and descriptions of people hoping to adopt special-needs children.

Exchanges also employ other recruitment devices, such as weekly newspaper columns or regular television newscasts that feature waiting children. Adoption parties or fairs may bring together social workers, prospective adoptive parents, experienced adoptive parents, and waiting children in informal settings. One exchange's trip to the zoo included a picnic lunch, a tour, and a chance for interested people to mingle, share information, and become more familiar with adoption. Although the children come to the event, there is no pressure for families to accept a child. Events such as this give children the chance to meet adults—and offer you the chance to find that special child.

STATE ADOPTION EXCHANGES

Many states operate some form of adoption exchange where agencies—both public and private—can list waiting children and, in some instances, waiting families (see appendix B for a state-by-state list). If an agency has a child needing to be placed in an adoptive home, but no suitable family, it can register that child with the exchange. Some states even mandate by law that agencies *must* register their children with a state adoption exchange if they fail to find an adoptive home within a specified period of time. The exchanges do not have children in their custody. Rather they take referrals and try to facilitate placements; both services are free of charge.

The Massachusetts Adoption Resource Exchange (MARE) is typical of a full-service exchange. Its programs include adoption information, referral (trying to match a referred child to one of their registered waiting families), photolisting (the *MARE Manual*), and recruitment (a waiting child series in the *Boston Globe* and other newspapers throughout the state and WBZ's television program, *Wednesday's Child*), exchange meetings, and adoption parties. In 1996, 340 children were registered with MARE (half of them were children of color) and 123 children found families through its efforts. MARE responds annually to thousands of inquiries. MARE focuses on waiting children who are more than six years old, sibling groups, children with emotional, physical, and intellectual challenges, children of color of all ages, and youngsters considered to be at legal risk. The *MARE Manual* provides a profile of the child through a detailed biography and photograph. Containing the write-ups of almost all the registered children, the manual is circulated to adoption agencies, community centers, public libraries, and parent groups—places where interested people might go for information.

As a person seeking a special-needs child, you should contact one or more exchanges. If waiting families are permitted to register with your exchange, then do so yourself or ask your worker to register you. Try to list yourself with other states' exchanges, particularly those nearby. Consult as many photolisting books as possible at frequent intervals. Find out whether your local parent group, or a local agency, has the photolisting books of other states' exchanges. (Some parent groups or agencies, particularly those with an interest in placing special-needs children, subscribe to out-of-state listing services.) You may not want to look at every exchange's books, but it's recommended that you look at the books of neighboring states, or states that have a large number of children in foster care. Remember, however, that the children listed in these books will be those for whom an agency has not been successful in finding a home locally.

Using a photolisting book, even for out-of-state children, can result in a successful adoption. Carol and Bob Wilson had been consulting their state photolisting book and those of several other states for several months. They saw the photos of the children who would be theirs—a brother and sister with developmental and physical handicaps (including congenital cataracts that severely limited the children's sight)—in another state's photolisting book. It took seven months and many interstate telephone calls; they had to contend with the reluctance of the children's social worker to place them out of state. But, says Carol, "persistence paid off." The caseworker confided to her afterward that the biggest selling point—what broke down her resistance to an interstate placement—were the letters that Carol sent expressing the family's sincere wish to adopt the children. All the other families under consideration had just provided factual information. "Our file was more personal," Carol says, " and that's what made the difference." That and the willingness to use a photolisting book, and the persistence to follow through.

REGIONAL EXCHANGES

Regional exchanges take referrals of children from several states and circulate information about adoption. Very often the children listed with the regional exchanges have problems that have made their placement more difficult. Agencies contact a regional exchange to seek wider exposure for such children and to recruit families. Like state adoption exchanges, regional exchanges usually register waiting children and families and distribute a photolisting book. They run recruitment programs and provide technical information to social service agencies.

You may want to contact your nearest regional exchange or the other regional exchanges around the country. A list of them follows.

ADOPTION CENTER OF DELAWARE VALLEY
1500 Walnut Street
Philadelphia, PA 19102; (215) 735–9988
Serves Delaware, District of Columbia, Maryland, New Jersey, Pennsylvania, Virginia, West Virginia.

THE ADOPTION EXCHANGE
925 South Niagara Street
Denver, CO 80224; (303) 333–0845
Serves Colorado, Missouri, Nevada, New Mexico, South Dakota, Utah, and Wyoming.

MASSACHUSETTS ADOPTION RESOURCE EXCHANGE
45 Franklin Street
Boston, MA 02110–1301; (617) 542–3678
Serves Connecticut, Maine, Massachusetts, New Hampshire, Rhode Island, Vermont.

NORTHERN NEW ENGLAND ADOPTION EXCHANGE
Department of Human Services
221 State Street
Augusta, ME 04333; (207) 289–2971
Serves Maine, New Hampshire, and Vermont.

NORTHWEST ADOPTION EXCHANGE
1809 7th Avenue
Seattle, WA 98101; (206) 292–0092
Serves Alaska, Idaho, Nevada, Oregon, Utah, and Washington.

SOUTHEASTERN EXCHANGE OF THE UNITED STATES (SEE US)
P.O. Box 1453
Greenville, SC 19692; (803) 242–0460
Serves Alabama, Florida, Georgia, Kentucky, Mississippi, North Carolina, South Carolina, and Tennessee.

THREE RIVERS ADOPTION COUNCIL
307 Fourth Avenue
Pittsburgh, PA 15222; (412) 471–8722
Serves Delaware, District of Columbia, Maryland, New Jersey, Pennsylvania, Virginia, and West Virginia.

NATIONAL ADOPTION EXCHANGES

June, a seven-year-old child with Down syndrome, was living in Georgia, awaiting adoption. She was registered with the state exchange, featured in the state photolisting book, shown on an Atlanta television show, and named child of the month in a local newspaper. All this was done to try to find an adoptive family for her. Finally her social worker registered her with **Children Awaiting Parents (CAP)** (see appendix A), a national photolisting service in Rochester, New York.

Bertha, a single woman in her fifties, was searching for a child to adopt in upstate New York. She looked through *The CAP Book* and saw June's photograph. She called her social worker; her social worker called June's social worker; Bertha's home study went to Georgia; June's biographical information came to New York. June's and Bertha's searches were over; a new adoptive family had been formed.

The CAP Book registers children from throughout the United States who need wider exposure. Workers must be willing to place the children across state lines. Both adoption social workers and families can contact the staff of *The CAP Book,* who serve as a clearinghouse and direct people to the appropriate agency and caseworker. All the children featured in *The CAP Book* are hard to place. Check your local adoptive-parent group or specialized agency for the book. For further information, you can also contact CAP.

The **National Adoption Center** (see appendix A) provides extensive information and referral services and operates a telecommunications network (the National Adoption Exchange) that lists waiting children and families, and links agencies around the country. This computer system can be accessed by adoption workers around the country whose agencies participate in the network. Using the telecommunications network, a social worker in Tallahassee, Florida, who is seeking an adoptive family for a ten-year-old boy with mental retardation can plug into the computer system and turn up interested families in Albany, Boise, or Albuquerque.

With that information the worker can then contact the families or their agency worker directly. Families with completed home studies can register themselves. Michael and Pam, a black couple stationed in Germany, used the electronic bulletin board after their efforts to adopt a young black child had been unsuccessful because of their posting overseas. They contacted the National Adoption Center, and their interest was listed on the electronic bulletin. A social worker in Wisconsin saw that message and got in touch: the agency had a ten-month-old child waiting for an adoptive family.

The National Adoption Center and CAP have also created an Internet photolisting book—*Faces of Adoption: America's Waiting Children* (http://www.adopt.org). The online photolisting contains basic information about each child—age, birth date, ethnicity, disabilities, state of residence, ID number—a photograph, and a verbal description. There are also hypertext links to other sites to provide you with further information. In the photolisting about a young boy named Ronald, for example, who is described as taking "medication to control attention-deficit/hyperactivity disorder," there is a hyptertext link to attention-deficit/hyperactivity disorder, while the description of Constance, who is "considered to be in the moderate range for mental retardation," has a hypertext link to mental retardation. You can search using various criteria (age, sex, disability). If you want to inquire about a specific child, you can speak with a *Faces* staff member. You may not find a specific child, but if you're Internet-savvy this is an excellent way to view a continuing selection of America's waiting children. Keep in mind that state and regional adoption exchanges also highlight special-needs children online.

Other excellent national resources are **Adopt A Special Kid (AASK) America** and the **National Resource Center**

for Special Needs Adoption (see appendix A). **AASK Midwest** (Toledo, Ohio) has also expanded its service beyond its Midwest core of Illinois, Indiana, Iowa, Michigan, Minnesota, Ohio, Wisconsin.

SOME SPECIALIZED REFERRAL PROGRAMS

In addition to state, regional, and national exchanges, there are specialized exchanges and programs:

CHILDREN WITH AIDS PROJECT OF AMERICA
4141 West Bethany Home Road
Phoenix, AZ 85019; (602) 973–4319
Recruits families, locates children, and does computer matches.

JEWISH CHILDREN'S ADOPTION NETWORK
P.O. Box 16544
Denver, CO 80216; (303) 573–8113
Links waiting Jewish children with waiting Jewish families.

A K.I.D.S. (KNOWLEDGE AND INFORMATION ON DOWN SYNDROME) EXCHANGE
56 Midchester Avenue
White Plains, NY 10606; (914) 428–1236
A voluntary adoption exchange providing services to birth parents, adoptive parents, and agencies. Accepts listings from agencies of children needing placement. Families seeking to adopt children can also list themselves. Can also help birth parents seeking to place a Down syndrome infant with an agency or independently.

DEAF ADOPTION NEWS SERVICE
7981 Northumberland Road
Springfield, VA 22153; fax: (703) 644–1827
Serves deaf parents and deaf children.

NATIONAL AMERICAN INDIAN ADOPTIVE SERVICE
Three Feathers Associates
P.O. Box 5508
Norman, OK 73070; (405) 360–2919
Serves Native American families.

NATIVE AMERICAN ADOPTION RESOURCE EXCHANGE
a.k.a. Indian Exchange, Council of Three Rivers
200 Charles Street
Pittsburgh, PA 15238; (412) 782–4457
Serves Native American children by providing recruitment and referral of adoptive Native American families. Families can apply for registration with the exchange if one or both parents are Native American. You will be expected to provide documented evidence of Indian ancestry, i.e., your enrollment number, census number, certificate of degree of Indian blood, or a letter from your tribe on tribal stationery. Be sure your home study also mentions the name of your tribe and your cultural lifestyle.

THE FRUSTRATIONS OF WORKING WITH EXCHANGES AND PHOTOLISTINGS

We first started looking at the Books (with an eye toward a two- to three-member sibling group around ten years of age) during the time we attended Parent Preparation Classes. By the time we received the letter from the agency certifying us as "perfect" prospective adoptive parents we already had selected a sibling group here we wanted to adopt. Several nervous weeks later we were told that unexpectedly relatives had come into the picture and those children were no longer up for adoption. But, "please try again."

We did. This time we chose two boys from another state's book we thought would fit into our home. It was several days later when we discovered that, unknown to the agency in our state, the boys were already in the process of being adopted. So, "please try again."

A week or so later one of the social workers from the agency called to say that she had just received a new exchange book, and that there were three siblings she felt were definitely suitable. We asked that she call about them rather than write, thus cutting down on the suspenseful waiting time. Within an hour she called back with the information that just the week before the children had appeared on Wednesday's Child *in another state. They too were already on their way through the adoption process.*

Shortly thereafter we chose two children from another state. The news from their social worker, "please try again."[7]

Alice's litany of woe is unfortunately not that unusual. Many people hoping to parent waiting children report that their search is long-running despite the fact that they've seen children listed for adoption, and that, like Alice, they have been willing to consider a wider range of children. "I would sit at our public library for four to five hours poring through photolisting books," recalls Cathy Beaver, who was hoping to adopt three siblings under the age of six. "I would walk out of there in tears. At one time I gave our social worker twelve choices, and the responses all came back 'hold' or 'placed.'" Parent-group newsletters often carry stories like Cathy's. People report that when they inquire about a specific child they are told that the child is on "hold." Yet months later these people report that they will still see the child's photo appearing in an exchange book.

You may find that social workers are reluctant to place children out of the county or out of the state, despite the fact that no adoptive family has yet been found locally. Stories like the one told by Ernesto Loperena of the New York

Council of Adoptable Children are not uncommon. A black family in New Mexico was interested in a sibling group of three in New York City. While the agency in New York that had custody of the children was interested in this family, the local New Mexico social service department turned down their request for a home study because the children were out of state. After Loperena's intervention, a home study was done, but then the New York State agency had second thoughts, expressing concern about moving the kids cross-country. "We've cut distance by fax machines, telephone, and jet airplanes," observes Loperena, "but we still think of New Mexico as a different kind of world." It was only after more arm-twisting that this adoption proceeded.

There is also the suspicion that social workers are "collecting" home studies, poring through as many as sixty before beginning to make a decision. Alice even found, when she inquired about one child in another state, that the social worker had only listed the child for adoption because the state had mandated it; the worker had no plans for placement and was surprised—and not very interested—when Alice contacted her. The statistics reflect this: in a study released by the Institute for Children in 1997 it reported that one-quarter of all foster children remain in care for more than four years and that children leave the foster care system to be adopted after an average stay of three-and-a-half to five-and-a-half years. The Adoption and Safe Families Act of 1997 may alter this situation: this federal legislation makes children's safety—rather than family unification—the primary goal. Under this, most children could be freed for adoption after a year in foster care and a "fast track" provision provides for greater speed in cases where the children have been severely abused or abandoned. (The legislation also rewards states with cash bonuses for each foster and special-needs child adopted.)

Be aware that a small percentage of the children legally free for adoption within a state or region may be listed with an exchange or photolisted. In states where listing is mandated by law, the number will be higher than where listing is voluntary.

UNDERSTANDING THE LABELS

Photolistings provide lively verbal snapshot portraits of children. But they may also contain code words, short-cut phrases, or jargon that you should understand, notes adoptive parent and advocate Rita Laws.[9] Just as there are red flags in independent adoption, so are there code words in special-needs adoption. "Very active, tomboy, impulsive" may indicate attention-deficit/hyperactivity disorder; "victim of neglect" could mean sexually abused; "developmentally delayed" could signify anything from mild learning disabilities to mental retardation, while "experienced families" could signal that the children are a handful and require constant attention. Be sure that you understand the diagnosis severity of any medical conditions described, as well as the treatments required. Having access to a good medical reference book or browsing online may help you sort out the terms. "Interpreting a photolisting takes practice," observes Laws. "Proceed with caution and ask lots of questions."

Exchange books, television appeals, and online photolistings that heighten a child's visibility are important tools in placement and recruitment. But, as people seeking to adopt will tell you, they can be hard on the families who respond to the appeal. Reporting on the impact of the local Connecticut television program, *Thursday's Child,* the Connecticut Adoption Resource Exchange noted that for three black brothers, ages six, five, and three, it had received forty-six calls; and for an eighteen-month-old girl of mixed parentage with developmental delays it got thirty-two calls.[8] In both cases one of the responding families became the children's adoptive parents. The television program worked but if you, as a family, set your heart on one particular child, you were likely to be disappointed.

SOME TIPS ON SEARCHING FOR THAT WAITING CHILD

To learn more about waiting children and special-needs adoption, get in touch with the **National Adoption Information Clearinghouse** (see appendix A). Its staff can provide you with basic factsheets and refer you to local agencies. If you'd like to read about some of the waiting children, try Gay Courter's *I Speak for This Child* or John Hubner and Jill Wolfson's *Somebody Else's Children*. Charlotte Lopez's moving autobiography *Lost in the System* offers the perspective of a teenager who spent her entire youth in foster care. The National Resource Center for Special Needs Adoption can also direct you to reading materials and local resources.

- Be sure that you understand who is a special-needs child. You may be searching for a child who is not likely to appear in the exchanges.
- Consider how flexible you are. See how much you can broaden your scope. Evaluate what behaviors or disabilities you can handle in a child.

- Decide if you are comfortable with a legal risk adoption, in which the youngster enters your home as a foster child whose parents may not have terminated their rights. If you are, say so.
- Be sure that you are listed with all local exchanges and informal exchanges available for your area.
- List yourself with the state exchange if possible.
- List yourself with the regional exchange if possible.
- Contact national exchanges to see if they have the type of child you are seeking.
- Use the Internet in your search and take advantage of the speed by which you can communicate.
- Be sure your home study is as complete as possible.
- Check your state photolistings (and others that you decide to consult) *frequently* and try to respond to *as many* listings as possible. Don't feel shy about requesting information on more than one child listed in the book. Let your agency know promptly about your interests.
- If you see a child who interests you in a photolisting, either you or your worker should call (or send an e-mail if that is possible), rather than write, to get some initial information about a child. If your worker has a problem making out-of-state telephone calls, see what special arrangements can be worked out. If you're still interested in a child after the initial inquiry, follow up immediately by sending out your home study.
- Note the date when you talk with your worker, and follow up. Your worker can get busy. Keep track of when you contacted the child's agency and be prepared to follow up.
- Don't wait to hear about one child before you inquire about another.

- Keep track of which children you inquired about, when you made the inquiry, whom you talked with, and what was done. Follow up.
- Encourage your worker to lobby on your behalf.
- When you are rejected for a particular child, ask why.
- Don't set your heart on one particular child you've seen featured. *Chances are you will be successful in adopting a child like the one who attracted your attention* rather than that particular child.
- If you are having trouble adopting a child who appeared in a photolisting book or a listing service, notify the exchange or listing service that you are having problems. They can often help expedite the process.
- If you are interested in adopting a special-needs infant, spread the word in the independent adoption grapevine. Tell people you are interested in the direct placement of a baby with significant medical problems or whose birth parents have a medical history that might be considered high risk.
- If you are interested in a transracial infant adoption, look beyond the agencies by utilizing the independent adoption grapevine.
- *Be persistent.* People who seek to adopt independently work hard to spread the word. You will need to do the same if you are looking for a special-needs child.

There are children who need you. It may take some time to make the connection.

6

PURSUING AN INTERCOUNTRY ADOPTION

◆

Ni Yan Yan, infant girl, Chinese, left at a few weeks old on a street and now six months old and living in an orphanage.

Hee Ra, infant girl, South Korea, living in a foster family.

Alfredo, infant boy, Guatemalan, living with a foster family.

Marta, four-year-old girl, living in a Russian orphanage.

Ionica, two-year-old girl, living in a Romanian orphanage.

Sharpla, infant boy, Indian, abandoned at birth weighing just three pounds.

Jose and Margarita, brother and sister, ages five and six, living in an orphanage in Peru.

Sompit, age three, female, living since infancy in an orphanage in Thailand.

These are just a few of the children, born abroad, who have been adopted in the United States. These children have found parents, but there are more like them still waiting to be adopted. The children needing permanent homes range in age from infancy up to their teens. They may be orphaned, abandoned, or have a parent or relatives who cannot care for them because of poverty or other conditions. Some may have lost or been separated from their families by war. Older children may have spent time living on the streets or may have spent all or most of their lives in orphanages. In some countries, agencies may attempt to place the infants in foster care, but that is not the general rule. Many of the children will have spent weeks, months, or even years living in orphanages. *All* children who come to the United States for adoption must meet the federal requirements for the designation "orphan" under federal immigration law (see chapter 8).

Intercountry adoption involves the placement for adoption in the United States of children born abroad. In the eighties the number of adoptees coming from abroad surged, rising from 4,868 children in 1981 to a high of 10,097 children in 1987, according to figures kept by the Immigration and Naturalization Service. South Korea alone accounted for half of those placements (5,910) with children also streaming in from India (807), Colombia (724), the Philippines (593), Guatemala (291), and Chile (238). Ten years later the foreign adoption picture had dramatically altered: while the total number had risen to more than 13,000, South Korean adoptions had dropped to 1,654, Colombian to 233, and those from the Philippines to 163. Following a stampede to Romania in 1991 (2,594 adoptions), both singles and couples journeyed to Russia in the mid-nineties (more than 9,700 adoptions between 1994 and 1997) and other former communist countries as the Iron Curtain lifted to reveal large numbers of children languishing in orphanages. Others traveled to the People's

Republic of China, whose one-child policy forced many Chinese families to abandon their baby girls. The numbers rose steadily: 856 in 1994, 2,193 in 1995, 3,318 in 1996, and 3,597 in 1997. By 1997, with more than 13,000 foreign adoptions, the new adoption picture was clear: about one-third were Chinese, one-third Russian, one-tenth Korean; the "top twenty countries" included Vietnam, Bulgaria, and Ethiopia.[1]

If you are contemplating an intercountry adoption, try to seek out people who have adopted children from abroad. Attend parent-group meetings, particularly ones where some of the children will be present. If that is not possible, be sure to look at photographs of these children. If you have access to the Internet, you can see photographs on families' home pages, in magazine articles and other resources on the World Wide Web.

This chapter describes the mechanics of intercountry placement. Although I focus on how the process works, keep in mind the reason that people concerned with children both here and abroad have supported intercountry placements. "Every child in the world needs a family," observed a priest working at a Chilean orphanage. For him and many others, intercountry adoption is one way to find "families for children, *not* children for families."

There are some basic matters that will affect your life as a family and your future child's life, and should therefore influence your decision regarding intercountry adoption. You will need to think about your motivation to adopt, your attitudes toward race, culture, and Americanization, and your acceptance of difference. How comfortable will you be when your family is the subject of frequent stares and questions?

IS INTERCOUNTRY ADOPTION FOR YOU?

Holt International Children's Services, whose experience placing children from South Korea goes back to 1956 and now serves children throughout Asia, Eastern Europe, and Latin America, devised a series of questions and comments that you should evaluate as you ponder intercountry adoption:[2]

1. What are your ideas about race? What characteristics do you think Asian, Indian, Latin American, etc. people have? Do you expect your child to have these characteristics? The children become Americanized; therefore try to visualize that cute little baby growing up into a child—a teenager—an adult—a parent. Think about grandchildren.
2. How do you feel about getting lots of public attention, stares, etc.? Possibly your adopted child will get too much attention and other children will tend to feel left out.
3. You will become an interracial family. Do you raise your child to have the same identity as you or your other children? How do you help him develop his own identity? Should his name reflect his national origin? What relationship will the name have to the sense of 'Who am I?' Imagine a child you know and love being sent overseas to be adopted? How would you want him raised? As an American in a foreign country? A native in that country?
4. How can you learn to know what it's like being nonwhite and growing up in a white society if you don't know this from your own experience? You

will have to find out how to teach or educate yourself to become sensitive to your child's world.

5. Your family will now be interracial for generations. Adoption of a child of another race or country is not just a question of an appealing little baby. How do you feel about interracial marriage? How does your family feel about interracial marriage? How do you feel when people assume that you are married to an Asian person?

In addition to your qualities and abilities as parents, it is important for you to understand your motivation for this kind of adoption. Do you feel you are doing a good deed for a poor, homeless child, who will perhaps be more grateful to you when he is older than if he were your birth child? This is poor motivation and not very realistic. If your primary orientation is to help the child become absorbed into your culture at the expense of his own, then transracial adoption is not for you. You must have an attitude of respect for the country and culture of the child.

Do you have the capacity to identify with this child, to see the world from his point of view and to lovingly supply his physical, mental, and spiritual needs? Do you want to learn more about the child's culture and heritage? If you do, then you can consider further the idea of intercountry adoption.

Consider the conversation that one mother had with a stranger about her daughter:

He: What is it?

She: She's a little girl—my daughter.

He: No, I mean, what is it?

She: She's a child.

He: No, where's she from?

She: She's from Korea.

He: You mean your husband's a Chink?

She: No, she's adopted from Korea.

He: Couldn't you just make a baby like normal people?[3]

You'll be asked: What do you know about her real parents? What's her real name? How much did it cost? ("I've heard that there's a lot of international baby buying.") Several people are likely to nominate you, in front of your child, for sainthood for rescuing the poor waif. They'll also tell her how lucky she is that you rescued her and adopted her. Someday, you may have the experience that another parent of a young Asian adoptee had:[4]

> *The usual questions continued throughout the dinner (in a restaurant filled with senior citizens)—'Where are the children from?' 'Are they related?' 'They speak English so well.' 'Don't you love their eyes.' As we prepared to leave, I took my daughter to the bathroom. She burst into tears—and I assumed that she hit her head on the door. When I asked what happened, she sobbed 'I'm not hurt in my head, I'm hurt in my feelings—why don't people leave us alone? I said—because you*

are cute children, who happen to look different. She said—'I don't want to look different, I want to look like you, Mommy.'

These issues are among the ones that will confront you as the parent of a child adopted from abroad. Many of the questions will be discussed in later chapters of this book. All of them should be explored by you *before* you adopt a child from another country.

HOW INTERCOUNTRY ADOPTION WORKS

In the United States, you may work with a local agency that places children directly from abroad, with a nonlocal agency that has an intercountry adoption program and networks with local agencies, or with a facilitator. Most of the intercountry adoptions today involve an agency in the U.S. that connects with an agency, attorney, government office, or orphanage overseas. For some countries, you may work directly with a contact abroad in what is known as a direct or parent-initiated adoption (this is becoming increasingly rare). You will still need to have someone, either a licensed social worker or an agency, do a home study of your family. Your child may be placed by a national department of social services, a government orphanage, a local orphanage, maternity home, private foundation, or other social-welfare organizations in the foreign country. Depending upon the laws of a country, judges, doctors, lawyers, social workers, and other people interested in child welfare, even relatives, friends, or business associates, may be involved in arranging intercountry adoptions.

Because you choose to work with an agency in the United States does not necessarily mean that your U.S. agency's intercountry adoption program will be connected to an agency or orphanage in the foreign country of your choice. *Some U.S. agencies work with attorneys and other individuals in a foreign country as well as with orphanages and other agencies.* Be sure that the U.S. agencies that you contact tell you exactly who their foreign counterparts are. You can get extensive valuable information about intercountry adoption around the world from the **Office of Children's Issues, Bureau of Consular Affairs of the U.S. State Department** (see appendix A). You will also want to get in touch with the **Joint Council on International Children's Services** (see appendix A). Many intercountry adoption agencies belong to the organization, as do some parent groups. And the *Report on Intercountry Adoption,* produced by **International Concerns for Children** (see appendix A) is a veritable gold mine of information. *The Report* is published annually and updated during the year so that you get current information.

To get a clearer sense of how intercountry adoption works, let's look at three families and see how their children's adoption proceeded:

Gena and Duane Moss adopted an infant girl from South Korea through a local U.S. agency working with a social welfare agency in South Korea. The local agency's worker met with them and conducted a home study. After the local agency approved the Mosses as prospective adoptive parents, it forwarded the home study and other documents to its counterpart in South Korea. A few months later Gena and Duane's worker called them into her office and showed them photographs of a five-month-old Korean girl in foster care. She also shared with them whatever records, particularly medical information, the Korean agency had provided. Gena and Duane were delighted and accepted the referral. They filled in some agency papers, including a statement that they would accept financial responsibility for the child, and processed their I-600 form with the Immigration and Naturalization Service (see chapter 8). They then waited while the South Korean agency did its share of processing forms (for example, obtaining the baby's Korean passport). Two months later their worker called to tell them that their daughter would be arriving on a flight later that week, brought by a volunteer escort.

Single parent Cheryl Hughes adopted an infant girl from China through a local U.S. agency, which had a Chinese adoption program. The agency's worker conducted a home study. After the local agency approved her as a prospective adoptive parent (and she had obtained any necessary approvals and other supporting documents), it forwarded the application, referred to as a dossier, to the China Adoption Center in Beijing, which oversees all adoption. The staff of the China Adoption Center reviewed the dossier and finally issued an approval accompanied by an assignment of a specific child in a specific province of China. Several months later Cheryl's social worker contacted her about the six-month-old baby girl who had just been referred for her. Cheryl knew that as part of her adoption process she would go to China because the Chinese require that families journey to the province where the adoptee lives and that they complete the adoption in the province. Some ten months after her dossier actually arrived in Beijing, after doing all the necessary paperwork in the U.S. and getting all the Chinese approvals she could in advance, Cheryl, along with several other families who were adopting through her agency, went to China. After the adoption in the local province, she traveled to Guangzhou to visit the U.S. consulate to obtain a U.S. visa for their daughter's entry to the United States.

Dana and Bill McCarthy adopted an infant girl in India with the help of a local agency, an agency in another state, and an Indian orphanage. They applied to the agency in another state because it had an intercountry Indian adoption program and would take applications from out-of-state people. Bill and Dana arranged for a local agency, approved by the out-of-state agency, to do their home study and serve as the "local service" agency. This local agency agreed to provide postplacement supervision of the child and work with the family toward finalization when the child arrived.

When their home study was completed, the local agency sent it to the out-of-state agency that had the international adoption program. The out-of-state agency also approved them as adoptive parents. This agency then forwarded the documentation to its counterpart abroad.

About a year after Bill and Dana submitted their application to this agency, their local agency received a child referral. This information was sent to them from the out-of-state agency via the interstate compact officer in the state's department of social services. All written communication, in fact, between the two U.S. agencies went through the interstate compact officer. Bill and Dana also filed papers with the Immigration and Naturalization Service and waited for word when they could travel abroad to do additional paperwork and pick up their child.

SEARCHING INDEPENDENTLY FOR A CHILD ABROAD

While the preponderance of intercountry adoptions involve a U.S. adoption agency, some people still choose to go it alone as much as possible. They may do so because they want a child of a particular nationality and there is no agency placing those children. Others have family or friends who make a connection for them. Still others feel that they want to do the adoption themselves—and that includes finding their own child abroad. Don't be surprised to discover that the orphanage or social welfare organization that you've chosen to work with independently abroad also has ties with several U.S. agencies.

Consider the experience of Robert and Carolyn Lange who arranged an adoption through business associates in a Latin American country where intercountry adoptions are rare. They flew to a remote, mountainous section of the country, half a day's distance from the capital. The next day, with a two-week-old infant in their arms, they found that the local passport office had been closed down by armed guards because officials had been selling passports illegally. Recalls Carolyn, "We tried to reach our attorney back in the capital for advice, but the telephones weren't working. We took a chance and flew back to the capital with our new baby, but without the passport."

There were more hitches: The mother's release for adoption didn't state that the baby was allowed to leave the country. Their attorney had to contact a lawyer in the baby's hometown to obtain a new declaration from her. Meanwhile, back in the capital, the Langes had to be interviewed by a court-appointed social worker in their hotel room, then wait for the worker to write up his report to the judge ("Would he approve of them?"), who then ruled on the placement. The baby had a bad case of diaper rash, so they went to see a local doctor. "Through all of this," says Carolyn, "the people were wonderful to us." When the Langes finally departed—having postponed their flight plans many times—the staff at the airline reservations office threw a party and gave them little gifts.

Five months later the Langes returned with the baby to the country's capital to appear before the judge for a postplacement visit. "Going back to court was scary," recalls Carolyn, "We were concerned that the judge might find something in the postplacement reports she didn't like and take the baby away from us."

"Flying without a net" is how Carolyn describes their adoption experience. "We learned as we went. The support system that people get from an agency—and that buffer—wasn't there. If something went wrong, we were the ones who found out."

With a direct adoption, the burden of bringing the adoption to fruition lies with you. If you toy with the possibility of arranging a legal, direct overseas adoption, you'll want to ask yourself:

- Is it important to have someone help me through the adoption process step by step?
- How much of the legwork am I willing to do myself? There may be a parent group to whom you can turn, but you will not be working with an established program in the United States.
- How much uncertainty can I live with?
- What is the state of my finances? If there are unanticipated expenses, can I absorb them? With an agency's

intercountry adoption program, many of the fees will be outlined.

- How self-reliant am I? You may have to deal with attorneys, bureaucrats, and other officials in a foreign country.
- What "risks" am I prepared to assume?
- What references can my adoption contact provide? Has this contact ever helped with a U.S. intercountry adoption before?

You will also have to determine:

- the legal steps you must take to realize the placement of a child and who will be doing your legal work abroad;
- the paperwork you will be required to do;
- the expected costs: Try to get a breakdown of probable expenses—lawyers' fees, court costs, foster care, orphanage or agency donation, medical care;
- the expenses, if any, that must be paid "up front": This is particularly relevant if you will be working with an attorney;
- when fees are to be paid: Be sure that you get a listing of *all* services and *all* fees *in writing;*
- how long the whole process is likely to take; and
- if you will be communicating by telephone, when is a good time to talk.

Be sure your contact overseas understands exactly what documents you will need in order to bring your child legally into the United States. Your contact may know the requirements for a legal adoption in his country; you may have to tell him what is required for U.S. immigration.

WAITING CHILDREN ABROAD

Just as in the United States, there are also waiting children and special needs children abroad. In another country children may be considered "hard to place" solely because of their age—and in some countries or in some circumstances, that may be a preschool-aged girl or boy. Young children may be considered hard to place if they are part of a sibling group or have a correctable handicap such as a cleft palate. The waiting children generally needing adoptive families are school-aged boys and girls, older sibling groups of two, sibling groups of three or more, and children of any age with significant medical needs. The medical needs that you might find include cleft palate, orthopedic problems, heart defects, blood disorders, cerebral palsy, major vision limitations, hearing limitations, seizure disorders, malnutrition, burns, significant developmental delays, and emotional problems.

If you've questioned whether adopting an older child would mean that you miss out on some of the infant experiences, consider the observations of Maggie Francis Conroy in *A World of Love*[5] about the adoption of Nadia, who'd spent her early years in an orphanage:

> *When we decided to adopt an older child, I sometimes worried that I would be missing important 'firsts' that make up a baby's initial years. The first smile, the first tooth, the first word. . . the first wave, the first steps; and all the other firsts that are not so exciting but equally important. . . during those first months with Nadia we got to celebrate firsts just like any other parents, firsts that were sometimes even more special because Nadia was marveling in them as much as we were and didn't take for granted as a tiny baby would. The first time Nadia called us Mama and Papa was just as thrilling at five as it would have been at eight months. For her to be able to iden-*

tify two adults as "Mama" and "Papa" was an amazing feat. She loved it too! Her first time in a grocery store was a thrill in ways that children who grow up in the United States will never experience. . . . I could tell she had never seen so much food in her life. . . .

We not only got the normal firsts that other parents have, but we got other firsts as well; firsts that could only come about in a child who has gone without and is discovering things thought unobtainable. We got our firsts. We got our special firsts, and more.

Some agencies have programs devoted to the placement of special needs children. If a special-needs child interests you, and your local agency does not have an active program, several agencies have nationally recognized programs for waiting children and will network with other agencies around the country. You might contact the Joint Council on International Children's Services or consult the *Adoption Photolisting* of International Concerns for Children.

REQUIREMENTS

For an intercountry adoption, you will need to meet the requirements of your state government, the federal government, and the foreign country. Chapter 8, which discusses paperwork, explores this at greater length. If you are considering a direct adoption, find out whether your state permits independent placements from abroad and what preadoption requirements must be met. The Hague Convention on Intercountry Adoption, a multilateral treaty that countries around the world are ratifying, seeks to ensure that the rights of adoptees, birth parents, and adoptive parents are respected. The Hague Convention is designed to remove barriers to intercountry adoption, establish basic adoption practices, criteria, and accreditation procedures, and smooth out the entire process. As the United States and other countries move toward full implementation of the Hague Convention, federal and international adoption requirements are likely to change.

Each foreign country, or possibly an individual district within the country, usually has its own laws about guardianship and adoption. These laws may govern such matters as your age, the length of your marriage, and whether or not previous divorce is permitted. If you are thirty-five and married for two years, you might be eligible to adopt in one country but not in another. A forty-five-year-old may be considered too old for adopting an infant in one country, yet seen as an excellent parental resource in another. There may be special requirements pertaining to such matters as your religious affiliation or your need to establish a residency abroad. To find out about the laws and procedures for a specific country (if you are not already linked to a U.S. agency program), the Office of Children's Issues, Bureau of Consular Affairs of the U.S. State Department has prepared country-by-country information sheets on international adoption. This information, which can also be found on the website, is frequently very detailed. You may be offered an overview of the process as well as specific adoption procedures required by the country, who regulates or oversees adoption in the country (often referred to as the adoption authority), the country's age and civil status requirements, documents required by the country, a list of licensed adoption agencies in the country—and embassy and consular contacts in the U.S. and abroad. Remember that agencies or orphanages within the foreign country may have their own requirements for prospective adoptive parents.

Some U.S. agencies with intercountry adoption programs also have special requirements. The most common, of course, is a geographic requirement—that is, an agency will work only within a specific area or state. Other common requirements involve age, marital status, and religion. (The willingness to travel abroad is not always expected of you for an intercountry adoption but it's increasingly part of the process.) Some countries require you to appear before a court or a social-welfare agency before they will place one of their children in your family; others do not.

THE COSTS OF AN INTERCOUNTRY ADOPTION

Intercountry adoptions can be costly, ranging from a minimum of six thousand dollars to upwards of twenty-five thousand dollars. Some agencies may charge less when you adopt a sibling group or a special-needs child; others do not. Expenses will vary depending on how many agencies are involved, whether you must travel to the country, and how long you must stay there. Some of the basic costs that you can anticipate with an intercountry adoption are outlined here. Expenses will differ by country and by program. Not all fees are due at once, and if there is an agency involved, there is likely to be a schedule for payment over a period of time.

GENERAL ADOPTION EXPENSES

- Home-study fee: home study required by U.S. and source of adoption in foreign country and foreign court
- Medical exams for you and your future child
- Fees for documents: e.g., birth and marriage certificates, divorce decree, passport, visa, both in the United States and abroad
- Photocopying fees
- Immigration and Naturalization Service fees
- Notarization fees required for some documents
- Postage, express mail, or courier fees

- Document-translation fees
- Document verification and authentication fees
- Long-distance telephone calls and other communication expenses
- Agency fees in the United States or in the foreign country (may be referred to as a contribution to an orphanage or institution)
- Foreign government fees
- Child care fees in the foreign country: e.g., for foster care
- Attorney and other court fees in the U.S. or abroad: possibly both pre- and postplacement expenses

ADDITIONAL ADOPTION EXPENSES WHEN YOU TRAVEL TO A COUNTRY

- Round-trip airfare for those who travel; possibly more than one trip overseas
- Airfare for your child
- Lodging expenses
- Meals
- Taxi and other transportation fees (you may have to travel within the country to pick up your child or to process documents)
- Donations or gifts
- Interpreters' or guides' fees

THE RISKS OF INTERCOUNTRY ADOPTION

All adoptions have risks. Let's explore some of the special issues that arise with intercountry placements:

Changes in Policy

Bob and Dawna saw a TV report on the plight of Romanian orphans. After doing the necessary paperwork in the U.S., Dawna flew to Bucharest and, as was the custom at the time, was referred by the Commission on Adoptions to an orphanage where she saw four-month-old Michael. She expressed her interest in adopting him and then returned to the United States to wait. Two months later the orphanage notified them that they could adopt Michael. But it wasn't simply a matter of flying back to Romania and picking up six-month-old Michael. There was more paperwork to do, and by then the Romanians, reacting to negative international publicity about their adoption process, stopped all intercountry placements. What Bob, Dawna, and Michael faced instead was a two-year wait, punctuated by calls in the middle of the night to Bucharest, to try to get his paperwork moving again. It finally did: Michael was two-and-a-half years old when Bob flew to Romania to bring him home.

Jennifer and Larry thought their dreams of becoming parents were going up in smoke when they turned on the evening news, saw government buildings in flames, and troops and tanks milling around the downtown of the city where they planned to adopt. They'd just returned from their first trip abroad, having done the initial adoption paperwork, and had held their infant son. But they'd had to leave him at the orphanage until the adoption was final. "It was horrible," recalls Jennifer. Their dreams were indeed "on hold" as the government regrouped and then rethought its adoption policy. But the delay was brief and their adoption proceeded after a few months' delay.

Strikes, bombings, a change in government, or revamping of adoption laws are risks associated with intercountry adoption. Negative media coverage about adoption may lead to a country's temporarily or permanently stopping intercountry placements. When foreign agencies are swamped with applications, they may temporarily stop their intake. U.S. agencies may stop placing from a particular country or agency for a variety of reasons, including long delays. "It's after the delays start coming at you from all sides that you become unglued," observed one adoptive parent, who unexpectedly spent three months in Peru completing her daughter's adoption. "Because disruption can come from so many sides, there's never any assurance of what may lie ahead. You're only sure of what's behind."

Health Concerns and Developmental Delays

On a very hot summer day, in a noiseless, crowded room packed with cribs in an orphanage in China, Carrie first saw her daughter Amy. At four months old, she was tiny, thin—weighing less than ten pounds—and suffering from chronic diarrhea. "She was very nonresponsive," says Carrie. "Her eyes were glazed and dead-looking."

Over the next few days, Carrie and the group of adoptive parents with whom she'd made the journey to China visited their children at the orphanage. "When we came to visit, I was frightened," she recalls, afraid that she'd be told that Amy had died during the night. But she didn't, and Carrie finally took Amy back to her hotel.

A transformation began after Carrie, who had communicated with her pediatrician by fax, switched Amy to soy formula. "She was so hungry," she recalls. "It was unreal how much she ate. She sucked so hard on the bottle that she broke out in a sweat."

When Amy's pediatrician finally examined her back in the U.S., she was diagnosed as suffering from chronic sinus and ear infections, hepatitis A, and malnutrition. "These are all things you can deal with," proclaimed the doctor. And they were: by Amy's second birthday she was no longer small for her age, just a healthy, active, and talkative two-year-old. "She is so wonderful," enthuses Carrie. Michael, Bob and

Dawna's son, also showed the wear and tear of orphanage life in Romania. "He would bite himself, rock, and hit his head on the floor," admits Dawna. "He's had some attachment problems but we see him blossoming. He's a survivor."

What can you expect if you adopt a child who has spent time in an orphanage? Dr. Dana Johnson, codirector of the International Adoption Clinic in Minneapolis, cautioned prospective adoptive parents in an article entitled "Adopting an Institutionalized Child: What are the Risks?" in the magazine *Adoptive Families*: "Let me be blunt. The chance of an institutionalized child being completely normal on arrival in your home is essentially zero."[6] From his experience examining children who have been in orphanages, Johnson reports that:

> *All institutionalized children fall behind in large and fine motor development, speech acquisition, and attainment of necessary social skills. . . . Physical growth is impaired. Children lose one month of linear growth for every 3 to 4 months in the orphanage. Weight gain and head growth are also depressed. Finally congregate living conditions foster the spread of multiple infectious agents. Intestinal parasites, tuberculosis, hepatitis B, chickenpox, middle ear infections, etc., are all found more commonly in institutional care settings.*

Many of the problems that foreign-born adoptees bring with them—acute infectious diseases such as ear and upper respiratory infections, sores, scabies, lice, parasites, deficient immunizations, lactose intolerance—are medical difficulties that are easily remedied. Some children may also be undernourished, have a low resistance to infection, or be anemic. In one study the International Adoption Clinic found undiagnosed—and curable—problems in two of every three children seen at the clinic.[7]

You'll want to make sure that your child has a complete medical evaluation (see chapter 9) after she has recovered from jet lag and immediate medical problems have been cleared up. Says Michigan pediatrician Jerri Ann Jenista, who has written about the health needs of adopted children: "We recommend an early 'quickie' visit to take care of ear infections and lice, followed by a calmer, more thorough visit after two to four weeks to do everything else."

Low birth weight and small stature in comparison to American children are not uncommon among foreign-born adoptees. If you are worried about a child's reported measurements, ask the people caring for the child abroad to provide your doctor with growth statistics for the child from at least two points in time, preferably a month or more apart. You're interested in learning if a child is "continuing to grow," rather than how she stacks up on an American growth chart.

Older children may be small for their age, arrive with few or no medical records, and are likely to have rotten teeth that must be filled or pulled. You may find that the age estimates given for older children by the agency have little to do with a child's actual chronological age. Agency staff may have guessed the child's age when he was placed in their care. Bone, dental, or endocrinological tests performed on children here may reveal that a child is older or younger than the agency and the adopting parent believed. It may, however, take months of nutritional rehabilitation before the age discrepancies are apparent.

There may also be inaccurate information. While researchers report that severe neurological problems are uncommon, despite the labels sometimes seen on foreign medical records, you should consider an orphanage child as *at risk*. Observed Dr. Lisa Albers in a study of children from Eastern Europe and the former Soviet Union:[8] "Because of the growth and developmental delays in these children, we suggest that children coming from these environments should be considered—at least temporarily—special needs children. Early intervention and special needs programs may assist these children to maximize their developmental potential."

Dr. Johnson urges families to educate themselves through adoptive parent support organizations and discussion with physicians and other knowledgeable people, to prepare in advance to rehabilitate their child, and to understand that there will be parenting challenges.

You should also consider whether you are comfortable adopting a child who may be found to be a carrier of hepatitis B. A viral infection, hepatitis B is a common infectious disease in many parts of the world, including Africa, Asia, Eastern Europe, and Latin America. In parts of Asia, including China, Taiwan, Hong Kong, and southeast Asian countries, the disease is endemic and transmitted predominantly during the neonatal and early childhood period, leading to a high carrier rate. A child may become a carrier at birth from an infected mother or later from child-to-child transmission, from blood transfusions, or injections or blood tests using inadequately sterilized needles.

The hepatitis B profile—blood tests that your child's physician can order—will reveal whether a child is a carrier. (Many intercountry adoption agencies also test children in their birth countries.) Infection can be prevented, however, by a vaccination, so that children in some countries are now being immunized. Children who are hepatitis B carriers may *not* have symptoms but *can* transmit the disease to family members. (If your child is a carrier, your family should be vaccinated before his arrival.) Carrier children are also at risk of future liver disease. To learn more about hepatitis B, contact the Centers for Disease Control in Atlanta, Georgia.

As for AIDS, the Immigration and Naturalization Service does not require AIDS testing of any immigrant under the age of fifteen. To assess the risk, ask yourself: What do I know about the prevalence of the disease in the country itself? (The regional office of the World Health Organization in Washington, D.C., and the Centers for Disease Control can give you data for individual countries on the number of reported AIDS cases.) Have you been given a profile of the birth parents and any information about possible high-risk behaviors? From what you know about the country, and your child's birth parents and situation, you should be able to make some determination about the likelihood of infection. Now, put this information into perspective: *you* reside in a country where there are thousands of AIDS cases annually. Have you submitted your test results to adoption personnel in the foreign country?

While you can nail down many details about your child, you must be prepared to take a "leap of faith," to be willing to take some risks. That leap was one Carrie made when she first saw her infant daughter in China and cradled her in her arms. At the hotel that night, Carrie wrote in her journal: "I think she looks just fine." Says Carrie: "I felt something deep in my heart about this child that I couldn't explain by any logic. I just knew she'd be okay."[9]

Adoption Scams

While the majority of intercountry adoptions proceed without difficulty, problems do arise. Complaints surfaced against a Pennsylvania adoption agency, for example, for having "charged fees in excess of those outlined in their agreements, failed to place children and misrepresented the length of time necessary to complete an adoption."[10] For the families who had placed their hopes—and their money—with this agency, foreign adoption had become a heartache.

Carol and Bob Trotter got into trouble when they decided to pursue a Latin American adoption through a facilitator. After the facilitator "assigned" them a baby girl, they were told to send the facilitator $5,200. First they heard nothing from her about the money; then word came back that she had received $4,100, not $5,200. No one seemed to know what had happened to the rest. There was still no indication as to when they might pick up their baby. They were led to believe that it would be a matter of weeks, but the weeks soon stretched into six months. Then the facilitator called and offered them another baby girl. Recalls Carol: "We asked what happened to the baby we'd named Karen Jo. We were told that the baby's mother had neglected to sign a paper and she'd disappeared."

With a feeling close to desperation, Carol and Bob said yes to the second baby offered them. But there was another catch: "We were told that the baby had been ill and that if we wanted her, we had to send an additional $1,600 to pay the hospital bill." They hesitated, and the arrangements fell through. Carol and her husband subsequently sued the facilitator to try to regain their original outlay of $5,200.

Barbara Adams also hooked up with a facilitator. She liked the woman's voice on the telephone and felt that this woman was reliable because "she had adopted children from Mexico." Since Barbara was told that the lawyer in Mexico placed newborns, "I went out and bought a crib and newborn clothing." There were the usual promises—a baby by Christmas, then in the spring, finally the fall. There was even the day when Barbara was told that her baby was expected to be born momentarily and she sat by the telephone all day. Finally, after months had passed, she and her husband decided to meet this woman, who lived in another state. A face-to-face meeting with the woman led Barbara to feel that "this was crazy" and she and her husband returned home and contacted a local agency that placed South Korean infants. A year later they welcomed their daughter home, and in subsequent years adopted two more children through the agency.

Carol lost $5,200. Barbara spent nine months on an emotional roller coaster. Carol's and Barbara's stories, unfortunately, are not unique. Recalls one prospective parent who entrusted money to a foreign attorney: "We were calling down to the office once a week. It was just promises, promises. I had gone through losing a baby and that just topped it off. We were just completely drained—financially and emotionally—by the whole experience."

Problems sometimes arise for people who pursue independent placement adoptions here and can plague people who use facilitators for adoptions abroad. The risks may increase if you try to do an adoption yourself abroad, particularly if you use a lawyer or other source *not proved to be reliable to you or others*. Even reputable foreign attorneys may run afoul of the law when they try to meet the insatiable demand from abroad (coming from couples in Australia, Canada, Western Europe, and Israel, as well as the United States). The attorneys may cut corners in an effort to help. The scams that Americans find themselves enmeshed in, reported an Immigration and Naturalization Service examiner, have included stand-in mothers (where women sell their babies to a midwife and then another woman claims she is the mother), forged documents (two babies have the same name and documents), and baby smuggling. An official in the Bureau of Consular Affairs at the Department of State reported that consular officers continue to hear about problems with people taking money: "either taking too much money and eventually delivering a child or stringing people along, sending pictures of a child, and not delivering."

MINIMIZING THE RISKS OF INTERCOUNTRY ADOPTION

You may be able to minimize your risks, notes Mary Sullivan of the National Adoption Information Clearinghouse, if you pursue an adoption in countries where there is a history of governmental oversight and monitoring intercountry adoption. If you pursue an adoption in a country where there is a history of scandal, and a lack of governmental oversight, you may be pushing the "ethical envelope."

Working with a reputable U.S. agency lessens the risk. You can check the agency out with the Joint Council on International Children's Services and the state licensing specialist (in the state's department of human services or social services) in its home state—and your state—that oversees adoption agencies. You can also contact the attorney general's office in both states to learn what complaints have been filed against an adoption agency. If something does go wrong with an agency's adoption program, observes Betty Laning of International Concerns for Children, "adoptive parents have some leverage. Parents stand a chance of getting some of their money back if no child is forthcoming. With facilitators or lawyers in a foreign country, there may be no refunds and no way to proceed legally to force a refund."

To minimize the chances of an intercountry adoption going sour, examine all sources very carefully. The Office of Children's Issues, Bureau of Consular Affairs of the U.S. State Department tracks adoption in more than sixty countries and can provide you with such detailed information as the number of children adopted from the country in the past few years, the country's adoption authority, procedures, embassy and consulate addresses, and overseas travel advisories. The consular officer abroad may be able to report on any complaints the embassy has received. To be blunt: *look at references just as you'd do before you would hire someone to work for you.*

Don't let your heart rule your head. If at any time you feel uncomfortable with the position you find yourself in, don't hesitate to bail out.

To help you minimize the risks, here are some questions to get answered:

- How long has the resource been in existence? How long has the particular program been in existence?
- How many children have been placed by the resource or the program?
- Are there written materials that describe the intercountry adoption programs?
- What experiences have other families had in working with the child-placing resource?
- What legal right does the resource have to place children?
- What information is the resource willing to reveal to you and what is not being disclosed?
- How much money overall is required? How much money is required initially? How much money is required before you get the child's papers? How much money is required before you see the child?
- What written agreements are there? What do they stipulate?
- What happens if there is a problem after the child has been offered to you? (e.g., The child has special needs that you feel uncomfortable handling.) Will there be another assignment if you choose not to accept this child?
- Can you get a refund? If you decide against intercountry adoption, what provisions are there for the return of your money?
- Has it ever been suggested that you can bypass federal or state immigration requirements?

- Has it ever been suggested that if you are unhappy with the child, you can still bring the child into the country and then the agency/person will find another family for the child?
- Has it ever been suggested to you that you put your name on the child's original birth certificate so that there would be no need for an adoption?
- What type of information is being offered to you about the child? What type of medical history is available? Are there details about the family available? Can you see photographs or a video of the child?
- Is the child-placing resource trying to answer your additional questions about the child?
- What has been promised to you about the adoption?

GETTING INFORMATION ABOUT YOUR CHILD

The day will finally come when you will receive a telephone call, a photo and description of a child, or even a short video clip. Be prepared that the images you see may not be the most appealing: they may be mug shots and out of focus. Don't be surprised if the information you receive is scanty rather than thorough. It is possible you will receive little background information about your child and few medical records. If you want to adopt a child about whom you can receive an extensive medical and personal history with detailed information about birth parents, then intercountry adoption is most likely not for you.

You should feel free, however, to ask for more information. The foreign agency, orphanage, or social welfare organization may not be able to give you much in the way of family medical background, but should be able to provide detailed information about your child's health since coming into care. You'll want to get specific growth measurements such as height, weight, and head circumference, and ask such questions as "Is the child alert?" and "Is the child learning new things?" If you have been sent a medical report, share it with a pediatrician or family physician (see chapter 9). If your doctor has questions, don't hesitate to refer them to your local agency or foreign resource. If your doctor feels that additional simple tests are needed, inquire about them. If you feel you need additional help in understanding the information provided, the **International Adoption Clinic** in Minneapolis (see appendix A) as well as several other specialized clinics, will examine faxed copies of your child's records.

If your child's placement is being handled by an attorney, social worker, or other helping professional, this person may well have met one of the birth parents or another relative. Under these circumstances you may be able to ask for more detailed medical and genetic information as well as general descriptions of the birth parents.

WHERE TO TURN FOR INFORMATION ABOUT INTERCOUNTRY ADOPTION

People you know who have adopted recently from a foreign country, people who have lived in another country, and people who have family or friends abroad can often serve as beginning sources of information about foreign adoption. But there are many other excellent resources to whom you can turn. As you get started, you'll want to:

- Check with adoptive-parent groups. Parent groups are crucial to successful intercountry adoptions since members can offer both support and up-to-date information. The National Adoption Information Clearinghouse has a state-by-state list of adoptive-parent groups. **Adoptive Families of America** (see appendix A) offers a wealth of resource material in its magazine *Adoptive Families* and can put you in touch with a local parent group whose members have done intercountry adoptions. **Families with Children from China** (see appendix A) answers all the questions you might have about Chinese adoptions, while **Families for Russian and Ukrainian Adoption** (see appendix A) provides support for families who have adopted or are adopting children from the former Soviet Union. You may also find that there is a local adoptive-parent group directly linked to the agency with whom you work.

- Check with the U.S. State Department, particularly the Office of Children's Issues and the State Department website. There are also twenty-four-hour State Department hotlines with recorded travel warnings (202) 647–5225.
- Contact the foreign country's embassy or consulates located in the United States. You'll find offices in Washington and New York City and, for some countries, in other locations around the U.S. In one day's telephoning, I found that I'd gathered quite a bit of information from the consulates, including lists of agencies abroad and descriptions of procedures to follow. You may also use the consulate to process your paperwork.
- Get in touch with family, friends, friends of friends, and business associates abroad. They may offer information and emotional support if you travel abroad.
- Read some accounts of intercountry adoption to get a sense of the process, including the feelings of parents and children as they form a family. Jill Smolowe's *An Empty Lap* takes you through the agonizing process of one couple's deciding upon adoption, her attempts to pursue both intercountry and domestic adoption, and finally, her journey to China to adopt her daughter Becky. Patty Dann's *The Baby Boat* describes in great detail her experiences

adopting an infant in Lithuania. Maggie Francis Conroy's *A World of Love* offers details about both Russian and Colombian adoptions. Gail Sheehy's *Spirit of Survival* chronicles the life of her daughter Phat Mohm in Cambodia and New York and gives you a sense of the challenges parents face when adopting older children. Single parent and Harvard Law professor Elizabeth Bartholet mixes political commentary with her personal experiences adopting from Peru in *Family Bonds*. Specialized guidebooks such as Barbara Bascom and Carole McKelvey's *The Complete Guide to Foreign Adoption,* Myra Alperson's *The International Adoption Handbook,* and Jean Nelson-Erichsen and Heinro R. Erichsen's *How to Adopt Internationally* document the process of intercountry adoption. Cheri Register's *Are Those Kids Yours?* examines the many postadoption issues, while Margi Miller and Nancy Ward's *With Eyes Wide Open: A Workbook for Parents Adopting International Children Over Age One* has excellent exercises to help you prepare.

- Contact U.S. adoption agencies about their intercountry programs. Remember that some agencies will have nationwide programs while others will only place children within a particular geographic region. An invaluable resource for information about intercountry adoption is the *Report on Intercountry Adoption* produced by International Concerns for Children.

WORKING WITH A U.S. AGENCY PROGRAM

Whether you write or call an agency, request information about *all* its programs. (If you call, keep in mind the agency's location and be aware of time zones.) Ask for an application. If you are told that the agency is not taking applications for a particular program, ask when intake will be open if that's the program you seek. Remember that the situation in intercountry adoption can change quickly, so try again within a few months. If you are willing to be a *pioneer* in a new program, indicate your interest. If you are willing to consider a special-needs child, say so and ask for information.

As you examine the information provided by the agency, ask some additional questions:

- What is your responsibility in completing the adoption and what is the agency's?
- How many children have been placed to date?
- How many children does the agency expect to place this year?
- How many people are on the waiting list?

Observed one parent support group leader: "We've known of agencies that have done four adoptions but had a waiting list of several hundred families." Look into program fees carefully as these can vary widely in intercountry adoptions. And remember that your licensed adoption agency in the United States may not necessarily be working with a licensed agency in the foreign country. You'll also want to have the agency delineate its policy if there's a problem abroad.

TRAVELING ABROAD

With many intercountry placements, families are asked to travel abroad: to finalize the adoption, to work out the guardianship, or to bring their child home. Everybody's travel experience is different, but there are some general guidelines that you can keep in mind:

- Contact an adoptive parent support group, such as Families with Children from China, before you go to learn about places to stay, things to take with you, local transportation, and the like. Wondering what to pack? A suggested packing list might detail clothes for you and your child, gizmos, medications, and travel gear. You're likely to get tips on communication, local hotels, taxi drivers, orphanage donations, even where to buy diapers.

- Contact the foreign embassy or foreign tourist office for information about the country. Ask your travel agent for material.
- Contact the office of Overseas Citizens Services in the U.S. Department of State in Washington, D.C. to find out about travel advisories for the country you are visiting.
- Read some guidebooks about the country you will be visiting.
- Contact the International Travelers hotline of the Centers for Disease Control in Atlanta, Georgia (to order a fax report: 888–232–3299 or website: http://www.cdc.gov). You can get details about vaccination requirements and recommendations as well as reports on disease outbreak abroad.
- Make sure that *your own* immunizations are up to date. Advises international adoption specialist Dr. Jerri Jenista: "All the childhood illnesses prevented by vaccine in this country are endemic in the countries you are likely to visit."[11] That means you need to discuss with your physician whether you've had the routine childhood immunizations for polio, measles, mumps, rubella, diphtheria, whooping cough, and tetanus, and any recommended boosters.
- If you are going to be around children or eating questionable food or water, you might also want to consult with your doctor about hepatitis vaccinations or getting a shot of gamma globulin. Special vaccines such as cholera, typhoid, or yellow fever are usually not required for tourist travel.

- Consult with your doctor whether you should bring along some diarrhea-prevention preparations, some hydrocortisone cream, a rectal or other thermometer to take your child's temperature, diaper rash medication, and Tylenol for you or your child. You might also discuss whether to take along anti-scabies or anti-lice medicines.[12]
- When you're in the country, take the time to see the sights. Show an interest in the country's customs. Take photographs of the country and also of the people involved in your child's adoption. And purchase some mementos that are characteristic of the culture. Your child will enjoy looking at these, and talking about them, as she grows up.
- Try to learn a little of the language. You may find it useful to listen to audiotapes designed for travelers that give you basic phrases and travel lingo. Don't be embarrassed to use a dictionary and point to words. People appreciate your making the attempt to communicate even if it isn't perfect.
- Dress and act appropriately for *their* culture, *not yours*. You represent adoptive parents and the image you project speaks for us all.
- Bring donations to the orphanages—clothing, medical supplies, formula, toys. Your local parent group can probably give you supplies to carry with you. If advisable, give a financial donation.
- Work at building bonds. Spend time at the orphanage. You'll probably want to bring small gifts to the people who have helped you with the adoption or cared for your child.
- *Don't complain.*

Be prepared to feel homesick, confused, and lonely. You're likely to be very excited, but you also can feel terribly unsettled. Parts of the trip may not feel like a vacation. When you're staying in a hotel or other accommodation, there's nothing romantic about having to boil baby bottles in a hot-pot rather than in a fancy sterilizer. Says one parent who traveled to Colombia: "Staying in a country club [which is where families adopting through one agency were housed] the American couples were operating in a social vacuum without supports. No family, no friends." Whatever your situation, she says: "You must understand that you are a *guest* in another country and understand their ways of doing things. They are giving you a precious gift."

FOLLOW UP CONTACT ABROAD

Once your child's adoption has been completed, there's a strong desire to "get on with living" and put the past behind you. That feeling may extend to failing to keep in contact with the people who helped in your child's birth country. You may not be legally required to keep in touch with the agency or court, but intercountry adoption advocates urge you to do so. Send cards on your child's birthday or at holidays. You may also want to send packages of clothing, small donations of money, and, of course, photographs that show your child's development. The judges and social workers in foreign countries who are involved in intercountry adoption are concerned about the welfare of those children who have left. Send letters not only the first year, but for the next five, ten, and fifteen years so that others can see that your child is loved and cherished. It's good for you, good for your child, and good for intercountry relations. A judge or an agency who never hears about the outcome of intercountry adoptions might just decide to stop approving placements to the United States.

◆

A precious gift—that is what your child adopted from abroad is. A gift from one country and one culture to another. Your journey to your child's country, and links you forge over the years, are the beginning of experiencing his heritage. Respect the people and their culture. From now on, your child's country is yours.

7

THE HOME STUDY

For all agency adoptions, for all intercountry adoptions, and for most independent adoptions, you will need a preadoptive home study. Although there is no prescribed format that a home study must follow, each state has guidelines on what must be covered.

The home study has traditionally revolved around a series of private meetings between the applicants and an adoption agency worker. Behind closed doors applicants discuss their lives and explore their feelings about adoption. It can be a time fraught with anxiety because prospective adopters worry that one misstep will lead the worker to decide they are unsuitable parents. Finally the worker produces a written report on the family (the home-study document itself) that becomes the basis for the agency's decision whether or not to place a child in the family and often the vehicle used to decide whether or not to place a particular child in the family.

But attitudes and practices have been changing, and the home study period is no longer seen by most agencies and workers as the time when applicants to adopt can be screened out. Rathcr it is treated as a time to prepare families for the challenges of adoptive parenthood. While some agencies still conduct home studies on an individual basis, many incorporate the group process into their home studies. Some require that applicants take an adoption information course sponsored by a local parent group as a prerequisite. Others hold a series of group meetings with prospective clients before the social worker meets with people individually. Still others conduct the whole home study in a group setting, but ask participants to do some individual homework assignments.

The home study process has evolved in this way partly because of the increased interest in placing special needs and older children. "Families need information to help them make realistic decisions about whether or not adoption is appropriate for them," observes Child Welfare Specialist Thomas D. Morton. "The process has to make maximum use of the family's role in decision-making, and it can only do so if the worker's role changes from that of investigator to educator, from judge to enabler."[1] In the Model Approach to Partnerships in Parenting (MAPP) program, for example, which trains potential foster and adoptive parents together in ten three-hour sessions, the group examines children's separation and loss experiences and how these impact on placement in a new family. The potential parents think about the strengths they will need to come with—or develop—to help their children cope. "With MAPP you have the opportunity," says adoption expert Toni Oliver, "to try on the foster parent dress or the adoptive parent dress and decide whether you need to make alterations ahead of time." Following the final session there's a home consultation with the family. "Although the agency has the final say," notes Oliver, "applicants are involved in the decision of selecting in or out. There's a greater likelihood that a family will select out than that a family will be turned down."

The group also helps people build a network of support that can be called upon both before, and after, their child enters their home. Since the discussion focuses on parenting issues, people enter the process with the assumption that there will be a child for them. The business at hand then is to decide what kind of child they can parent, what arrangement they will be comfortable with, and how they can get ready for the task.

The written home-study document is also changing. Although agency staff check references, visit homes, and write reports of their impressions, a part of the home study is often created by the prospective adopters. They contribute autobiographies or statements expressing their beliefs on various subjects and fill out worksheets about the type of children they hope to adopt and their attitudes and expectations. And as adoption has become more open—bringing both birth parents and other agencies into the process—these home-study documents serve as the family's passport to the outside world.

WHO CONDUCTS THE HOME STUDY?

Within an agency, the person who prepares the home study or who leads the group meeting may be a certified social worker, a caseworker, or even another adoptive parent under the supervision of a social worker. Although home studies have usually been conducted under agency auspices, not all states require that a home study be done by an agency. In some states, and for some types of adoptive placements, you may be able to have a home study prepared by a licensed social worker not affiliated with an agency. If this is possible, you'll want to find out from your state adoption unit what the state's rules and requirements are. Before you sign on with a worker, you'll want to find out about her qualifications, the format of the study, her fees, and how long she expects the study to take. Will the worker be available to you after your child arrives and can she handle postplacement visits and court reports? While your state may allow you to use an independent social worker, be sure to find out whether the state or country whose laws will govern your child's adoption accepts a home study prepared by an independent social worker. Does the worker have an affiliation with an agency if you find you need to affiliate with an agency to complete the adoption? And on what basis would the worker *not* approve a family for placement of a child?

In selecting an agency for a home study, you'll want to consider the process they use, how comfortable you are with their approach, and how their timetable fits yours. If you are networking with another agency or with a child-placing source in a foreign country, you'll want to be sure that the local agency's home-study process meets the requirements of the child-referral agency.

THE HOME-STUDY PROCESS

A question was put across the table to the birth mother attending a group home-study workshop. "If the adoptive parents invited you to a baby shower for the baby, would you come?"

For days Tom and Sheila Hawkins had been mulling the idea over—Tom thought it would be neat to invite the birth mother; Sheila felt it was putting pressure on her—and now he popped the question to Vicky Knight, a young birth mother sharing her experiences of open adoption with a group of prospective adoptive parents. Nothing was off-limits in the three daylong group discussions held at this agency. In addition to meeting with birth parents and experienced adoptive parents, the group examined their fears and fantasies of open adoption, the mixed emotions they might feel as they got to know a birth mother, and the painful but exhilarating experience they were likely to share with the birth mother at the time of the baby's birth. There was also a discussion of specifics: how to compose a profile of themselves, how to react if a birth mother called them on the telephone, what questions were important for them to ask the birth mother and her social worker. By week's end Tom and Sheila were confident that open adoption was for them—although they still hadn't resolved the matter of the baby shower—and were eager to proceed.

Meeting at an agency, which concentrated on placing special-needs children, Joan and Michael Arthur, along with several other couples, looked through photolisting books featuring children needing adoption and marked in the books the children who interested them. Over a period of time the group members talked about how children behave when they enter a new home, how it feels to be rejected, how a child already in their home might react to a new sibling, and how each of them would handle questions about adoption. The sessions stressed developing individual self-awareness, building commitment, identifying what is involved in parenting a "challenging child," and finding techniques to work with that child. Experienced adoptive parents and community resource people were also introduced to the group members. "It was interesting," says Joan. "A good parenting course." At the conclusion of the series, Joan and Michael visited a family who had already adopted a child with a profile similar to the youngster they were hoping to adopt.

At another agency Kate and Tony Fales participated in group counseling that was referred to as a "self-education experience." They shared information about their life histories and the people who shaped their lives, their marital relationships, their childlessness and how it affected them. The couples in the group role-played situations to help them identify with birth parents, adoptive parents, and adoptees. One couple found themselves playing the birth parents who showed up at the adoptive parents' front door many years later asking to meet her child, while Kate and Tony were confronted with a fifteen-year-old who announces that she was going to go live with her "real" parents. Recalls Kate: "The group meetings were a matter of getting you used to accepting an adopted child."

While the specific content of a group home-study process varies agency by agency, there is an increasing emphasis on family preparation and self-awareness. Whether through role-playing, listening to adopters relate their experiences in panel discussions, or getting to know one family in a buddy system, the home studies seek to challenge the adoptive parents before their child ever enters the home. (The process of preparing adoptive parents is constantly evolving: another method, just finding its way into practice, involves a strength-based family assessment.)

What happens if your agency or worker prefers to conduct the home study along more traditional lines? In that situation you can expect to have your first meeting with your caseworker as a couple at the agency. Then, typically, the caseworker will meet separately with you and your spouse at the agency office. One or more additional interviews will follow at your home. If you have older children, the caseworker is likely to interview them and may also interview each of them individually. (In some instances, particularly when it's done by a social worker on a freelance basis, the home study may be a daylong discussion of adoption issues rather than a series of meetings.) Finally the caseworker will draw up a written report, based on the interviews and documents you submit.

Whether your home study is done in a group setting or on an individual basis, there will be some basic paperwork (see chapter 8), an extended discussion about adoption, including a look at your motivation for adoption and your attitudes, and a visit to your home. During the home visit the worker is not looking for dust balls under the beds but does want to come away with a picture of the environment the child will be entering. "I will ask people about their reality—how they will fit, for example, into a one-bedroom apartment," acknowledges New York City social worker Phyllis Lowinger, who does private home studies. But Lowinger emphasizes that her main concern is to "make the home study an educational experience."

While the home study may cause you anxiety at the outset, says social worker Debra Smith, you're likely to find that the process helps you crystalize your ideas about parenting, in general, and adoptive parenting in particular. Recalled one couple about the process: "After the homestudy, we compared notes to see if our answers were consistent. We found several areas of philosophical difference in childrearing practices which led to further discussion. The homestudy actually became an important learning experience."[2]

Whatever the circumstances of the home study, your worker will eventually offer a written evaluation and a summary report to accompany documents that you submit. Says Debra Smith: "The home study is thorough—not because social workers like being intrusive and invasive—but because they want to be sure they have done their best to prepare parents and that a child will be going to a place where he or she will be loved, safe, understood, and able to realize his or her full potential." "What everyone has to come to grips with," emphasizes adoption expert Kay Donley Ziegler, "is that the agency and the caseworker have the ultimate responsibility for the choice that's made. They are going to have to deal with the placement of the child." As Lowinger puts it: "My home study has to say that these people are ready to parent a child now."

WHAT'S EXPLORED DURING THE HOME STUDY

Whether your study takes place in individual meetings with the caseworker or in group sessions, you can expect to discuss the following:

YOURSELF

- Your strengths and weaknesses
- Your personality: level of patience, flexibility, attitudes toward life, anxiety levels, sense of humor
- Your health, medical problems that you have had, and how you have resolved them
- Your upbringing
- The kind of parenting you had and how you feel about it
- If you've been divorced: its causes, your relationship with your ex-spouse, your relationship with your children from a previous marriage
- Your financial picture, your employment history, your insurance coverage, your ability to support a child
- How you have handled crises in your life
- How you have resolved a fertility problem, if you have one
- How you handled the loss of a child due to miscarriage, stillbirth or some other cause, if such has occurred, and your feelings about it

YOUR FAMILY

- Your marriage: its strengths and weaknesses; how you handle family disagreements
- Your family plans for working or for staying home with your children; if both parents are planning to continue working, your child care plans

- Your relationships with family, friends, neighbors: your extended families' feelings about adoption and what support you can draw from them
- Any past history of abuse in the family: sexual/child abuse, substance abuse, domestic violence
- Your past experiences with children
- How your children, if you have any, will adjust to a new sibling and how you are preparing them for adoption

YOUR LIFESTYLE

- Your home and neighborhood: your housing situation
- Your lifestyle and how a child will fit in
- Your awareness of, and willingness to, tap community resources

YOUR FEELINGS ABOUT ADOPTION

- Your reasons for adopting a child
- Your expectations of adoption and of your new child: how you will feel if your adopted child doesn't live up to your expectations
- How you have handled situations in which your expectations were not met
- What special needs in a child you feel you can handle and what you are willing to consider
- How you will handle your child's questions about adoption and birth parents
- Your understanding of, and feelings about, birth parents
- Your preparation for adoption: reading, knowing others, parent-group involvement

If you have a history of previous drug or alcohol use, "you've got to be up front about it," urges adoption expert Susan Freivalds. "It's more harmful to you to lie to any agency than to disclose previous chemical use." The agency worker will want to know how long it's been since you overcame the problem and whether you are in a support group today. And the worker will probably probe into your family for any history of drug abuse. The same advice applies if you've been in therapy or had infertility or other counseling. Notes one adoption agency in their literature describing the home study: "*Any history of counseling, alcohol and drug abuse and/or any arrest records must be addressed in the home study consistent with the expectations of the foreign government.* These conditions do not mean the prospective parents can not adopt. The home study must address them."

SINGLES AND HOME STUDIES

In addition to the points raised already, if you are single, you will be asked to evaluate what age child you want to consider and what type of child will best fit your situation as a prospective single parent. You can also expect your home study to explore the following in addition:

- Your lifestyle and a child's impact on it
- Your family and friends: your support system, your extended network, and the alternatives they can provide in the event of your illness or death
- Who will provide the opposite sex role model for your child
- Your daily plan for the child: how you expect to handle matters from day to day, what arrangements

you can make for day care, for after school, for weekends

- Your finances: how you are going to provide for the child over time
- Why you are not married and whether you have had long-term relationships before; you may also be asked about your sexual orientation
- What would happen in the future if you married; how you think a prospective partner would react to the fact that you are a single adoptive parent; if you are you worried that adopting will prevent your getting married
- Your work: how flexible it is; how much time you can take off from work when the child arrives
- How you foresee you and your child handling the special situation of adoptive single-parenting. You are going to have to explain to your child—and to the outside world—adoption and why there's only one parent in your family

The worker will also want to go over the provisions you have made for the care of your child in the event of serious illness, death, or other circumstances that prevent you from carrying out your duties. You'll be asked to discuss your insurance plans and your benefits as well as name the specific guardians for your child.

GETTING REFERENCES

As part of your home study you will also be asked to submit some references. The agency will want to know how your references feel about your potential parenting ability and whether they perceive you as a mature individual. The people you may be asked to use as references include your family, your employer, your clergyman, your friends, and your neighbors. Each one may have to submit a letter on your behalf, talk by telephone with the social worker, or even come to the agency for an interview. Your references may be cited in your home study by name, and your social worker may quote from the interviews and from letters that were submitted.

Think carefully about the people you will list as your references. Good friends do not necessarily make good references. How do they feel about adoption? How do they feel about your adopting a child? How do they feel about your adopting a particular type of child? Talk with them and explore their feelings and perceptions. Do they think that you will make good parents? Why? Do they think that you are making a mistake? Don't hesitate to give them some pointers as to what you would like them to emphasize about you, and don't be embarrassed to ask your references to read you their letters before they submit them to the agency.

Whom should you choose as references? When the Williamses were applying for their first child to an agency that specialized in intercountry adoptions, they asked one friend who taught nursery school and with whom they liked to talk about raising children. They also asked a friend who had an interracial marriage and could testify to the Williams' respect for ethnic differences. Their caseworker also insisted on meeting one of their references. They asked the woman who had introduced them ten years before; she was an experienced journalist, a television producer used to talking with people. Three years later when the Williamses were applying for their second child they chose a different reference—a neighbor whose son frequently played with their son and who had observed their parenting day in and day out.

Doctors such as your family physician, infertility specialist, psychologist, or psychiatrist may also be asked to comment on your application to adopt. Be sure that you talk with them and explain your reasons for adopting. If you're committed to adoption, you don't want your fertility specialist elaborating on all the other courses that he believes you should pursue. Your physician should provide a medical analysis only and understand fully that adoption is your decision.

If you have had psychological or infertility counseling, your therapist may be asked to submit a report stating why you had the counseling and how he evaluates you today. Some Latin American agencies will also request a statement about your mental health. For Latin American adoptions the reference from your doctor should state that you are in good physical *and mental* health and free of all communicable diseases. Physicians and mental health practitioners should also state in references for Latin America who licenses them and should provide their licensing number or a photocopy of their license.

References and other documents submitted to an agency abroad may very likely have to be notarized, verified, and authenticated (see discussion, chapter 8). To make the process easier, you may want all your references to come from the same state. And you'll want to ask them to refer to you in any written recommendations by your *given* names—those that appear on your birth and marriage certificates—rather than any nicknames. Your primary concern, however, should be that your references are able to talk comfortably about you.

RÉSUMÉS

You may be asked to prepare an autobiography, a one-page résumé-like letter, or a multipage scrapbook that might be shown to birth parents. Your social worker may give you guidance as to content or even provide you with forms. Here's some general advice: An autobiography or résumé needs to contain some basic information about yourself—your jobs, education, home, community—and your desire to become parents. But it should be written in an open, appealing manner and convey your personality. Do you play tennis? Do you enjoy movies? Do you have a pet? Do you come from an extended family that gets together frequently? What is important to you in raising a child? How has your desire to parent a child affected you? What makes you unique?

The résumé should make a person want to get to know you. You will want your readers to feel that they can envision a child's future with you. To round out your profile, you'll probably want to attach an inviting, good color photograph of yourself, your other children—and, if you have them, your pets.

THE HOME STUDY AS YOUR PASSPORT

At a training session of social workers, several families' home studies were offered as sample reading material. The workers then commented on their understanding of each of the families' strengths, weaknesses, resources, and readiness to adopt a special-needs child. After the group had completed its discussion, one worker revealed that she had prepared one of the home studies and that she was dismayed at the conclusions drawn by the group about the family. "That's not at all what the husband and wife are like," she said, "and not what I was trying to convey about them."[3]

As this worker learned, what she wanted to say about the family was not what the other members of the group gleaned from her summary. That's why many adoption experts have urged that families take as active a part as they can in the creation of the home-study document, particularly when it is to be used as their ambassador beyond the agency's doors. Observes adoptive parent Pat Shirley: "Studies seldom say negative things but often give inadequate information, sometimes are written in a superficial or less than readable style. Many children's workers are going to read it and it should make your family as real as possible."[4]

Try to read your completed copy and to review all documents connected to it. At some agencies that is now an accepted part of agency practice. (Some states mandate that you be shown a copy.) Be sure your home study is clearly, cleanly typed with a good overall appearance. It should be dark enough that it can be successfully photocopied. Any supporting documents such as autobiographies should also be clearly typed. If your home study is going to be mailed out, you don't want the child's worker to ignore your study because it is unreadable.

Examine your home study for typographical or spelling errors. In one home study for an intercountry adoption the social worker spelled "Chile" as "chili" and "Colombia" as "Columbia." Check the chronology of your life (e.g., dates that you attended school, where, what you've done) and other facts carefully. (To ensure accuracy in reporting factual details about your life, you might give your worker an autobiographical profile at the beginning of your home study.) If you object to any description of your family, say so. Mary Beth Gart was distressed at the way events in her life were handled. The stillbirth she'd lived through several years earlier was described as "stormy." Her home study dwelled on her childhood and her late father's alcoholism. Her worker reported that she and her husband were motivated to adopt a South Korean child "because they were unable to adopt a white child." She approached the social-work supervisor and asked that the home study be revised. Mary Beth rewrote certain sections, correcting factual errors. The agency took out the objectionable language.

Warning: If you move or your family circumstances change after your home study is completed, you'll need to have it updated. Families who've moved have found themselved delayed in China when their documents and home studies haven't matched.

There are other things that you can do to ensure that your home study presents as full a picture of you as possible. Since most agencies will not know your agency and the child's worker may be reluctant to trust another worker's home study, you'll want to:[5]

- Insist that your home-study packet contain multiple copies of photos of you as a family, of your home, and maybe of your activities as a family. It should also contain autobiographies written by you. State your experience with adoptive-parent group meetings and activities.
- Be sure that the entire home-study packet is sent every time you apply for a child. Ask that your worker inspect the packet when it is sent. Offer to pay for copying costs or postage. (If you get the costs you will know whether the entire package has been sent.)
- Include with the package any specific plans for the child's therapy if it will be necessary. Indicate what local resources are available.
- Volunteer to meet with the child's worker in person.

Since the child's agency may not have worked with your agency, ask that your agency include with your home study a brief description of their home-study process and also their plan for follow-up should your family be chosen. Recognize also, writes Pat Shirley, that in a special-needs adoption "your chances for a placement may indeed be lessened when your traditional home study is on the table next to a study done by an agency using the group home study concepts."[6]

If you will be sending your home study to a foreign country, keep in mind the value system of that culture. You may have discussed with your worker that you and your husband lived together before marriage—a practice more accepted in our society than in others. Not everything discussed in a home-study interview needs to be written up. One adoption agency found that the mention in a home study of a father's labor-union membership was questioned by a foreign agency since labor unions were illegal in that country. What is regarded as an indicator of stability in one culture can be seen as subversive in another.

You may want your worker to focus on the multi-ethnic character of your community, if that is so, and how you can take advantage of its resources. Discuss the opportunities your child will have to meet with other people from his birth country and also how he will meet with other adoptees. If you come from a small community, explain how you will help maintain his cultural and racial identity.

It is up to you, and your agency, to convince a child's adoption worker that you have given a lot of thought, and time, to the adoption route you are pursuing.

COMMON PROBLEMS AND SOLUTIONS

If all goes well, you will contact an agency, arrange for a home study to be done, and be satisfied with the result. But sometimes things don't work out as you think they should. What do you do? You have rights. You are a consumer of an agency's services whether you pay for them directly in a fee or whether they are funded through your tax dollars. The agency and the workers are there to provide you with a service, and you have the right to question those services.[7]

IF AN AGENCY SAYS THAT IT IS UNABLE TO DO A HOME STUDY

- Find out why. If you are told that there are long waiting lists for the type of child you seek, think about broadening the categories of children you will consider.
- Determine whether state law requires the agency to do a home study and, if so, within what period of time.
- Sometimes a local agency will not do a home study for an intercountry placement unless it receives a request from a foreign agency, while the foreign agency will not accept an application from you unless it sees your home study. If you are caught in the catch-22, see whether the local agency will accept a letter from the foreign agency indicating its willingness to consider placing a child with you upon its receipt of your home study.
- Find out whether state law permits you to work with a licensed social worker without agency affiliation. If you are networking with an out-of-state agency, find out if they will accept your using an independent social worker.

IF YOU DON'T GET ALONG WITH YOUR CASEWORKER

- Discuss your problems with other adoptive parents who have previously worked with the agency or worker. They may have suggestions on how to proceed.
- Discuss your problems with your worker.
- Talk with the adoption supervisor.
- Request a new worker. Your home study may take longer, but it may make a difference in the outcome.

IF THE AGENCY TURNS DOWN YOUR APPLICATION FOR A CHILD AFTER YOUR HOME STUDY IS COMPLETED

- Find out why.
- Get the decision in writing.
- Appeal the decision within the agency or beyond. Many states have established appeal procedures.
- If there are specific deficits given, offer a plan to address these deficits in your appeal.
- Don't take the agency's decision as the final answer to your decision to adopt. Some agencies can be more flexible in approving families than others.

8

PAPERWORK

◆

Paperwork and adoption go hand in hand. Whether you are adopting a child in this country or abroad, you will at some point have to amass documents: birth and marriage certificates, financial statements, the birth parents' releases. With intercountry adoption, the paperwork expands since you must meet the requirements of a foreign country, the U.S. government, and your state government. This chapter focuses on the basic paperwork and how to go about obtaining it.

DOCUMENTS YOU CAN EXPECT TO OBTAIN FOR AN ADOPTION

When an agency sends you an application for adoption, or when a foreign country requests information, you will be asked to submit documents about yourself. At some point you can expect to show the following:

- Certified copy of your birth certificate
- Certified copy of your marriage certificate
- Certified copy of any divorce decree or annulment
- Certified copy of the death certificate of any deceased former spouse

- Medical statement from physician about your health (agency may provide forms). You may also be asked to submit a statement about your mental health (may need to be on physician's letterhead stationery)
- Medical statement about infertility, if applicable (may need to be on physician's letterhead stationery)
- Financial statements, including letters from banks describing your accounts, an accountant's report, a statement of liability and assets, and a notarized copy of your most recent income-tax returns (you may be asked to have these statements notarized)
- Verification of your employment stating salary, position, length of employment, and stability of your position (may need to be on employer's stationery)
- Letters of reference from friends or colleagues

You may also be asked to provide:

- A statement from your local or state police records bureau stating that no criminal records exist for you or, if they do, explaining those that do
- Child abuse clearance letter from state department of social services
- A summary of your traffic record from the Bureau of Motor Vehicles
- Fingerprint check from local, state, or federal authority
- Certified copies of your children's birth certificates
- Medical statements for members of your family
- Decree of name change, if any
- Lease or deed to residence
- Letters certifying that you have attended a child care class, infant CPR class, or adoptive-parenting class
- Verification of health insurance/life insurance coverage

- Autobiographies, including discussion of life experiences, marriage, parenting
- Photographs of yourself, your children, your home, your neighborhood (may need to be a certain format and size)
- Power of attorney that is used by another person on your behalf—if your spouse, for example, will not be traveling abroad with you to pick up your child, you will need this

If you are a naturalized citizen, you will be asked to show proof of your naturalization. Some states may also require a check for a police record or may send your name to a central registry that lists people who have been accused of child abuse.

As you begin thinking about adoption, you should begin actively working on your documentation. Certified copies of birth, marriage, death, and divorce certificates can take time to acquire since they must be obtained from the state in which the event took place. Since these documents certify a past event, they usually do not have to be updated so that you can and should request several copies of each document at one time. One family ordered five copies of the relevant documents and were able to use them for two adoptions. The extra money spent may save months in paperwork. (If you are planning an intercountry adoption, find out whether the foreign country must have copies that have been recently certified. Some countries require this; others do not.) You should also try to figure out in advance how many certified copies of each document you are likely to need for any given adoption. (The Immigration and Naturalization Service will accept photocopies of the original documents.)

You may also want to arrange for your physical examination as soon as possible. Some agencies require that the physical examination forms be submitted before a home study begins. As you inquire about adoption procedures, find out about an agency's medical exam requirements—particularly about lab tests, such as the tuberculin test, the blood test for syphilis or HIV, an electrocardiogram, or statement of infertility. You can often have the physical done and then, within a few weeks or months, ask your physician to fill in the form. Be sure to find out how current the examination must be.

OBTAINING BIRTH AND MARRIAGE RECORDS

The chart that follows lists where you can get information about certified copies of birth and marriage certificates. Call first to find out about the procedures for obtaining certified copies and what the fees are. In some states certified copies of marriage licenses must be obtained from local courts.[1]

BIRTH/MARRIAGE RECORDS AGENCIES

ALABAMA

Center for Health Statistics, State Department of Public Health, P.O. Box 5625, Montgomery 36103–5625; (334) 206–5418

ALASKA

Bureau of Vital Statistics, Department of Health and Social Services, P.O. Box 110675, Juneau 99811–0675; (907) 465–3391

ARIZONA

Vital Records Section, Arizona Department of Health Services, P.O. Box 3887, Phoenix 85030; (602) 255–3260

ARKANSAS

Division of Vital Records, Arkansas Department of Health, 4815 West Markham Street, Little Rock 72201; (501) 661–2336

CALIFORNIA

Office of Vital Records, Department of Health Services, Box 730241, Sacramento 94244–0241; (916) 445–2684

COLORADO

Vital Records Section, Colorado Department of Health, 4300 Cherry Creek Drive South, Denver 80222–1530; (303) 756–4464

CONNECTICUT

Vital Records, Department of Health Services, 150 Washington Street, Hartford 06106; (203) 566–2334

DELAWARE

Office of Vital Statistics, Division of Public Health, P.O. Box 637, Dover 19903; (302) 739–4721

DISTRICT OF COLUMBIA

Vital Records Branch, 800 Ninth Street, SW, Washington 20024; (202) 645–5962

FLORIDA

Office of Vital Statistics, Department of Health and Rehabilitative Services, P.O. Box 210, 1217 Pearl Street, Jacksonville 32231; (904) 359–6900

GEORGIA

Vital Records Service, Georgia Department of Human Resources, 47 Trinity Avenue SW, Room 217-H, Atlanta 30334; (404) 656–4900

HAWAII

Office of Health Status Monitoring, Vital Records Section, State Department of Health, P.O. Box 3378, Honolulu 96801; (808) 586–4533

IDAHO

Vital Statistics Unit, Center for Vital Statistics and Health Policy, 450 West State Street, P.O. Box 83728, Boise 83720–0036; (208) 334–5988

ILLINOIS

Division of Vital Records, Illinois Department of Public Health, 605 West Jefferson Street, Springfield 62702–5097; (217) 782–6553

INDIANA

Vital Records Section, State Department of Health, 2 North Meridian Street, Indianapolis 46206; (317) 233–7274

IOWA

Vital Records Section, Iowa Department of Public Health, Lucas Office Building, 321 East 12 Street, Des Moines 50319–0075; (515) 281–4944

KANSAS

Office of Vital Statistics, Kansas State Department of Health and Environment, 900 SW Jackson Street, Topeka 66612–2221; (913) 296–1400

KENTUCKY

Office of Vital Statistics, Department for Health Services, 275 East Main Street, Frankfort 40621; (502) 564–4212

LOUISIANA

Vital Records Registry, Office of Public Health, 325 Loyola Avenue, New Orleans 70112; (504) 568–5152

MAINE

Office of Vital Records, Maine Department of Human Services, Station 11, State House, Augusta 04333–0011; (207) 287–3184

MARYLAND

Division of Vital Records, Department of Health and Mental Hygiene, Metro Executive Building, 4201 Patterson Avenue, P.O. Box 68760, Baltimore 21215–0020; (410) 225–5988

MASSACHUSETTS

Registry of Vital Records and Statistics, 470 Atlantic Avenue, Boston 02210–2224; (617) 753–8600

MICHIGAN

Office of the State Registrar and Center for Health Statistics, Michigan Department of Community Health, 3423 North Logan Street, Lansing 48909; (517) 335–8655

MINNESOTA

Section of Vital Statistics, Minnesota Department of Health, 717 Delaware Street, SE, P.O. Box 9441, Minneapolis 55440; (612) 623–5121

MISSISSIPPI

Vital Records, State Department of Health, 2423 North State Street, Jackson 39216; (601) 960–7450

MISSOURI

Bureau of Vital Records, Missouri Department of Health, 930 Wildwood, P.O. Box 570, Jefferson City 65102–0570; (573) 751–6400

MONTANA

Vital Statistics Bureau, Montana Department of Public Health and Human Services, Helena 59604; (406) 444–4228

NEBRASKA

Bureau of Vital Statistics, Department of Health and Human Services, 301 Centennial Mall South, P.O. Box 95065, Lincoln 68509–5065; (402) 471–2871

NEVADA

Division of Health—Vital Statistics, Capitol Complex, 505 East King Street, Carson City 89710; (702) 687–4480

NEW HAMPSHIRE

Bureau of Vital Records, Health and Welfare Building, 6 Hazen Drive, Concord 0330l; (603) 271–4654

NEW JERSEY

Bureau of Vital Statistics, State Department of Health, South Warren and Market Streets, CN 370, Trenton 08625; (609) 292–4087

NEW MEXICO

Vital Statistics, New Mexico Health Services Division, P.O. Box 26110, Santa Fe 87502; (505) 827–2338

NEW YORK

Vital Records Section, State Department of Health, Empire State Plaza, Tower Building, Albany 12237–0023; (518) 474–3075. **For New York City**: Division of Vital Records, New York City Department of Health, P.O. Box 3776, New York 10007; (212) 619–4530 or (212) 693–4637; Marriage records through City Clerk's Office in borough where license was issued.

NORTH CAROLINA

Vital Records Section, NC Vital Records, P.O. Box 29537, Raleigh 27626–0537; (919) 733–3526

NORTH DAKOTA

Division of Vital Records, State Capitol, 600 East Boulevard Avenue, Bismarck 58505–0200; (701) 328–2360

OHIO

Bureau of Vital Statistics, Ohio Department of Health, P.O. Box 15098, Columbus 43215–0098; (614) 466–2531

OKLAHOMA

Vital Records Section, State Department of Health, 1000 Northeast 10th Street, P.O. Box 53551, Oklahoma City 73152; (405) 271–4040

OREGON

Vital Statistics Section, Oregon Health Division, P.O. Box 14050, Portland 97214–0050; (503) 731–4095

PENNSYLVANIA

Division of Vital Records, State Department of Health, Central Building, 101 South Mercer Street, P.O. Box 1528, New Castle 16103; (412) 656–3100

PUERTO RICO

Demographic Registry, Department of Health, P.O. Box 11854; Fernandez Juncos Station, San Juan 00910; (787) 728–7980

RHODE ISLAND

Division of Vital Records, Rhode Island Department of Health, 3 Capitol Hill, Providence 02908–5097; (401) 277–2811

SOUTH CAROLINA

Office of Public Health Statistics and Information Systems, South Carolina Department of Health and Environmental Control, 2600 Bull Street, Columbia 29201; (803) 734–4830

SOUTH DAKOTA

Vital Records, Department of Health, 445 East Capitol, Pierre 57501–3185; (605) 773–3355

TENNESSEE

Tennessee Vital Records, Department of Health, Central Services Building, 421 5th Avenue, North, Nashville 37247–0450; (615) 741–1763

TEXAS

Bureau of Vital Statistics, Texas Department of Health, P.O. Box 12040, Austin 78711–2040; (512) 458–7111

UTAH

Bureau of Vital Records, Utah Department of Health, 288 North 1460 West, P.O. Box 142855, Salt Lake City 84114–2855; (801) 538–6105

VERMONT

Vital Records Section, Box 70, Vermont Department of Health, 108 Cherry Street, Burlington 05402; (802) 863–7275 for records since 1981. For records prior to 1981: Division of Public Records, US Route 2-Middlesex, 133 State Street, Montpelier 05633; (802) 828–3286

VIRGINIA

Office of Vital Records and Health Statistics, State Health Department, P.O. Box 1000, Richmond 23218–1000; (804) 786–6228

WASHINGTON

Center for Health Statistics, Department of Health, P.O. Box 9709, Olympia 98507–9709; (206) 753–5936

WEST VIRGINIA

Vital Registration Office, Division of Health, State Capitol Complex Building 3, Charleston 25305; (304) 558–2931

WISCONSIN

Vital Records, 1 West Wilson Street, P.O. Box 309, Madison 53701; (608) 266–1371

WYOMING

Vital Records Services, Hathaway Building, Cheyenne 82002; (307) 777–7591

CONSENTS

Before an adoption can be approved by a court of law, certain consents must be obtained. The child will be asked to consent to the adoption if he is legally old enough to do so. (This will vary state by state, but the age of legal consent is typically at least twelve years.) The consent of the birth parents, both mother and father, is expected. If the parents are dead or have abandoned the child or lost their custody judicially, then the consent of the guardian, next of kin, court-appointed "friend," or an authorized agency will be used. If you are adopting a child through an agency, the agency will be sure that the necessary surrenders are obtained. The agency will then be authorized to consent to the adoption. If you are adopting a child independently, you or your attorney must make sure that the necessary surrenders are obtained. Be sure that if a father is known (whether or not he is actually married to the birth mother), you obtain his consent. If you cannot readily locate him, the court in some states may ask you to show that you made an effort to find him. In some states that may mean searching for him by placing an advertisement in a newspaper. Many states are now establishing putative-father registries by which a birth father can record his interest in his child. The state must then inform the father of legal proceedings that affect the well-being of his child.

States may also have regulations stating the length of time (a waiting period) that must elapse between a child's birth and the parents' relinquishment. (It is unusual for a state to permit a birth parent to consent to the adoption prior to the child's birth.) There may also be provisions stating the length of time in which a parental release is revocable or can be withdrawn.

Medical Consent Forms

If you are adopting a child independently, before you take custody of the child, have the birth mother sign a medical consent form stating that you can legally provide medical treatment for the child. Adoption agencies normally provide you with their consent for treatment.

THE INTERSTATE COMPACT

Sometimes families will identify a child in another state whom they would like to adopt. These adoptions are carried out under the Interstate Compact on the Placement of Children. The compact is a uniform law enacted by all the states, the District of Columbia and Puerto Rico. It establishes procedures for the transfer of children and fixes specific responsibilities for those involved in the placement of the child. At each step of the adoption process, your documents, and a prospective child's, are passed through the state's Interstate Compact Administrator. The interstate compact is designed to protect children and parents to make sure that everyone knows what is happening. Any interstate placement, whether done through an agency or independently, must follow compact procedure. Failure to comply violates the law and could result in your child being ordered returned to the first state.

For a fuller explanation of procedures, contact the Administrator in your state's social service or public welfare office. You might also want to request a copy of the *Guide to the Interstate Compact on the Placement of Children,* available from them or from the **American Public Welfare Association** (see appendix A).

FINALIZING AN ADOPTION

Since a legal adoption is a procedure that establishes a relationship of parent and child between people who are not biologically related, you will have to go to court to finalize an adoption. This may be in your state of residence, your child's place of prior residence, or even the agency's place of (business) operation, depending upon state laws. If you are involved in an intercountry adoption, you may be adopting your child abroad. *If your child left his or her country of birth under a guardianship, not a final adoption, then you must adopt in the United States.*

Some states require a waiting period before you may petition the court to initiate formal adoption proceedings. In other states, you may be able to file your court papers immediately but must still wait a period of time before finalizing the adoption. The process usually begins when you submit to the court a petition for adoption. This petition, signed by the people seeking to adopt, sets out information about them, the child, and the biological parents. It asks the court to approve the adoption and may also include your request for an official change of your child's name. Along with the petition, you are usually asked to provide birth certificates, documents concerning guardianships, statements of the consent or termination of rights by the biological parents, the (older) child's statement of consent to the adoption, and the agency's consent to the adoption. The court may require that the consents (of birth parents, agencies, etc.) be submitted with the petition for adoption or at a hearing.

The court usually requires a postplacement investigation and the investigator's report before approving an adoption. (They will be looking at how your child is doing in your home.) If a child is placed through an agency, the agency will probably already have done its own postplacement follow-up. If a child has been adopted independently, the court will probably arrange for a postplacement study of your home.

The court usually holds a hearing. It may be in a closed courtroom or in the judge's chambers, and you may or may not be present. After the hearing, the court, having approved the adoption, issues an order or decree. The nature of the decree depends upon state law. It may be a final decree or an interlocutory decree (a temporary one stipulating that at a later date—perhaps six months or a year—the court will again consider the application). Practices may vary by locality and by state. Which court actually considers your petition will also depend on local statute. It may be the probate court, district court, family court, superior court, or even the county court.

Once you have legally adopted your child, you can apply for a social security number from the Social Security Administration. To file with Social Security, you'll need proof of the adoption and proof of residency.

Readoption

If your child has been legally adopted abroad, the adoption is valid. State courts are not required to recognize a foreign adoption decree; it is possible in your state that you will have to readopt. Even if your state recognizes the foreign adoption, most adoption authorities recommend that as an additional safeguard you readopt your child in the United States under the laws of your state. This will also give you readily available evidence of the validity of your child's adoption. Some states may not permit readoption, so check locally to see if this can be done.

GETTING LEGAL HELP

Attorneys usually handle the court paperwork. In selecting an attorney to handle an adoption, inquire around and do some comparison shopping. Be sure to:

- Find an attorney who is experienced with adoption law. The more adoption cases an attorney handles, the more familiar the attorney should be with the forms, the courts, and the local clerks.
- Ask for recommendations from parent groups, the local chapter of the American Bar Association, the American Academy of Adoption Attorneys, and the clerks at the courts that handle adoptions in your community. You can get some biographical information about a lawyer from the Martindale-Hubbell legal directory (available at your local library and on the World Wide Web). The American Bar Association in Chicago maintains a National Discipline Data Bank which is a nationwide listing of public disciplinary actions of attorneys, including public censure to temporary suspension to disbarment.
- Ask your adoption agency for recommendations since there is often a list of recommended lawyers. If the agency directs you to "its" lawyer, however, you may want to ask some questions. The agency attorney may have an arrangement to handle adoptions for a set fee. You may find an equally competent attorney who charges less. The agency attorney, because he also handles all agency legal matters, may be very busy and finalizing adoptions may be a low priority on his agenda.
- Ascertain what the attorney's fees include. Are you billed for the time spent, or is there a set fee for every adoption? Watch out for hidden fees. One attorney, when asked to break down fees, said that he charged two hundred

dollars to handle a foreign-born adoptee's application for citizenship. You can do this paperwork yourself.

- Ask what other expenses, beyond fees, you can anticipate.
- Find out how long it will take the attorney to get to the paperwork. Courts may be backed up, but if an attorney's caseload is too heavy, there may be delays because he or she simply does not have time to work on your case.
- Find out who will be working on your case. Will there be junior attorneys or paralegals involved in some of the administrative work and, if so, will there be a lower rate?
- Check into an attorney's local reputation. Some adoption attorneys may not be well regarded by the court because of the poor quality of their paperwork or their questionable legal practices.

Should you use an attorney to handle your child's adoption? Some jurisdictions may permit you to file your own adoption papers, particularly the papers for finalization. Be sure to consult with other adoptive parents who have finalized their children's adoptions, with your local parent group (which may have sample completed forms for your area or state), and with your agency.[2]

Before you consider doing your own adoption, however, think it over carefully. Observes adoption attorney Blanche Gelber: "No two of my adoptions have been the same, and despite all my experience, the variations on the theme seem unpredictable and endless." Independent adoptions, particularly, are complex and often very intricate. Gelber points out that each judge may have his own beliefs and ways of approaching adoption.

Consider the experience of three families in one state. The Tellers used the forms that an attorney—whose child had also been adopted from Chile—had obtained from the local court and had successfully used. They essentially filled in the blanks. Their son's adoption went through the local court without a hitch. However, in passing on the "sample" papers to a third family—who also had a Chilean child but lived in another jurisdiction—things went awry. This family's judge was adamant in his insistence that the family provide evidence of having tried to obtain the putative father's consent in Chile. So this family hired an attorney both in the United States and in Chile and advertised for the putative father.

These three families, living just ten miles apart but in different counties of a state, had different adoption experiences. If you will be following in the steps of someone else, particularly on a road *well trod* and with your agency's support, then adopting without an attorney may be a viable alternative.

If you are pursuing an independent adoption, you'll have some special questions to ask an attorney. These are explored in chapter 3.

THE SEALED RECORD

With the issuance of the final order of adoption, the adoption proceeding is completed and the case is legally closed. The legal practice has been to keep the adoption records confidential. In the past they have been available in most states for inspection by court order only. In most states the child's original birth certificate and the other documents collected for the adoption petition are placed in sealed court files. (Agency records are not necessarily sealed, but some agencies do not release the information.) Access to this basic information can thus be limited, even to adult adoptees.

The laws surrounding the records of adoption are changing. In some states, adoptees can receive "non-identifying" information about their birth parents. They can request identifying information (name of child before placement, parents' names, most recent address of birth parents), but this information will not be released until the state receives statements of consent from the birth parents (in some states the consent of the adoptive parents is also required). To keep track some states maintain a central adoption registry, a file of birth parents' and adoptees' consents or denials to release information. When all the necessary parties have consented, then the state discloses the names and addresses to everyone. In still other states no registries exist, and no information is disclosed. For a state-by-state listing of reunion registries, see appendix B. Under federal law a foreign-born adoptee can obtain the records that were filed with the Immigration and Naturalization Service.

Several chapters discuss at length the importance of getting information about a child. Keep in mind that any information that you turn over to the court may indeed be sealed and no longer be accessible. If you are concerned about sharing with your child information about his background, keep a copy of whatever information you have received and push your agency or contact to share information with you.

OBTAINING A NEW BIRTH CERTIFICATE

It is customary, upon the adoption of a child, for the state to issue a new birth certificate or an amended birth certificate giving the new name of the adopted child. The certificate will usually give your child's name, will list you as parents, and may give the child's birthplace and other details. The new birth certificate will not reveal any information about the child's birth parents, nor does it usually state that the child is adopted.

Your attorney may handle this routinely as part of the adoption process. If you are not using an attorney, check with your state office of vital records. It is always a good idea to order more than one certified copy of the new birth certificate, as your child may need the birth certificate when entering school, when obtaining a driver's license, and when marrying.

If you have adopted a child abroad, some states will permit you to apply for a state birth certificate without readoption, while others will insist upon readoption. Some states will issue a birth certificate for foreign-born adoptees upon their U.S. citizenship; others permit parents to submit a copy of the child's translated birth certificate and a translated copy of the child's final adoption decree. Check with your state's Vital Records office.

Some states will issue a foreign-born child a birth certificate that is the same as the birth certificate issued to all people born in the state. Other states issue "certificates of foreign birth."

THE SPECIAL PAPERWORK OF AN INTERCOUNTRY ADOPTION

The amount of paperwork increases exponentially with an intercountry adoption. Even if you will be working with an agency, you must be well-informed, well-organized, determined, and willing to assemble what in advance may seem like an awesome array of personal documents. It can be done and has been done by thousands of people. The paperwork is extensive because *you are meeting the requirements of a foreign country, the federal government, and your state system.*

Everyone bringing a child into the United States for the purposes of adoption must file documentation with the U.S. Department of Justice's Immigration and Naturalization Service (INS). The INS operates a toll-free number (800–755–0777) through which you will be apprised of basic procedures as well as the location and telephone number of the INS office near your home. You can request basic forms through another toll-free number (800–870–3676) or consult your telephone directory (under U.S. Government) to see if there is a special local phone number designed to handle document requests. The INS's website has updates as well as forms you can download. You can also get detailed explanations of paperwork procedures through the **Office of Children's Issues, Bureau of Consular Affairs of the U.S. State Department** (see appendix A).

You must have an INS-approved petition as well as a visa issued by the State Department before you can bring a child into the country for the purposes of adoption. The federal FORM I-600—Petition to Classify Orphan as an Immediate Relative—is filed with the INS, which has offices throughout the United States.

When you file form I-600 with the INS, you will need to submit a variety of supporting documents and pay a filing fee by check or money order. The I-600 form also states that you must meet certain federal requirements:

- The term "orphan" under the immigration laws means a child who is under the age of sixteen years at the time the petition in his behalf is filed and both of whose parents have died or disappeared, or who has been abandoned or otherwise separated from both parents.
- Under the INS definition an orphan may also have one sole surviving parent. If the child has one parent, that parent must be incapable of providing for the child's care and must have in writing irrevocably released the child for emigration and "adoption." *WARNING: If there are two known parents, then the child does not qualify as an orphan under the I–600. A foreign country's determination that a child is an "orphan" does not mean that the child will be considered an orphan under American immigration law as the foreign country may have different criteria.*
- To enter the United States, the orphan either must have been adopted abroad or must be coming to the U.S., for *adoption* by a U.S. citizen and spouse jointly, or by an unmarried U.S. citizen at least twenty-five years of age.

Your spouse does not have to be a U.S. citizen but must agree to the adoption. *WARNING: If you are a legal permanent resident or a long-term non-immigrant visa holder, under American immigration law, you will not be able to adopt abroad and then bring that child immediately into the U.S under an orphan visa.*

- The I-600 also states that you must *meet state preadoption requirements,* and that if the child has not been adopted abroad, you must certify that he will be adopted in the United States.
- *There is no bypassing an I-600.* Children brought in for medical procedures are brought in on different visas. If you try to bring a child into the country on a temporary visitor's visa, then you are asking for trouble. *WARNING: While your heart may go out to the abandoned children in orphanages of a particular country, whom you see in heartrending photos, you cannot just fly abroad, locate a child for adoption, show up at the U.S. embassy, and request a visa for your new-found child. You will not be able to bring that child into the U.S. unless you have complied with U.S. immigration procedures, which are very detailed and specific.*

When submitting paperwork to the INS, send it via FedEx, UPS, or another airborne carrier that permits you to track it. The INS will accept legible photocopies of the original documents required. Be sure you copy both sides of any document. You will need to send with these copies a signed and dated statement that states that "Copies of documents submitted are exact photocopies of unaltered original documents and I understand that I may be required to submit original documents to an Immigration or Consular official at a later date." (Some people prefer to do this step in person to insure delivery and receipt.)

PROCESSING THROUGH THE IMMIGRATION AND NATURALIZATION SERVICE

Long before your child arrives in the United States—even before a particular child may be assigned to you—the paperwork for adoption begins. You should begin gathering your documents in advance so that your application can proceed. Accompanying the I-600 will be the documents that describe you and your child.

The I-600 requires that you submit the following for yourself:

- Proof of U.S. citizenship of the petitioner
- Proof of marriage (and proof of any previous divorce)
- Home study favorably recommending adoption. (The INS requires that there be an in-person interview, as well as other information, with every adult member of your household.)
- Fingerprints (Form FD-258)
- Application Fee

To speed the INS paperwork process, you may begin by submitting Form I-600A, the Application for Advance Processing of Orphan Petition, to INS *before you have identified a specific child.* You present your documents, the I-600A, and a nonrefundable filing fee. Thus, INS can run the fingerprint check on you (fingerprint cards are sent to the FBI) and look at your documents. You can even file the I-600A before your home study is completed. (The home study must be submitted to INS within one year of the filing date of your application for advance processing.) *WARNING: If your family situation changes or you move, you will need to update your homestudy after the change.*

You must have your fingerprints at INS-registered law

enforcement agencies and INS offices that do fingerprints. INS procedures have been changing: the service is in the process of setting up Application Support Centers (ASC). According to Maureen Evans of the Joint Council on International Children's Services: "Once the Application Support Centers are set up, all applicants needing to submit fingerprints will apply to the INS, which will send the applicant a letter with a designated week during which the applicant can go to the ASC for fingerprinting."[3] (For further details, call 800–876–3676.) When you go to the law enforcement agency registered with the INS, you must take identification and an envelope large enough to hold the fingerprint card (eight inches square). After your fingerprints are taken, you will be asked to sign the card and it will then be placed in the envelope, sealed and given to you for submission to the INS. A fingerprint check processed by the INS can take weeks or months.

Sometimes fingerprint checks reveal a record of a previous arrest. Convictions for drunk driving, trespassing, participating in an antiwar demonstration—even if they are many years past—will show up. When this occurs, you will have to submit additional documentation to the INS to clear the record. It's recommended that to avoid this delay you reveal this information in advance to your social worker so that your home study can indicate knowledge of this, as well as a statement that you are approved for parenting an adopted child.

If the INS approves your I-600A application, you will receive a "notice of favorable determination." This approval is valid for eighteen months. When you obtain your child's documents, you file an I-600, and the I-600 is processed. You do not need to resubmit with the I-600 the material that was presented to the INS for the I-600A.

Advance processing can shorten your wait. Nothing is more frustrating than to get a child referral, know that your child is ready to emigrate, but be held up because your documents are not in order. For an I-600 application, you will also be showing your child's documents to the INS for approval. If your child's documents are in a foreign language, you must provide a translation in English. For the child that you are planning to adopt you must show:

- Proof of age of orphan (e.g., birth certificate)
- Certified copy of the adoption decree together with certified translation, if the orphan has been legally adopted abroad
- Death certificates of the child's parents, if relevant
- Evidence that the sole or surviving parent is not able to provide for the child's care and has in writing irrevocably released the child for emigration and adoption
- Evidence that the child has been unconditionally abandoned to an orphanage, if the child has been placed in an orphanage by his parent or parents
- Evidence that your state's preadoption requirements have been met if you will be adopting the child here

If you are adopting more than one child, you must file a separate I-600 for each child.

You will also be expected to submit Form I-864, an affidavit of support. You must provide copies of the most recent three years worth of tax returns and a letter documenting proof of employment. The letter must indicate that your income is 125 percent of the federal poverty level (or meet an alternative through evaluation of your assets); if not, your visa request will be denied.

Once the INS has approved the I-600 application, an official can notify the embassy in the country where the child is located that he or she has permission to enter the U.S. and that the adoptive parents (or their representative) can apply for a visa. If you are traveling abroad to complete the adoption there, you can submit the completed I-600 to an INS service office abroad or to the US embassy in your child's birth country. If you file the I-600 in the U.S., the INS will cable the visa-petition approval to the embassy. Ask for confirmation from the INS. If you are not traveling to pick up your child, you will want to follow up with the agencies to be sure that the visa approval was received. To receive a visa, there must be a "visual inspection" of the child by a consular officer and a medical examination of the child by a designated physician. When the consular section schedules the final visa interview, you'll be expected to provide:

- notification by the INS of the I-600 or I-600A approval
- final adoption decree or proof of custody from the foreign government
- child's birth certificate
- child's passport issued by the country of the child's nationality
- completed and signed medical examination report
- required photographs of the child
- visa application (Form OF-230)
- completed I-600 (if it was not previously approved)

If you will be adopting your child abroad, the submission of the I-600 may come at the end of your wait, when your child is already with you, and you and your child may enter the U.S. shortly afterward. As the State Department notes in its International Adoption literature:

Although the final visa interview appears to involve a single action which may be completed quickly, the consular officer must perform several different steps required by law and regulation. The officer must review the I–600 petition, verify the child's status as an orphan, establish that the prospective parents have legal custody, survey the child's medical condition and confirm that the child has the required travel documentation.

Meeting State Preadoption Requirements

To meet preadoption requirements, some states may demand that you submit certain documents—for example, your home study, your child's birth certificate, the release for adoption, a police report or fingerprint check—to them before they will approve the child's entry. Not all states have preadoption requirements, but be sure to inquire with your state's department of social services and the state's interstate compact administrator about requirements and procedures to follow. If your child is entering the United States with a final adoption decree, you do not need to meet state preadoption requirements.

Notarization, Verification, Authentication

Some documents may need to be "notarized, verified, and authenticated." A document that is notarized bears the seal of a notary public, who attests that the signature of the person on the document is valid. The county clerk of the county in which the notary is registered or the secretary of state (whose office is in the state capitol) for the state in which the notary resides verifies that the notary's seal and signature are valid. (Birth and marriage certificates are certified copies, so that they do not usually require this step). Your notarized and verified documents, with translations if required, then go to the consul for the country to which you are applying for authentication. The consul of the country to which you are applying can tell you what documents must be authenticated and will also attest to their authenticity before your submitting them abroad. Some countries may require that everything you submit—your references, your birth certificates, your home study, your doctor's report—be notarized, verified, and authenticated. Some countries will also require an additional step before authentication takes place: the U.S. Department of State must also certify the notarized and verified documents. (You can obtain details about State Department authentication, from the Authentications Office, 518 23rd Street NW, State Annex 1, Washington, D.C 20520.; 202–647–5002.)

Don't be surprised if costs mount to several hundred dollars. You'll want to have this procedure done when you are sure of your adoption plans. Be sure you call ahead to the consulate in advance to ask about hours and costs (cash payment may be expected) and to make an appointment if necessary.

Be prepared that you may have to leave the documents and have them returned to you by mail. You'll want to make copies of all documents, as well as the final fully authenticated documents, so that when you travel abroad you have your own set.

Translations

Your documents may have to be translated into a foreign language. Your child's documents will have to be translated into English. If you are working with an agency, they may have the translations done. If you are asked to arrange this yourself, be sure to use a competent, experienced translator, preferably someone working in his or her native language. Your translator will need to provide you with a statement of competency bearing an official raised seal. The statement might read: "I, _________, hereby certify that the above is a complete and accurate translation of the original and that I am competent in both English and _________ to render such a translation."

Legwork

As the volume of paperwork grows with intercountry adoption, so, too, does the time it takes to process the papers. If you live near the offices of the Immigration and Naturalization Service, or indeed within any reasonable distance, it often pays to do your paperwork in person. Be sure to call ahead to find out opening and closing hours, lunch hours, and the days when the people you need to see will be on vacation or out of the office.

Many families carry as many of their documents as possible by hand. They may spend one day in their state capitol, another at the foreign consulate getting the papers authenticated, and still another filing papers with the INS. You can also use an express mail service. (When using express mail services to communicate abroad, ask your local parent group or agency for a specific recommendation as some services have a better track record handling foreign correspondence than others.) If there is a specific person who will be handling your documents, such as the interstate placement officer, you may want to follow up your letter with a telephone call a week later.

As you do the paperwork for an intercountry adoption, it's useful to talk to people who have recently completed the process. They can give you tips about whom to contact at the INS, what process to follow, and how long things will take. Many parent support groups have written up the local INS or foreign-consulate procedures.

If you will be traveling to pick up your child, you will need a valid passport. You can apply for a passport at a regional passport agency of the U.S. Department of State, at federal or state courts, or at some U.S. post offices. With the application you must present proof of U.S. citizenship such as a certified copy of your birth certificate, a prior passport, or your naturalization certificate. You will also need two recent identical photographs of a specified size, evidence of your identity such as your driver's license, and a fee. If you are applying for a passport for the first time, you must apply in person. For further details, call the recorded message of the Department of State, Office of Passport Services (202–647–0518).

Since passports for adults are valid for ten years, apply for your passport as soon as you can. Some Latin American agencies will ask for your passport number on their applications, and the foreign consulate may ask to see your passport when you present your documents. Even if you do not plan on traveling abroad, you should have a valid passport so you can travel if a situation arises that requires your presence. The child you adopt will need a passport issued by his birth country to travel to the United States. If you are adopting through an intercountry program, your agency will help make these arrangements.

You may need a visa to travel. Check with the foreign consulate, the airline that you will be traveling on, or the Office of Children's Issues, Bureau of Consular Affairs of the U.S. State Department.

If you will be traveling to pick up your child, you may have to appear before foreign authorities and do some paperwork at that time abroad. You may be asked to do such things as submit affidavits to a department of welfare or documents to the court, obtain statements from a physician about your child's health, or file an application for your child's passport. Your agency or attorney abroad may do this, or you may have to do this yourself.

Alien Registration

When your child immigrates to the United States, he or she enters as an alien, not as an American citizen. You will receive from the INS an alien registration card. This card should be carefully safeguarded along with other important papers. Until your child becomes a U.S. citizen, whenever you move, you must notify INS of the change of address.

CONFERRING U.S. CITIZENSHIP ON YOUR CHILD

If you adopted your child abroad, you can apply to the INS to make him or her a citizen immediately. Otherwise, as soon as your child has been legally adopted in the U.S., you can take this step. You must obtain INS Form N-643, Application for Certificate of Citizenship in Behalf of Adopted Child. The application is filed at the INS office that has jurisdiction over your child's place of residence and you will have one interview (at which you sign an affidavit before an interviewing officer), following which your child, who must be under the age of eighteen, will receive the certificate of citizenship. To file for a certificate of citizenship, you must be a U.S. citizen, your spouse must be a citizen, and the two of you must be the child's adoptive parents. You'll need to file with the application:

- photographs of your child that meet INS specification
- child's alien registration card
- child's birth certificate
- final adoption degree
- proof of name change if child's name has been changed
- evidence of U.S. citizenship of adoptive parent(s).
- marriage certificate of adoptive parents
- divorce certificates from any previous marriages

There is also the long-standing method of naturalization, in which you submit to the INS Form N-402, an Application to File Petition for Naturalization in Behalf of Child. The application must be accompanied by a fee and photographs.

At a later date you are called for a hearing before an Immigration officer. Bring your child's birth certificate, a certified copy of the child's adoption decree (if your child was adopted abroad, be sure that you have the adoption decree translated and that you have your translator's statement of competence), your various documents (birth, marriage, divorce certificates), the alien registration card, your child's passport, and your child. Even if the INS fails to tell you to bring your documents, do so.

Only one parent needs to file the naturalization petition (Form N-402). If there is a family emergency—or illness—only the parent who filed the petition must attend the hearing and naturalization. (If only one parent is a U.S. citizen, this is the form to use to obtain your child's citizenship.)

Some time after your meeting with the Immigration official, you will be summoned to the "swearing in" naturalization ceremony. It is for all new citizens, not just adoptees. Must a young child be present for this ceremony? It is the parent, rather than the young child, who takes the oath of allegiance. Most parents want their children present, but it is apparently not mandatory. Sometimes after the naturalization, the INS will send you a naturalization certificate for your child.

What happens if your child doesn't become a U.S. citizen? Maureen Evans of the Joint Council on International Children's Services notes that under recent American immigration laws: "Parents who wait to get U.S. citizenship for their children until it means something to the child or for any other reason face the possibility of their child being deported back to the birth country, if the child runs into trouble with the law after the age of 16." If your child, for example, gets involved in a felony drug conviction and is not a U.S. citizen, he could be deported after age sixteen.

Once your child becomes a U.S. citizen, you will also want to check with your adoption agency or with the foreign consulate whether your child holds dual citizenship. If that's the case, you will want to complete the paperwork to nullify the other citizenship. It's unlikely, but an adopted child who has not become a U.S. citizen or whose citizenship has not been renounced could be required to serve in their birth country's armed forces. (The Korean government, for example, requires notification of U.S. citizenship.)

KEEPING TRACK

You will want to devise a method to keep track of all the documentation you need to accumulate. Be sure to keep copies of all correspondence and all documents.

Remember that you are preparing *at least* three sets of documents: one for the agency or person who is handling the placement of your child; one for the Immigration and Naturalization Service; and one for yourself (a duplicate set that you can use if necessary).

How do adoptive parents feel about what often seems like an endless stream of paperwork? Wrote one adoptive parent: "If all these procedures and requirements seem daunting, take heart—remember that you've already been through a seemingly complex myriad of procedures, survived, and have been rewarded with the smiles of your child. This is merely one of the last stops on the journey."[4]

9

PREPARING FOR YOUR CHILD

◆

Dear Lynne,

Do you think the day will ever come when we will exchange letters filled with frustrations of being stuck at home with babies? Do you think we will ever write to each other about how our instincts pushing us toward motherhood were right? About how fulfilled we feel, how happy? I am feeling very pessimistic these days. Very.

It's so easy for both of us to lose sight of our strengths in the midst of all this exasperating waiting. . .

My best to you, friend,
Barbara[1]

In her letter to her friend Lynn Sipoiora, Barbara Shulgold captures the anguish that prospective adoptive parents feel as they anticipate the future. All adoptive parents have to go through the wait—whether for a few days, a few weeks, a few months, or years. Waiting is a critical part of adoption: Children wait for homes; parents wait for children. When you've done all that paperwork, when you've done all the preliminaries that you need to do in order to make your adoption happen, you may still have some waiting to do.

Keep busy. If you're working, keep working. If you plan to take time off for parenting, wait until your child is ready to enter your home; don't quit your job, or start your leave, in anticipation of your new status. Do other things that you'd planned: don't defer a vacation or other project "because the adoption call might come." Let your life continue.

Get involved in your adoptive-parent group. Others have been through the waiting and they may help. "Looking back, the waiting period was just a few months," observed one adoptive parent. "but those months were the longest, most stressful, emotionally turbulent months of my life." For this parent, the monthly meetings of New York Singles Adopting Children were critical: "Seeing the children helped to reinforce that 'it will happen.' Those who had been through the wait could understand as no others could. I met others whose wait began around the time of mine, so we went through it together. And, when the placements came, we shared each other's joy."[2]

The waiting period should be the time when you sit down and read about child care and adoption. Think about the future. How do you see yourself as a parent? What do you think your life will be like once your child arrives? What roles will your spouse, other children, family, and friends play in the upcoming adoption? How will your relationships with them change? What do you expect of your new child? "Waiting parents," says Claudia Jewett Jarratt, "are wise to discuss openly their dreams and fears and plans for their coming child."[3]

Consider those first days and weeks after your child arrives. If you are working, will you be taking time off? If so, how much? Do you want help at the beginning from a spouse, parent, or friend? What kinds of support will you require? When? This chapter outlines some of the things that you will want to get done in preparation for your role as an adoptive parent. You may want to change insurance policies and wills, arrange for a leave of absence from work, meet with a prospective doctor for your child, and, if your child is older, a dentist. If you are adopting an infant, you may want to set up your child's room and do some shopping. If you are adopting an older child, you may want to do some fixing up yourself and leave some things to do with your child. Time is likely to be in short supply once your child arrives.

LEAVES OF ABSENCE AND ADOPTION BENEFITS

In 1983 Carole Fezar wanted to take an unpaid maternity leave to spend time with her infant daughter—a common request among working mothers. But unlike most mothers, Carole had to file a grievance with her union to get that opportunity. For Carole had adopted her daughter. A federal arbitrator ruled that she was entitled to her leave. He said:

> *It is apparent that the term maternity does not singularly embrace conception and childbearing but rather that it encompasses the duties and responsibilities of motherhood. The very fact that maternity leave can cover a period of time up to one year in duration serves to establish the fact that it sets a major portion of the time for child-rearing. It must follow then that the adoption of an infant child requires the same care, the same responsibility as would be with an infant born to a natural mother.*[4]

Fezar might have less of a struggle today. The federal Family and Medical Leave Act mandates twelve weeks of unpaid, job-guaranteed leave for childbirth, adoption, or illness of an employee or family member with employee benefits continuing while away. The law, which took effect in

August 1993, covers nearly 55 percent of U.S. employees, including all public sector workers and those of private companies with fifty or more workers. Some states also require that employees be offered leave. Keep in mind, however, that adoption leaves are almost always *unpaid* leaves of absence, while maternity leaves, which are subject to the federal Pregnancy Discrimination Act of 1978, typically provide some disability benefits, including financial compensation, for time off. Federal and state law set only minimum requirements: your employer may have a more generous leave policy.

Recognizing the strains placed on a family and their budget when they adopt a child, some employers are also now offering adoption assistance that ranges from telephone advice hotlines, lunchtime seminars, books, videos, and pamphlets to a ten-thousand-dollar reimbursement for the costs of adoption. In a 1996 study of work and family benefits, the independent consulting firm Hewitt Associates found that 23 percent of 1,050 major U.S employers provided their employees with some form of adoption assistance with the typical benefit having a maximum payout of between two thousand and three thousand dollars. While employees typically could request reimbursement for their agency, legal, and medical fees, some employers provided lump-sum payments instead. There may be other restrictions: the U.S. military, for example, provides for adoption expense reimbursement of up to two thousand dollars per child but does not extend this to adoptions arranged by attorneys, non-agency persons such as doctors or clergy, or for-profit agencies.

Paid adoption leave is not common. "That's next on the horizon," predicts Suzanne Camp of the Adoption and the Workplace initiative at the **National Adoption Center** (see appendix A). "People are asking for it even more than for financial reimbursement." If your employer provides a benefit, you'll be asked to document your expenses. Don't be surprised if you're also asked to wait until your child's adoption is finalized.

If you are a working parent waiting to adopt a child, then you will want to explore your employer's leave and benefit policies. Start by looking at your employer's human resources booklets outlining benefits and then talk with one of your company's human resources counselors. Be sure that you get the policy outlined to you *in writing* and that you understand it fully. In your research, you will need to find out:

- Does your employer grant adoption leave? If so, to whom, and under what circumstances? Are both men and women eligible? Are there restrictions? If you are adopting an infant who is not a newborn, can you take a leave? If you are adopting an older child, can you take an adoption leave?
- Is your employer's adoption leave a formal policy or has it been granted informally, on a person-by-person basis?
- What are the specific provisions of the adoption leave?
- Are there differences between your employer's maternity leave, adoption leave, and family leave? If so, what are they?
- How many weeks of adoption leave are you entitled to? Are you entitled to paid weeks of adoption leave? If so, how many?
- How far in advance must you request an adoption leave?
- Are you guaranteed your job—or a similar job—when you return?
- How are your health insurance, disability, and other plans in which you participate affected while you are on leave? Who pays for them?
- Is there a restriction on the number of adoption leaves, or the frequency of leaves, that you can take?

- Does your company offer adoption benefits? How does the benefit package work? Is there reimbursement for specific, itemized expenses? If so, what's covered? Is there a dollar ceiling set for each adoption, regardless of your actual expenses? When are you eligible to apply for reimbursement under your company's benefit package?
- What other forms of adoption assistance does your company offer? Is there a resource and referral service?

If you find that your company is not in compliance with federal or state law, contact the U.S. Department of Labor or your state Department of Labor. The Adoption and the Workplace initiative at the National Adoption Center can also offer guidance. You might also, as Carole Fezar did, ask your labor union to back your request. Enterprising adoptive parents have also asked their unions to include an adoption assistance program as part of the contract negotiations. If you negotiate for yourself a leave, be sure to get all the terms of the leave in writing.

If you want to advocate for adoption benefits within your company, Adoption and the Workplace can help by sending you—and your company—information about benefit policies at companies nationwide. Among their recommendations:

- Learn what's common within your industry.
- Research current "family-building" benefits in your workplace such as maternity, parental leave, or resource and referral. Compare these with whatever adoption assistance is offered.
- Identify the key people within your company, such as the work/family coordinator, who can back your request.
- Find other adoptive parents or prospective adoptive parents in your company and enlist their support.

- Send a letter or memo, along with your backup documentation, to the vice president, director, or other senior managers in your company's human resources department. Request a meeting to discuss adoption benefits.
- Follow up with telephone calls and supportive material that Adoption and the Workplace will send to your employer.

You'll also need to decide when to inform your employer about your adoption plans and your interest in taking a leave. When you discuss your plans, you may find that your employer has some difficulty dealing with the timing of an adoption leave. Employers and benefits managers are accustomed to having people tell them that "My baby/my wife is due on March 5 and I want to leave work two weeks before that." Employers understand that medical complications may force a person to leave work earlier than planned. It's much more difficult to grasp the reality of adoption: that people often don't know when the blessed event will take place; that families will not have much notice; that working parents can't give much notice. Your employer may be stymied by a statement like "We don't know when the agency will contact us." You may also have difficulty getting people to understand that you won't have time for a while to come back to the office to take care of things unexpectedly left hanging. You'll need to explain that you're going to be swamped at home for a while. You may not be exhausted from the birth of your child, but that's only a small part of new parenthood. Adjusting to a new child—whether by birth or adoption—will require your full attention.

HEALTH INSURANCE

Before your child enters your home, you should be sure that you have proper medical coverage. Some agencies may require a statement about the exact coverage that you have. If you are adopting a child with special needs, be sure you understand the details of any health coverage or subsidy that the child will receive. In all cases you want to be sure that your child will be covered upon "placement," upon "arriving" in your home, or from the time that you are responsible for care—rather than upon finalization. Federal law requires most employer-sponsored group policies to pay medical expenses, including for preexisting conditions, from the time you assume legally binding financial responsibility for the child. If your company is not in compliance, you may contact your state insurance commissioner.

Check with your health insurance company or health maintenance organization to find out about your plan's coverage for dependents and get the details in writing. Some plans cover foster children; others do not. Find out what you must do to get your child covered under your policy. Be sure to explain that the child is not adopted at the time he enters your home but that you are fully responsible for the child's well-being. If there is a gap in your health insurance coverage, you may need to take out additional coverage through your insurance company, or else contact other insurance carriers to arrange for separate coverage for your child. (An insurance broker or your agency or adoptive-parent group may be able to help you find a company. A sympathetic employer might put pressure on your insurance carrier or HMO to change its policy so that coverage is available.) Get a letter from the insurance company verifying your coverage for preexisting conditions, both diagnosed and undiagnosed. Military families will want to be sure that they understand the coverage that is available to them under CHAMPUS.

If you have individual coverage under a group plan (sometimes spouses are covered individually by their employers), you'll need to convert to *family* health insurance coverage.

This is particularly important if you are a single parent, because you will need to have a family policy in order to cover your child. Check also whether there is any waiting period before coverage begins. For most policies, federal law now prohibits a waiting period as long as parents have notified the plan within thirty days of adoption or placement for adoption of their child. You might also want to find out who holds the guardianship of your child in the period between placement and finalization.

While states may prohibit insurance companies from discriminating against adoption—stipulating that adopted children be treated on the same basis as other dependents, there are many loopholes in insurance coverage and differential treatment occurs. In the past few years, under pressure from adoption advocates, state laws and insurance practices have been changing. To find out the situation in your state and whether your health care provider is in compliance, check with your state's insurance commissioner, your elected state representatives, and adoption advocacy groups.

WILLS

If you don't have a will, you'll want to write one to be sure that from the time your child arrives in your home he's provided for. Your will gives you a chance to name the executor of your estate as well as the guardian of your child and your child's property. In naming guardians, you will need to explore with them their feelings about adoption and about raising an adopted child. Just as seriously as you prepared for adoption, you will want to talk at length with the people who might end up raising your child.

You'll need to look closely at your will to be sure that it protects your child. Wills and trusts sometimes include terms like *issue, heirs of the body, born to, next of kin,* and *descendants,* which are not always legally understood to include adopted as well as biological children. To protect your child, you should insert a clause stating that all biological and adopted children are to be considered equally as heirs and beneficiaries. One family's wills state that "whenever the terms *child, children,* or *descendants* are used or are relevant under this will and in the disposition of my estate, adopted children shall be considered and treated in all respects the same as natural children." A clause such as this protects your adopted child, but not necessarily during the period before you've been to court to obtain the final order of adoption.

Some attorneys recommend that to protect your children fully, you should state their names (both the names under which they are currently known and any other names they have had in the past). If you do that, however, update your will whenever you add a child to your family.

You may want to ask relatives, such as grandparents, who may be making bequests in their wills to your *descendants* or *issue* to insert similar clauses to ensure that all your children inherit equally.

LIFE INSURANCE

Life insurance policies may also use terms such as *descendants* or *issue* or *heirs of the body,* so be sure that you are covering your adopted children. It is also recommended that you advise your insurance company in writing (keeping a copy) that you have adopted children and request confirmation that the policy applies to them. Also check into the provisions of your pension plan and any company death benefits.

Some adoptive parents have also taken out life insurance policies for their children. "When our son was an infant," Laura said, "we took out a ten-thousand-dollar life insurance policy. We had adopted our child from abroad and had used up our savings. We felt that if something were to happen to our child, we would not otherwise have the financial resources to undertake a second adoption. We felt funny taking out the policy, but we did it."

ADOPTION INSURANCE

Participating in a networking plan of an out-of-state adoption agency, Liz and Matt Bayer located a birth mother through newspaper advertising and paid for her medical, living, and legal expenses. By the time the baby was born, and they'd traveled to Texas to take their new daughter home, their out-of-pocket expenses had reached twenty thousand dollars. Then came the devastating news: the birth mother had decided against adoption. Their policy, obtained at the start of the placement process, provided for fifteen thousand dollars' worth of coverage for a cost of fifteen hundred dollars. It absorbed most of their financial loss.

Adrianne and Ron Gilligan had a similar experience when their independent adoption plans went awry. Their insurance, obtained through their attorney, provided coverage up to ten thousand dollars (after a 10 percent deductible) that included the birth mother's expenses. Even though they were present for the baby's birth, the birth mother later changed her mind. "We filed a claim several weeks later, submitting documentation for medical expenses, phone bills—even the hotel room and a pager service we used," says Adrianne. To their delight the insurance policy covered these expenses. "We were able to try again and adopt our son Matthew," she says, "because we had the adoption insurance."

Does adoption insurance make sense for you? "You're insuring yourself against a potentially catastrophic loss," observes Washington, D.C., adoption attorney Mark McDermott. "The larger the expenses you lay out, the more reasons to buy adoption insurance."[5] Determine the costs of your prospective adoption and consider the insurance if the dollars you are likely to spend on the birth mother's medical and physical needs are high and state law doesn't restrict the amount you can subsidize her. You can purchase **Adoption Cancellation Expense Insurance** through MBO Insurance Brokers in Menlo Park, California (800–833–7337). The policy, providing for coverage for a premium is available for agency and independent adoptions. The birth parents' expenses and yours, minus the agency's and legal fees and a deductible, are eligible for reimbursement if your attempt at adopting fails. Separate riders cover some of the coverage gaps.

FINANCES

Landmark federal tax legislation, passed in 1996, entitles adoptive families to a tax credit of up to five thousand dollars (six thousand dollars if the child has special needs) for qualifying expenses paid to adopt a child. Qualifying expenses include "reasonable and necessary adoption fees, court costs, attorney fees, traveling expenses while away from home, and other expenses directly related to, and whose principal purpose is for, the legal adoption of an eligible child." You can also exclude up to five thousand dollars (six thousand dollars for a special-needs child) from your gross income if you receive financial assistance for adoption from your employer. This combination—a tax credit and a tax exclusion for the expenses of adopting an eligible child—is a powerful financial package. Let's see how this works:

Example 1: Your qualifying adoption expenses for the credit for adopting a healthy baby are $1,000 for 1998 and $6,000 for 1999. You file for a tax credit of $1,000 for 1998 and $4,000 for 1999 ($5,000–$1,000).

Example 2: You pay $3,000 of qualifying adoption expenses in an effort to adopt a child but the placement falls through. You then incur an additional $4,000 of qualifying expenses when you successfully adopt a different baby. You are permitted to carry over the $3,000 and treat the total expenditure of $7,000 as one adoption effort. You apply for the maximum tax credit of $5,000 ($6,000 special needs).

Warning: there are restrictions, combinations, and permutations that you'll need to comprehend. If you pursue an intercountry adoption and adopt a foreign-born child, for example, you cannot file for the credit or exclusion until the adoption becomes final. You can, however, take the credit or exclusion before finalization—or even if the adoption never becomes final—if the child is a U.S. citizen or resident. The tax credit and exclusion are also linked to your family's modified adjusted gross income (AGI). If your modified AGI is $75,000 or less, you get the entire credit or exclusion; if it's more than $115,000, you are not eligible. If your modified AGI falls between these figures, your credit or exclusion is proportionately reduced. After December 31, 2001, the adoption tax credit and exclusion apply only to the adoption of a domestic child with special needs.

To understand the process fully, obtain Publication 968, *Tax Benefits for Adoption,* from the Internal Revenue Service at the Department of the Treasury. (You can request this publication by calling 800–TAX–FORM or going to their website—http://www.irs.ustreas.gov.) You can ask the IRS, an accountant, or another qualified person for help. Some states also offer income tax deductions, credits, or exclusions for adoption. Check with your state's department of revenue to learn what your state offers.

On your income taxes you can take a dependency exemption for your child, just as you would for a biological child, as long as you are providing more than half of your child's support. This exemption is not tied to finalization of the adoption. There may be other deductions or credits for which you qualify.

Federal tax law requires you to list your child's social security number on tax forms but the Social Security Administration will not let you apply for a number on your child's behalf until the adoption is legally completed. To circumvent this hurdle the Internal Revenue Service will permit you to write "U.S. adoption pending" in the exemption section of your tax form instead of your child's social security number. You must also attach documentation confirming your child's legal placement in your home.

Even with these tax breaks the costs of adoption for many families can quickly mount up. If you're wondering how you are going to finance your adoption, there are other sources you can tap:

- The **National Adoption Foundation** (see appendix A) offers grants and loans, in partnership with MBNA America, to adopters. Although the number of outright grants, averaging two thousand dollars, is small, the Foundation has disbursed unsecured adoption loans since 1994. First Union Bank of Rockville, Maryland offers families nationwide home equity loans as well as unsecured loans.
- You may be eligible for a home equity loan from a local bank. (Keep in mind that you are putting your house at risk.) You may be able to borrow against a 401(k) plan, insurance policy, retirement plan, or credit card. Family and friends may lend you money.
- You may be able to refinance your mortgage.
- Find out whether your agency will permit you to pay out the adoption expenses over time. Some will set up an

installment plan that permits you to spread the payments beyond finalization.

You will find an informative discussion of the finances of adoption in the **National Endowment for Financial Education's** *How To Make Adoption An Affordable Option*. This booklet can be found online at NEFE's website (www.nefe.org) or obtained through the Consumer Information Center (719–948–4000; request item #602-E).

GETTING MEDICAL ADVICE AND ARRANGING FOR MEDICAL CARE

You'll want to line up a pediatrician or family physician before your child arrives. If you are considering a child with a special need or a child who will be coming from abroad, you may consult a physician before you apply for a specific child or at the time you receive a child referral. Says Peggy Soule of *The CAP Book*: "Be sure to let your physician tell you the *facts* about specific diseases or handicaps. The doctor should tell you what to expect but should not put his own value judgment on whether or not you should adopt. That is your decision. Too often because the doctor would not adopt a child with the specific handicap you are considering, she will advise the family not to do it."

Ask other physicians, family members, coworkers, and particularly parents whose children may have the same needs as your prospective child, about their experiences with local physicians. When selecting a physician, take the time to have a sit-down discussion about your child. (Some doctors will talk with families on the telephone, but many will not.) A meeting at a doctor's office may mean that you will have to pay for a consultation, but it's well worth it. If you are a new parent, you're going to want to find out about the medical practice. Among your questions: What are the office hours?

SUBSIDIES FOR SPECIAL-NEEDS CHILDREN

All states have developed adoption subsidies (sometimes referred to as "adoption assistance") based on the special needs of children. The subsidy provides the financial base for a family so that the adoption of a special-needs child will not result in expenses beyond the reach of many adoptive parents and insures that the child receives required services. Coverage includes medical assistance, psychological counseling, day care, and tutoring, for example. The federal government mandates that states provide nontaxable subsidies for eligible children.

If you're considering a child for whom a subsidy may be possible, you'll want to find out:

- What children are eligible for subsidy?
- Are there monthly cash stipends for the child?
- Are there payments for specific medical, surgical, psychiatric, or other costs?
- How long is the subsidy designed to last? A subsidy may be paid for a specific period of time or it may continue until a child reaches maturity.
- Are there one-time, nonrecurring expenses, such as legal fees, that will be paid?
- How do you apply for subsidy?
- Can the subsidy go with the child if you move to another state? What must you do?
- Is the state requiring that adoptive parents submit financial information about themselves as a "means"

test? (In 1992 the U.S. Department of Health and Human Services' Children's Bureau released an official statement indicating that families can reapply for subsidy after finalization if a family had been previously denied assistance because of a means test. If you're asked to submit to a means test, you should question this.)

- Would subsidy be available after the fact if you can identify that there was a preexisting condition?
- Obtain as much information as you can about your child before the placement. Request a subsidy for your child—even if you think that you may not use it. Get a written subsidy agreement and try to spell out the financial aid, medical coverage, and social services your child will receive as well as what nonrecurring medical expenses will be reimbursed.

Subsidies vary state by state: some states have restricted programs; others, more inclusive programs. The **National Adoption Assistance Training, Resource and Information Network** (NAATRIN) at the **North American Council on Adoptable Children** (see appendix A) can provide you with detailed information about subsidy programs. You can also contact your state's department of social services to learn about your state's subsidy program. If you are considering adopting an out-of-state child, check with the social services department of the state where your potential child resides. A foreign-born special-needs child may occasionally be eligible for subsidy. Ask your agency or parent group for help.

How are phone calls handled? When you call in, will you speak with the doctor or the nurse? Are there special "call-in" hours? What happens when your child is sick? Who will treat your child at night or on weekends? If the doctor is part of a medical group or HMO, will you normally see your doctor? When do you meet the associates?

If you are a working parent, how does the doctor feel about someone other than you bringing your child for checkups or sick-child visits?

Try to visit during office hours so you can also meet other parents and children and observe the routines. How long are patients kept waiting? How are sick and well children handled? You can also discreetly ask the parents in the waiting room about their experiences.

But you'll also have some more adoption-specific questions:

- Does the doctor see other adopted patients in his practice?
- Has the doctor treated foreign-born adoptees? Your physician should be aware, for example, that a child adopted from abroad might not have reached the developmental milestones or the weight and height that American children of the same age have. Does your physician have any particular expertise that might be useful?
- How does the physician feel about adoption? What has been the doctor's experience with adoption? One family learned their pediatrician's opinion about adoption when he discovered a heart murmur in their newborn and recommended that the family not keep the baby.
- Is the doctor willing to read articles or medical materials that you bring in, especially those that concern the special medical concerns of adopted children?

- How many patients in the doctor's practice have been in foster care? What are the doctor's opinions of foster care?
- What is the physician's expertise with the special needs that your child presents? What is the physician's attitude? What does the doctor know about prenatal substance abuse and its effect on children?
- What is your physician's policy about Medicaid? If you will be receiving a subsidy for your child and if it involves Medicaid, be sure your physician will accept it.
- How does the physician feel about receiving incomplete medical records? There may be a lot that is unknown about children who have been in foster care in the U.S. and about children born abroad. There may also be inaccurate information. Dr. Dana Johnson of the International Adoption Clinic reports that "there is a habit in Eastern Europe of putting down a lot of diagnoses. . . . [W]e found that most referrals [85 percent were from Russia] had one or more neurological diagnoses, such as perinatal encephalopathy or spinal trauma. Most also stated that the child was developmentally delayed. . . . Parents and their physician must look beyond these diagnoses to ascertain whether a child has a significant condition."[6]
- Will the physician share what is in the medical records with you?
- How much support do you expect to receive from this physician?

Raise issues that concern you. You may want to discuss child care, childrearing, circumcision, even your plans for feeding. Linda had told her pediatrician about the uncertainty of her child's arrival from South Korea and had raised the possibility that her daughter might arrive on a Saturday. Would the doctor see her? Sure, he said. But when she called her physician on a weekend night to tell him that her daughter would be arriving the next day and that the agency had requested that the baby be seen because of a rash, she found out differently.

She recalls: "The pediatrician refused, saying that he did not have office hours and that he didn't trust an agency's opinion about whether a child should be seen. This agency had brought thousands of Korean children to the U.S. and had called us long distance to urge us to make medical arrangements. Here was a pediatrician doubting our word. We switched pediatricians."

If you are adopting a child from abroad, you will want to be sure that your child's doctor does a few basic tests on your child when he arrives. Dr. Margaret Hostetter and Dr. Dana Johnson reported in 1997 that "in a survey we're currently conducting, we've found that less than 50 percent of children adopted in this country from Eastern Europe and less than 20 percent of children from China have been adequately screened."[7] (There are basic tests recommended by the American Academy of Pediatrics that your child should have.) If you are working with a U.S. agency that has an intercountry adoption program, your agency will probably tell you if there are additional tests they recommend. You will want to ask that your child's physician do a:[8]

- Hepatitis B profile, to include HBsAG, anti-SBs and anti-HBc
- Mantoux (intradermal PPD) skin test with Candida control for tuberculosis. Notes Dr. Jerri Ann Jenista: "This is the 'blister under the skin test,' not the four-prong TINE quick test." Be aware that in some countries children are vaccinated at birth against tuberculosis—the BCG vaccine—and may test positively. It also has been found not to provide complete protection. Note Drs. Hostetter and

Johnson: "The AAP has now advised physicians that children who have received BCG vaccination can be screened with a Mantoux test. Interpretation of the test is the same as in non-immunized ."[9]

- Complete blood count with erythrocyte indices
- Stool examination to check for ova and parasites
- Stool culture for bacterial causes for diarrhea
- Blood test for syphilis
- Urinalysis and urine culture
- HIV-1 and HIV-2 testing by ELISA in children older than eighteen months and by ELISA and culture in children younger than eighteen months.
- Vision and hearing screening
- Developmental assessment. Keep in mind that children who have been institutionalized in an orphanage may be developmentally delayed.

Offer your physician some of the specialized adoption literature that's available. You might want to subscribe to Dr. Jenista's *Adoption Medical News* (see appendix C). Many U.S. agencies have prepared factsheets about the health and care of the children they are placing. The staff at the International Adoption Clinic at the University of Minnesota will provide you with reprints of their articles and will consult by mail or telephone. Their information is also available through their website. You can also contact the International Adoption Clinic at the New England Medical Center in Boston, and the Evaluation Center for Adoption at Schneider Children's Hospital in New Hyde Park, New York.[10] And you might suggest that your child's physician consult the American Academy of Pediatrics' recommendations for internationally adopted children. You'll also find a discussion of health-care issues in Lois Ruskai Melina's *Raising Adopted Children*.

If you are adopting a child who is not an infant, you will probably want to take your child to a dentist within a few weeks of his arrival. Indeed, since older foreign-born children often have extensive tooth decay, you may want to talk with a dentist in advance.

GETTING BACKGROUND INFORMATION ABOUT YOUR CHILD

Whether you are adopting through an agency either here or abroad, a birth parent, or an intermediary, try to get *as much information* about your child as you can. Don't shy away from asking questions fearing that you might rock the boat and upset the adoption. Ask about the birth parents' names and ages, ethnic group, religion, education, occupation, personality, temperament, medical and psychiatric history, and intellectual capacity. Find out the circumstances of the birth parents prior to your child's birth (Were they married? Is the birth father known? Was the birth mother raped?) and the reasons for the relinquishment. What can you learn about the birth grandparents? What were their feelings and their involvement in the adoption decision?

Try to get as much medical information about the birth parents—and their family—as possible. While it may be awkward, ask about drinking and drug habits (Did she ever drink during her pregnancy? Has she, or a family member, ever been in Alcoholics Anonymous?). Be aware that if you're told that "when the birth mother found out she was pregnant, she stopped drinking or taking drugs," it's also a signal that for a period of time, perhaps as many as several months, the birth mother was involved in substance abuse.

Push your worker or intermediary for any personal descriptions (e.g., "She enjoys singing"). There are also the "little" details in a birth parent's life that you might want to inquire about. When did the mother get her first menstrual period?

Does she bite her nails? When did she cut her first tooth? When did she first talk? Has she had a weight problem?

If you had a child by birth, you might ask your parents some of these questions about yourself as you tried to think about what family traits your child has inherited. So ask your child's birth parents for him. If you're wondering how your child might look when he grows up, then requesting photographs—or meeting—can offer clues. At the very least, get a good physical description, including eyes, hair color, height, weight, body build, voice, gait, posture, and special characteristics.

If you adopt your child as a newborn, then you should have detailed information from his very first hours. But if your child is older, whether it be two weeks old or ten years old, you'll want to know the experiences of this child from birth on, and there is a line of questioning to pursue. Was the child born in a hospital? How long was the child in the hospital? Who did the child live with after leaving the hospital? How long did the child live with them? What was the child like as a small baby? Are there pictures that can be shared? Were there other places the child lived? When? Why? With whom? Who have been the important people in this child's life? Why? If the child was separated from these people, why? Are there people who have information about this child that will be crucial to you and your family? Says Adoption Consultant Kay Donley-Zeigler: "It's important for children to understand how many places they lived until they came to live with their mom and dad."

Get the information in writing. Don't trust your memory. Take detailed notes during any meetings or telephone conversations, and be sure to save your notes. (If you're a poor notetaker, ask permission to use a tape recorder to preserve the conversation.) Make sure that your adoption worker also shares with you any notes she makes of her conversations with you. If you are adopting a child from abroad, you may find the names of birth parents or other relatives on your child's documents. Be sure to keep copies of all documents for your child and that you get full translations of them. Keep any attorneys' letters, health reports, even medical bills that you may have been sent. And politely push your agency or intermediary for any further information they can provide; let the agency or intermediary know that you are asking for this information for your child's well-being, not because of your anxiety. It's a lot easier to get the information during the adoption process than five, ten, or fifteen years later when your child is pushing for answers to many questions.

If you are adopting a U.S. special-needs or older child, your agency should tell you the reason the child came into foster care and provide copies of your child's health history records, school records, mental health records (psychological and social evaluations), and any residential setting records. You should be informed of the number of placements the child has had, of any sexual abuse the child has been a victim of, and of any unusual traumas, such as death or divorce. Get as much detail as possible about the child's experiences in foster care.

What have been the foster parents' impressions of this child? Ask the worker: Is there information in this child's history that would indicate high risk for future developments that could be problematic? While you may worry that your worker will interpret your question as showing reluctance to take the child, you need to know the facts.

You'll also want to find out what possessions belong to your child. Are there photographs, mementos, toys, or other items that have traveled with him during his childhood?

What about clothing? Ascertain what belongs to him—and make sure that it makes the move with him when he enters your family.

Insist on full disclosure—that all available information about your child be shared with you. Then, urges Ernesto Loperena of the New York Council on Adoptable Children, "double check any information the agency provides. Have your own physician do a physical workup. Have your own child psychologist do an analysis." These independent evaluations may turn up other facts that could lay the groundwork for Medicaid or subsidy. Be sure that you ask about the number of moves that your child has made and that you find out what kind of therapy the child has received. "Insist that the agency provide an assessment of the child's current attachment to the present caretaker and whether she was attached in the past to other caretakers," urges Holly van Gulden, coauthor of *Real Parents, Real Children*. (For additional information on attachment issues, see chapter 10.)

Be prepared that a child's condition may have been misdiagnosed—hence the labels attached to a child may not adequately reflect his situation. Children who are identified as "retarded" or "slow learners" may just be reflecting the lack of stimulation that existed in their previous environment. Paula describes what she learned when she took her son, identified as a slow learner and a behavior problem, for a full medical checkup:

He had a 60 percent hearing loss because of a fibrous tumor in one ear that had gone undetected in his fourteen foster homes. He was an underachiever because he couldn't hear. He's actually quite bright and taught himself to lip-read, which is why the tumor went undetected for so long.

You may also find that a worker tries to gloss over a problem or not disclose full information if she feels that it could jeopardize a child's placement. Agencies are often reluctant to reveal whether a child has been abused because of the issue of confidentiality. Jewett Jarratt, in *Adopting the Older Child*, notes:

> *One of our daughters came to us from a foster home that was being suddenly closed because it had been determined that the children there had been exposed to sexual abuse. Hesitant to share this information, our daughter's worker deliberately omitted mentioning the abuse to our agency or to us. This information would have made no difference in our willingness to adopt our child, but it would have saved us valuable time and lessened our concern at her seemingly unreasonable terror of men and of bedtime.*[11]

For an older child Jewett suggests that prospective adoptive parents ask:

- Why is this child not living with his biological parents?
- What has the child been told about his first family? What was his last contact with them?
- How old was the child when he came into care? Where has he lived? If he has lived in more than one other family, what were the reasons he moved?
- How is the child's physical and emotional health? What is his history—shots, allergies, dental care?
- How well does the child's worker know him? How long has she been assigned to him?
- How does this child feel about himself? How does he respond to other people?
- How does this child handle failure, anger, anxiety, fears, happiness, success, pain, disappointment, sadness, affection, discipline, daily routines?

- What does this child understand about adoption? About foster care?
- How has this child said "good-bye" to people left behind? How has this child left other families?
- How has this child said "hello" to new people? How has this child entered other families?
- Why was this child picked for me?

As you gather information about your child and his birth family, you should also ask if the agency or state has a centralized mechanism for birth parents to update medical and family information in the years ahead. Explore how you can insure that, if the birth parents want to provide further updates, you will be apprised of the family's desire to communicate with you as well as the information they shared.

PREPARING FOR AN INFANT

When Susan McGovern learned that she was pregnant, she began eight months of planning and reading about infants before her baby arrived. Closer to her due date, she and her husband took a class in prepared childbirth. Although the classes focused on the childbirth experience, the last session included a film about an infant's first three months. The instructor gave her a checklist of things to pack for the hospital and things to have at home for the new baby. Susan took a class at the hospital to prepare herself for breast-feeding. After her daughter was born, she was kept busy in the hospital with a series of classes: the feeding of infants; general child care (e.g., how to diaper a baby, how to bathe a baby); infant development. When she took her daughter home, she felt shaky but informed about her new role.

Prospective adoptive parents often find themselves less well-informed and feeling adrift.

Francine Elman had read some books about child care but lacked much experience. She enrolled in an infant-care course at her local American Red Cross, but withdrew the first day when she found that everyone else was eight months pregnant. "Too awkward," she recalls. So, she says, "When I traveled to Chile to pick up my baby, I knew very little about babies. I'll never forget my first diapering of her—alone on an airplane, not too sure which end went where. Nor did I know how much formula she should take, how frequently to feed her, and how to burp her."

Amanda Khan has another story that she likes to tell about her adoption experience: "I didn't know what a bunting or a layette was. When we were expecting Jonah, we bought newborn-size clothing. Since he was seven weeks old when we brought him home, he outgrew it all in a week."

Recognizing that prospective adoptive parents need to be better informed, there are now special "expectant adoptive-parent classes." While some programs focus more on providing hard-core information and hands-on experience, others meld together such topics as basic infant care, infant development, CPR, choosing baby toys and baby clothes, with adjustment to parenting and adoptive parenting. Observes adoptive parent Mickey Lutz, whose classes have been attended by adoptive families in the Northern Virginia area: "This is the first place that people think of themselves as expectant adoptive parents. Here, joining others in a similar situation, they feel safe. They don't worry about jinxing the process. The classes focus them on something positive and cement the adoption in their minds."

To find a class in your community, start by checking with adoptive-parent or infertility support groups and adoption agencies. In some communities you'll find these specialized classes offered through continuing education programs at community colleges, Y's, and other community centers, and local hospitals.

If you have friends with infants, spend some time with them. If you feel competent alone, volunteer to baby-sit for a few hours or an evening so that you can get some "hands-on experience." Take a look at some of the books about infant care and select a few to own. You can also write to the magazine *American Baby* (PO Box 53093, Boulder, CO 90322; give your "expected due date") to request a complimentary subscription. Expectant and new adoptive parents are eligible for this free offer.

You might also want to explore the possibility of breast-feeding your baby. Even if your new baby is two months old, experts say that it's possible to nurse. While breast-feeding will probably not satisfy your infant's total nutritional needs, it offers the chance to enrich the parent-child relationship through this special physical relationship. Although women can stimulate the breast to produce some milk, most have to supplement their milk through the use of nursing supplementers such as the Lact-Aid® Nursing Trainer System or Supplemental Nursing System. These bottle-like devices hang from around the mother's neck, hold the formula, and feed the infant through very fine flexible tubes. When a baby sucks at the breast, he takes the tube in addition to his mother's nipple into his mouth and gets nourishment through the tube. If you are interested in breast-feeding, you'll want to learn as much as you can about it before your baby arrives and obtain the necessary equipment from the manufacturers. For further information, contact the lactation consultant at your local hospital and **La Leche League International** (1400 North Meacham Road, Schaumburg, IL 60173; 847–519–7730). La Leche has pamphlets about breast-feeding an adopted infant and can put you in touch with a local leader who will work with you toward your goal.

If your baby is known to have been exposed to cocaine, alcohol, or other drugs prenatally, you'll want to do some reading about the possible effects of these substances on infants and the special needs these children may have. These infants, who are often born prematurely with low birth weights, may be irritable, startle easily, sleep poorly, have a high-pitched cry, and have difficulty feeding and sucking. For the baby who is easily overstimulated by loud noises, bright lights, and excessive manipulation, as perinatally crack-exposed infants sometimes are, swaddling in a blanket and offering a pacifier can be calming. Rocking or jiggling and singing at once can be too much, as can walkers and jumpers. Gentle rocking in an up-and-down motion is advised. Roughhouse play must also be toned down with slow, gentle swinging through the air replacing rapid movements through space. You also need to be aware of early distress signals—yawns, sneezes, hiccoughs, motor agitation, color changes, frowns, and eye aversions. If you notice these, your baby needs time out and even help in calming down.[12] For further information and referral to local specialists, contact the **National Association for Families and Addiction Research and Education** in Chicago, Illinois (see appendix A).

PREPARING FOR A CHILD FROM ABROAD

As you prepare for your foreign-born child, "know your child by his culture," says intercountry adoption specialist Cheryl Markson. Find out about the child-care practices in his culture, and try to use them to ease him into your home. Do some reading about the country; you might also want to listen to music of the country to get an idea of how the language sounds. If you know people from his birth country, ask them what they found strange when they first came to the United States. Talk about differences in cultural patterns between the two countries. Ask about family relationships and how they differ. Ask other adoptive parents and older foreign-born adoptees about their experiences. Reports Cheri Register in *Are Those Kids Yours?*: "Soon Hee Truman remembers her surprise when her new family walked into the house with their shoes on." For Silvia Kowalski, who was twelve years old when she was adopted from Colombia, the shock came from seeing her mother undressed. "I thought she was totally disrespectful to *me*. The Hispanic culture is very private, and that was the ultimate to me."[13]

If your child has been used to physical closeness with adults or other children, even sleeping with them at night, then he is likely to be petrified of sleeping alone in a bed or crib. Korean infants or toddlers are usually carried on their mothers' backs; if your child has been with a foster mother, carrying your child in a backpack may provide a soothing and familiar manner of locomotion. If your child has been in an institution, then you need to learn about orphanage life. Babies who have been in orphanages may have lain on their backs in their cribs for endless hours: don't be surprised if the back of your infant's head is flattened. They may seem listless, willingly allow strangers to handle them, and have developed their own patterns of self-stimulation, such as rocking, if they had limited handling by caretakers. Infants may have shared a crib with others. Orphanage children may not have received much individual attention and may never have been alone. All their days and nights may have been spent in the company of other children.

The lives of older children in orphanages may have been so tightly regulated that they are not adept at making decisions, knowing how to use free time, or playing independently with toys. "Children are spoon-fed and dressed beyond the age in which children born into families learn these skills," note the editors of the *Report on Intercountry Adoption*. "Just imagine trying to re-button 20 little smocks or clean up after the attempts of 20 children to feed themselves." Many children also will not have had anything they could call their "own" and therefore have no concept of personal possessions—either theirs or yours. The world of the orphanage child may have been orderly, circumscribed, and governed by rules and routines.

Your child may be fearful. If your infant has been in a foster home where no man was present, he may be scared of men. Even if he's been around men, the differences in appearance from what he's used to, including a full beard, may frighten him. The physical size of adults, which may be radically different from those in his previous environment, may be upsetting. He may be scared of pets, particularly dogs, since in some cultures they are used as guards or run wild in the streets. And, of course, he will have to cope with dietary changes. You can help him by having familiar foods on hand. It's worth keeping in mind that some children from Asia and Latin America will have a lactose intolerance or sensitivity, and that infants from these areas may need soy-based formulas. This is something you should discuss with your child's doctor.

If you are adopting an older child (toddler and up), learn some basic words and phrases in your child's language so you can communicate with her in both her language and yours. Even if you're adopting a baby, if you are traveling to the country to pick up your child, some basic language skills will be helpful for communicating with your child's caretakers. While you're waiting, you might enroll in a foreign language course offered at a local college or community center or by a company like Berlitz. You could also check local public libraries, bookstores, or adoptive-parent support groups for foreign-language audio- or videotapes that you might obtain and listen to at home.

You might also want to line up an interpreter who can help explain things in the early weeks. One parent whose Korean-born daughters have served as translators for other adoptees says that they were able to "answer children's questions, relay parents' questions and messages, and help clear up misconceptions. One child, for instance, wanted the two boys 'visiting' her new home to go to their own house and was surprised to learn that they were her brothers." Be sure, however, that you let your translator know exactly what you want communicated. Says Markson: "You don't want your translator to tell your child that 'you must behave or they'll send you back.' And you do want your translator to tell your child that 'it's OK to cry.' You must *educate* your interpreter."

Ask your agency and people in your parent group for help. Some offer workshops that focus on preparing. The Internet can connect you with families around the world. You'll find extensive information, for example, at the website of the support group **Families with Children from China** (see appendix A), in computer chat groups and bulletin boards, and the Adoption Forum of America Online. You might also inquire whether it's possible to correspond with the foster parents caring for your child or the caretakers at the orphanage, whether they could jot down for you some information about your child's habits and care, and whether you'll be able to talk with them when you receive your child. Not only can caretakers give you detailed information about your child's daily routines, but their correspondence—and perhaps photographs—will also help your child at a later point fit together the various pieces of his life. And, if your child's old enough to flip through it ahead of your meeting, you'll want to send a book of photographs depicting yourself, your family, and community.

Cheri Register's *Are Those Kids Yours?* explores how the emotional bonds between parent and child are "sealed, maintained, and tested in families formed across racial and cultural boundaries." The book utilizes the author's experience as the adoptive parent of two Korean children and that of other adoptive parents and older foreign-born adoptees to discuss how families come together and deal with the questions of race and identity. *The Complete Guide to Foreign Adoption,* by Barbara Bascom and Carole McKelvey, focuses extensively on the experiences of Romanian children and presents rather graphic descriptions of orphanage life. Margi Miller and Nancy Ward's *With Eyes Wide Open: A Workbook for Parents Adopting International Children Over Age One,* created by the Children's Home Society, offers a variety of interesting written exercises that will give you insight into the intercountry adoption experience. Adoptive parents have also reported that personal accounts helped them prepare. Appendix C lists these and other books.

PREPARING FOR AN OLDER CHILD

As you prepare for the arrival of your child, particularly an older child, you've got to try to put yourself in his place. It is important that you keep in mind the environment that he came from and the environment he will be entering. Think about the impact that moving has had on you and on other families that you know. How might a child react to change? What can you do to ease the transition?

"Parents have to be prepared to deal with the child who should not be happy to come to their house," observed one therapist. "They're glad that these people have said that they'll be their parents, but they're not glad to be adopted."[14]

For kids who have not known permanence, adoption is just another move. In fact, since adoption is described as a "forever family," a youngster may feel that he is permanently trapped. Says the therapist: "You need to be in touch with what your kid's expectations are."

How are children helped to make the move? As part of the adoption preparation process, your child may have created a "life book," which tells the story of his life through pictures, drawings, and other materials. His social worker will have used this to help him talk about his life. Children's lifebooks, writes Claudia Jewett Jarratt, may "include pictures and comments about foods that they love and hate; people that they love and hate; things that make them feel good and bad; some of the things that they are afraid of." The book will "express feelings, so that the child is less concerned about what his new parents will think of the things he considers unacceptable about himself, less fearful that his new parents wouldn't want him if they knew what he was like inside."[15]

What are some of the steps you will want to take as you get ready for your child?

Read Some Adoptive Parenting and Child-Development Books

Claudia L. Jewett's *Adopting the Older Child* has served as a primer for adoptive parents for many years. It's a balanced, insightful book, based on case studies, that will help direct your thinking. So can her *Helping Children Cope with Separation and Loss,* which deals with the child's response to grief when he loses a family member, whether through death, divorce, or separation from his birth family. Holly van Gulden and Lisa Bartels-Rabb's *Real Parents, Real Children* offers practical suggestions on moving children from one home to another, as does Gregory Keck and Regina Kupecky's *Adopting the Hurt Child*. The writings of Vera Fahlberg (*Helping Children When They Must Move, Attachment and Separation, Residential Treatment—A Tapestry of Many Therapies*) also cover older and special-needs adoption. Mary Hopkins-Best's *Toddler Adoption: The Weaver's Craft* focuses on the issues that confront parents who adopt children aged between one and three. Gay Courter's *I Speak for This Child: True Stories of a Child Advocate* paints a vibrant picture of the tumultuous lives of children in the American foster care system, while Ann Kimble Loux's *The Limits of Hope: An Adoptive Mother's Story* chronicles her family's struggle.

If you're interested in the child's perspective on adoption, look at Jill Krementz's *How It Feels to be Adopted*. The children Krementz interviewed shared their fears and fantasies and discuss their relationships with their adoptive parents, their siblings, and their birth parents. While some of the children were placed as infants, several were older. Maxine Rosenberg's *Growing Up Adopted* offers the insights of eight children and six adults, while John Y. Powell's *Whose Child Am I? Adults' Recollections of Being Adopted* features the memories of adults who were adopted as older children. His interviewees reflect on the strengths and perils of older-child placement.

Be sure you also do some reading about child development. You want to understand a child's behavior at the age of your future child—how he thinks, acts, feels—and the common developmental landmarks. Some of your child's behavior may be typical of his or her age group rather than a response to the move to your home. If your child has learning disabilities, talking with other parents or reading about learning and behavior patterns is helpful.

You will also want to look at material that discusses sexual abuse in children. Bernard and Joan McNamara's series of pamphlets and books on adoption and the sexually abused child can provide you with an overview, as they discuss both the impact of sexual abuse on adopted children and offer helpful tips and information. For a quick orientation, try the factsheet prepared by the **National Adoption Information Clearinghouse**.

Line Up Postplacement Support

Building a family is hard work. You and your child may need help initially, and in the long run. Your parent group, where you can talk with families who have adopted older children, will be an invaluable resource. You may also want to turn to a therapist for help. Insists adoption expert Barbara Tremitiere: "You can't drop these kids in cold."

Larry Jones, a parent whose four-year-old son almost started a fire in their house, describes how he and his wife floundered. "We planted our own seeds of failure," he recalls, "because we didn't understand what was going on. We'd been told that our son had a deprived background. What we found was that the things that we accept as part of our everyday life (how to eat at a table, how to interact with others, how to take a bath), he hadn't been taught." He and his wife were embarrassed to talk to their social worker about their problems. "I was scared that people would think I was a rotten father." The relationship deteriorated: "It was like drowning in molasses. You couldn't move fast enough to get out. There was no one to throw a rope."

Two and a half years after their son was placed with them, Larry and his wife relinquished their adopted son. Looking back Larry says: "Now Jamie would be no problem. In foster care we've had thirteen different children. We've had children who've been physically and sexually abused, children who've been physically and emotionally handicapped. We've learned a great deal about how children work and how children think. We adopted one of our foster children, a girl with spina bifida. Today I spend a good deal of time talking and sharing with others."

The **National Resource Center for Special Needs Adoption** (see appendix A) in Southfield, Michigan is designed to improve the availability and quality of adoption and postadoption services for children with special needs and their families. The center's primary focus lies in the training of agency workers and providing support services to agencies, parent groups, and other organizations, rather than helping individual families directly. It does, however, distribute resource material and staff members can refer you to agencies, therapists, and other mental health professionals in your community with an expertise in adoption. You'll also want to check with the National Adoption Center in Pennsylvania and the National Adoption Information Clearinghouse.

Observe Other Children

If you have never parented an older child, observe children about the age of your expected child to familiarize yourself with their interests and behavior. Perhaps you could volunteer at your local school, community center, or Scout troop.

If you are adopting a child who is developmentally delayed or physically challenged, you'll want to get to know children of the same age who present similar challenges. By locating the local foundation or organization that works with these children, you can attend functions where you can observe the children and talk with their parents about their experiences.

If Possible, Visit with Your Child

When an agency places an older U.S. child, the prospective parents and the child may meet, perhaps a few times or over an extended period of time, before the child moves. First visits might revolve around outings to a park, zoo, or other neutral surrounding. It's helpful to visit your child at his foster home where he may feel more at ease and where you can observe his environment and have the chance to talk with his foster parents. Children may also spend time in your home, including weekend sleepovers.

There is no prescribed way or specific length of time that visiting will take place before the child is placed in your home. The circumstances vary with the individual child. Don't feel pressured to assent to a child's move to your home until you feel you're ready. (You'll have to ask yourself: how do I know that *I'm* ready?) Take the time you and your child need.

Think about How Your Household Operates

If this will be your first child or your first older child, consider your household and the rules that you will want observed. When is bedtime? What about homework? What about television? What household chores will he be asked to perform? Keep in mind that your child's understanding of tasks may be different from yours. You'll need to give clear messages about your expectations. When you tell a child to "clean your room," you may mean that you expect him to pick up the trash from the floor and make his bed. In your child's previous home that may have meant to wash down the walls.

Visit the School Where Your Child Will Be Going and Talk with the Staff

Since school will play an important role in your child's life, you should begin working with the school before his arrival. What is your child's educational background? Will the child attend your neighborhood school, or do you need to look further? Does the school you are considering offer special services that you can tap? Do you anticipate that your child will need an after-school tutor to provide additional support?

Try to visit the school to see what it is like. Can you meet with the principal and the guidance counselor to learn about the school and to acquaint them with your child's situation? Is there a special education coordinator, a learning disabilities specialist, or an English as a Second Language (ESL) teacher whom you should meet? Keep in mind that under U.S. Public Law 94-142, all children with handicapping conditions, including mental, physical, sensory, emotional, or speech and language difficulties are entitled to a free appropriate public education. The school system must provide it or alternatively pay an external agency for services.

What can you learn about the teachers on the grade? Can you observe them in their classrooms? Have you talked with some parents with children in the school to learn about their experiences? From the staff and parents, find out how you can have some input into your child's classroom placement.

When you share background information about your child with the staff, make it clear to them this is "for their eyes only" and must be treated as a "professional confidence." If your child has been sexually abused, you'll want to share this, although you don't need to go into the details. Imagine what could happen to your family if you didn't disclose this information, and your child were to say "my daddy sleeps with me." She's referring to the dad she left behind, but school personnel, knowing nothing about her past, will assume she's describing the present.

Prepare a Book of Photographs That Features Your Family, Your Home, and Your Neighborhood

All children appreciate photographs to look at, but this is particularly important if you will be unable to visit. Sending photos and letters before your child enters your home gives him an introduction to you and helps to familiarize him with his new surroundings. He can thumb through them as much as he wants, just as you are probably looking at his photograph and spinning dreams based on it. Your book might say: "This is the mom in the family. She likes to do X, Y, and Z. She likes a child who does X, Y, and Z. Here is the dinner table, and here is where you will sit." Says Claudia Jewett

Jarratt: "Kids look at these books and try to find a place for themselves in the family." For foreign-born children, you'll also want to include photographs of things that might be "strange" to them: the car seat, the four-poster bed, stairs, the bathtub, snow on the ground. Reports one adoptive mother: "Seat belts horrified my older kids."

If several weeks or months will elapse before your child arrives, you will want to continue the contact, just as your agency is probably sending you updates. If you are adopting a toddler or young child, ask your agency if you can send a toy or other item that he can bring with him as a transitional object.

Fashion a Cover Story for Your Child and Yourself

From your child's first day in your home, he and you will be asked by playmates, neighbors, friends, teachers, and others in your community about himself and his past history. Rather than have him and you flounder, or even betray personal information that should not be shared, you'll want to prepare a "cover story," a bland, all-purpose summary that is offered to the world.

Imagine the potential questions—"Where did you come from?," "Why couldn't you live with your parents?" "Tell me what you *know* about him"—and review the appropriate information that can be shared. It's helpful to make a list of the likely questions, who might ask them, and the possible situations where they will come up (e.g., introducing your child to a neighbor, the first day of school, meeting new relatives). Then you prepare some simple responses: "My name is John Doe. I used to live in Miami, but I'm living here now because my family had problems. I'm being adopted because I couldn't live with my other family anymore." Finally role-play the questions and answers. You'll also want to teach your child how to deflect people's questions: "So, where are you from?" "I'm sorry, but you'll have to ask my mom that question." Says adoption specialist Kay Donley-Ziegler: "Every child entering a new living situation needs this preparation."

Adopting older children is complex, and this section sketched out a few of the many issues. Adoption experts believe that successful adoptions are more likely to occur when parents and children are realistically prepared. *Do your homework.*

NAMING YOUR CHILD

Bestowing a name on a child is one of the fundamental ways parents claim children as theirs. For adoptive parents, however, the matter of naming a child can be problematic. If they've had a relationship with the birth mother, as is the case with many infant adoptions today, should she have a say in naming the child? If so, what? "Jennifer, Jane, and I each shared several ideas before we collectively settled on Aaron Alex," reports Carl Tonn in *Adoption without Fear*. "The naming process symbolized our determination to work together in Aaron's behalf." The adoptive parents of David Christopher Thomas gave him his first name, but it was his birth mother Chris who chose Christopher, saying that she wanted to leave him a part of herself.[16]

If you're involved in an open adoption, you'll want to work out an arrangement with the birth parents that is comfortable for all of you. Nothing could be worse for your child than the situation that arose in the legendary Baby M surrogacy case where Mary Beth Whitehead insisted on calling her daughter Sara, while Bill and Betsy Stern used the name Melissa.

What do you do if your child already has a name by which he's identified and that he recognizes? Mused one parent:

> *When my son arrived from India at age three-and-a-half, he was wearing what was probably his first pair of shoes—used, too small, and with no socks they were rubbing his toes raw. But he would not give them up. Only through much hand waving could I convince him that the removal of his shoes was temporary, and only then did he part with them in order to take a bath. They had to be returned to his feet immediately following—over the sleepers with the built-in feet—and then into bed with him. How little and simple were his possessions! The other item he was attached to was the bag (you know, the one on the airplane for emergency use) he was carrying with two pennies in it. His shoes, the bag, and pennies, and, yes, his name, were his only possessions—his security. And I wanted to change his name. The shoes he gave up for brand new ones. The bag was eventually set down and lost in the shuffle. But the name? Something he had for three-and-a-half years? How would I? How could I take that?*[17]

By the time children are school-aged most parents realize that a name-change would be hard—that names are very much tied up with a child's sense of self. Keep in mind that children, even before their first birthday, know their first names and respond to them. What type of confusion will occur if you change the name? Observes Lois Melina: "A preschooler may have a particularly difficult time adjusting to a new first name. A young child's identity is so closely tied to her first name that changing it during the preschool years can cause a child to think she is not really the same person, or that one name goes with being a good person and one name with being a bad person. A name change can make it more difficult for the child to integrate her past life into her present."[18] Cautions Vera Fahlberg, who has written extensively about children and attachment: "Adopted children have enough issues to deal with without having to understand what it means to have their names changed."[19]

You, as a parent, may feel strongly the need to give your child a name that you—rather than a birth parent, a social worker, or someone else—chose. After all, you've waited for the day when you could confer a name upon *your* child. You may feel that it helps build attachments. Your family may have a naming tradition. You will have to weigh your needs with your child's.

You may want to consider renaming a child, however, if there is already a child in the family with that name. Parents of foreign-born children sometimes change their child's name when it is difficult to say or spell, retaining the child's original first or last name as a middle name. Rachel and David Abrams changed the name of their Colombian infant from Jesus to Joshua, because, says Rachel, "We are Jewish and he would have had difficulty being accepted in a Jewish community today with that name." If your child has an unusual name—one that might lead to teasing or ridicule from his peers—he might welcome a nickname or an additional middle name that he might choose to use at a later point.

If you do decide to change your child's name, then consider picking a name that's similar to the original. You might keep your child's original first name—or last name—as your child's middle name, or make the new name the middle name that becomes your child's nickname. You'll also want to ease your child into the name change gradually, using the new name as well as his original given name, in conversation.

You will probably want to call your child by your family last name from the day that he is placed in your house. (While it's not unusual for mothers and fathers to have different last names today, their children usually carry their joint last names or one of the parents' surnames as their surnames.) You may have to battle with your child's school, however, to recognize this name change before the adoption is finalized. Adoptive parent Gloria Peterson brings the point home most graphically: "One of our children was not riding the school bus for weeks. I was at work when our son arrived home on foot and was unaware of the situation. When it was discovered, the answer was that his bus pass was in his old name and he simply refused to show it to anyone and so he walked."[20]

Even here, however, there are two sides. One therapist has pointed out that youngsters who have bounced around from one situation to another have one thing which traveled with them—their name. Their reaction to adoption may be "and now you even have to give up your last name."[21]

PREPARING FAMILY AND FRIENDS

If you have older children, you began preparing them at the time of the home study. You've talked about adoption and the type of child that you're hoping to adopt. If you are adopting an infant, then you'll need to help your children understand what infants are like. A young child will have to learn to share his parents and toys.

If you are adopting an older child, make your children aware that the new sibling may seem less than overjoyed at joining their family. Indicate that there are likely to be rocky times ahead and that the new child's behavior may be different from what they expect. They should realize that the child may hoard, hit, or act as if he doesn't like them. Says Cheryl Markson: "Prepare the siblings for the worst, just as if you were bringing home a new baby and wanted to educate your child in advance." Ann Loux, in *The Limits of Hope* provides some telling examples of the disruptions and turmoil that her biological children experienced as they worked at integrating four-year-old Margey and three-year-old Dawn into the family.

There are also some children's novels that focus on the foster care experience and the feelings of children moving to a new home. These books are listed in appendix C. Your children might want to read one of them before their new sibling arrives. Keep in mind that your children will be faced with a difficult transition. They may be resentful and jealous and feel that the new sibling is receiving preferential treatment.

If you are traveling abroad to pick up your child, you may want to take your other children along with you. The trip will give them a chance to see their sibling's birth country and to forge their own special bonds. "When the orphanage directress went to get the baby, she took our three-year-old son with her," recalls Lisa. "To this day Michael still remembers that he was the first one to see his brother." Lisa also feels that the trip "helped give Michael a perspective" and "now he writes letters to the orphanage when I do." Lisa's brother and sister-in-law have also adopted through the orphanage. Reports Lisa: "Our whole family went down with them for a week. The orphanage directress fussed over our kids, and the two boys spent time at the orphanage. That really reinforced their feelings about Colombia and adoption."

Adoptive grandparents also need preparation and a chance to vent their feelings. Even the most eager grandparents-to-be, like prospective adoptive parents, have their own grieving to do over the lost biological grandchild. "I was disappointed to a degree that my son and his wife didn't have their natural child," admits Jerry, whose son Tom and daughter-in-law Kathy adopted a newborn independently. "But the adoption was to be a fact, and I was very much in favor of it." Mary, whose son adopted two school-age children from Chile, admits that, she did feel a tinge of regret that the family's bloodline would not be carried on: "But it wasn't a big point.

If you can't have the next generation one way, you're very happy that you can have it another."[22]

Prospective grandparents also have to deal with their own lack of knowledge about adoption and their particular prejudices. Learning about Kathy and Tom's plans to advertise for a baby, her father Ed's reaction was: "What is this? You put an ad in the newspaper? What about the kooks?" Ed also admits to having "reservations about the child's medical history. I worried about AIDS, that maybe the mother didn't know who the father was, and everything else that can affect the baby's health."

There are other feelings that grandparents-to-be may leave unspoken to their children. After Tom and Kathy started speaking with a pregnant woman about an independent adoption, the prospective grandparents feared that the adoption might fall through. "That was the hardest part," recalls Tom's mother Jean. "I worried that the mother would change her mind, which would break Kathy's and Tom's heart." Kathy's mother Pam found the days just after the baby's birth particularly trying: "Tom and Kathy were so many miles away, living in a hotel with a brand-new baby. It was scary." A possible open adoption makes grandmother Shirley nervous: one fell through when the birth mother reclaimed the baby after several months. She knows that this is rare, but says "it was like a death in the family, and I don't want this to happen to my daughter again."

Lois Melina in *Raising Adopted Children* and *Making Sense of Adoption* offers some helpful suggestions for preparing the extended family. She recommends introducing the idea of adoption gradually, rather than springing it on them, and being sure to provide ways for the family to get information. You might, for example, invite prospective grandparents, aunts, or uncles to join you at a meeting of an adoptive parents group, give them a subscription to an adoption newsletter or magazine, or arrange for them to talk with experienced adoptive grandparents by telephone. Perhaps your local adoptive parent group could hold a special workshop or panel discussion for adoptive grandparents. Just how critical that can be was underscored by one prospective grandparent who announced at a workshop: "I've been so in the dark. This is the first time my daughter has shared with me her adoption plans."

If you will be involved in an open adoption, talk about the feelings that various extended family members have. How do the birth grandparents as well as the adoptive grandparents feel? Will contact be maintained in the years ahead with birth grandparents, aunts, and uncles? You'll also need to talk about what happens during labor, delivery, and the hospital stay.

If you are still coming to terms with your infertility, take a look at Linda Salzer's *Surviving Infertility* and Gay Becker's *Healing the Infertile Family*. You might also find helpful Patricia Johnston's *Understanding: A Guide to Impaired Fertility for Family and Friends*.

As you prepare everyone for the adoption, however, think carefully about revealing to others the background information that you have about your child: this is information for you and your child (for a full discussion, see chapter 11). As you enthusiastically share details about the adoption process, exercise some caution. Ask yourself: What facts are "private" and belong to just my child and me?

It is to be hoped that the family member or friend who worried about "not knowing what you'll get" or perhaps expressed concern about "diseased children from abroad" when initially talking about adoption later changes his mind. Counsels Melina: "Forgive relatives for any insensitive remarks they made while they got used to the idea of adoption. Adoptive parents forget that there was a time when they, too, may have had doubts about adoption, told racist jokes, or thought there was no choice but to conceive a child."[23]

The day may come when you'll get a letter saying: "We are counting the days when we will come to you and hold the darling in our arms. We keep looking at the picture all the time."

10

ADJUSTMENTS

◆

I knew this was supposed to be the happiest day of my life, and that made me feel even worse. This was nothing like I pictured. What about those images of exhausted, beaming, brand-new mothers holding tiny infants to their bloated chests? This wasn't that. . .

I'd better adjust to having a baby, I had to accept that he was a boy, I needed to get used to dark brown skin, and I'd better come up with a name for this kid—and all before someone caught on to my feelings of pure panic.

I kept looking toward the backseat to make sure there was still a baby with us. He didn't exist three days ago, and now he was here for good. Just because I had wanted a baby all these years didn't mean I was ready for him. I didn't have nine months to feel him inside—not a cramp, not a single kick to warn me. Not only was this stranger staying in my home, but he needed to be fed, and changed, and held, and probably a lot of other things I didn't know about a year ago. It was very strange and disconcerting to be an instantaneous parent.[1]

Jana Wolff's account of the adoption of her newborn son in *Secret Thoughts of an Adoptive Mother* gives us a sense of the mixed feelings adoptive parents may have at the time of placement. The arrival of her son, she knew, was supposed to be a joyous occasion, and in her book Wolff shares her excitement. Yet we also have a sense of the stress of the independent adoption process: waiting for the baby to be born for three weeks; being in the delivery room for the birth; interacting with the birth mother and her family at the hospital; caring for her son in a hotel room; coming home.

In our society, with its focus on the early bonding of parents and infants, adoptive parents are sometimes hesitant to discuss what they felt when their families were formed. They will acknowledge that the process is different, but how it differs and how they worked at creating a family can be private topics. People who have adopted older children may be more open about acknowledging the problems they encountered. The press has chronicled some of those difficult times, publicizing tales of attachment disorder, of children who abuse themselves, of parents groping to control them, of parents "devastated, stunned and confused," of the straining to build a bond between parent and child.

Parents of newly adopted infants may be less comfortable talking about any mixed feelings they had or the difficulties they encountered in the early weeks or months. The outsider may be left to believe that "love" and "rapport" magically occurred. Perhaps you've even heard an adoptive parent say: "Everything has been golden." Or you've seen a television report on intercountry adoption that featured an airport lounge festooned with banners and balloons and smiling adoptive parents cooing over their newly arrived babies. This is the silk from which adoption mythology has been spun.

What is it like to form a family through adoption? While many adoptive placements go smoothly, with parents feeling a close connection to their children from the start, this chapter will examine some of the bumps in the road. For there are other tales to be told, where things do not go as well as expected, and families stumbled as they formed attachments. To bring these stories into the daylight is not to suggest that you'll have the same feelings or experience. Rather, if you do find that the road to family-building is steeper than you'd expected, be reassured that you're not alone. Consider the story of the adoptive parent who traveled to Chile, facing a scene quite unlike any she'd imagined, experiencing negative feelings toward her new child and wanting to bail out:

> *I was ready to pack our bags and leave. That was my first reaction to the baby we had traveled so far to adopt. Here we were in Santiago, Chile, tired, anxious, no sleep in two days, and faced with a screaming, sweaty, red-in-the-face, quite unpleasant, almost 7-month-old little boy. The only thing that prevented me from leaving was having to face friends and relatives upon our return home.*
>
> *The weeks before our trip were filled with excitement. There was furniture to buy, wallpaper to hang, curtains to sew. I made tons of stuffed animals, interviewed doctors, and bit my nails. I also spent many hours drooling over the pictures. Throughout this time people continually asked, "Aren't you nervous?" My answer was, "Well, a little," but in truth, I felt pretty calm. I only fell apart when we were introduced to our son—a tired, screaming, ugly baby.*
>
> *I was unprepared for negative feelings towards the baby we longed for. . . . Needless to say, my trip was not very enjoyable. I saw no sights, unfortunately for our son bought no souvenirs, got no sleep and easily lost five to seven pounds in four days.*

The plane trip home, though uneventful for the baby, was a very anxious time for me. I was only able to relax when we landed in Miami.[2]

In the weeks that followed, as the baby drank his bottle, played with his toys, and smiled at his new parents, the "happy, smiley, and full of fun" baby that this mother had fantasized about emerged, and the bond between parent and child developed. "I'm *so* glad that I didn't pack and leave without him," she finally enthused.

This chapter looks at how parents and children experience the coming together into an adoptive family. For adoptions, like marriages, need time for the ties to cement, and the transition, while joyful, can also be difficult and stressful.

EXPECTATIONS

Parents awaiting the birth of a baby often fantasize about their child-to-be, talk with family and friends about their impending parenthood, and engage in nesting behaviors such as preparing their infant's room and buying clothes. When the baby arrives, there's a flurry of activity, with grandparents, siblings, and friends dropping in to offer congratulations and support.

For adoptive parents the experience may be quite different. While chapter 9 discusses the preparations prospective adoptive parents can make, many do much less. Before their child's arrival, not knowing when, where, or whether the adoption will occur, adoptive parents may be reluctant to plan and fantasize. "It's hard to picture nothing in your mind," observed Kate Burch about her difficulty in imagining the siblings whom she hoped to adopt. "Maybe they'd be two girls, maybe two boys, maybe the children would be five and six, maybe eight and ten. We just didn't have any idea, and we couldn't imagine anything." Parents involved in an independent adoption may avoid dreaming at all, fearing that the placement might fall through. Recalls one mother who adopted independently: "Part of me wanted to be really excited and part of me wanted to hold back." Expectant adoptive parents may also delay sharing their adoption plans with family and friends, and when they do, they may receive less than wholehearted support. Even parents involved in an open adoption can keep their emotions at arm's length. "I looked at this more from a business perspective," remembers one adoptive father who was present at his son's birth, "making sure that all the i's were dotted and the t's were crossed with the paperwork." Observes psychologist David Brodzinsky: "Unlike nonadoptive parents, whose parental status is warmly welcomed by all, adoptive parents frequently must justify to others why they have made their particular decision."[3]

Traditional rituals, such as baby showers to celebrate the impending arrival, are often skipped. Familiar steps of validation and attachment that families follow before a child's arrival are thus absent or short-circuited in adoptive families.

When the child finally arrives, the circumstances of the child's entry into the family may be less than idyllic. Linda's daughter arrived from South Korea the day after her husband returned from a week-long hospitalization. After waiting for three months, they were notified on a Tuesday that the baby would be brought to the U.S. on Saturday. "The timing was terrible; the baby wasn't well, wouldn't sleep, and cried every time my husband tried to touch her," recalls Linda. For Betty, a single mother who traveled to South America to pick up her daughter, it is the airport scene on her return that sticks out in her mind: "We entered the country covered with shit. She had diarrhea. At the airport, all I wanted to do was get out of there, go with my parents, go to a hotel room, and take off my clothes. I didn't want to stand around an airport and celebrate. I needed to get to a private place."

How these children looked and reacted to their new surroundings must surely have influenced these mothers' feelings. It can be hard to fall in love instantly with a child who is smelly, weak, covered with sores, and generally unappealing. Illness can have a dual effect: It fosters togetherness between parent and child, but it also creates tension because of the demands and the worries put on the parents. An anxious stay in a motel room far from home or in a foreign country, where the parent or parents are alone, without supports, coping perhaps with the intricacies of a legal system, not to mention the rigors of the journey itself, may also increase the stress of the initial adjustment.

Barbara Shulgold, who experienced a failed adoption after the baby had been in her home, captures the feelings of uncertainty in her letters to her friend Lynne Sipiora in *Dear Barbara, Dear Lynne*:

> *Bonding... it takes time, and that can happen to anyone—biological or adoptive parent. . . . Truth is, we both feel as if we are babysitting still. . . . But for now, some secret thoughts that shame me: I wonder if she will be pretty (would our biological child have been?) or smart. . . . In other words, can I and will I love her 'as if' she is my own. . . . [C]an I make her my own? From what every other adoptive mother I know has told me, my fears are common. You get past them, to the point where you cannot imagine the child as anyone else's; she or he was meant for you. I am not at that place yet.*
>
> *. . . I think bonding was and is slower for me because of already having lost a baby. It felt very risky for a long time to love Miriam.*[4]

COMING TOGETHER

As the child moves into the family, parent and child interact. Now is the time for the new parents to get acquainted with their child, to love, cherish, and nurture their new son or daughter. Yet newly adopted children may not want the closeness that the parent offers. Christine describes her first months with her eighteen-month-old daughter: "I was not prepared for the anger. She wasn't able to accept comforting for four months. She'd wake up at night and be frightened. I'd pick her up, she'd stiffen, and I'd have to wait until she'd exhausted herself. She'd go into these rigid tantrums—deep breath, arms straight out." This behavior puts a distance between parent and child and can form a part of the attachment process as it goes on. For many parents, closeness and distancing interplay—the parents wanting to make the attachment; the stress of the new parenting role and the child's actions making it difficult and exhausting. The adoptive mother of two Korean sisters, aged two and four, tells this story about the first few months:

> *Sleeping: What's that? Why is Kendra inconsolably sobbing NIK-O-YAH for three hours? A call to our Korean friend at 11 P.M. fails to resolve this tiny question. Oh, she wants to sleep with her little picture book we had sent to her in Korea. How could we be so stupid? But, at least Kendra, aged four, liked to sleep. With Lisa, aged two, nothing worked. She screamed, raged, rolled all over until one night, in desperation, I spanked her legs. INSTANT silence. So, that's what they must do in Korea. Well, it may work for a few nights but forget it. One night, we let her follow me around the house. I walked in a circle for 45 minutes from 10 o'clock to nearly 11. Was she tired? Of course not.*[5]

This mother's tale raises another basic issue in adoptive parenthood. How does it feel to take on the instant role of mother or father? Despite having read all the parenting books you could find, you are now confronted with your child—not the hypothetical child—whose habits, likes, and dislikes you barely know. All parents must come to terms with their child. The parents of newborns can follow some basic advice: if the baby's wet, change him; if he's hungry, feed him. Parents who adopt non-newborns may grope around for other answers.

One adoptive mother describes how it felt to take on her new role:

He was two years old when he arrived from South Korea. The day after he came, we were in a restaurant. I got ready to order breakfast for my two kids—Carol, my two-year-old birth daughter, and John, my new son. I knew what to order for Carol, but I had no idea what to order for him. I felt terribly inadequate. Since he spoke Korean, there was no way to communicate with him. Because I had become his "mother," I felt that there was something inborn that I should have had but I didn't have it.

Mothers of infants can have these same feelings. "I didn't fall in love with our baby at first sight," recalled one mother. "She cried and cried, and I couldn't comfort her. For the first 100 hours we were together, she cried or slept—exhausted. I felt I was too much for her. She startled or blinked at sound, withdrew from touch. I didn't know her. I felt ashamed."[6] Says adoptive mother Paula: "When I started to talk with other mothers about my son, I felt terribly unsure of myself. My son and I had a lot to learn about each other."

BEGINNINGS

The questions always come up: When you bring your child to your house, who should be with you? Should you celebrate? Should you take your child around to meet family, neighbors, and friends immediately? Or should you stay at home for a while just to acclimate yourselves?

This is a time of transition. Your family may profit from some private time. If you are adopting an infant and feel that you'd like a more experienced hand around, such as a grandparent, then go ahead. But an older child may appreciate the time to become acquainted with you and your house before being asked to relate to the larger family network or to the neighbors. There is, after all, a lifetime ahead.

People should understand that this is a time when you may need to be alone. While your child is settling in, you may not want to feel obliged to entertain company.

POSTADOPTION STRESS

> *Before Adam came I had read everything I could get my hands on about cerebral palsy. I was prepared for his not walking and his speech difficulties. However, reading about a disability and living with a child on a daily basis who has that disability are two different things. All of a sudden I was overwhelmed with it all—not overwhelmed with joy and happiness; instead I was overwhelmed with fear and guilt and tremendous feelings of failure. The last thing in the world I felt like celebrating was 'Mother's Day' when I was feeling so inadequate as a mother (or anything else for that matter).*[7]

That's not the way it's supposed to be. Or is it? Most people have heard about postpartum depression, but postadoption blues? Is it possible that you could endure years of fertility treatments, wait for months to adopt a child, and then feel depressed, irritable, fatigued, tense, inadequate, and overwhelmed? Everything seems up in the air, in turmoil. And why not?

Your family is changing. It's disorganized. New relationships are being established. The waiting and the tension surrounding the wait are gone. Now you wonder when things will ever settle back to normal. But what is normal? Not the way it used to be. A new family constellation is emerging, but you don't yet know how it will work. You're unsure of yourself and your child.

The family has to set up new routines and find ways to establish authority and control. Your new child keeps "testing" you to see how things work in your home. He's got to figure out how the hours and days are organized in your family, what's off-limits and what's not, who disciplines, who nurtures, and which of his actions will be punished. Your other children are jealous of the new sibling and act up, testing to see where they fit into the new scheme of things. Life is exhausting.

If you experience feelings of incompetence, don't let them get you down or cause embarrassment. Try to view these feelings as simply a sign that you've got learning to do: while you can prepare in advance for a child in some ways, most of the learning process begins when your child is in your home..

Ann Kimble Loux in *The Limits of Hope* describes the strains of bringing two sisters into a family with birth children:

> *In December, six months after Margey and Dawn came, it was time to go to court and formalize the adoption. The whole family dressed up and appeared in the courtroom. The judge asked Mark and me if we would swear to become the legal parents of Margey and Dawn, to care for all their needs, to love them as*

our own children. We each swore to do so, but it was impossible not to have serious doubts about our abilities to fulfill such an ambitious oath.

Mark and I asked each other a thousand 'what if' and 'if only' questions. What if we'd had another baby and never thought about adoption? What if we'd gotten an African-American or Asian child? What if we'd taken foster children instead of adopting? Mark was so discouraged; one decision and six months, he felt, had taken away so much of our joy as parents. Would we ever regain that pleasure, he kept asking. I kept thinking, if only we could break through and get the girls to listen, to obey. If only we could let go, not care so much. If only we could find help, for the whole family. We both wished we could discover how to keep from getting so angry; we were horrified by how terrible our tempers had become. Was there no way out, no way to return to 'normal'?[8]

If you've adopted an infant, you may find that holding your new baby suddenly makes you confront, once again, your infertility and your feelings of biological loss. You may think about the birth child you never had and how life might have been different. If you've lost a child, as one mother did when an independent adoption fell through, your new baby could trigger feelings about that other child. Recalled Janet: "Getting Caroline has brought Michael to the front of my mind. I wonder where he is now."

Sometimes postadoption blues hit when you least expect them. Barbara Shulgood describes the joyous day that her daughter's adoption was finalized, the ceremony in the judge's chambers, and the celebration following. "Everyone left by two," she records:

WHAT'S DIFFERENT?

Studies of the experiences of new adoptive parents are scarce but there is a richer literature examining the experiences of families created through birth. For two decades Professor Jay Belsky of Pennsylvania State University has recorded the effects of a child on a marital relationship, how marriages change when the first child arrives, and what accounts for these changes. Drawing on interviews, surveys, and observations of two hundred and fifty couples entering the transition to parenthood, Belsky and John Kelly, in *The Transition to Parenthood: How A First Child Changes a Marriage*, offer useful guideposts to answer the question that *all* new families confront: Why does my marriage feel different after the baby's arrival? Observes Belsky:

> *It turns out that the 'faceless something' that produces this unpleasant sense of differentness has a very concrete source. It arises from a couple's handling of the six transition domains—Self, Gender Ideology, Emotionality, Conflict Management, Communication, and Expectations. Quite simply, husbands and wives who know how to make most of these domains work see their marriage improve, while those who don't see theirs decline.*[11]

In the course of the book Belsky creates picture portraits of several representative couples to chart their transition experiences, sketching out their feelings before the baby's birth through to the family's third year. While the anecdotes at the outset are pregnancy-related, the larger issues they raise are valuable for all newly emerging families. Consider this example:

> *Tina said she had been convinced that no one ever felt as* incompetent *[emphasis added], unattractive and overweight as she had that afternoon. But several years ago, when Dr. Candace Smythe Russell of the University of Minnesota asked a group of new mothers, 'What aspects of the transition do you find most stressful?' three of their top five complaints were similar to Tina's. The women said they were very unhappy about their figures and general appearance and* very concerned about their parental competence. (Their other two top concerns were tiredness and unpredictable mood swings.) *Dr. Russell also found that, like new mothers, new fathers tended to worry about the same things. In one way or another all of the men she interviewed cited intrusive in-laws, lack of sleep, loss of free time, and all the new chores the baby had created as their top transition concerns.*[12]

Belsky reports that new parents very much agree as to what the transition uppers, as well as the downers, are. The top satisfactions: "the baby and all the new love he has brought into my life, the way he has changed my feelings about myself, the new sense of closeness I feel toward my spouse and my own mother and father."[13]

Sound familiar? Belsky also notes that where new parents differ enormously is how they weigh the two aspects of the transition—does the positive or the negative prevail?

I read your letter and then just plain collapsed.

Five years. Five damn hard years. It all came crashing down on me, that it was over. I think this is what is called postadoption depression. I cried and cried and then slept for the rest of the afternoon. I have been a zombie since then. I've spent two days stretched out on the couch, watching Miriam and sleeping when she sleeps. I'm in a kind of shocked, dazed state. Though it is not bad per se, it just feels like a process I have to go through to get my balance back.[9]

Recognize what is happening. Seek out supports. Be sure to leave some time for yourself. Do what you feel you can; leave what can wait until tomorrow. Observe Holly van Gulden and Lisa Bartels-Robb in *Real Parents, Real Children*: "The first few months of parenting a new child can present a myriad of emotions, affecting each parent individually and their relationship with each other. The emotions and stresses are much the same for parents who have adopted and those who have given birth."[10]

CHILDREN TALK ABOUT THEIR FEELINGS

"I asked them how far away I was from home, and they told me it was miles and miles and miles away and it was over the ocean. I yelled out, 'Why did you let them do that to me?'"[14]

Those were the words of adoptee Armando Jordan, who was separated from his mother in Colombia when he was nine years old. Fright, not joy at the new life awaiting him, was Armando's reaction to the new home and family in America. For some children there is the fear instead that the long-awaited adoption might fall through. "I guess the hardest thing for me in the first year was when I had to go back to the agency for follow-up visits," Melinda confides in Jill Krementz's *How It Feels To Be Adopted*. "I was always terrified that I would see my other mother there and she would want to take me home with her again. That's because when I was in foster care we had monthly visits—my mother and I—in the playroom at the agency."[15] Renee, who by age eight and a half had lived in eight different foster families in just three-and-a-half years, expresses similar concerns in Maxine Rosenberg's *Growing Up Adopted*: "When I first came to Mommy's house, I felt sure she would also give me up like the other families I had stayed with. When I told her this, she said to me, 'This family is it!' Deep down I'm starting to believe her. . . . Once we sign the adoption papers, I'll feel better."[16]

THE EXPERIENCE OF INFANTS

When I held my nine-month-old daughter, Amanda, for the first time at the agency, she burst into tears and wouldn't let me hold her. She stopped crying when her foster mother picked her up. For our next visit, her foster mother brought her to our house. She didn't want to be held. She let herself be on the floor. She still cried almost the whole time. So, for the next visit to our house, her ten-year-old foster sister brought her. She still cried every time I picked her up.

Amanda reacted just as you would expect an infant to react to strangers. She cried. But these strangers who kept approaching her were her new adoptive parents. After moving to her new home she did form a strong connection with her new mother. In fact, for the next two years, she had major difficulty separating from her mother, and she slept fitfully, frequently tossing and turning, crying in her sleep, waking up and wanting to be held. "We did not sleep through the night," reported JoAnn, "until she was past two." Her pediatrician suggested it might be teething. When her teeth came in, he gave the explanation that many one year olds had trouble sleeping. JoAnn feels, however, that Amanda was grieving for her foster mother: she didn't have the words, only the body language, to explain how she was feeling.

ATTACHMENT

Developmental psychologist John Bowlby once observed that:

> *By [a baby's] first birthday he is likely to have become a connoisseur of people. Not only does he come quickly to distinguish familiars from strangers but amongst his familiars he chooses one or more favorites. They are greeted with delight; they are followed when they depart; and they are sought when absent. Their loss causes anxiety and distress; their recovery, relief and a sense of security. On this foundation, it seems, the rest of his emotional life is built—without this foundation there is risk for his future happiness and health.*[17]

In 1958 psychologist Harry Harlow removed eight tiny rhesus monkeys from their mothers and placed them, instead, in cages where they were alone. Alone except for the company of two surrogate mothers. One was a block of wood, softened with a sponge-rubber coating and a terry-cloth cover, and equipped with a circular face with large eyes and a light bulb that shed warmth. The other was more spartan, a wire mesh contraption with a face and light bulb. Four of the monkeys were fed by the cloth-covered surrogate; the others, by the wire mesh. Harlow observed that the monkeys, while accepting nourishment from either, persistently clung to the cloth mothers. And when they were moved to unfamiliar surroundings—a "strange situation"—they sought out the cloth mother, clinging to her and rubbing against her. The baby monkeys also used the cloth mother as a base for exploring their surroundings. The cloth "mothers," though inadequate in providing for their children, "meant the world to these little monkeys." From this study, and other pioneering ones by James Robertson and John Bowlby, emerged an understanding of attachment, of the ties binding parents and child.

Mary Ainsworth extended this understanding with a series of descriptions of how young children respond to the "strange situation." Ainsworth observed infants in a room equipped with a one-way mirror for observation, chairs, and a bunch of toys. What would happen to children, Ainsworth asked, when mother and child are in that environment, when a stranger enters and leaves, when the mother leaves the child with the stranger, when the child is left alone, and when the mother returns?

From her observations Ainsworth posited a continuum of attachments that youngsters have. Children with secure attachment show signs of missing their mother, seek closeness to her upon reunion, but also resume play or exploration. Children with insecure/ambivalent attachment are very distressed during her absence; upon her return, however, they may be inconsolable, obsessed with her or vacillate between their need for closeness and the expression of their anger. They may cling but may also resist physical contact. Children with insecure/avoidant attachment exhibit the most confusing behavior. An outburst of anger may be followed by a turning away from the caretaker, a refusal to make eye contact, a resistance to closeness. Yet these children, seeming fearless, are willing to be taken home by a stranger.

Understanding attachment—and the problems, such as reactive attachment disorder that children may have when the attachment is insecure, incomplete, disoriented, ambivalent, or avoidant—lies at the heart of modern child development theory. As an adoptive parent, you'll need to focus on the process of attachment to better comprehend how your child experiences the world around her. As Robert Karen notes in his excellent overview of the literature, *Becoming Attached: Unfolding the Mystery of the Infant-Mother Bond and Its Impact on Later Life*:

> *Starting with a simple concept—that a child needs to be lovingly attached to a reliable parental figure and that this need is a primary motivating force in human life—the work of Bowlby and Ainsworth and the many others they inspired has helped fill an unseen void. It's a void that still exists in many respects, and it's a concept that still meets with resistance: It doesn't always fit comfortably with the lives we have built for ourselves. But the need for proximity, for felt security, for love; the need to be held, to be understood, to work through our losses; these basic themes of attachment are to some degree built into us biologically. We have mixed feelings about them. But they are there."*[18]

Consider the experiences of the parents of Jane, who was born in South Korea and joined her new family when she was four months old:

> *At first her parents were delighted that she did not cry or appear frightened. They became concerned, however, when she*

failed to respond to them or to anything around her. She neither laughed nor cried for several weeks. Alert and watchful, she indicated awareness by stiffening up when she was moved or spoken to. After about two months she smiled at her brother, Joe, then two years old. Shortly thereafter she began to respond to her mother, but it was about a year before she responded to her father. This withdrawal and isolation concerned and frustrated her parents and caused tensions between them.[19]

Her mother feels that the disruption in her care—and the need to adjust to new patterns of child care—caused deep feelings of insecurity which continued for several years. She feels that she underestimated the adjustment needs of her daughter "because of the myth of the adaptability of infants." She had expected her baby "to be happy and to trust" her. Instead, her first year with her new parents was "unsettled and difficult."

"A parent should expect rejection or withdrawal as part of the infant's adjustment to the new situation," says parenting expert Dr. T. Berry Brazelton.[20] The adjustment period may stretch for "weeks or months." Adopted infants can be expected to grieve. They have suffered a major dislocation in their lives. They have left behind familiar sights, sounds, smells, and people as well as established sleeping and eating patterns. They cannot verbalize their feelings but they can vocalize them and act them out. They may cry; they may withdraw; they may refuse to smile. Glum infants who sleep almost all the time, who wake up for short periods to eat and play, and who never really laugh and smile, are in mourning for the life they left behind. They are reacting normally to the changes that are going on in their lives. As a parent you will need to help them work through their grieving.

For guidance, try Patricia Irwin Johnston's *Launching A Baby's Adoption* and Mary Hopkins-Best's *Toddler Adoption.*

While the general parenting literature does not focus on adoption issues, if you dip into it, you'll get a sense of a young child's physical and emotional development.

ADJUSTMENTS AND THE FOREIGN-BORN ADOPTEE

Foreign-born children must cope with moving from one country and one culture to another, from environments that are dramatically different. Some of the shifts are clear-cut: Asian children, for example, travel through many time zones to get to their new homes and may have sleeping problems because, for them, days and nights are reversed. The child's schedule may straighten out in a week, but his sleep may remain troubled. Infants who have lain in a crib on their back may have a flattened head in the back. For the child who has been malnourished, food and eating may be very important. Recalls one mother:

> *There was a period of time after he came from South Korea when our two-year-old son would wake up at night and hold his stomach and talk about the ghost in his stomach. He also typically hid food. We'd find rotten oranges around the house. And he guarded his food. We'd had him for a couple of months, when one night he dove onto the table to prevent us from taking his plate away. Kind of a flashback. Talk about two grown-ups dancing around the kitchen showing him that there was food all over.*

This child's preoccupation with food lasted many years, and seven years later, his mother was still careful to pack a snack whenever he went out.

Children may cling to one parent and reject the other. Often the parent who traveled abroad to pick up the child will be the person to whom the attachment is formed. But the opposite may also take place: A child whose first contact was with the adoptive mother might choose, nevertheless, to attach to the father, because of the painful memory of the loss of the birth or foster mother. One parent is then left in the "odd-man-out" position, while the other is the round-the-clock caretaker. Either way, it hurts, exhausts, and causes tension.

"Neglect is the sine qua non of institutional life," comment Barbara Bascom and Carole McKelvey in *The Complete Guide to Foreign Adoption*. "All physical, developmental, and mental health problems that occur in children as a result of institutionalization represent some form of neglect."[21] In addition to medical challenges, parents of orphanage infants must be prepared that they may rock, bang their heads, or stare at their hands (a means of self-stimulation); lie quietly in their crib or bed (not letting you know they've awakened); vocalize infrequently; have poor motor skills; be slow to respond to stimuli; and withdraw or avoid interaction with their peers or siblings. Consider the scenario that Bascom and McKelvey paint:

> *Imagine such a child on his first night in an adoptive home. The new father picks him up and joyfully lifts him over his head, or tumbles him in play on a bed. Our baby cannot respond normally due to his deprivation and does what one might expect. He grabs for anything he can find (usually, a handful of hair) to cling to and holds on for dear life. A tiny misunderstanding enters into a fragile, beginning relationship.*[22]

Older children who grew up in orphanages may have difficulty making decisions, recognizing feelings, and showing emotions. Observes adoptive parent Barbara Holtan: "Knowing pleasure from pain, knowing sensation, and knowing how to make a choice, are acquired, learned. . . . Gazing at that tall, lanky eleven-year-old and realizing that he needs to master two-year-old skills is difficult for us. For the orphanage child, these attributes may not only have been untaught but positively frowned upon."[23] Holtan's son, Seth, who came from an orphanage at age seven, had to be helped to distinguish what was "fun" and what was not. Recounts Holtan:

Every night at dinner time, each of us was expected to tell three good things that had happened to him or her that day. When it was his turn, Seth was silent for many nights running. He truly had no idea how to separate the good from the not-so-good. Gradually as we identified things ranging from 'Amy gave me two stickers at school' to 'I made a base hit at baseball practice,' Seth began to make the connection that life has categories.

The kaleidoscope of life began to take form, to show patterns for him. When, at last, at his turn he mumbled, 'I liked lunch today,' we were jubilant. We did the same things for the bad things that had happened and decisions we had made during the day.[24]

Colorado adoption expert Cheryl Markson points out that the foreign-born child may also communicate more in physical terms. Since language creates a barrier, the child will have to show you through his actions how he feels. One older child tried to run away several times in the first days after he arrived, a graphic statement about how unhappy he felt.

If your child has spent time in an orphanage, inquire about infant-stimulation, early-intervention, and language-stimulation programs in your area. Learn about opportunities for occupational therapy so that your child can focus on jump-starting lagging motor and sensory skills. A multitude of programs, designed to help "deprived" children catch up, may be provided free or at little cost to your child through local hospitals or social service agencies in your community.

THE ADJUSTMENT OF THE OLDER CHILD

In 1974 Laurie Flynn and her husband adopted two teenagers, ages fourteen and twelve. The teenagers came with a history of many foster homes and needed love and security. Writing about her experiences in an article entitled "Why Would Anyone Adopt a Teenager?" Flynn notes: "We knew they would resist much closeness for quite a while. After all, they had no reason to trust adults. The traditional concept of family held little meaning to them."[25]

During the next few years, her son experimented with drugs and alcohol, ran away from home repeatedly, and was arrested for theft and vandalism. He was eventually ordered by the juvenile court to a residential treatment facility. Her daughter also had a difficult time adjusting to the family. "Sometimes she withdrew," writes Flynn, "and wouldn't speak to us for days at a time." Flynn balances her description by saying that they also had many "great times"—taking their son to his first real restaurant, throwing the first party for their daughter, having family picnics and camping trips. Affection did develop and "once in a while, they would open up a little and share some of their deepest feelings. And slowly and gradually, trust and caring grew between us."

The "adoption of the older child is a lot like marriage," Flynn writes. "If we are lucky, maybe the child will choose to change. But the changes belong to him, not to us. What matters most is that he have the chance to learn and grow through what we have to offer. To be effective parents, we must learn to accept risks and approach them as challenges. That essentially is how we made it with our teenagers."

Children who move into adoptive families need to work through their experience of separation. Whether they are separated from their foster parents, birth parents, or a caretaker in an orphanage, they will have to come to terms with what has happened to them before they can fully make new attachments. They will need help to open up, to talk about and share their feelings. The process of recovery from the separation, and then forging new links, will be gradual and can take years.

Gregory C. Keck and Regina M. Kupecky in *Adopting the Hurt Child* challenge us to look at the experience from the child's point of view.

> *Imagine a lazy summer evening at home where your spouse is dozing on the sofa and your two children playing quietly with their toys. A stranger suddenly comes to the door, grabs you and whisks you away. You're deposited at a new home—beautiful, affluent, where everyone smiles and is loving. The stranger 'assures you that this new family will love you forever. And all they expect in return is for you to love them back.' Your reaction: you are moving through a dream. This new family may be wonderful—they may be superior to your old family in every way—but they're not your family. You don't even know them, how can you be expected to love them?*[26]

Experts liken the child's grieving and attachment process to the experience that we have when a loved one dies.[27] The process may begin with an attempt to deny that this has happened. Or it may start with what is called the "honeymoon" period: The child and the parents are on their best behavior; things are calm. This is the time when parents are likely to report that the child made a rapid adjustment into the family.

However, the calm is deceptive. You could compare it to how you might feel on an extended trip away from home and everything familiar to you. At some point the exhilaration wears off. You feel frightened, overwhelmed, tired. You say to yourself: "I want to be where I can relax, where I can understand my world." You long for the familiar. In the child you may begin to see two responses: withdrawal and rage. These are normal reactions to a new situation.

Be it two weeks or two months after the child enters the home, the "testing" period will begin. The child will show his anger, often violently, and stop being obedient. He will exhibit a range of behaviors, both good and bad, and see how the parents react and deal with the behavior. It is not uncommon for children to have behavioral problems, acting out through temper tantrums, running away, stealing, lying, or setting fires. The children are testing you, seeing how much you will tolerate before you will throw up your hands and say "enough," as others have done in the past, and throw them out. During this "testing time" the children are trying to fit themselves into the family, figuring out what the rules and routines in the household are and how they affect them. They need to learn what you expect of them, to be told "hitting your brother is unacceptable," and "running away from home is not how we solve problems."

Children will also regress. Their behavior will tell you: "I need attention; I am insatiable." They may have eating and sleeping problems. They may wet the bed or soil themselves. They may have difficulty separating and will have fears. Bedtime may be particularly trying. Adoptive parents often report that their children want to go through the stages of their childhood that they may have missed. One parent reports: "When I put my eight-year-old daughter to sleep at night, she wanted to try to nurse on my lap. She needed to sit on my lap and cuddle. She needed this so badly." Some parents are upset by such behavior. But it is part of the child's need for parenting—to relive pieces of his life. One mother who refused to cuddle her ten-year-old daughter at the time reflects now: "I should have given her the comfort that she missed from that part of her life."

According to Claudia Jewett Jarratt, an older child entering a family can act several different ages at one time. Parents may find it difficult to respond to the child because they may not recognize what age a child is being at any given moment. She writes: "It's almost as if your kid has to crawl back into the womb and act through all of the time that you haven't shared together. So if you get an eight year old, he's going to go through parts of being 1, 2, 3, 4, 5, 6, and 7 with you." The child may act like a four-year-old for one week, for example—but, writes Jewett, "you're going to have that week, if that's what it takes him.[28]

Keeping in mind, that "just as everything is new to the adoptive family, so is it new to the child. School and siblings, food and clothing, family rituals and religious preferences—all present new experiences and challenges." Keck and Kupecky, in *Adopting the Hurt Child,* offer specific strategies for the process of "getting used to each other."[29] They urge parents to:

- Stay in charge, utilizing a few clear-cut rules that you follow through on. "The fewer and simpler the rules in a family," they note, "the more likely it is that the child will comply with those expectations. All unnecessary rules should be abandoned." The messy room may disgust you but it can be endured simply by shutting the door. "It is only by letting go of many unnecessary rules that parents can help their child comply with the rules that are really important. These rules must be enforced at all costs, so the child learns that his parents are serious."

  You must also recognize that your new child is struggling to sort out your family's unwritten rules—its rituals, means of communication, unspoken practices—and will have trouble deciphering them.
- Take care of yourselves. For parents, "as their child's

needs become all encompassing, it can seem overwhelming—even impossible—to find the time or space to care for themselves. But they must," urge the authors. You can do this by taking a coffee break away from home, spending a night out, or even verbalizing a fantasy about flying off to Maui without kids.

- Get support, whether from other adoptive parents, buddy groups or a respite service.
- Find a therapist who can help the family and the child.

Over the months and years, when the initial adjustment process is long over, adoptive parents find that certain events, such as the anniversary of the child's removal from his birth family or the anniversary of his placement with his new family, may trigger a child's regressive behavior and the family may go through a mini-adjustment process again. It's not uncommon for children to experience "prefinalization jitters"; old and new behaviors surface as they deal with guilt about abandoning others from their past or worry that they may not be able to fulfill the expectations of their new parents. Adolescence is another predictable crisis period.

Much is involved in the integration of older or special-needs children into a family. Parents and children may have to deal with issues of health, school, change of birth order, and the acceptance of the family and community. I have touched on a few of these issues in this book. The reading you should be doing and the contact you have with adoptive parents will help you identify others. By the time your child enters your home, you should have made extensive preparations, including identifying support services in your community. Claudia Jewett Jarratt says that:

Parents often come out feeling that the older child's adoption has been one of the most significant experiences of their lives. They talk about a sense of enormous personal growth, of satisfaction at having sought a meaningful challenge and met it, and of the privilege of having shared something of lasting value with another human being. Most are convinced that the rewards of their adoptions were well worth the hard times, and that they wouldn't have missed out on their experiences for anything.[31]

SIBLING RIVALRY

Dear Betsy,
I can't believe Mom and Dad ever adopted you. They already had five of us and did not need you. Why couldn't they be happy with us? What did we do to deserve you? You've made my life a living hell. My friends won't come over because of you . . ."

I HATE YOU. Ben[30]

Imagine finding that letter, written from one of your birth children to his adopted sibling, on your dining room table. While a new adoptive sibling may be welcomed enthusiastically, parents are often unprepared when their other children start acting up and out. All children have a critical need for their parents' time and attention and a new sibling is a usurper of that.

Your children may feel that "it's not my problem," since you, not they, made the commitment to adopt. The children already in your family have experienced a loss, a changed environment that they must adjust to. Getting your other children to talk or write about their experiences, to join a support group or to participate in family therapy may help. Making sure that you find the time for all your children is vital.

DEALING WITH THE CHILD WHO'S EXPERIENCED SEXUAL ABUSE

Some of the children in foster care in the United States have been the victims of sexual abuse. They may have been abused in their original homes—even placed in foster care because of a reported incidence of sexual or physical abuse, or they may have experienced abuse while in foster care, either by an older child or an adult. Older children adopted from abroad may also have had sexual experiences. In some circumstances sexual interaction may have been a culturally acceptable way of life for children who spent time on the streets, in orphanages, and in prisons (where some societies will keep older children). Foreign-born adoptees may also have been abused while in foster care.

"Abused children are hurt and traumatized children, and require resources of security, stability, and support beyond the love and attention that adoptive parents are going to give them," says adoption expert Joan McNamara of Family Resources in Greensboro, North Carolina. "Parents need to become comfortable talking with their children about past issues of sexual abuse and present issues of family rules, roles, and routines. They've got to educate their children about personal safety, sexuality, and sexual abuse. That is very difficult."

As a parent, you must deal with your child's reality. A few suggestions:

- *Try to get in advance whatever information you can about your child's sexual history.* Be aware that caseworkers may not know or that they may not record this information in a child's record. Children are often reluctant to disclose past incidents of abuse, fearing they'll get in trouble if they admit this "badness" in themselves or if they feel guilty that they allowed this to happen to them. If their "telling" resulted in their removal from their family, they may also feel that their placement was their punishment. It's not unusual for children to be in a home for several months or years before they reveal this secret. Hard as it may be for parents to hear the sordid details, the telling itself is a sign that the child trusts his new parents sufficiently to unearth the past.

- *Talk with other adoptive parents about their experiences.* Belonging to a parent support group, and having your child involved with group activities, is important for the healing process. You'll also want to do some reading about sexual abuse, and provide your child with therapy. Your adoptive parent group, the **National Adoption Information Clearinghouse**, and the **National Resource Center for Special Needs Adoption** (see appendix A) should be able to help you find a therapist who's versed in both adoption and sexual-abuse issues.
- *Know some of the common signs of sexual abuse in children.* They may be fearful of adults, suffer from nightmares, be afraid of the dark, and have difficulty sleeping. Their sexual knowledge may be advanced for their age; they may act seductively towards adults or peers and even imitate some of the abusive behavior they've been taught. Some children dislike being touched; others tend to be clingy. Some masturbate excessively and in inappropriate places.
- *Be aware of how sexually abused children may behave.* Feeling they are "damaged" and low in self-esteem, these children may be untrusting and find it hard to establish a relationship with others. They may have a range of defensive behaviors that are hard to breach. Abused children may also lash out and be abusive to others, including friends and adoptive siblings; they may try to involve

others in inappropriate sexual behavior. They may also withdraw, either physically or emotionally, experience mood swings, and have fits of anger, with the adoptive parent the target.

- *Give your child guidance as to how grown-ups and children are expected to act.* The child needs to understand that rules are made to keep children safe, not to punish them.
- *Recognize that your child will need help in sorting out what abuse, sex, love, caring, and intimacy mean.* Your child may have a distorted perception of how parents or other adults act towards children. Your child will need to learn to differentiate between "good touch" and "bad touch." While you'll want to hold your child's hand, bestow kisses and pats on the shoulder, and put her on your lap, she may resist or stiffen. Saying what you are doing ("I like being close" and "You feel good to be near") helps. Brushing a child's hair, applying nail polish, or helping her hold a tennis racket are other, less physically threatening ways to come close. Both you and your child will need to find the means to express feelings.
- *Talk with the other children in your household about their new sibling.* Help them understand that this is a hurt child whose mixed-up feelings sometimes lead to inappropriate behaviors. Your children should understand that if they see inappropriate sexual behavior, or are asked to touch—or are touched—in an inappropriate way, they should say "no" and inform you of what transpired. Make clear that they won't be punished for telling; you can't help their sibling unless you know. You'll also want to discuss the situation with members of your extended family and other adults who may have considerable contact with the child. "Privacy is fine," advises McNamara, "but there should be no more secrets."

POSTADOPTION SUPPORT

The adjustment process may take months, but it can also take years. Just because a family "finalizes" an adoption in court doesn't mean that the adjustment process is ended. Children's and families' timetables are different from those of agencies and courts. As the next chapter makes clear, there are special issues that adoptive families must deal with. Building a family by adoption is different from building a family by birth, and adoptive families must meet adoption-related issues head-on. Often you will handle them within your own family. At other times, however, you may want to turn to others for support and guidance.

What types of situations prompt people to seek help? Perhaps there's a recalcitrant teenage girl, an only child who's acting up in school and whose teacher or counselor thinks the problem is adoption-related. Or a continual struggle between father and son. Or a mother who's unnerved when her child says "You're not my real mother. Leave me alone." Or a parent who does not feel "bonded" to the child, even if the family relationship is long-standing. Or a child who says "What am I doing in this family?" Observes Judith Schaffer, coauthor of *How To Raise an Adopted Child*: "There's a temptation to wonder: Is this adoption-related? There are all kinds of doubts." With those doubts is the need to talk and to share.

You may have joined a parent group before you ever identified your child. Now that your child is in your house, the temptation may be strong to let your membership lapse as your family settles in. Parent groups are not for plucking information from and discarding once you achieve the goal of a child. A parent group gives you the chance to talk with people who've had similar experiences, to share with them your knowledge, and to draw upon them for support. Groups with an intercountry focus often sponsor cultural events for families. You can also raise the questions that vex you. And your child can get to know and interact with other adopted children.

If you are experiencing any adjustment problems, a parent group can be indispensable. Some groups have developed a buddy system, pairing experienced adoptive families with new families so that the buddy family provides insight and moral support. Others provide respite families who, when a family is experiencing difficulty with a child, will take the child to their home to give the adoptive parents and the child some breathing space. There may be telephone hot lines for adoptive parents to talk with more experienced adoptive parents as well as postadoption workshops and discussion groups. Many groups try to bring in speakers from around the country to talk with their members on adoption-related issues, or hold annual daylong or weekend conferences that focus as much on how to raise an adopted child as how to find one.

Some parent groups also offer special support groups for school-aged children and teens. "The kids' support groups introduce them to other adopted kids, so they can learn that their particular situations are not as unique as they may seem in the community at large," reports one parent whose children participated in a youth group. She also feels that the group provided "a sounding board—adults who are not 'parents' and other kids of about the same age who are safe to talk to about how they really feel." If you're interested in starting a group, the **North American Council on Adoptable Children** (NACAC; see appendix A) has created a training program, "Family Preservation: The Second Time Around" that prepares mental health professionals, adoptive parents, and adult adoptees for working with parents and children on adoption issues. The curriculum materials are available from NACAC. Says NACAC Executive Director Joe

Kroll: "People need to talk about adoption issues before they hit crisis situations and not wait until someone blows up."

The number of agencies that see adoption services as extending through the lifetime of the adoptee is growing as attitudes toward adoption continue to evolve and policies about disclosure change. Special workshops at agencies might range from discussions of the questions children ask to the use of a positive adoption vocabulary. For the family with children adopted from abroad you may find preteen and teen support groups or special event days, such as the Children's Home Society of Minnesota's Korean Children's Day (a social event for children and their parents that includes a Korean meal, arts and crafts, and storytelling). The agency also provides counseling services, booklets, videos, and books, including the excellent *With Eyes Wide Open: A Workbook for Parents Adopting International Children Over Age One* (written by Margi Miller and Nancy Ward; see appendix C).

Check with the agency that placed your child or another local agency about their postadoption services. Try also adoption umbrella organizations, particularly those that promote special-needs adoption. The Three Rivers Adoption Council in Pittsburgh, for example, operates an Adoption Support Network: its programs include a therapist referral service, a twenty-four-hour hot line, and two newsletters—one for adults and the other for kids. Don't forget to call your state's adoption office. Some states are now underwriting, or even offering, postadoption support programs. You can also check community centers and colleges for postadoption classes. You can subscribe to Lois Melina's monthly *Adopted Child,* and to *Adoptive Families,* the bimonthly magazine of Adoptive Families

CREATING A LIFEBOOK

Lifebooks, a chronicle of a child's past and present, are used by social workers and parents to create a permanent record. With the child as the centerpiece, the lifebook collects disparate pieces of information about a child and offers a child the opportunity to take hold of, and think about, his history. The lifebook, unlike a baby book that starts with the birth, follows a child's journey through life and might be assembled on paper, audio- or videotape.

What might be preserved in a lifebook?

- original birth certificate and other birth information, a baby picture (or a photo of the hospital where the child was born or other early helpers)
- data about the birth family, including siblings
- notes you took when you learned about your child, health or other reports that you may have been sent about your child, photos of the orphanage and other materials you took when you picked up your child
- mementos, photos, or other information about the previous families and places where the child has lived (both good and bad details as a child needs to understand why an adoption plan was made)
- documentation from the past (copies of court records, passports, letters, souvenirs)

In the age of high technology, you may want to use duplicate photographs and copies (including color laser copies of photographs) in the lifebook and store the originals in a safe place.

of America, which has a strong focus on postadoption issues (see appendix C). Internet bulletin boards highlight postplacement issues and enable you to reach out and touch someone.

The goal of postadoption support is to forge links and to help people understand that their family situation is not unique. Says Reuben Pannor, coauthor of *The Adoption Triangle*: "I worry about the people who are out there on their own."

DISRUPTION

By summertime, we hoped that a major adjustment time was past and that after six months our living pattern was familiar and secure to Ken. However, each day it was as though it was Ken's first day in our family routine.

It was one thing after another. Ken talked out loud to himself continuously at school, at home, and everywhere. We talked about how to act every place we went. Ken could not seem to remember from one time to the next how to act, whether it was at the store, at church, or just visiting. Day after day, there was no significant change.

We became so disheartened, guilty, and frustrated. My life became a see-saw of hope and despair. I became very afraid of what would happen to us during those critical adolescent years. I began to realize that the uncertainty of Ken's behavior was more than I could cope with. I knew he needed time, but I had invested so much of my life and self in trying to help us make it so far, I had no further resources left to give him. This handsome, kind child whom we loved was so confused and fearful within himself. Could we finalize this adoption and make it?[32]

Ken's family chose to disrupt the adoption. His parents felt that the toll that the placement was taking on their family life and on their other children was more than they could handle.

They had tried for a year and a half, had gone for counseling, but the family had still not begun to fit together. They talked with their social worker and their adoption counselor and learned that Ken, a seven-year-old boy, would be able to find another placement. A new adoption plan was made; Ken's new family met with him several times and finally, he left to begin another life. Ken's first adoptive mother continues: "We experienced a mixture of sadness and relief: sadness that our hopes for this adoption had not worked out; relief that Ken was moved and was settled with another family. We had come to realize that we were not a family who could survive the continuous emotional upheavals."

Not all adoptions proceed to finalization. Research shows that older children are likely to have more problems, and the more problems children have and the more moves they have made, the greater the likelihood the adoption will disrupt. While thorough preparation of adoptive parents and the provision of postadoption services give families a better chance of success, adoption experts believe that there will always be some risky placements.

One failed adoptive placement does not mean, however, that a child is unadoptable nor that the adoptive parents will be unsuccessful in their parenting of another child. "In view of the emotional baggage that children bring to a placement, the multiplicity of factors in the home environment, and the flaws in our ability to predict their interaction, it is inevitable that some disruption will occur," observes Trudy Festinger, author of *Necessary Risk: A Study of Adoptions and Disrupted Adoptive Placements*: "Disruptions do not end the hope for, nor likelihood of, a later successful adoption. In the process, children, families, and workers can learn how to improve the chances that the next placement will hold."[33] Conclude the authors of *Adopting the Hurt Child*: "A child sometimes disrupts one family, only to move on and be adopted successfully by another family. Sometimes this is because the child received help to better prepare him; sometimes it is because he feels more 'at home' in the second adoptive home. Just because one adoption experience fails, a child is not necessarily doomed to repeated failure, nor is the next family to adopt him consigned to chaos and defeat."[34]

◆

The challenges of adoptive parenthood are enormous, but so, potentially, are the emotional rewards. "I'm still 'hooked on adoption,'" concluded one adoptive parent after chronicling the rocky road she'd traveled. "It's just that I'm learning that sometimes the joy takes a little longer to surface." When that joy does come, you'll be glad you are around.

11

RAISING THE ADOPTED CHILD

◆

I thought of my origins as a vacuum. I possessed a birthdate: March 9, 1935; a birthplace: Borough of Manhattan, New York City; and a beginning: July 1938.[1]

Katrina Maxtone-Graham tells us in her memoir, *An Adopted Woman*, that she always knew she had been adopted when she was three and a half. She knew that in those few years before her final placement, she had lived in several foster homes and had one adoption disrupted. What she could not integrate were her memories—a name by which she had previously been called, images and feelings from those early years that she could not pin down. For her, this information was not enough:

I had thought of my loss at all times, and since as long ago as I can remember. Every moment, every breath, I was consumed with wondering, and longing and searching. Each stranger on the street, each house along the road, posed the same questions: Where? Why? Who? There were no answers; and so my yearnings were without resolution, a confirmation of my inadequacy.

At the age of thirty-eight Maxtone-Graham sets out to fill that vacuum. It is a long struggle for knowledge that begins with a search for basic information, includes meeting her birth mother, learning about her deceased birth father, and visiting a foster parent. It is a struggle that pits her against the agency that placed her as a toddler and takes her to court. One of the first pieces of information that she gains, on the day that she meets the agency's social worker, tells us exactly how isolated she has been:

> *It is a remarkable experience to sit across from a person who knows who your parents are when you do not; to hear, at the age of thirty-eight, someone tell you simple facts about your own private spectres. 'Your father was six foot one, brown hair, blue eyes, a college graduate.'*
>
> *Just like that you* ***know*** *something. Not six foot two, not six foot even. Six foot one. 'Brown hair.' Your own hair is brown, too—what a glorious coincidence! You try to imagine what a man with brown hair and blue eyes and six foot one* ***looks*** *like. You had not even expected to hear anything about your father; you had not thought his identity was even known. And now, 'six foot one.' I could go home, mark a spot on the wall six feet and one inch from the floor and proclaim a victory, 'There, there is my* ***father****.'*

There are many memoirs written about adoption's impact on the individual and the family: J. Douglas Bates's *Gift Children: A Story of Race, Family, and Adoption in a Divided America,* Michael Dorris's *The Broken Cord: A Family's Ongoing Struggle with Fetal Alcohol Syndrome,* Florence Fisher's *The Search for Anna Fisher,* Tim Green's *A Man and His Mother,* Betty Jean Lifton's *Twice Born,* Ann Kimble Loux's *The Limits of Hope: An Adoptive Mother's Story,* Maxtone-Graham's *An Adopted*

Woman, Susan Wadia-Ellis's *The Adoption Reader: Birth Mothers, Adoptive Mothers, and Adopted Daughters Tell Their Stories*, and Jan L. Waldron's *Giving Away Simone: A Memoir* (see appendix C for details of these and other similar titles). These books highlight the inner turmoil some birth parents, adoptees, and adoptive parents face, the disconnectedness and anomie felt by some adoptees, and the strong need some adoptees feel to search for their biological roots. You may feel uncomfortable reading these chronicles, for they emphasize the strains experienced within adoptive families and touch on the issue of shared parenthood—one that many adoptive parents would like to forget.

Consider these books instead as ones that parents can use to help them understand some of their children's needs. Many adoptees live with the thirst for knowledge about themselves. They are missing the "who, what, where, when, why, and how" about their lives that people born into a family take for granted.

What prompts an adoptee to start pushing for the answers? One fifty-year-old adoptee says that his search started when he was sitting in a new doctor's office, confronted once again with a questionnaire asking him for his family's medical history. As he kept writing "Don't know," he decided, "I want to know." Others say that it was the birth—or impending birth—of a child that made them wonder about their own genealogical history. Or a contemplated marriage and the fear of inadvertently marrying a birth sibling. Or the death of a parent.

But the need to know is not limited to the adult. Wondering about birth parents is a theme that echoes through Jill Krementz's interviews with youngsters in *How It Feels To Be Adopted*. Reports one twelve-year-old: "There is one time when I do always think about my biological mother, and that's on my birthday. How does she feel on this day? Does she think of me, or does she just pretend that I was never born and it's any other day? Is she sad, or is she happy?"[2] A five-year-old foreign-born adoptee, when asked by an adult who was traveling to his birth country what he wanted as a souvenir, requests: "Can you bring me a photo of the hospital where I was born?" And a seventeen-year-old adoptee reports:

> *I think that I have always wanted to know about my roots but pushed it out of my mind. I became aware of this about two years ago when my grandfather was visiting. We had one of those big family dinners and he kept talking about relatives that did great things. Everyone started to trace our ancestry. It struck me then that I really needed to know about myself. I want to be able to tell my children and grandchildren about their ancestors. I don't want to leave my parents or go back to my natural parents. I just want to ask them a million questions.*[3]

SHARING INFORMATION

All parents have to come to grips with some basic questions:

- When and what do you tell your child generally about adoption?
- How do you tell your child about adoption?
- If your child does not ask questions, do you initiate them?
- How much information do you share with your child about his past?
- How old should your child be when you tell him about his adoption?

- If there are unpleasant facts, do you reveal them? If so, when?
- How should you present the birth parents?
- Should you tell the *whole* truth and *nothing but the truth*?
- If your child has memories of his birth parents, do you encourage him to share them with you?

There are some additional questions that parents will also face—those that their children ask them:

- What is adoption? What does it mean that I was adopted?
- Why do some children need or want to be adopted?
- How do people go about adopting a baby?
- Why couldn't I be born to you?
- Why didn't my mother/father keep me?
- Where is my mother now? What about my father?
- What did my parents look like? What were their names? Were they married?
- Did I have another name when I was born?
- How do you know my birthday?
- Did I have any other brothers or sisters?
- Who is my *real* mother?
- Did you buy me?
- Why did you adopt me?
- What did the social worker, adoption agency, or lawyer do?

Not all the questions will be asked at one time. Rather they are likely to come up at different times—sometimes at odd moments—and at different stages of development in your child's life.

Children must be told about adoption and must be helped to understand it in order to grow. As a parent, you must be open and accepting of adoption. You must acknowledge that your family is built by adoption, and that the process of family-building by adoption is different from that of building families by birth. You must also accept that you are involved in a shared parenthood experience. Adopted children have a set of parents, whether known or unknown to them and you, who gave them life. Your child may also have had foster parents to whom he formed attachments. Adopted children's interest in their parents is natural. Adopted children will fantasize about them and ask questions: curiosity about origins is normal.

Those touched by adoption must also confront the issue of loss: birth parents must grapple with the loss of the child born to them, adoptive parents with the fantasy birth child, and the adoptee with the loss of the first, and perhaps also the foster, family. Psychologist David Brodzinsky has posited that "adopted children's adjustment is determined, in part, by their appraisal of adoption-related losses."[4] While Brodzinsky and others stress the centrality of loss to the adoptee's identity formation, which is accompanied by the normative process of adoptive grieving, Peter L. Benson, Anu R. Sharma, and Eugene C. Roehlkepartain, in their study of adopted adolescents, *Growing Up Adopted,* have questioned this hypothesis: "for most, adoption is seen as a fact of life that carries no heavy meaning. It is neither a burden nor a celebration. It just is."[5]

There is invariably an ebb and flow in a child's interest in, and willingness to talk about, adoption. In *Being Adopted: The Lifelong Search for Self,* nine-year-old adoptee Elizabeth says: "I know that I'm adopted: it's part of who I am. When people ask about me and want to know about me, one of the things that comes to my mind is that I'm adopted. Sometimes I tell them and sometimes I don't."[6]

Recognize that children and parents have different tasks: *yours* is to tell your child about adoption and the circumstances of his adoption; *his* is to understand. As a parent you will also want to listen to what your child tells you about the experience of adoption. As your child grows up, you may be asked the same questions again and again, plus many new ones. What your child needs and wants to know, and what your child understands, will deepen with age. Observe Mary Watkins and Susan Fisher in *Talking with Young Children about Adoption*: "The parent must listen for how the child's understanding is evolving to know at what point she is eager and able to understand something that a few months before would have held little interest for her."[7] Make sure that openness and communication are an integral part of your adoption telling.

Telling a child about adoption is not something you save up until a child reaches a certain magical age. Nor is it something that you reveal in one fell swoop at a very young age, thereby getting the "telling" over with and behind you. You are involved in a lifetime process of sharing information about family-building.

This chapter touches on the core issues parents confront in raising adopted children. For more in-depth discussions, you can look at David M. Brodzinsky, Marshall D. Schechter, and Robin Marantz Henig's *Being Adopted*, Lois Ruskai Melina's *Making Sense of Adoption* and *Raising Adopted Children*, Cheri Register's *Are Those Kids Yours*?, Judith Schaffer and Christina Lindstrom's *How To Raise an Adopted Child*, Holly van Gulden and Lisa M. Bartels-Rabb's *Real Parents, Real Children*, and Mary Watkins and Susan Fisher's *Talking with Young Children about Adoption*.

CHILDREN'S UNDERSTANDING OF ADOPTION

Child: Adoption is when you are born.

Adult: What do you mean?

Child: You came out of a lady.

Adult: Tell me more about that.

Child: Well, then you go to live with your parents.

Adult: Which parents?

Child: Your adopted parents. You came out of one lady, but she's not your mommy.

Adult: Is that true for all children?

Child: Sure, that's how it is.

Adult: Are all children adopted?

Child: Of course they are.

Adult: You mean that all kids are born to one set of parents, but then are adopted by other parents?

Child: That's what I said, didn't I?[8]

Here's one precocious four-and-a-half-year-old adoptee's explanation of birth and adoption. "Too often we are fooled by the child's words," observes David Brodzinsky. "Children can talk to us about things that suggest they have a real understanding, having learned to apply a vocabulary to a particular topic. It's a working vocabulary without much substance behind it. The surface knowledge is there, but when you scratch the surface, the real understanding of what is going on is missing." Brodzinsky and other researchers have found that the depth of a young child's understanding of adoption parallels her understanding of birth and reproduction.

Even if preschoolers can rattle off some of the facts of life, they actually have a limited comprehension of where babies come from. Their concept of family, then, tends to be fairly simple: a group of people who live in the same place—whether they are biologically related or not.[9]

Not until the elementary school years, when children are ages six to eleven, do they begin to appreciate the genetic and kinship ties connecting families. As their understanding of the birth process comes into clearer focus, their questions about adoption sharpen. They observe that most of their friends are not adopted and that they're different. It is the child of eight or ten—not the preschooler—who asks those pointed, specific questions: Why couldn't my mother keep me? Was there something wrong with me? Was I so bad? These are the children who are grappling with the key issue: Why did my birth mother give me up? Brodzinsky and his co-authors note in *Being Adopted*:

> *Middle childhood is often the period when being adopted is first seen as a problem. This is when the youngster begins to reflect on the meaning of being adopted—which often leads to feelings of confusion, and to feeling odd or different. And this is when the child, because of his growing capacity for logical thought, begins to realize that there's a flip side to his beloved adoption story—that in order to be 'chosen,' he first had to be given away.*[10]

As elementary-school-aged children start problem-solving and figuring out relationships, the questions multiply. They may be able to empathize with the birth parent but can't truly understand *why* a woman might choose not to parent. (Imagine some of the child's possible responses: "But Mommy, my friend Jane's mommy isn't married." "But

Mommy, if she didn't have enough money to take care of a baby, couldn't somebody just give her some money?" "She couldn't take care of a baby; why didn't she get someone to teach her how to take care of a baby?") Equally hard for a child to comprehend is why a birth parent might release one child for adoption and choose to raise another. Research has also shown that until children are about eleven years old, they do not understand how the legal system protects them from being taken away from their adoptive parents and insures an adoption's permanency. Adopted children may need reassurance in the meantime that the adoptive parent is really the *forever* parent.

It's not uncommon for school-aged children to daydream about their birth parents. ("What's my birth mother like? Would life be better with her? Would my birth mother make me pick up my room and go to bed so early?") Children may blame themselves for the adoption ("She didn't keep me because I have a crooked smile.") and have a negative self-image. Comparing themselves with others, adopted youngsters realize that they have lost a set of birth parents (whom they very likely never met) and grieve for them. Feelings of anger, directed at the birth parents and the adoptive parents, are possible. Maintain the researchers at the Rutgers University Adoption Project:

> *Many school-aged adopted children are actively struggling with issues of separation and loss. . . . Rather than representing emotional disturbance, or poor adjustment to adoption,* these attempts by school-aged children to understand the basis for their relinquishment—which often include overt displays of sadness and anger—actually are normal, age-appropriate, and probably inevitable components of the adoption experience. *Like reactions to*

parental death and divorce, they represent children's grief and bereavement in response to parental loss.[11]

As youngsters reach adolescence, their understanding broadens so that they comprehend that adoption entails a legal transfer of rights and responsibilities between parents. They can grasp why their birth parents chose to make an adoption plan, and why infertility or a desire to help children led their adoptive parents to adoption. Adolescence is also a time for self-discovery and questioning, a time when youngsters contemplate who they are, who you are, what makes them alike and different, what others think of them, and what gives their parents authority. It is a time when youth think about how life might have been different for them and when they attempt to put some distance between themselves and their parents, asserting their independence. For some youngsters it can be a time of emotional vulnerability and one when some youngsters will crave additional information and desire to search for their birth parents. Maintain the authors of *Being Adopted*: "when adopted teenagers ask themselves 'Who am I?' they are really asking a two-part question. They must discover not only who they are, but who they are in relation to adoption."[12]

While we may fashion for our children a simple explanation of adoption, the concept itself is complex and difficult to comprehend. Children must come to understand birth and reproduction and what a family is. They must develop an awareness of, and sensitivity to, interpersonal motives. They must assimilate why, for example, a parent chooses to place rather than parent a child. And they must comprehend the roles that societal institutions, such as agencies and courts, play in the adoption process. This information-gathering and processing, begun when your child was a toddler, continues throughout the elementary school years: while the adoption process was fuzzy to the four-year-old, it's crystal clear to the twelve-year-old:

Adult: Suppose an important decision had to be made about the child after it was adopted. Who should make that decision—the adoptive parents or the birth parents?

Child: The adoptive parents, of course.

Adult: Why?

Child: Once you give up a child and he's adopted, then he doesn't belong to you anymore. You don't have the right to say he should do this or that.

Adult: Why is that?

Child: It wouldn't be fair to the adoptive parents. The child is theirs and they have to take care of him. They're the ones who are responsible for how he should grow up. Besides it would really mix up the adopted kid if the other parents suddenly came back into his life.

Adult: But what if the birth parents really wanted the child back?

Child: No way. When they signed the adoption papers, that's that. The laws say it isn't their child anymore and they don't have the right to try and get him back and upset the whole family.[13]

TALKING ABOUT ADOPTION

Adoptive parents often start talking about adoption long before their children are able to understand what it means.

While there have been a few writers who argue against an early telling, most adoption experts believe that adoptive parents should use the term "adopted" in their home from infancy on—but appropriately. Looking at photographs in a scrapbook that show your first meeting with your child you can mention "adoption" just as you might use the word "born" when looking at a photo of your child at the hospital on the day he was born. Perhaps you've been told to look at your baby and say "Oh, my beautiful adopted baby." Would you look at a birth child and say "Oh, my beautiful birth baby?"

Recognizing that young children may not fully understand adoption, it's still important for parents to explain from the start that adopted children aren't different from anybody else: they are conceived and born the same way other children are, and don't come from adoption storks, adoption agencies, or airplanes. The preschool-aged child needs to know how she came into the world ("A man and a woman made a baby and that baby was you. You grew inside that woman, just like all babies do, but not inside me.") and that she was adopted ("Sometimes people can't take care of the children they give birth to, so other parents raise them. That's how you came into our family.").

School-aged children need to understand that birth parents are people who were in a difficult situation and had to think hard about their problem and come up with a solution that would give their child a fuller life. Be aware that your child must deal with rejection, since his birth parents, no matter how loving, chose not to raise him. Don't place the burden of the rejection on his shoulders, however; don't even unwittingly lead your child to believe that some flaw in him led his parents to decide on making an adoption plan. Saying "Your mother couldn't take care of *you*" suggests that he wasn't worthy of care. Better to say, "Your mother couldn't take care of any child at that time." It's also important for you to listen to your child's concerns and to be open to the feelings that they express.

Try to be honest, matter-of-fact, and nonjudgmental in your explanations, since you are also conveying your own attitudes about adoption. Steer clear of loaded words such as abandoned, rejected, lucky, special, and chosen. Avoid speaking in hushed tones that suggest secrecy or shame, or imply that your child should feel sorry for being adopted. Peter Benson of the Search Institute reports that the 1994 study of adopted teens showed that "what's particularly important is the way parents deal with adoption in the family. In the families that are thriving adoption is a fact of life that is accepted and affirmed, not dwelt upon. Quiet, open communication about adoption seems to be the key."[14] In your discussions you might also want to mention some of the different types of families your child knows, pointing out Aunt Sally's and Uncle Joe's blended family where there are step children.

Always answer your child's questions. If he's capable of asking them, you're capable of answering them. "In talking with very young children," cautions Brodzinsky, "answer what they are asking. Most of the times parents overexplain and overinterpret the question." Give real answers to real questions, and don't make up stories. Don't tell your child that her mother made a loving "plan" for her if she abandoned her in a city square in Shanghai. Telling a child that her birth parent gave her up because she loved her so much can also be problematic: your child may get the idea that being loved leads to being given away. Your child may also ask questions when you least expect them. "One of the most consistent 'findings' across the stories we report," observe Mary Watkins and Susan Fisher in *Talking with Young Children about Adoption,* "is that conversations about adoption most often occur informally, at times and in places between other activities: in the car, at bedtime, on walks."[15] Eliza tells the story of how she was driving on an interstate highway when her three-year-old son asked, "Did I grow in your tummy?" She answered "No" and braced herself for the next question. Her son's response: "Mommy, did you see that dump truck?"

PRESERVING YOUR FAMILY STORY

Families preserve their joint history through stories, photographs, videotapes, mementos, and traditions. If you have a camera, use it as your child joins your family. If you meet the birth parents or their extended family, photograph them with their child, with you, and by themselves. Ask for photographs from your agency or foster family. Keep drawings, mementos, or other keepsakes for your child. Perhaps the birth parents have written a letter—or letters—to their child that you can preserve and share.

You might want to buy one of the special memory books created for children or you can create your own. Traditional baby books work best for families who have adopted newborns. More adaptable are calendars that track a child's development over the first year (and can be started on the day of the baby's arrival into the family) or a memory book that asks the child to fill in basic birth data and also answer questions about himself: for example, "The people who were in my family when I was first brought home." You can check *Adoptive Families* magazine (see appendix C) and other adoption mail-order catalogs for alternative books.

Consider making your own lifebook or storybook with your child (see also chapter 10, p. 337). Lifebooks, which have traditionally been used to prepare older children for moving to a new family, reconstruct important instances in childhood. The book chronicles key events—birth, foster

RITUALS IN ADOPTION

What about commemorating the adoption? In open adoptions, some agencies hold a birth parents' farewell/adoptive parents' welcoming ceremony, what is often referred to as an "entrustment ceremony," at the agency, the hospital, in a chapel or church, or in the family's home. Notes Lois Melina in *Adopted Child* magazine: "An entrustment ceremony at the time of placement gives public notice and affirmation of the child's move from one family to a new one, just as a wedding acknowledges and witnesses the creation of a new family by members of two separate families."[16] Families may choose, for example, to light candles, say blessings, trade keepsakes, or plant a tree of life in a special location.

Some families celebrate a child's joining their family with a party or a religious ceremony after the child has settled in. Christians often baptize or rebaptize their children; some churches have a special adoption service. Jews may formally convert their children to Judaism if their birth mothers were gentile. Boys undergo a *brit milah* (circumcision) and a *tevilah* (immersion at a ritual bath); girls a *tevilah* and a naming ceremony at the synagogue.[17]

Ten-year-old Josh discusses the importance of his family's celebrations in Maxine B. Rosenberg's *Growing Up Adopted:* "Mom says that they invited seventy people to this big party just to meet *me.* Of course, I don't remember any of it, but I still like hearing the story."[18] These are all formal ways of linking the child with the family, and they are events that a family can remember and talk about in the future.

Some families also celebrate the anniversary of their child's arrival as a family holiday. That's what Josh's family has done each year: "Usually the four of us go out for dinner, and the child whose day it is gets to pick the place." Holly van Gulden and Lisa Bartels-Rabb propose a candle-lighting ceremony that's treated as a family anniversary. They suggest getting a large, long-burning candle that will stand for the whole family and can be relit many times. Along with this candle you use a smaller candle to represent the child's birth family, and taper candles that will be held for each member of the family. The family then talks about the child's entry into the family and says "Today, we celebrate the day you came home, the day we became family." This ceremony, say van Gulden and Bartels-Rabb, can be performed on the birthday of those who entered the family by birth and on the anniversary of the day of those who entered the family through adoption.

"Whether Adoption Day should be celebrated on the actual day the child came home or the day the adoption was finalized is an individual decision that depends on which day feels like the day the family was created,"[19] observes Lois Melina in *Adopted Child*. Melina offers concrete suggestions on how to celebrate the day you choose—and what rituals you might design.

Parents of foreign-born children may want to commemorate their child's citizenship by asking their congressional representative or senator to arrange for a flag to be flown over the U.S. Capitol in the child's honor. (Contact the congressional office several weeks ahead and specify your child's name, the date, and the occasion. You'll be asked to pay for the flag and will get it as a souvenir with a note saying that it was flown in honor of your child.) Later on your child can bring the flag to school for show-and-tell when the class talks about citizenship. If you adopt an older child, you will want to involve her in the planning of any celebrations. Consider also the creation of new family rituals and the incorporation of her traditions into yours. Ask your child about the holiday traditions in her birth and foster families, or at the orphanage where she lived. You can then work some of her favorite practices into your family celebrations, linking her past with your present.

Families have also created special ceremonies to mark a disrupted adoption. After the birth mother reclaimed their seven-week-old baby, Jeanne and Harvey Hammer had a service, developed in conjunction with their pastor, for closure. "We read psalms and expressed our feelings of anger," recalls Jeanne.

To stimulate your thinking about rituals, try Evan Imber-Black and Janine Roberts, *Rituals for Our Times* and William J. Doherty's *The Intentional Family: How to Build Family Ties in Our Modern World.* Lois Melina discusses rituals in her various books and in several issues of *Adopted Child.* You can order reprints of her articles, as well as a list of resources on rituals, through *Adopted Child* (see appendix C). Mary Martin Mason has created *Designing Rituals of Adoption for the Religious and Secular Community.* Jewish families may find useful *The Resource Book: A Guide to Jewish Adoption Issues* (contact Jewish Family and Children's Service of Greater Philadelphia; see under Pennsylvania in appendix B).

care, moving to a new house, starting school, vacations, adoption, getting a pet—and people. The child puts the book together, drawing pictures, writing, adding clippings, photographs, and mementos. Adults work with the child, filling in details and helping to ensure accuracy. You'll find that as your child works on his lifebook, it's a natural time to pull out those pictures, letters, and other items from his birth family (or your trip to his birth country) that you'd stashed away. All adopted children can gain from creating a lifebook, since it gives them a chance to talk about their past. Making the book also lets you talk about adoption and explore your child's knowledge and feelings.

Family stories about the adoption itself are also to be cherished. Says one mother:

> *The older they get, the more they want to hear their story. Thomas likes to hear about our going in a taxi to pick him up at the agency. We tell him how I held him in my lap and he smiled at me. It's important to Sandra that we changed her into certain clothing. That we painted her crib. She wants to know what people said about her when we first saw her. Each child has his own story. They hear their story. They are beginning to retell their story. It's folklore.*

Folklore is important for families. But there's a side to the adoption folklore that parents must guard against, for, as parents emphasize the adoption story, children may lose the sense that they were ever born. Betty Jean Lifton tells us:

> *Sometimes when I'm with nonadopted friends, I will spring the question, 'Did you ever think you weren't born?' I get quizzical looks as to my seriousness or sanity, but always the reply, 'Of course, I was born.' For without knowing it, while*

they were growing up, they heard random fragments about how they kicked in the womb, how Mama almost didn't make it to the hospital, and without understanding it, they were receiving direct confirmation about their entrance into the universe and their place in the flow of generations.

But the Adoptee says: 'I'm not sure I ever was born.'[20]

The focus in adoption stories is on children's entering into their families, not on their entrance into the world. For children to understand how they entered the world, they need to know about their birth families. Chapter 9 discussed the importance of getting background information for your child. How can you respond to your child's questions if you have not tried to get the answers?

One mother decided to travel to South Korea to search for additional information about her children because "what would their chances be after almost twenty years had passed to find records, addresses, and people halfway around the world."[21] In the agency records, she found out more about her daughter's birth date and name. The agency also arranged for her to meet one of her children's foster mothers. But the highpoint of her trip came when, using her son's documents, which gave the names and addresses of the people who had signed his relinquishment, she located her son's grandmother (who had cared for her son after his birth) and visited her at her house. She writes:

My son's grandmother told me that she had met him often in her dreams and that she worried about him greatly, even whether or not he had lived. She had told me he was so sick when she gave him away, she thought he would die. She lives in peace now, for she always had thought she would die not knowing if he was happy. When she got out the family album, there in a place of honor were pictures of our son. Mark, also, now has invaluable pictures of his grandparents, aunt, and father.

Jeannette Watkins had never met the birth mother of her son, but she did have her name. One night when her son was three years old, she called his birth mother. "She was just dumbfounded," Jeannette recalls. "She was really glad to hear about him. She asked questions about him. I sent her photos and then she sent photos."

As it turned out, the birth mother was about to get married and did not want to stay in touch. (She did, however, give Jeannette her new surname and address.) Jeannette learned how valuable that one contact had been, however, when, six years later, her son started asking probing questions about his adoption. "One day he was overwhelmingly possessed with it," she says, "whining, crying. I said, 'Let's go to the bank and see what's in the safe deposit box.' He studied the picture of his mother, we talked about it, and then we came out. He hasn't pushed the issue again." As Jeannette learned, the appropriate time to share photos and other documents with a school-aged child is when the child *needs* it—not on a "special occasion" set aside to discuss adoption issues. Maintains Lois Melina: "This material belongs to the child—it is not a gift from you."[22] If you have on hand *copies* of letters, photographs, and other documents pertaining to their birth families (preserving the originals in a safe deposit box), your child can study them whenever he wishes.

For your child to build a strong identity, he needs to have the basic building blocks. In families formed through birth ties, children have a family and a genetic history to link up with. As they grow up, they may choose to affirm or deny that history. They have the knowledge, and thus can make the choice. Should not children in a family formed through adoption have the same opportunities? Writes Lifton:

Adoptive parents can help their children by returning to the agencies or professionals who arranged the adoption and requesting all missing information. By preparing in advance, they can give their children the feeling they are working on their side, not against them, that as parents they care about them in the deepest sense possible—which means having empathy for their needs.[23]

UPDATING INFORMATION

As your child grows, you may want to inform the agency, the intermediary, the birth parents directly, or the other people who were involved with your child's adoption about his development. You might want to send periodic photos and letters describing your child. If you did not work out a means of communication with the birth parents at the time of your child's placement but now wish to have the updates shared, be sure that you specify to the agency or intermediary that these updates are to be placed in your child's file and that you give permission for them to be available to the birth parents. (If you're willing for identifying information to be provided, ask the agency about its policy. Will they leave it in or insist on blacking it out?) If you wish the updates to be forwarded to the birth parents, be sure that you make this clear—and follow up to determine whether this has been done. Find out whether your state has a centralized registry or other service that allows for you and the birth parents to update medical and family information.

If your child develops a medical condition such as diabetes that has a possible genetic link, be sure to let people know and find out what the intermediary's or agency's policy is in relaying such information on to the birth family. Such information should be passed on to the birth parents, who might like to know this if they have other children. "We had a very sad situation where the child died at age seven," recalls Marlene Piasecki about a challenge she faced when she worked at the Golden Cradle agency. "The couple contacted us, and we tracked down the birth mother and told her. This wasn't an open adoption and there had been no contact, but our perspective on all the parties was that they have a continued interest in one another."

You should also let your agency or intermediary know that you would like any updated information provided by the birth parents. And you should be prepared that your child's birth parents, even if you participated in a closed or semi-open adoption, may request photographs and additional information from you. Reports Piasecki: "The woman who placed eight years ago is going to decide to ask for an update. We're seeing that all the time. Openness not only has an impact on new adoptions, but on adoptions that took place before." Emphasize the importance to the agency or intermediary that any attempts by birth or adoptive parents or adoptees to initiate contact, and open up the adoption, are to be respected. Observes Mary Sullivan of the National Adoption Information Clearinghouse: "More and more families are finding that they both contacted the agency or attorney separately with requests to establish more open contact only to have their requests be ignored."

If you are vacillating about whether to update information or request it, consider the story of adolescent Jane, in Jill Krementz's *How It Feels to Be Adopted.*[24]

> *When I was five, I developed epilepsy and the specialists were always asking questions about my medical history. My father and my doctor both wrote to the adoption agency requesting additional medical data, but the agency people never responded. We had very little information and it was extremely frustrating.*

Jane's birth mother, independent of the agency, later tracked her down. Jane reports:

> *The most upsetting part of our conversations was learning that she had written to the adoption agency in Rochester several times asking if my parents wanted any more medical information. They always told her no, even though my doctors had been asking—and begging—for updates because of my epilepsy.*

Try to put yourself in the birth mother's shoes. One woman whose social worker contacted the adoptive parents of the girl that she had relinquished eighteen years earlier says: "Just knowing that she's alive and well and happy is quite a relief, but I shouldn't have had to wait eighteen years to find out so small a fact."

If your child is adopted from abroad, don't assume that there's no information available and that updating is not possible. Adoptive parents of South Korean children have found that even in circumstances where South Korean children were listed as "abandoned" on their documents, there may be some data—or photographs—in the Korean agency's files. Some children are "technically abandoned" (they do not have legal documents comparable to a birth certificate). Children's records coming out of South Korea in the nineties have had more information about the birth parents than those provided in earlier years.

When Sarah obtained additional information about her daughter, she learned that the baby had been brought by her birth mother to the South Korean child welfare agency that arranged the adoption. In her daughter's case file was the original intake file compiled eight years earlier. The documents revealed the birth mother's name and age, her education and employment, her reasons for placing the baby, and who joined her at the agency when she released the baby.

While the amount of additional information in your child's file may not be extensive, some may be forthcoming. If your child was born in a hospital, it's possible that there are separate birth records you can obtain. There may also be an intake worker's file that contains notes from an interview with the birth parents that was not put into your child's case history. "You play detective," says social worker Sherry Simas. To get more information, you might be in touch with the U.S. agency that placed your child, or contact the agency, orphanage, or intermediary in the foreign country directly. If you have friends in the foreign country, don't feel shy about asking them to help you find any additional records pertaining to your child. If you write, enclose a list of specific questions, a letter describing your child today, and some photographs of your child. Finally, keep in mind that at some agencies, it's possible that some information may be shared with the adoptee who visits the agency as an adult that was not provided to the adoptive parents. Both Korean adoptees and birth mothers have been returning to the Korean agencies, asking for information, and initiating contact between each other.

It's also possible that, just as birth parents in the United States are seeking out adoptees, birth families abroad may contact the orphanage, agency, or court that placed their child years later, ask for additional information, and request a meeting.

A DUAL PERSPECTIVE: BIRTH MOTHER AND ADOPTIVE MOTHER

Barbara North was nineteen when she gave birth to her son in December, 1966. She didn't decide on adoption until her eighth month of pregnancy: "It was a very difficult decision. I knew that I couldn't provide for the child, and I didn't think it was fair to have my parents do it." She saw the baby in the hospital—"I walked down every day, but didn't want to hold him. I knew that I wouldn't be able to give him away"—and then went home. "I was told by the agency 'don't ask us any questions because we won't give you any answers.' That's the way it was back then, so I never asked any questions."

Within a year Barbara had met her husband-to-be and married. While many birth mothers have a replacement child soon after the surrender, she did not. Although she wanted a child, she discovered she suffered from secondary infertility. Finally she and her husband approached the agency through whom she'd made her adoption plans and inquired about adoption for themselves: "I was afraid that the agency wouldn't let us adopt because I had placed." Her fears were unfounded, however, and they ultimately adopted two children. When she expressed interest about her son, her social worker shared with her some non-identifying information from the file about her son's adoptive parents.

Still, Barbara couldn't get her first child out of her mind: "I went through all the stages mentally with him that you do with your own children." She wondered what he was up to in school, whether he was playing sports, and later if he was attending college. "There were so many things that I thought I needed to know," she says, "but couldn't ask."

She also grew increasingly depressed: "Every birthday I was crying, and the holidays were really hard. I'd be a real crab throughout the Christmas season. No matter how hard I would try to be happy and make it a joyful event, I wasn't putting my heart into it. Every year it got worse. All I could think about was him."

She updated medical information about herself at the agency, and left a letter in his agency file for him. When her son finally contacted the adoption agency asking for more information about his birth family, her letter was forwarded to him. The two did not get in touch, however, until he was twenty-two, when both listed information about themselves with an adoption registry. Her son has now visited her home; his family has given her a photo album of his childhood, and the families have vacationed together. "It makes me feel wonderful," says Barbara. "A two-ton weight has been lifted off my shoulders."

When it comes to her adopted children's birth parents, Barbara confesses, "I don't think we've acknowledged them like we should have. We've always talked to our children about being adopted. You would think that with me being a birth mother, I would have thought about their birth parents more than I have. I was so wrapped up in my feelings, I really didn't stop to think about how other birth parents may feel."

Barbara would be comfortable exchanging letters with her children's birth parents right now (they've told the agency about their willingness) and would support her children if they wanted to meet their birth parents when they are older. "Birth mothers don't forget, and the unknown is always worse because you imagine things," says Barbara. "If I had been able to know every five years, I think that would have been plenty for me. To not know anything for so long was much worse."

SHARING INFORMATION BEYOND THE NUCLEAR FAMILY

Dave and Katherine Wilcox happily announce the adoption of a baby daughter estimated to have been born on March 5 (she was discovered, abandoned, on a road in China on March 8).

That arrival announcement was sent to friends of the joyful adoptive parents. How would they have felt several years later if the daughter of one of these friends, who was having a fight with their daughter, told her: "You were dumped in the street. My mommy told me."

Before your child arrives, you need to sit down and consider who should be informed about your child's adoption and exactly what details they should be given. The background information that you have about your child is his and yours. If there is information that you want to share with your child alone, don't discuss it with others. Even people with the best of intentions, including grandparents, aunts, and uncles, may later slip parts of your child's history to your child or others. "I'm quite willing to answer people's questions about the adoption process, the practices of different agencies, our reasons for adopting, and how my children reacted to what was a major change in their life," notes Lois Melina in *Making Sense of Adoption*. "I consider information to be 'private' if it refers to a child's genetic and social history."[25] Her rule of thumb: Would you readily share that information about yourself?

In the beginning everyone who knew you before the adoption took place will know that you have adopted a child. But as time passes, as you meet new people, move, or enter new situations, not everyone will necessarily know that your child is adopted. You'll have to decide who to tell, when, and for what reason. Does your baby-sitter need to know? Does your mailman need to know? When someone who doesn't know you well comments on your child's curly, blond hair (and yours is straight and brown), what do you say? Do you automatically say "That's because she's adopted?" Observes Melina: "The person who asks, 'Where did she get those blond curls?' probably has no interest in the child's heredity, but is merely remarking on the child's attractive hair. Parents should therefore respond to the remark in the way it was intended, saying, for example, 'Yes, isn't her hair lovely?'" In the same vein, the person who says "Oh, you have a new baby. What obstetrician did you use?" may be seeking a referral to a doctor rather than information about your adoption. Putting the question into context, therefore, is important. "Parents are under no social or moral obligation to reveal personal and potentially stigmatizing information about themselves to casual acquaintances or strangers," says Melina.[26]

What exactly do you tell the school? If you have adopted an older child, you have probably worked closely with the school in getting him established in your community. But if your child entered your family as an infant, the school may not know about his adoption. Parents may be reluctant to tell the school or an individual teacher because they feel that some people associate adopted children with problems. If openness is a part of your life, however, not telling the school will present you with quite a dilemma. What kind of message are you delivering to your child about adoption if you conceal it now?

"A child's adoptive status is part of his social history," counsels Melina in *Raising Adopted Children*. "And schools need to know the social histories of their students."[27] When you share any history, however, ask the school personnel to consider this as "privileged" information: it is not to be talked about with others. If you provide the teacher with any background details that you have not discussed with your child, be sure that you make this known.

HANDLING TROUBLESOME SCHOOL ASSIGNMENTS

I can't do my homework tonight. My teacher told me to look at both my parents and decide from which parent I inherited my brown eyes and which parent gave me my red hair. And then I'm supposed to look at my brother and see what traits we have in common. How can I do that?

◆

I have to write an autobiography and my teacher told us to start with our birth and tell where we were born, what time it was, and how our parents felt. How can I do that?

◆

Our teacher told us to bring in a baby photo for the bulletin board. We don't have any baby photos since I wasn't living with you. And that first photo you have of me—from the orphanage with a number slung around my neck—is yucky. What do I do?

◆

We have to do a family tree and the teacher gave us a form. What do I fill in?

◆

We're going to do reports on the countries connected to our family heritage. I told my teacher that your parents were Irish and dad's were Polish. My teacher insists that I do China because I'm Chinese. I don't want to study China; I did a big country report on it last year. Why can't I study Poland?

Time and again adopted children face assignments in school that pose challenges for them. Autobiographies, family trees, family histories, family time lines, lessons focusing on genetics, heredity, and ethnic origin are difficult because they demand that your child come up with information that is missing, incomplete, or noticeably different from his peers. What he discloses could be embarrassing or reveal details that you believe should be kept private. Should he then, as teachers sometimes suggest, "do the best he can," "just make it up," or "just use present family relatives"? Those responses in themselves may raise your hackles since they may make your child feel different or ashamed. And then you wonder, will the assignment open him up to questions about adoption that he's not prepared to answer publicly?

What can you do to circumvent this? Try to schedule a parent-teacher conference at the beginning of the school year to talk about your child's needs and the potentially problematic assignments. Meeting the teacher in advance, says Virginia educator Carol Dolber McMurray, who lectures on adoption and the schools, gives you a chance to get a sense of the teacher. Don't assume that the teacher or other school personnel are knowledgeable about adoption or have spent much time thinking about possible curricular pitfalls. Their ignorance is probably not from a lack of interest or prejudice, just a lack of exposure. Chances are your child's teacher will welcome your sharing general materials about adoption and particularly those that explain how children experience and understand adoption at different ages. You can also help by putting adoption into a broader societal perspective: there are many family configurations in our society today and a family tree, for example, could prove equally problematic to a foster child, a child of divorced parents, a child living with a step parent and step siblings, the biological child of a single mother, or the child being raised by grandparents.

Explore with the teacher why a particular assignment has been devised. "When a parent understands the educational objective of a given assignment, s/he is in a better position to suggest alternatives," observe Nancy Sheehan Ng and Lansing Wood in *Adoption and the Schools*. "To use the ubiquitous family tree as an example, kindergartners might work on family trees to study the basic concept of family. Sixth graders might be assigned a family tree as part of a social studies class. Freshman Biology students may be asked to complete a family tree to study genetics and heredity." Ng and Wood's *Adoption and the Schools* (available from FAIR, P.O. Box 51436, Palo Alto, CA 94303; 650–328–6832) offers practical ideas for classroom presentations, alternatives to problematic assignments, and advice on learning disabilities and special education.

Understanding the purpose of a project and exploring alternatives with the teacher—and with your child—is key. Let's take a closer look at a few assignments and how they could be changed:

- *Genetics:* Rather than focusing on a youngster's relationship to his parents and siblings, students might be asked to choose any biologically related group—other family members such as an aunt, uncle, and cousins, friends, neighbors—to investigate inherited traits.
- *Autobiography:* A youngster's "lifeline" could be entitled *When We Were Young* or *My Life* and offer choices (e.g., what I remember about myself, things my parents have told me about myself, toys, rituals, memorable days, the first time I. . .). Rather than creating a rigid, linear time line, the autobiography reveals facets of the child's personality. It doesn't matter if the child's self-portrait spans the child's entire life or a shorter time frame.
- *Baby Pictures:* For the assignment that attempts to show how children change over time, a photo of a child at an earlier moment or younger age, rather than infancy, serves the same purpose. If the intention is to create a guessing game (such as match the child with the baby photo) and your child is going to be singled out because she's the only Chinese child in the class), the assignment might be broadened to use word clues or favorite things rather than photos for identification.
- *Family Trees:* What are they trying to show? Are they designed to make linkages between members of a household or a family? Ng and Wood depict many variants: the loving tree (where members of the family are drawn), the caring tree (people who have cared for the child, including physicians, teachers, and foster parents), the rooted tree with roots below and branches above (the present family above and the birth family below), the genealogist's half wheel (with the child at the center and the birth family on one side of the circle and the adoptive family at the other), the genogram, or a diagram that shows "important people in my life."

Each family's—and child's—solutions may be different. There will be times when your child will be eager to share information about his adoption, and others when he just wants to blend in. Talk with your child about how he wants to handle a particular assignment. If he's uncomfortable adapting it to fit his particular situation, let him do it the way the other kids do. Give him the freedom to make that choice (rather than what you may feel is the "politically correct" solution). Beyond looking for adaptations, you can explore with the school how to build their resources. Perhaps there are books about foster care and adoption available in the class and school library that the teacher might like to highlight? (See appendix C for some suggestions.) They might be grouped together permanently or displayed during November's National Adoption Week. How about some videos that focus on adoption themes? You can also offer to be a resource to the classroom teacher and the school about adoption. Would the school be interested in your giving a presentation to teachers that touches on adoption-related issues. Perhaps the Parents Association would like to offer evening workshops on a variety of subjects, with adoption being one of the topics offered? Does the school have support groups where youngsters meet to discuss issues of common concern? Does your child want you to come to the classroom to read a favorite book about adoption or help with a cultural celebration? Before you venture into the classroom, however, check with your child about his feelings. If your discussion of adoption at school embarrasses him, you'll want to work behind the scenes only.[28]

ADOPTION PREJUDICE

Another six-year-old said to Jason: 'You don't have a mother; you're adopted.' Jason did not say anything. His teacher overheard the conversation and said, 'Why do you think he doesn't have a mother? Who do you think is standing outside waiting to take him home?'

Doesn't have a mother. . . adopted. The words ring in your ears. Jason's teacher handled the situation by stepping in and speaking out. She also called Jason's mother and asked her to bring in a book about adoption for the class to read. And Jason's mother also worked with him on a "cover story"—a simple, basic explanation about adoption.

Your family is likely to have such experiences. Elementary-school-aged children like Jason are often subjected to questions and outright teasing from their peers. After all, kids at this age are problem-solving and figuring out relationships, thinking about what sets some children apart from others. As part of *their* development, they're checking out the idea of adoption.

H. David Kirk reported in the provocative *Shared Fate*, published in 1964, that more than half of the adopters he surveyed had encountered the following statements:

- Isn't it wonderful of you to have taken this child? (92%)
- This child looks so much like you he (she) could be your own (92%)
- He (she) is certainly lucky to have you for parents (87%)
- Tell me, do you know anything about this child's background? (82%)
- He (she) is a darling baby, and after all, you never know for sure how even your own will turn out (55%)[29]

Kirk includes the story of one couple who returned their questionnaire with the note "You will probably be amused to know that when I first scanned your questionnaire I found these questions anachronistic. Adoptions, I said to myself, are accepted in our community. Those questions are not in good taste or ever asked. Yet when my wife and I carefully reviewed them I was surprised that we had been asked at least five of them."

These questions and others are still being asked. In a 1997 study of Americans' attitudes about adoption, half of the respondents believed that adopting was "better than being childless, but it is not as good as having one's own child."[30]

Has someone referred to your child's birth parents as the "natural" parents or "real" parents? Does that make you "unnatural" or "unreal" or "not his mother"? If you have children by birth, how do people refer to them? Are they your "real" children or "your own" as distinguished from your "adopted children?" When people use phrases to describe adoption that you don't like, tell them. Often they are just repeating what they've grown up hearing. They may not be aware of the implications of their remarks, nor the alternatives like "birth mother" and "birth father."

While it is often difficult to come up with a tart retort to an impertinent question, there *are* some rejoinders that you can try. To the person who asks about your child's background, Holly van Gulden suggests rattling off the entire family's background in great detail, starting with your grandparents or further back. Counsels van Gulden: "By the time you get to the child in question, the asker will either have gotten the message or become bored or irritated with the answer." If you're asked "When did you get him or Where did you get him," talk about the present—"We just came from school." As for the question, "How much did she cost," try turning the question around and inquire about the questioner's child or grandchild. That, advises van Gulden, is a helpful technique to deal with intrusive questions.[31]

THE QUESTIONS YOUR CHILD MAY BE ASKED

Out of your earshot your child is likely to handle his peers' awkward questions about adoption. Social worker Ronny Diamond of Spence-Chapin Services to Families and Children in New York, who leads workshops for youngsters, offered some examples in *Adoptive Families* magazine of the questions kids report encountering and some of their solutions:[32]

"Does it feel weird to be adopted?"

The sarcastic answer: "Does it feel weird not to be adopted?"

"Why didn't your real parents keep you?"

The humorous retort: "Do you think my parents are fake?"

"Is that your real brother?"

The response that says little: "Would we fight like this if we weren't really brothers?"

Or the direct answer "He's my brother through adoption, but we weren't born from the same parents."

◆

Diamond says that kids are most comfortable giving open, honest answers when they feel close to the question or the kid senses that the inquisitor is genuinely curious.

RACIAL PREJUDICE

In addition to coping with our society's sometimes thoughtless attitudes about adoption, some adoptees must also confront the prejudices that people may hold against their ethnic group. "I can recall being teased constantly about my slanted eyes and flat little nose. I even heard the words 'chop chop' and 'aw so' and all the degrading rhymes associated with Orientals," recalled one adult Korean adoptee.[33]

Adoption therapist van Gulden cautions that parents of transracially adopted children must be especially sensitive to the racial prejudices that their children may encounter. Even preschoolers, says van Gulden, "know that there are differences and can tell the hierarchical differences in our society." Within the community, school, and perhaps within their own family, they may hear racial slurs, or at least unfeeling comments about different groups. At school a child may refuse to play with your child or even to hold your child's hand because he's been told to stay away from those "chinks." One parent tells the story of the day when her son, a black Amerasian, excitedly invited a girl to his junior prom. The girl, a close school friend, eagerly accepted. Three days later, however, she declined the invitation because "my dad won't let me go out with blacks." Imagine if this were your child. Or consider the experience of a Korean adoptee who has been active in her Jewish youth group:

> *I was adopted from South Korea when I was nine months old and really do feel wholly 'American,' although I suppose it is odd to see an Asian girl at temple. I don't mind questioning, but sometimes people have been inquisitive to the point of being rude or pushy. This feeling was magnified into a queer kind of self-consciousness in Israel, where I actually got blunt stares and some, not really insulting, but quite ignorant com-*

ments. At the end of the trip one of my counselors even admitted to me that he had never met an Asian before and was actually scared of me when he first met me.

This adoptee handled the incidents when they came up and didn't reveal the details to her parents until she discussed adoption in a college application essay.

HELPING CHILDREN BUILD THEIR SPECIAL IDENTITIES

I wish that I was white because everybody else in this family is white.

Barbara's four-year-old Chinese daughter told her this as she stared at the white, blond, blue-eyed child on the Cheerios box. Had Barbara failed as a mother? Was her daughter seriously disturbed? If you look at the daughter's situation from her vantage point, her comment shouldn't stun you. Young children want to be like the adults around them, so it's natural for Barbara's daughter to wish that she looked like the rest of her family. Most of her friends probably look like their parents (and she's probably heard comments about her cousins like "Oh, he's got the Jones family nose"). Why shouldn't she want this? Children at whatever age do not like difference. Said one transracially adopted black youth: "It's hard enough growing up. Growing up as a black child in a white family is harder. Being 'other' isn't funny."[34]

"The history of oppression and discrimination that black Americans have had to endure requires that white parents adopting a black American child must make sustained efforts to understand what their child may come up against outside the home," note Judith Schaffer and Christina Lindstrom in

How to Raise an Adopted Child.[35] They must be prepared for racial slurs, stares from strangers when the family is out together, and shopkeepers who keep close tabs on them in stores. At an adoption conference a panel of black adolescent adoptees who had been raised by white parents discussed their feelings about transracial adoption. They felt that families who chose to adopt transracially should live in integrated neighborhoods and participate in interracial groups. The parents should have black friends and help the child explore the richness of the black community and his black heritage. The adoptee should be able to spend time with other adopted children, particularly with others who are growing up in racially heterogeneous families. Parents and children must talk about how it feels to be black in a white family.

Families with children adopted from Asia or Latin America also need to consider issues of identity. In its adoption literature Holt International Children's Services has touched on how children may feel growing up in an interracial home:[36]

- *Preschool Years.* The people he loves the most look different from him. It will be natural for him to want to resemble those he loves, or else understand why he is different, and to learn that difference is not a bad thing.
- *School Age.* The child will need help in understanding his heritage and background so he can explain and feel comfortable about his status with his pals. He needs to be able to answer their questions: "What are you?"
- *Adolescence.* This is the time he tries to figure out "Who am I?" Curiosity about his original parents or background may become stronger. We share with adoptive families everything that is known to us about the child. At best the information on family background is limited, and for abandoned children there is none. The child will need

help in accepting this lack of factual information. Questions about dating arise, and you should look at your community and try to guess how many of your friends or neighbors would wholeheartedly accept their children dating your child. How would you feel if your child developed a special interest in his homeland, identified himself as a foreigner, and got involved in a group for Asian, Indian, black, or Latin American teens, or wanted to visit his original country?

- *Moving into Adulthood.* "Whom will I marry?" This is sometimes a different answer than "Whom will I date?" as dating is not seen as serious or permanent. Do you have an idea now that your child would probably marry a white person, or a person of his own background? Why? Would you recommend for or against an interracial marriage for your child?

Transracially adopted children who grow up in small communities can feel particularly isolated. "I spoke, ate, lived American," recalled a nineteen-year-old Californian who was adopted when she was two years old, "but I definitely looked Korean. This had bothered me since I was a little girl."[37] To help their children feel less isolated, some parent groups around the U.S. hold summer culture camps for younger foreign-born adoptees. At these camps children can learn about their birth country and meet with other adoptees. Holt International Children's Services of Oregon, for example, runs sleepover Heritage Camps in Oregon and New Jersey for youngsters aged nine to fifteen years old. The counselors are older adoptees, and they share their experiences of growing up adopted. "At Holt Camp, adoptees learn to feel good about Korea," says Susan Soon Keum Cox. "They recognize how they are part of the global community." And what do the kids think? Camp, enthused one ten-year-old, "was a fun experience with lots of activities. Good food and nice counselors. You cook traditional Korean dishes and get to taste them. There's fan dancing and tae kwon do. You learn and sing songs. You learn Korean art and culture. You get to meet other Koreans and children of your heritage."

If you're interested in having your child participate in a camp, or starting one in your area, check with **Adoptive Families of America** (see appendix A) for information on where camps are held. Several adoption agencies also sponsor "motherland" tours for older teens and adult adoptees, and "family tours" for parents and younger adoptees. On Holt's Motherland Tour, for example, participants spend time in South Korea at Holt's Il San Center, sightsee around the country, look in their files at the agency, meet with Korean families—and sometimes reunite with members of their birth family. "Everything I saw and experienced, heard and tasted, felt and smelled," wrote one adoptee afterwards, "served to be the sources to gain the knowledge and pride I had so badly desired."[38] If you're interested in this type of travel experience, check with the intercountry adoption agency that placed your child, as well as Adoptive Families of America.

SEARCH AND REUNION

Some adoptees' need for information goes beyond their desire to know as much factual information as possible about their birth families. It evolves into a need to search out and arrange for a meeting with their birth parents, birth siblings, and other members of their birth families. Says adoption expert Linda Yellin: "A lot of search is dealing with unfinished business. Reunion allows the reworking of many issues."

ETHNIC DOLLS

How about an ethnic doll for your child? "When children are able to see dolls that have a similar ethnicity to them, or just see dolls of diverse ethnicity, they can identify a lot better," says Dr. Michael J. Barnes, a clinical psychologist at Hofstra University who has looked at the impact of white dolls on black children. "They are able to see the world in the pluralistic way it is."[39] You can find black, Hispanic, and Asian versions of dolls, including realistic-looking baby dolls. Check with your specialty toy store or with your department store about their selections. You might also enjoy looking at Loretta Holtz's *How-to Book of International Dolls*. This heavily illustrated book surveys dolls around the world and is filled with information about costumes, crafts, traditions, and holidays. Holtz discusses, for example, the bread-dough dolls of Ecuador and the chain-stitch dolls of Peru, and shows you how to create your own.

Although many adoptive parents are comfortable with their childrens' need to search, others fear that their children are seeking to forge new families centering on their birth parents. They may see the search as a rejection, as a symbol of their failure as parents. If those are your fears, consider the words of Jean A. Strauss in *Birthright: The Guide to Search and Reunion for Adoptees, Birthparents, and Adoptive Parents*:[40]

There are adoptees who never feel they fit into their selected families, but I always felt I belonged, wholly and completely. The fact that I was not "born" of Betty and Lou seemed to be of no significance to me. I never found them lacking as parents because we didn't share the same DNA codes. They were my parents and I was their daughter.

Why did I feel I had to search? If I was so comfortable with my parents and with my childhood, why would I pursue such a quest? The reality for me was that I was never looking for parents. I was looking for answers. There was an empty chamber in my mind full of question marks. My curiosity changed as I grew older, until I no longer just wanted to know about my origins, I had to and needed to find answers.

At the time I felt that I was searching for three reasons: I was curious, and believed my origins were my business—my birthright. I wanted to learn my medical history. And lastly, I felt a strong urge to contact the woman who had given birth to me. I felt she deserved to know I had survived childhood, to know I was happy and doing well. I wanted her to know she had done the right thing. Somehow, I was sure she needed to know.

Birth parents, also, are clear that they don't seek to replace the adoptive parents. Says Diane whose daughter, Laurie, found her twenty-five years after placement: "I'm coming in with a clean slate. I can talk to Laurie a lot more comfortably about things than the girls I raised because we didn't go through the traumatic high school years together. To come in and say to her adoptive mother 'you did a good job and now I want to be her mother,' is very presumptuous." For Diane, Laurie "is this grown-up adult friend of mine, this really good friend."

Meeting birth parents may, in fact, lead to stronger bonds between the adoptee and his adoptive parents. Arthur D. Sorosky, Annette Baran, and Reuben Pannor claimed in *The Adoption Triangle* that most adoptees emerged from the search and reunion experience with "a deeper sense of their love and appreciation for their adoptive parents, whom they viewed as their true 'psychological' parents."[41]

Just as there are adoptive-parent groups, there are adoptee support groups. These groups provide both expertise and emotional support, and your family will want to link up with one of them. To find local groups, or to get more information about search issues, you can contact the **American Adoption Congress;** the **Adoptees' Liberty Movement Association**; and **Concerned United Birthparents** (see Appendix A). The **National Adoption Information Clearinghouse** can also provide you with information. The **International Soundex Reunion Registry** lists birth parents, adoptees, and other family members willing to exchange information. Write to them (enclosing a self-addressed, stamped envelope) to learn the details about registration. To help clarify issues, take a look at Jayne Askin's *Search,* Betty Jean Lifton's *Lost and Found*, Sorosky, Baran, and Pannor's *The Adoption Triangle*, and Strauss's *Birthright* (see appendix C for details of these and related titles).

What should you do if your adult son or daughter expresses a desire to search? If honesty has been the cornerstone in building your family, you should share whatever information you have. If you have not previously contacted the agency or the person who handled the adoption, then you will want to help your son or daughter do so now. By writing to your state's Bureau of Vital Statistics, you may be able to obtain additional birth data. If there is a state mutual consent adoption registry that matches identifying information of adoptee and birth parents, encourage your child to register. While these registries are not always effective, in some states they are one of the few routes available. *If the state registry requires your signature to release records, be sure you give your permission.*

Should your response be different if your school-aged child or teenager expresses a desire to search for information about his birth family? Curiosity about birth parents is normal, report researchers at the Search Institute in Minneapolis. In their study of adopted teens they found that 40 percent of the adolescents wanted to know more about their birth history, 55 percent wanted to know more about their birth mother, 46 percent about their birth father, and 65 percent said that they would like to meet their birth parents. Their reasons: to find out what they look like (94 percent), to tell them I'm happy (80 percent), to tell them I'm OK (76 percent), to tell them I'm glad to be alive (73 percent) and to find out why I was adopted (72 percent). "Finding their birth parents—either discovering more information about them or actually making direct contact—can be an enormous relief for a teenager," counsels David Brodzinsky and his coauthors in *Being Adopted*. "A search can help simplify the adolescent's task of separating from the family."[42] The search can take many forms—going back to old agency files, learning more about the place where your child was born, making a pilgrimage to the birthplace or country. Some clinicians even advocate an "imaginary search" where the teenager writes letters to the birth parent and then writes the responses—a process that allows youngsters to think about their birth families and express their feelings about adoption.[43]

In *Gift Children,* Douglas Bates recounts the excitement his family experienced when they journeyed to Yakima, Washington, to search out additional information for their grown daughter Liska (born Tina Lynn Jackson), who had joined their family as a three-year-old after bouncing around foster homes. On microfilm they discovered a front-page article in the Yakima newspaper heralding their daughter's birth ("Miss Yakima county 1969—Nurse Mrs. Lester George holds the first baby born in a Yakima County hospital this year. . . . The little girl, Tina Lynn Jackson, weighed five pounds ten ounces at birth.") and a prominently displayed photo of the newborn. It was the family's first glimpse of baby Liska. "A couple of enormous teardrops landed on the photocopy as I finished reading it," Bates writes. "Liska was weeping so hard her body was shaking. . . . 'That's you, Liska,' I said. 'Now we know what you looked like as a baby. You were a cutie, weren't you.'" At the hospital Liska was treated as a celebrity; the hospital staff pinned her baby picture to a bulletin board chock-full of other Yakima Hospital babies and assembled a package of materials that included photos of the hospital from 1960 and of the physician who delivered her. The family visited the maternity ward, and Liska peered at the newborn visible through the nursery window: "Liska was silent as she resumed her stroll around the ward, a little subdued, pausing only once to say, softly, 'This is where I was born.'"[44]

What should you do if your youngster's search proceeds to a plan to meet his birth parents? If you've had indirect contact through letter-writing or an intermediary, or if you've updated information by recontacting the agency, it might be a natural step to move on to direct contact. If you are considering opening up an adoption, you will want to have some professional counseling. Cautions open-adoption expert Sharon Kaplan Roszia:

> *The older children are, the more we have to keep in mind that they too have a need for control in their lives and need to be involved in the process carefully. It's different for children who grow up knowing their birth parents than for children who suddenly have to make a major right-hand shift in life. I'm not saying 'don't do it,' but we need to be much more aware of the therapeutic issues involved.*

You may want to proceed gradually: communicating first by letter, then by telephone, and finally arranging a face-to-face meeting after everyone is comfortable. Beatrice, a birth mother whose fifteen-year-old daughter's adoptive parents initiated the opening up of the adoption through a search counselor, describes how complicated a dance it was for her as well:

> *The easiest way for me to deal with Wendy all those years was to make her a closed chapter in my life. What's made this slightly awkward for me is how I've dealt with it all these years. She's known that she was adopted from the beginning. She's been raised knowing about the adoption—all her friends and all of her family know that. Whereas none of mine do. I'm opening a whole new door in my life to everyone who knows me.*
>
> *I spent the year of 1987 getting to know the counselor, writing letters, and talking to Wendy's parents. Then I met Wendy. I didn't want my kids (who are younger than Wendy) to know anything about Wendy until I was sure that our relationship was going to grow rather than be a passing little thing. I didn't want to have* my *children get to know her and then be tossed aside. I didn't want my kids to be disappointed.*

Keep in mind that there may be some rough patches ahead as you all work out a relationship that's comfortable. Professional counseling is likely to ease the transition. Advises Patricia Martinez Dorner, who counsels on how to open an adoption: "People are re-entering each other's lives without a previous history of contact. They may have different communication styles, different values, different ways of looking at the world. They need to learn about each other and build trust."[45] For additional guidance, try Melina and Roszia's *The Open Adoption Experience*. Birth mother Jan L. Waldron's *Giving Away Simone* chronicles her delicate dance after she met the teenage daughter she had relinquished. In the years since their reunion, she writes:[46]

We have been inquisitors, we have searched and destroyed—each other and ourselves—for the answers that would make sense of a life's worth of missing, weaving in between our necessary truces until the next rueful outpouring, brittle silence, or giddy afternoon. And we love each other beyond speech—against a backdrop of doubt, across an unbridgeable distance. How do I answer the looming question she lives with: Why? And the doubt that nags me. What do I owe her, how do I give it?

Her daughter, Rebecca, has the last word:

Now, almost fifteen years after reuniting, Jan and I trust each other. Our love is finally kind. And the reasons for this are clear. We have created, through love and our struggle, a language for our relationship that was and continues to be desperately needed. Without language, there is no communication, and what cannot be communicated cannot exist.

This book began with information about how to get started on the road to adoptive parenthood and how to find the children who will complete your family. It has come full circle with information about seeking out birth parents.

Your family will have its own special history. As adoptive parents, we all share important rights and crucial responsibilities that we must exercise for the sake of our children. If this book has given you a clearer perspective on adoption today, and if it has set out some guideposts that will point you toward your own informed decisions, then it will have done its job.

APPENDIX A

GETTING ADVICE

The following organizations can answer questions about adoption and put you in touch with adoption agencies, parent groups, and other experts. Keep in mind that there are several hundred parent groups in the country.

Adopt a Special Kid (AASK) America, 1332 E Street NE, P.O. Box 77672, Washington, DC; (202) 396–2916. Special needs adoption.

Adoptees' Liberty Movement Association (ALMA), P.O. Box 727, Radio City Station, New York, NY 10101; (212) 581-1568. Search and support organization.

Adoption Exchange Association, 820 South Monaco Parkway, Suite 263, Denver, CO 80224; (303) 322–9592. Special needs adoption.

Adoptive Families of America, 2309 Como Avenue, St. Paul, MN 55108; (612) 645–9955 or (800) 372–3300 (http://www.adoptivefam.org). Adoption support organization.

American Academy of Adoption Attorneys, P.O. Box 33053, Washington, DC 20033–0053; (202) 832–2222. Membership organization of attorneys with an interest in adoption.

American Adoption Congress, 1000 Connecticut Avenue, NW, Washington, DC 20036; (202) 482–3399 (http://www.american-adoption-cong.org/). Educational network concerned with openness and honesty in adoption.

American Public Welfare Association, 810 First Street NE, Washington, DC 20002; (202) 682–0100 (http://www.apwa.org).

American Society for Reproductive Medicine, 1209 Montgomery Highway, Birmingham, AL 35216–2809; (205) 978–5000 (http://www.asrm.com). Infertility advice.

The **Centers for Disease Control,** in Atlanta, Georgia. Call toll free, (888) 232–3278 (http://www.cdc.gov)

Child Welfare League of America, 440 First Street NW, Washington, DC 20001; (202) 638–2952 (http://www.cwla.org). Social welfare organization concerned with setting standards for agencies, publishes the journal *Child Welfare*.

Children Awaiting Parents (CAP), 700 Exchange Street, Rochester, NY 14608; (716) 232–5110. National photolisting service; publishes *The CAP Book,* and an Internet photolisting service *Faces of Adoption* (for website and details see National Adoption Center).

Children with AIDS Project of America, 4141 West Bethany Home Road, Phoenix, AZ 85019; (602) 973–4319 (http://www.aidskids.org). Special needs adoption.

Concerned United Birthparents (CUB), 2000 Walker Street, Des Moines, IA 50317; (515) 263–9558 or (800) 822–2777. Nationwide support organization for birth parents.

Evan B. Donaldson Adoption Institute, 120 Wall Street, 20th Floor, New York, NY 10005; phone: (212) 269–5080; fax: (212) 260–1962; e-mail: geninfo@adoptioninstitute.org (http://www. adoptioninstitute.org). Focuses on research in adoption.

Families for Private Adoption, P.O. Box 6375, Washington, DC 20015; (202) 722–0338. Independent adoption support group.

Families for Russian and Ukrainian Adoption, P.O. Box 2944, Merrifield, VA 22116; (703) 560–6184 (http://www. frua.org). Intercountry adoptive parents' support group.

International Adoption Clinic, University of Minnesota, Box 211, 420 Delaware Street SE, Minneapolis, MN 55455; (612) 626–6777 or (800) 688–5252 (http://www. cyfc.umn.edu/Adoptinfo/iac.html). Medical advice for intercountry adoption.

International Concerns for Children, 911 Cypress Drive, Boulder, CO; (303) 494–3333 (http:/www.fortnet.org/icc). Intercountry adoption information.

International Soundex Reunion Registry, P.O. Box 2312, Carson City, NV 89702; (702) 882–7755 (http://www.okynsute.cin.isrr). Links adoptees with birth parents and other family members.

Joint Council on International Children's Services, 7 Cheverly Circle, Cheverly, MD 20785; (301) 322–1906 (http://www.jcics.org). Consortium of intercountry adoption agencies.

National Adoption Center, 1500 Walnut Street, Philadelphia, PA 19102; (215) 735–9988 or (800) TO ADOPT (http://www. adopt.org). Promoting special-needs adoption is a fundamental concern of the center, as is their adoption-in-the-workplace initiative. Publishes the Internet photolisting book *Faces of Adoption* in collaboration with Children Awaiting Parents (access via the NAC website or send e-mail to nac@adopt.org).

National Adoption Foundation, 100 Mill Plain Road, Danbury, CT 06811; (203) 791–3811. Focuses on the finances of adoption.

National Adoption Information Clearinghouse, 330 C Street S.W., Washington, DC 20447; (703) 352–3488 or (888) 251–0075 (http://www.calib.com/naic). Just what the name says—a clearinghouse providing free adoption publications and other services. A one-stop service that can't be beat for referrals.

National Association for Families and Addiction Research and Education, 200 Michigan Avenue, Suite 300, Chicago, IL 60601; (800) 638-2229. Special needs children.

National Council for Single Adoptive Parents, P.O. Box 15084, Chevy Chase, MD 20825; (202) 966–6367 (http://www.adopting.org/ncsap.html). Clearinghouse for information for singles interested in adoption.

National Federation for Open Adoption Education, 391 Taylor Boulevard, Pleasant Hill, CA 94523; (510) 827–2229. Organization that promotes the practice of open adoption.

National Foster Parent Association, Information and Service Office, 9 Dartmoor Drive, Crystal Lake, IL 60014; (800) 557–5238 or (815) 455–2527 (http://kidsource.com). Support organization for foster parents.

National Resource Center for Special Needs Adoption, 16250 Northland Drive, Southfield, MI 48075; (248) 443–7080. Offers advice on special-needs adoption.

North American Council on Adoptable Children (NACAC), 970 Raymond Avenue, St. Paul, MN 55114–1149; (612) 644–3036 (http://members.aol.com/nacac). Adoption advocacy organization, composed of parent groups and individuals, promotes special-needs adoption and reform in adoption policies.

Office of Children's Issues, Bureau of Consular Affairs of the U.S. State Department, phone: (202) 736–7000 or (202) 647–3444; automated fax: (202) 647–3000 (reached by dialing from your fax machine); and website: http://travel.state.gov.

One Church, One Child, 2811-2-E Industrial Plaza Drive, Tallahassee, FL 32301; (904) 488–8251. Promotes the adoption of black children.

Resolve, 1310 Broadway, Somerville, MA 02144–1731; (617) 623–1156 (http://www.resolve.org). Provides infertility counseling and referral services for infertility and adoption.

RESOURCES ON THE INTERNET

Using computer links you can send messages to an adoption e-mail pal, request further information, download applications, fill out forms, and do a variety of other tasks that you might accomplish through telephone, letter, or fax communication.

Using one of the search engines (Yahoo!, AltaVista, Infoseek), type in keywords such as adoption, intercountry+adoption, foster+care, or open+adoption, and glean hundreds of websites touching on your subject.

The search engine Yahoo! can lead you to adoption classified advertisements (http://www.yahoo.com/Business and Economy/Classifieds/Adoption/Seeking to Adopt).

Keep in mind that *privacy is not guaranteed on the Internet*. When you provide your name, address, and other details about yourself, there is no guarantee that the information will not be shared with others.

For a printed source of information that includes government sites as well as support groups and agencies, see the *Adoption Guide to the Internet,* produced by the **National Adoption Information Clearinghouse** (http://www.calib.com/naic).

APPENDIX B

ADOPTION DIRECTORY

A STATE-BY-STATE GUIDE

This list gives basic information about adoption in each of the states and the District of Columbia. It is derived, primarily, from information gathered by the National Adoption Information Clearinghouse (see Appendix A) and published in its *National Adoption Directory* (December 1997). I have edited the data into my own format and dropped several categories, including a county-by-county listing of public agencies and a state-by-state listing of adoptive parent groups. The Clearinghouse updates its comprehensive directory twice a year. You can obtain an updated, complete version by requesting a copy ($25) in book form or on computer disc. The Clearinghouse will also provide you with free information about individual states.

This directory includes information about agency adoption (public and private) and independent adoption. I start with the state agency that oversees adoptions in your state. You'll probably want to begin, however, by contacting the county, district, regional, or city agency that is the local representative of the state office. This agency is usually listed under "Adoption" or "Child Welfare" or "Public Welfare" or "Social Services" in your telephone book and has children to place. Your state agency can answer your questions about adoption in your state and, in some states, may be eager to provide you with information. Its staff can also tell you about your state's adoption registry (listed below) and what steps adult adoptees, adoptive parents, and birth parents must take to request information from adoption records.

The state adoption exchanges do not place children but do help waiting parents find waiting children. You, or your worker, can contact them. Check to see if you can list your family with them. The state exchanges often function as the "adoption information centers" for the state and will try to answer questions, even if you are not thinking about a special-needs adoption. Those states that do not have their own exchanges often list children with the regional exchanges. If you find that you are having trouble getting help at the state level, you may want to contact the regional exchange. Find out also if you can list your family with the regional exchange.

This directory also indicates whether independent adoption is permitted in a state. For more complete information about independent adoption, contact the National Adoption Information Clearinghouse. In some states independent adoption is legal, but using an intermediary to make a link or to maintain confidentiality between the birth parents and the adoptive parents is not. Remember also that state regulations about independent adoption are often revised, so you'll want to check with local authorities. Many states will also permit identified adoption, also known as designated adoption, if independent adoptions are restricted or not permitted. Some states will permit newspaper advertising, others will not.

Finally, this directory lists private agencies in each state that are involved in adoption. Remember, some agencies place children of all ages; some have specialties. Some agencies will have geographic or religious restrictions; others will not. Start with your local or neighboring agencies, but if you need to, don't hesitate to check with other agencies in your state, or possibly out-of-state. Agencies that have been involved with intercountry adoptions are designated by an asterisk (*).

A few cautionary notes from the National Adoption Information Clearinghouse's directory bear repeating here:

> *The National Adoption Information Clearinghouse has collected information on licensed adoption agencies. . . as a service to the adoption community. We cannot vouch for the services provided by these agencies or individuals. It is always advisable to get recommendations from former clients of the agency or individuals before making any financial commitment. . . .*
>
> *Prospective adoptive parents should check with the State licensing specialist on the status of an agency before dealing with the agency. We recommend that once prospective adoptive parents narrow down to 1–2 agencies they want to work with, they should contact the state attorney general's office to see if there are complaints on file regarding agencies they are considering.*

Although this directory strives to be comprehensive and up-to-date, keep in mind that state agencies reorganize, shuffle personnel, and change their telephone numbers. Laws concerning adoption change, and local agencies may move or change their programs. Agency license status can change. Since the primary source for the data in this directory came from a published source in December 1997, you may want to double check the information with the appropriate telephone information service before you place your call or write your letter.

Some of the sources listed in this directory can be contacted by e-mail and have Internet addresses and websites. I have not listed those addresses, but you may want to check for them using Internet search engines.

A little persistence pays off. And don't hesitate to turn to others for advice. There's a wealth of material at your fingertips.

ALABAMA

State Agency: Adult, Child, & Family Services Division, Department of Human Resources, 50 North Ripley Street, Montgomery, AL 36130–4000; (334) 242–9500

State Exchange: Alabama Adoption Resource Exchange (see above)

Independent Adoption: Permitted

Private Agencies

Alabama Baptist Children's Home, P.O. Box 19792, Birmingham, AL 35219; (205) 945–0037

Alabama Baptist Children's Home and Family Ministry, P.O. Box 429, Troy, AL 36081; (334) 566–2840

Association for Guidance, Aid, Placement, and Empathy, (AGAPE), 2733 Mastin Lake Road NW, Huntsville, AL 35810; (205) 859–4481

Association for Guidance, Aid, Placement, and Empathy (AGAPE), 6300 Airport Road, Mobile, AL 36685; (334) 343–4875

Association for Guidance, Aid, Placement, and Empathy (AGAPE), P.O. Box 230472, Montgomery, AL 36123; (334) 272–9466

Catholic Family Center of Concern, 1010 Church Street NW, Huntsville, AL 35801; (205) 536–0041

Catholic Family Services, 2164 11th Avenue South, Birmingham, AL 35205; (205) 324–6561

Catholic Family Services, 733 37th Street East, Tuscaloosa, AL 35405; (205) 533–9045

Catholic Social Services, P.O. Box 759, Mobile, AL 36601; (334) 438–1603

Catholic Social Services, 4455 Narrow Lane Road, Montgomery, AL 36116–2953; (334) 288–8890

*Children of the World, 201 Oswalt Street, Fairhope, AL 36562; (334) 928–5597

Children's Aid Society, Birmingham, AL 35222; (205) 251–7148

Family Adoption Services, 631 Beacon Parkway West, Birmingham, AL 35209; (205) 290–0077

Lifeline Children's Services, 2908 Pumphouse Road, Birmingham, AL 35243; (205) 967–0919

Special Beginnings Adoptions, 600 Azalea Road, Mobile, AL 36609; (334) 666–0747

United Methodist Children's Home, P.O. Box 859, Selma, AL 36702; (334) 875–7283

*Villa Hope International Adoption, 6 Office Park Circle, Birmingham, AL 35223; (205) 870–7359

ALASKA

State Agency: Department of Health & Social Services, P.O. Box 110630, Juneau, AK 99811–0630; (907)–465–3631

State Exchange: Northwest Adoption Exchange, 1809 Seventh Avenue, Seattle, WA 98101; (206)–292–0092

State Photolisting Book: See above

Independent Adoption: Permitted

State Reunion Registry: None

Private Agencies

*Adoption Advocates International, 218 Martin Drive, Fairbanks, AK 99712; (907) 457–3832

*Catholic Social Services, 3710 E 20th, Anchorage, AK 99508 (907) 276–5590

*Fairbanks Counseling and Adoption, 753 Gaffney Road, Box 71544, Fairbanks, AK 99707; (907) 456–4729

Kawerak Adoption Agency, P.O. Box 948, Nome, AK 99762; (907) 443–5231

*Western Association of Concerned Adoptive Parents (WACAP), P.O. Box 81865, Fairbanks, AK 99708; (907) 479–2895

ARIZONA

State Agency: Department of Economic Security, P.O. Box 6123, Phoenix, AZ 85005; 602–542–2359

State Exchange: Arizona Adoption Exchange Book, c/o Arizona Families for Children, P.O. Box 17951, Tucson, AZ 85731; (520) 327–3324

State Confidential Intermediary Service: Arizona Confidential Intermediary Program, Arizona Supreme Court, 1501 W. Washington, Phoenix, AZ 85007; (602) 542–9580

Independent Adoption: Permitted

Private Agencies

Adoption Care Center, 8233 Via Paseo Del Norte, Scottsdale, AZ 85258; (602) 922–8838

Aid to Adoption of Special Kids (AASK) of Arizona, 501 E. Thomas Road, Phoenix, AZ 85012; (602) 254–2275

*Arizona Children's Association, 2700 S. Eighth Avenue, Tucson, AZ 85713; (520) 622–7611

Arizona Family Adoptive Services, 346 East Palm Lane, Phoenix, AZ 85004–1531; (602) 254–2271

Birth Hope Adoption Agency, 3225 N. Central, Phoenix, AZ 85012; (602) 277–2860

Black Family and Children Services, 2323 N. Third Street, Phoenix, AZ 85004; (602) 256–2948.

Catholic Community Services of Western Arizona, 690 E. 32nd, Yuma, AZ 85365; (520) 341–9400

Catholic Social Services of East Valley, 18 E. University, Mesa, AZ 85201; (602) 964–8771

Catholic Social Services of Flagstaff, 201 W. University Drive, Flagstaff, AZ 86001; (520) 774–9125

*Catholic Social Services of Phoenix, 1825 W. Northern Avenue, Phoenix, AZ 85021; (602) 997–6105

*Catholic Social Services of Tucson, 155 W. Helen, Tucson, AZ 85703–5746; (520) 623–0344

*Catholic Social Services of Yavapai, 116 N. Summitt, Prescott, AZ 86301; (520) 778–2531

Christian Family Care Agency, 3603 N. Seventh Avenue, Phoenix, AZ 85013–3638; (602) 234–1935

*Commonwealth Adoptions International, Inc., 4601 E. Ft. Lowell, Tucson, AZ 85712;(520) 327–7574

*Dillon Southwest, 3014 N. Hayden Road, Scottsdale, AZ 85251; (602) 945–2221

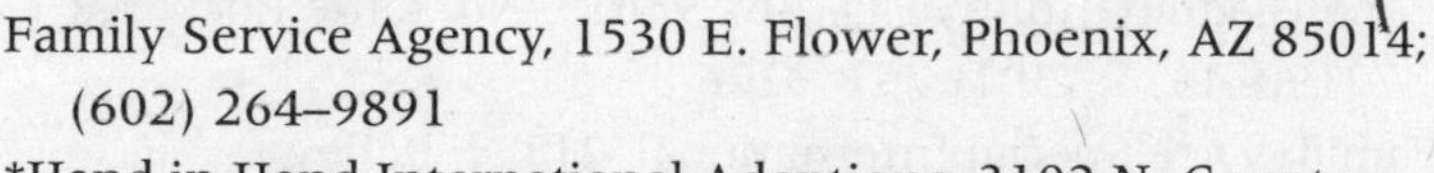

Family Service Agency, 1530 E. Flower, Phoenix, AZ 85014; (602) 264–9891

*Hand in Hand International Adoptions, 3102 N. Country Club, Tucson, AZ 85716; (520) 743–3322

LDS Social Services, P.O. Box 856, Snowflake, AZ 85937; (520) 536–4117

LDS Social Services, 5049 E. Broadway Boulevard, Tucson, AZ 85711; (520) 745–6459

LDS Social Services, 235 S. El Dorado, Mesa, AZ 85202; (602) 968–2995

Lutheran Social Ministry of the Southwest, 919 N. First Street, Phoenix, AZ 85004; (602) 258–7201

*One-World Adoption Services, 8260 E. Raintree Drive, Scottsdale, AZ 85260; (602) 567–1232

ARKANSAS

State Agency: Department of Human Services, P.O. Box 1437, Slot 808, Little Rock, AR 72203; (501) 682–8462.

State Exchange: See above

State Reunion Registry: Arkansas Mutual Consent Voluntary Adoption Registry, P.O. Box 1437, Slot 808, Little Rock, AR 72203–1437; (501) 682–8462

Independent Adoption: Permitted

Private Agencies

*Adoption Services, Inc., 2415 N. Tyler, Little Rock, AR 72207; (501) 664–0340

*Bethany Christian Services, 1100 N. University Avenue, Little Rock, AR 72207–6344; (501) 664–5729

Children's Home, Inc., Church of Christ, 1502 E. Kiehl Avenue, Sherwood, AR 72120; (501) 835–1595

Children's Home, Inc., Church of Christ, 5515 Old Walcott Road, Paragould, AR 72450; (870) 239–4031

*Edna Gladney Home, P.O. Box 94615, No. Little Rock, AR 72190–4615; (501) 791–3126

*Families Are Special International, 213 N. Bailey, Jacksonville, AR 72076; (501) 985–0172

Highlands Child Placement Services, P.O. Box 300198, Kansas City, MO 64130–0198; (816) 924–6565

*Holt International Children Services (*see* Oregon)

LDS Social Services of Oklahoma (*see* Oklahoma)

Searcy Children's Home, Church of Christ, 900 N. Main Street, Searcy, AR 72143; (501) 268–5383

*Small Miracles International (*see* Oklahoma)

Southern Christian Home, P.O. Box 556, Morrilton, AR 72110; (501) 354–2428

Volunteers of America (*see* Louisiana)

CALIFORNIA

State Agency: Adoptions Branch, Department of Social Services, 744 P Street, Sacramento, CA 95814; (916) 445–3146 or (800) 543–7487

State Exchange: California Waiting Children-Photolisting Service (see above)

State Reunion Registry: Mutual Consent Registry, California Department of Social Services, Adoption Systems Unit, 744 P. Street, M.S. 19–31, Sacramento, CA 95814; (916) 322–3778

Independent Adoption: Permitted

Private Agencies

*ACCEPT, 339 S. San Antonio Road, Los Altos, CA 94022; (650) 917–8090

Across the World Adoptions, 399 Taylor Boulevard, Pleasant Hill, CA 94523; (510) 356–6260 or (800) 610–5607

Adopt a Special Kid (AASK) of California, 287 17th Street, Oakland, CA 94612; (510) 451–1748

*Adopt International, 121 Springdale Way, Redwood City, CA 94062; (650) 369–7300

*Adopt International–East Bay Office, 5927 College Avenue, Oakland, CA 94618; (510) 683–8600 or (800) 610–5607

Adoption Advocates, 795 Farmers Lane, Santa Rosa, CA 95405; (707) 575–8201

Adoption Center, 15450 Ventura Boulevard, Encino, CA 91403–3000; (818) 789–3477 or (800) 637–7999

Adoption Connection, Jewish Family and Children Services, 3272 California Street, San Francisco, CA 94118; (415) 202–7494

*Adoption Horizons, 302 Fourth Street, 2nd Floor, Eureka, CA 95501–0302; (707) 444–9909 or (800) 682–3678

*Adoption Options, Inc., 5101 Glen Verde Drive, Bonita, CA 91902–2625; (619) 267–4090

*Adoption Services International, 2021 Sperry Avenue, Ventura, CA 93003; (805) 644–3067

*Adoptions Unlimited, 11800 Central Avenue, Chino, CA 91710; (909) 902–1412

Alternative Family Services Adoption Agency, 25 Division Street, San Francisco, CA 94103; (415) 626–2700

*Bal Jagat Children's World, Inc., 9311 Farralone Avenue, Chatsworth, CA 91311; (818) 709–4737

*Bay Area Adoption Services, Inc., 465 Fairchild Drive, Mountain View, CA 94043; (650) 964–3800

*Bethany Christian Services, Inc., 14125 Telephone Avenue, Chino, CA 91710–5771; (909) 465–0057

*Bethany Christian Services Northern Region, 3048 Hahn Drive, Modesto, CA 95350–6503; (209) 522–5121

*Bethany Christian Services Southern Region, 11929 Woodruff Avenue, Downey, CA 90241–5601; (562) 803–3454

Better Life Children Services, 1337 Howe Avenue, Sacramento, CA 95825; (916) 641–0661

Black Adoption Placement and Research Center, 1801 Harrison Street, 2nd Floor, Oakland, CA 94612; (510) 839–3678

Black Adoption Placement and Research Center, 508 Couch Street, Vallejo, CA 94590; (707) 552–3658

Catholic Charities Adoption Agency, 349 Cedar Street, San Diego, CA 92101–3197; (619) 231–2828

*Catholic Charities of the Archdiocese of San Francisco, 814 Mission Street, 5th Floor, San Francisco, CA 94103; (415) 778–6111

Children's Bureau of Los Angeles, 3910 Oakwood Avenue, Los Angeles, CA 90004; (213) 953–7356. There are several district offices as well.

*Children's Home Society of California, Regional Office, 300 S. Sycamore Street, Santa Ana, CA 92701–5792; (714) 542–1147

Children's Service Bureau, 6950 Levant Street, San Diego, CA 92111; (619) 565–3011

Christian Adoption and Family Services, 1698 Greenbriar Lane, Brea, CA 92821; (714) 529–2949

*Chrysalis House, 2134 W. Alluvial Avenue, Fresno, CA 93711; (209) 432–7170

Families First, 2100 5th Street, Davis, CA 95616; (916) 753–0220. There is also a Hercules office, (510) 741–3100.

Families for Children, 3650 Auburn Boulevard, Sacramento, CA 95821; (916) 974–8744

Family Builders by Adoption, 528 Grand Avenue, Oakland, CA 94610; (510) 272–0204

*Family Connections, P.O. Box 576035, Modesto, CA 95367–6035; (209) 869–8844. There are several branch offices.

*The Family Network, Inc., 307 Webster Street, Monterey, CA 93940; (408) 655–5077

Future Families, Inc., 3233 Valencia Avenue, Suite A–6, Aptos, CA 95003; (408) 662–0202

*God's Children International Adoption Agency, 19389 Live Oak Canyon Road, Trabuco Canyon, CA 92679; (714) 858–7621

Guadalupe Homes Adoption Agency, Suite 455, 1111 Howe Avenue, Sacramento, CA 95825; (916) 646–1256

*Hand in Hand Foundation, 2401 Robertson Road, Soquel, CA 95073; (408) 476–1866

*Heartsent Adoptions, Inc., 6 Oak Lane, Orinda, CA 94563; (510) 254–8883

*Help the Children, Inc., Suite 2, 1350 W. Robinhood Drive, Stockton, CA 95207–5512; (209) 478–5585

*Holt International Children's Services, 3807 Pasadena Avenue, Suite 170, Sacramento, CA 95821; (916) 487–4658

*Holy Family Services—Counseling and Adoption, 1403 S. Main Street, Santa Ana, CA 92707–1790; (714) 835–5551. There are offices in San Bernardino (909) 885–4882 and Pasadena, (626) 432–5686.

Holygrove Foster Care, 815 N. El Centro, Los Angeles, CA 90038.

Independent Adoption Center Central Office, Headquarters, 391 Taylor Boulevard, Suite 100, Pleasant Hill, CA 94523; (510) 827–2229 or (800) 877–6736. There are branch offices in Sacramento, Los Angeles, and Santa Clara.

Indian Child and Family Services, P.O. Box 2269, Temecula, CA 92593; (909) 676–8832 or (800) 969–4237

Infant of Prague, 6059 N. Palm Avenue, Fresno, CA 93704; (209) 447–3333

Institute for Black Parenting, 9920 La Cienega Boulevard, Suite 806, Inglewood, CA 90301; (310) 348–1400 or (800) 367–8858. There is another office in Riverside (714) 782–2800.

*International Christian Adoptions, 41745 Rider Way, #2, Temecula, CA 92590; (909) 695–3336

Kinship Center, 507 E. First Street, Suite D, Tustin, CA 92780; (714) 544–7646. There is another office in Monterey (408) 649–3033.

LDS Social Services—California North Agency, Fresno Office, 1425 N. Rabe Avenue, Suite 101, Fresno, CA 93727; (209) 255–1446. There are offices in San Jose (408) 243–1688, Concord (510) 685–2941, and Colton (909) 824–0480.

LDS Social Services—California South Agency, Fountain Valley Office, 17350 Mt. Herrmann Circle, Fountain Valley, CA 92708; (714) 444–3463. There are offices in Van Nuys (818) 781–5511, Citrus Heights (916) 725–5032, and San Diego (619) 467–9170.

*Life Adoption Services, 440 W. Main Street, Tustin, CA 92680; (714) 838–5433

Lilliput Children's Services, 1455 Response Road, Suite 210, Sacramento, CA 95814–4849; (916) 923–5444. There are offices in Stockton (209) 943–0530 and San Leandro (510) 483–2030.

Los Angeles Orphan's Home, 1200 E. Alosta Avenue, Glendora, CA 91740–6360.

Mooretown Rancheria, 1 Alverda Drive, Oroville, CA 95966–9379; (916) 533–3625

*North Bay Adoptions, 862 Third Street, Santa Rosa, CA 95404; (707) 570–2940

*Partners for Adoption, 4527 Montgomery Drive, Suite A, Santa Rosa, CA 95409; (707) 539–9068

*Sierra Adoption Services, 117 New Mohawk Road, Suite A, Nevada City, CA 95959; (916) 265–6959. There is an office in Sacramento (916) 368–5114.

*Vista Del Mar Child Care Services, 3200 Motor Avenue, Los Angeles, CA 90034; (310) 836–1223

COLORADO

State Agency: Department of Human Services, Child Welfare Services, 1575 Sherman Street, Denver, CO 80203–1714; (303) 866–3209

State Exchange and Photolisting: Colorado Adoption Resource Registry (see above)

State Reunion Registry: Colorado Voluntary Adoption Registry, Colorado Department of Health, 4300 Cherry Creek Drive South, Denver, CO 80222–1530; (303) 692–2188

Independent Adoption: Permitted

Private Agencies

*AAC Adoption for All Children Adoption and Family Network, 735 East Highway, Berthoud, CO 80513; (970) 532–3576

*Adoption Alliance, 3090 S. Jamaica Court, Suite 106, Aurora, CO 80014; (303) 337–1731

Adoption Centre, 234 Quail Ridge Circle, Highlands Ranch, CO 80126; (303) 470–7842

Adoption Choice Center, 729 Cascade, Colorado Springs, CO 80903; (719) 444–0198

Adoption Connection, 702 S. Nevada Street, Colorado Springs, CO 80903; (719) 442–6880

Adoption Consultants, Inc., 200 Union Boulevard, Suite G-16, Lakewood, CO 80228; (303) 988–4226

Adoption Option, 2600 S. Parker Road, Suite 2-320, Aurora, CO 80014; (303) 695–1601

Adoption Services, Inc., 1108 N. Star Drive, Colorado Springs, CO 80906; (719) 632–9941

Adoptions: Advocacy & Alternatives, 2500 South College Avenue, Fort Collins, CO 80525; (970) 493–5968 or (800) 813–5868

Adventist Adoption and Family Services (see Oregon)

*Bethany Christian Services of Colorado, 9185 E. Kenyon Avenue, Suite 190, Denver, CO 80237–1856; (303) 221–0734 or (800) 238–4269. There is an office in Colorado Springs (719) 591–7595.

Catholic Community Services of the Diocese of Colorado Springs, 29 W. Kiowa, Colorado Springs, CO 80903; (719) 636–2345

Catholic Social Services, Inc. Family Counseling Center, 302 Jefferson, Pueblo, CO 81004; (719) 544–4234

Children of Promise Adoption, 2140 CR 41, Bellvue, CO 80512

*Children of the World, 363 S. Harlan Street, Denver, CO 80226; (303) 922–3433

*Chinese Children Adoption International, 6920 South Holly Circle, Englewood, CO 80112; (303) 850–9998

Christian Family Services, 1399 S. Havana Street, Suite 204, Aurora, CO 80012; (303) 337–6747

Christian Home for Children, Inc., 1880 S. Cascade Avenue, Colorado Springs, CO 80906–2590; (719) 632–4661

*Colorado Adoption Center, 1136 E. Stuart Street, Suite 2040, Fort Collins, CO 80525; (970) 493–8816. There is an office in Wheatridge (303) 467–3128.

Colorado Christian Services, 4796 S. Broadway, Englewood, CO 80110; (303) 761–7236

*Covenant International, Inc., 2055 Anglo Drive, Suite 104, Colorado Springs, CO 80918; (719) 531–5100

Creative Adoptions, 2329 W. Main Street, Suite 220, Littleton, CO 80120; (303) 730–7791

Denver Catholic Community Services, Inc., 2525 W. Alameda, Denver, CO 80219; (303) 742–0828

Designated Adoption Services of Colorado, Inc., 1420 Vance Street, Suite 202, Lakewood, CO 80215; (303) 232–0234

*Family Extension, 525 Third Avenue, Longmont, CO 80502; (303) 776–1224

Family Structuring, 1015 S. Gaylord, #185, Denver, CO 80209; (303) 575–1115

Family Ties Adoption Agency, 7257 Rogers Street, Golden, CO 80403; (303) 420–3660

*Friends of Children of Various Nations, 1562 Pearl Street, Denver, CO 80203; (303) 837–9438

*Hand in Hand International Adoptions, 615 N. Nevada Avenue, Colorado Springs, CO 80903; (719) 473–8844

*Hope's Promise, 309 Jerry Street, Suite 202, Castle Rock, CO 80104; (303) 660–0277

Innovative Adoptive Solutions, 1395 Bellaire Street, Denver, CO 80220; (303) 355–2107

LDS Social Services, 3263 Fraser Street, Suite 3, Aurora, CO 80011; (303) 371–1000

*Littlest Angels International, 1512 Grand Avenue, Suite 216, Glenwood Springs, CO 81601; (970) 945–2949

Loving Homes, 212 West 13th, Pueblo, CO 81003; (719) 545–6181. There is an office in Denver (303) 371–9185.

Lutheran Family Services, 503 Remington, Ft. Collins, CO 80524; (970) 484–5955

Lutheran Social Services of Colorado, 3707 Parkmoor Village Drive, Suite 101, Colorado Springs, CO 80917;(719) 597–0700

Lutheran Social Services of Colorado, Inc., 363 S. Harlan Street, Denver, CO 80226; (303) 922–3433

*MAPS Colorado, 400 Cascade Circle, Silverthorne, CO 80498; (970) 262–2998

Parent Resource Center, 7025 Tall Oak Drive, Colorado Springs, CO 80919; (719) 599–7772

Professional Adoption Services, 1210 S. Parker Road, Suite 104, Denver, CO 80231; (303) 755–4797

*Rainbow House International, 547 Humboldt Street, Denver, CO 80218; (303) 830–2108

*Small Miracles, 555 Denver Tech Center Parkway, Suite B-21000, Englewood, CO 80111; (303) 220–7611

Top of the Trail, 3760 J 75 Road, Paonia, CO 81428; (970) 527–4385

Whole Family, 190 E. Ninth Avenue, Suite 210, Denver, CO 80203; (303) 863–8443

CONNECTICUT

State Agency: Connecticut Department of Children and Families, Office of Foster & Adoption Services 505 Hudson Street, Hartford, CT 06106; (860) 550–6463

State Exchange and Photolisting: see above
State Reunion Registry: see above
Independent Adoption: Not permitted; identified adoption permitted

Private Agencies

*A Child among Us, The Center for Adoption, Inc., 2410 New London Turnpike, South Glastonbury, CT 06073; (860) 657–2467

*Adoption Services of Connecticut, 769 Newfield Street, Suite 2, Middletown, CT 06457–1815; (860) 635–0003 or (800) 537–6230

Casey Family Program East, 1 Corporate Drive, Suite 515, Shelton, CT 06484; (203) 929–3837 or (800) 332–6991. There are offices in Bridgeport (203) 334–6991 and Hartford (860) 727–1030.

*Catholic Charities—Catholic Family Services Archdiocese of Hartford, 467 Bloomfield Avenue, Bloomfield, CT 06002; (860) 242–9577

Catholic Charities of Diocese of Norwich, 11 Bath Street, Norwich, CT 06360; (860) 889–8346

Catholic Charities of Fairfield County, 238 Jewett Avenue, Bridgeport, CT 06606; (203) 372–4301

*Catholic Charities—Hartford District Office, 896 Asylum Avenue, Hartford, CT 06105–1991; (860) 522–8241

*Catholic Charities—New Haven District Office, 478 Orange Street, New Haven, CT 06502; (203) 787–2207

*Catholic Charities—Waterbury District Office, 56 Church Street, Waterbury, CT 06702; (203) 755–1196

Child Adoption Resource Association, Inc., 7 Vauxhall Street, New London, CT 06320; (860) 442–2797

*Children's Center, 1400 Whitney Avenue, Hamden, CT 06514; (203) 248–2116

Downeyside, 829 Wethersfield Avenue, Hartford, CT 06114; (860) 296–3310

*Family and Children's Aid of Mid-Fairfield County, Inc., 9 Mott Avenue, Norwalk, CT 06850; (203) 855–8765

*Family Life Center, Shady Brook Lane, Norwalk, CT 06850; (203) 698–1808

*Family Services, Inc., 92 Vine Street, New Britain, CT 06052; (860) 223–9291

*Franciscan Family Care Center, Inc., 271 Finch Avenue, Meriden, CT 06450; (860) 237–8084

Hall Neighborhood House, 52 Green Street, Bridgeport, CT 06608; (203) 334–3900

Highland Heights, 651 Prospect Street, Box 1224, New Haven, CT 06505; (203) 777–5513

*International Alliance for Children, Inc., 23 S. Main Street, New Milford, CT 06776; (860) 354–3417

*Jewish Family Services, Inc., 2370 Park Avenue, Bridgeport, CT 06604; (203) 366–5438

*Jewish Family Services Infertility Center, 740 North Main Street, West Hartford, CT 06117; (860) 236–1927

*Jewish Family Services of New Haven, 1440 Whalley Avenue, New Haven, CT 06515; (203) 389–5599

LDS Social Services, 1000 Mountain Road, Bloomfield, CT 06002; (800) 735–0149

*Lutheran Social Services, 2139 Silas Deane Highway, Suite 201; Rocky Hill, CT 06067; (860) 257–0303

*Professional Counseling Center, 1 Eliot Place, Fairfield, CT 06430; (203) 259–5300

Quinebaug Valley Youth and Family Services, 303 Putnam Road, Wauregan, CT 06387; (860) 564–6100 or (800) 953–0295

*Thursday's Child, Inc., 227 Tunxis Avenue, Bloomfield, CT 06002; (860) 242–5941

The Village for Families and Children, Inc., 1680 Albany Avenue, Hartford, CT 06105; (860) 236–4511

Wheeler Clinic, Inc., 91 Northwest Drive, Plainville, CT 06062; (860) 527–1644

*Wide Horizons, 34 Connecticut Boulevard, Suite 7, E. Hartford, CT 06108; (860) 291–8610

DELAWARE

State Agency: Delaware Department of Services for Children, Youth, and Their Families, 1825 Faulkland Road, Wilmington, DE 19805; (302) 633–2655

State Exchange and Photolisting: Deladopt (see above)

State Reunion Registry: None

Independent Adoption: Not permitted

Private Agencies

*Adoptions from the Heart, 18-A Trolley Square, Wilmington, DE 19806; (302) 658–8883

*Bethany Christian Services, 308 Possum Park Road, Newark, DE 19711; (302) 737–2890 or (800) 238–4269

Catholic Charities, 442 S. New Street, Dover, DE 19901; (302) 674–1600

Catholic Charities, 21 Chestnut Street, Georgetown, DE 19947–2164; (302) 856–9578

*Catholic Charities, 2601 West 4th Street, Wilmington, DE 19805; (302) 655–9624

*Child and Home Study Associates, 101 Stone Crop Road, Wilmington, DE 19810; (302) 475–5433

Children and Families First, 2005 Baynard Boulevard, Wilmington, DE 19802; (302) 658–5177. There is an office in Milford (302) 422–8013.

Children's Choice of Delaware, 910 B Walker Road, Dover, DE 19901–2759; (302) 678–0404

LDS Social Services, 502 West Chestnut Hill, Newark, DE 19711; (302) 456–3782

*Madison Adoption Agency, 1009 Woodstream Drive, Wilmington, DE 19810; (302) 475–8977

Tressler Center of Delaware, 2 Centerville Road, Wilmington, DE 19808; (302) 995–2294

Trialog Children's Bureau, 2005 Baynard Boulevard, Wilmington, DE 19802; (302) 658–5177

*Welcome House, Inc., 910 Barley Drive, Wilmington, DE 19807; (302) 654–7683

DISTRICT OF COLUMBIA

Public Agency: Child and Family Services Agency, 609 H Street NE, Washington, DC 20002; (202) 724–8692

Exchange or Photolisting: No

Reunion Registry: No

Independent Adoption: Permitted

Private Agencies

*Adoption Center of Washington, Suite 1101, 1726 M Street NW, Washington, DC 20036; (202) 452–8278 or (800) 452–3878

*Adoption Service Information Agency (ASIA), 7720 Alaska Avenue NW, Washington, DC 20012; (202) 726–7193

*American Adoption Agency, 1228 M Street NW, Washington, DC 20005; (202) 638–1543

*Barker Foundation, 1200 18th Street NW, Washington, DC 20036; (202) 363–7751

Catholic Charities, Archdiocese of Washington D.C., 1438 Rhode Island Avenue NE, Washington, DC 20018; (202) 526–4100

*Datz Foundation, 4545 42nd Street NW, Washington, DC 20016; (202) 686–3400

Family & Child Services, 929 L Street NW, Washington, DC 20001; (202) 289–1510

*Holy Cross Child Placement Agency, Inc., 1915 I Street NW, Suite 500, Washington, DC 20006; (202) 332–1367

*International Children's Alliance, 1101 17th Street NW, Suite 1002, Washington, DC 20036; (202) 463–6874

*International Families Inc., 5 Thomas Circle NW, Washington, DC 20005; (202) 667–5779

Lutheran Social Services, 4406 Georgia Avenue NW, Washington, DC 20011; (202) 723–3000

*New Family Foundation, 3615 Wisconsin Avenue NW, Washington, DC 20016; (202) 244–1400

Progressive Life Center, 1123 11th Street NW, Washington, DC 20001; (202) 842–4570

World Child, 4300 16th Street NW, Washington, DC 20011; (202) 829–5244

FLORIDA

State Agency: Florida Department of Children and Families, 2811-E Industrial Plaza Drive, Tallahassee, FL 32308; (850) 487–2383

State Exchange and Photolisting: *Florida's Waiting Children* (see above) and Adoption Information Center Daniel Memorial, Inc., 134 E. Church Street, Jacksonville, FL 32202–3130; (904) 353–0679 or (800) 962–3678

State Reunion Registry: Florida Adoption Reunion Registry, Florida Department of Health and Rehabilitation Services, 2811-E Industrial Plaza Drive, Tallahassee, FL 32301; (850) 353–0679 or (800) 962–3678

Independent Adoption: Permitted

Private Agencies

ACA Adoption Project of ACA, 6226 Presidential Court, Suite D, Fort Myers, FL 33919; (941) 433–3137

Action Youth Care of Florida, Inc., 4175 E. Bay Drive, #160, Clearwater, FL 34624; (813) 530–7284

Adoption Advisory Associates, 299 Camino Gardens Boulevard, 2nd Floor, Boca Raton, FL 33432; (561) 362–5221

Adoption Advocates, Inc., 11407 Seminole Boulevard, Suite D, Largo, FL 33778; (813) 391–8096

*Adoption Agency of Central Florida, 200 W. Welbourne Avenue, Winter Park, FL 32789; (407) 644–2117

*Adoption by Choice, St. Andrew's Square, 4102 W. Linebaugh Avenue, Suite 200, Tampa, FL 33624; (813) 960–2229 or (800)421–2229

Adoption Placement, Inc., 2734 E. Oakland Park Boulevard, Suite 104, Ft. Lauderdale, FL 33306; (954) 564–2950

*Adoption Resources of Florida, P.O. Box 14655, Suite 206, Clearwater, FL 34629; (813) 726–3555

Adoption Services, Inc., 3767 Lake Worth Road, Lake Worth, FL 33461; (407) 969–0591. There is an office in Palm Springs (561) 969–0591.

Advent Christian Home for Children, P.O. Box 4309, Dowling Park, FL 32062; (904) 658–3333

*Advocates for Children and Families, 16831 NE 6th Avenue, North Miami, FL 33162; (305) 653–2474

All About Adoptions, Inc., 505 East New Haven Avenue, Melbourne, FL 32901; (561) 723–0088

American Adoption Advisors, Inc., 3111 Stirling Road, Suite 135, Ft. Lauderdale, FL 33312; (954) 985–4117

Baptist Home for Children, 2332 Bartram Road, Jacksonville, FL 32207; (904) 721–2711

Bond of Love Adoption Agency, Inc., 2520 S. Tamiami Trail, Sarasota, FL 34239; (941) 957–0064

Boys Town of South Florida, 3111 South Dixie Highway, Suite 200, West Palm Beach, FL 33405; (561) 366–9400

Catholic Charities, 900 54th Street, West Palm Beach, FL 33407; (561) 842–2406

*Catholic Charities Bureau, 134 E. Church Street, Suite 2, Jacksonville, FL 32202–3130; (904) 354–3416

*Catholic Charities, Inc., 6533 94th Avenue, North Suite 1-East, St. Petersburg, FL 33710; (813) 345–9126

Catholic Charities of the Diocese of Venice, Inc., 2210 Santa Barbara Boulevard, Naples, FL 33963; (941) 455–2655

Catholic Community Services, Inc., 1300 S. Andrews Avenue, Fort Lauderdale, FL 33316; (954) 522–2513

Catholic Community Services, Inc., 1505 NE 26th Street, Wilton Manors, FL 33305; (954) 630–9404

Catholic Foster Services, 18601 SW 97th Avenue, Miami, FL 33157; (305) 238–1447

Catholic Social Service of Bay County, 3128 E. 11th Street, Panama City, FL 32404; (850) 763–0475

Catholic Social Services, 319 Riveredge Boulevard, Suite 109, Cocoa, FL 32922; (561) 636–6144

Catholic Social Services, 40 Beal Parkway Southwest, Fort Walton Beach, FL 32548; (850) 244–2825

*Catholic Social Services, 1771 N. Semoran Boulevard, Orlando, FL 32807; (407) 658–1818

Catholic Social Services, 855 W. Carolina Street, Tallahassee, FL 32309; (850) 222–2180

Catholic Social Services of Pensacola, 222 E. Government Street, Pensacola, FL 32501; (850) 436–6410

Center for Family & Child Enrichment, Inc., 1405 NW 167th Street, Suite 200, Miami, FL 33169; (305) 624–7450

The Centre for Innovative Solutions, Inc., 1851 W. Indiantown Road, Jupiter, FL 33458; (561) 746–4154.

There are offices in Indianalantic and Plantation (954) 370–2151.

CIII—Therapeutic Foster Home, 10300 SW 216th Street, Miami, FL 33190; (305) 271–4121

*Children's Home Society of Florida Administrative Offices, 5700 54th Avenue, North, St. Petersburg, FL 33709–2095; (813) 223–5383. There are offices in Rockledge (561) 636–0126, Fort Pierce (561) 489–5601, Jacksonville (904) 398–3265, Orlando (407) 422–4441, Clearwater (813) 546–4366, Fort Lauderdale (954) 763–6573, Ocala (850) 629–7597, Tallahassee (850) 921–0772, Daytona Beach (904) 255–7407, Lakeland (813) 688–7968, West Palm Beach (561) 844–9785, Miami (305) 271–5700, Fort Myers (941) 334–2008, Pensacola (850) 494–5990, and Tampa (813) 855–4435.

Children's Psychiatric Center, 9380 Sunset Drive, Suite B-125, Miami (305) 271–5700

Chosen Children, 3924 A Avenue, Lake Worth, FL 33461; (561) 969–0591

*Christian Family Services, Inc., 4001 Newberry Road, Suite A-1, Gainesville, FL 32601; (352) 378–6202

Christian Home and Bible School, West 13th Street, Mt. Dora, FL 32757; (904) 383–2155

Clear Choice, 2727 Ulmerton Road, Suite 2D, Clearwater, FL 34622; (813) 578–4447

Daniel Memorial, 134 E. Church Street, Jacksonville, FL 32202; (904) 353–5077

Developmental Center, 6710 86th Avenue, North, Pinellas Park, FL 34666–2562; (813) 822–6914

Devereux Foundation, Inc. Therapeutic Foster Home, 2626 Edgewater Drive, Orlando, FL 32804; (407) 425–4491

Faith House, Inc., 602 E. Palm Avenue, Tampa, FL 33602; (813) 228–9644

Family Based Treatment Homes, 134 E. Church Street, Jacksonville, FL 32202; (904) 737–1677

Family Continuity Programs, Inc., 21218 Mariner Plaza, Suite 105, Lutz, FL 33549; (813) 948–3010. There is an office in St. Petersburg (813) 321–3007.

Family Enrichment Center, 6013 N. 40th Street, Tampa, FL 33610; (813) 628–4432

Family Service Centers, 2960 Roosevelt Boulevard, Clearwater, FL 34620; (813) 531–0482

Father Flanagan's Boys Town of Central Florida, 950 N. Central Avenue, Oviedo, FL 32765; (561) 366–3667. There is an office in Tallahassee (850) 385–1074.

First Coast Counseling, 3601 Cardinal Point Drive, Jacksonville, FL 32257; (904) 448–1933

*Florida Adoption and Children's Center, Inc., 11410 N. Kendall Drive, Building B, Suite 306, Miami, FL 33176; (305) 274–2811

Florida Baptist Children's Home, 7748 SW 95th Street, Miami, FL 33156–7599; (305) 271–4121. There are offices in Tallahassee (904) 878–1458 and Fort Myers (941) 275–4121.

Florida Baptist Family Ministries, 1015 Sikes Boulevard, Lakeland, FL 33802; (813) 688–4981

Florida Key's Children Shelter, P.O. Box 2574, Tavarnier, FL 33070–2005; (954) 852–4246

Florida Sheriffs Youth Ranches Administrative Offices, Central Office Boys Ranch, State Road 795, Live Oak, FL 32060; (904) 842–5555. There are offices in Safety Harbor (941) 725–4761, Bradenton (941) 745–2553, and Bartow (941) 533–0371.

Gift of Life, Inc., 136 Fourth Street, North, St. Petersburg, FL 33701; (813) 822–5433

*Global Adoption Link, Inc., 100 N. Biscayne, #2812, Miami, FL 33132; (305) 371–6478

Gorman Family Life Center, Inc., 315 N. Wymore Road, Winter Park, FL 32789; (561) 628–5433

Gulf Coast Community Care, 14041 Icot Boulevard, Clearwater, FL 34620; (813) 538–7460

*Hearts and Homes for Children, 6315 Presidential Court, Suite D, Ft. Myers, FL 33919; (813) 481–4548

Henry & Rilla White Foundation, 6112 Arlington Road, Jacksonville, FL 32211; (904) 745–3060

His House Children's Home, Inc., 7000 NW 53rd Terrace, Miami, FL 33166–4804; (305) 888–3181

Homes for Children—Lutheran Ministries, 1989 Wood Hollow Lane, Sarasota, FL 34235; (941) 371–0011

*International Adoption Agency, 20801 Biscayne Boulevard, Aventura, FL 33180; (305) 933–9684

*International Children's Foundation, 8620 NE Second Avenue, Suite 207, Miami, FL 33138; (305) 751–9600

Jewish Adoption and Foster Care Options, 300 S. Pine Island, #246, Plantation, FL 33324; (954) 424–6734

Jewish Family & Community Services, 3601 Cardinal Point Drive, Jacksonville, FL 32257–5582; (904) 446–1933

Jewish Family Services of Greater Miami, Inc., 1790 SW 27th Avenue, Miami, FL 33145; (305) 445–0555

*Jewish Family Services, Inc., of Broward County, 2719 Hollywood Boulevard, Hollywood, FL 33020; (954) 927–1297

Lake County Boys Ranch, P.O. Box 129, Altoona, FL 32702; (904) 669–3252

LDS Social Services, 1020 N. Orlando Avenue, Suite F, Winter Park, FL 32789; (561) 628–8899

Life Management Center of NW Florida, 525 E. 15th Street, Panama City, FL 32401; (850) 769–9481

*Lifelink Child and Family Services Corporation, 1031 S. Euclid Street, Sarasota, FL 34237; (941) 957–1614

LifeNet, Inc., 6408 E. Fowler, Tampa, FL 33617; (813) 988–2889

Lutheran Ministries of Florida, 2456 Jackson Street, Fort Myers, FL 33901; (941) 332–2251. There is an office in Pensacola (850) 453–2772.

The McIntyre Foundation, Inc., 10235 W. Sample Road, Suite 103, Coral Springs, FL 33065; (954) 345–0900

My House is His House, 20000 NW 47th Avenue, Building 22, Opa Locka, FL 33055; (305) 888–3181

New Beginnings of SW Florida, Inc., 2700 S. Tamiami Trail, Sarasota, FL 34239; (941) 954–0454

Northside Centers, Inc., Professional Parenting Program, 12512 N. Bruce B. Downs, Tampa, FL 33612–3807; (813) 977–8700

*One World Adoption Services, Inc., Crown Center Complex, 1451 W. Cypress Creek Road, Suite 300–2, Ft. Lauderdale, FL 33309; (954) 498–2702

Pinellas Emergency Mental Health Services, Inc., 11254 58th Street, North, Pinellas Park, FL 33782; (813) 545–5636

Ruth Cooper Center Good Homes Project, 2789 Ortiz Avenue, SE, Fort Myers, FL 33905; (941) 275–3222

Shepherd Care Ministries, 9280-3 College Parkway, Fort Myers, FL 33919; (941) 433–1929. There are offices in Lake Worth (561) 588–3649 and Hollywood (954) 981–2060.

St. Augustine Youth Services, 50 Saragossa Street, St. Augustine, FL 32084; (904) 829–1770

St. Vincent Adoption Center, 18601 SW 97th Avenue, Miami, FL 33157; (305) 445–5714

*Suncoast International Adoptions, Inc., 14277 Walsingham Road, Largo, FL 33774; (813) 596–3135

The Sunrise Program Mental Health Care, Inc., 5707 N. 22nd Street, Tampa, FL 33610; (813) 237–3914

*Tedi Bear Adoptions Inc., Suite 204, 226-5 Solano Road, Ponte Verde Beach, FL 32082; (904) 280–0056

Therapeutic Group Home for Girls/Boynton, 317 S. Seacrest Boulevard, Boynton Beach, FL 33462; (561) 736–4554

Therapeutic Group Home/Lantana, Holley Hospital, Lantana, FL 33462; (561) 582–7255

*Universal Aid for Children, Inc., 1600 S. Federal Highway, 2nd Floor, Hollywood, FL 33020; (954) 925–7550

GEORGIA

State Agency: Georgia Department of Human Resources, State Office of Adoptions, 2 Peachtree Street, NW, Atlanta, GA 30303–3142; (404) 657–3550

Adoption Exchange and Photolisting: *My Turn Now* (see above)

State Reunion Registry: Division of Family and Children Services, Permanency Support Unit, Attention: Reunion Registry, 2 Peachtree Street, NW, Atlanta, GA 30303–3142; (404) 657–3559

Independent Adoption: Permitted

Private Agencies

Adoption Care, 1447 Peachtree Street, Suite 511, Atlanta, GA 30303; (404) 897–1766

Adoption Planning, Inc., 17 Executive Park Drive, Suite 480, Atlanta, GA 30329; (404) 248–9105

Adoption Services, Inc., P.O. Box 155, Pavo, GA 31778; (912) 859–2654

All God's Children, Inc., 1120 Athens Road, Winterville, GA 30683; (706) 742–7420

*Atlanta International Family Services, Inc., P.O. Box 422117, Atlanta, GA 30342; (404) 845–0007

*Bethany Christian Services, 1867 Independence Square, Suite 201; Atlanta, GA 30338–5152; (770) 396–7700 or (800) 238–4269

Bethany Christian Services of Tennessee, Inc. (*see* Tennessee)

Catholic Social Services, Inc., Adoption Program, 680 W. Peachtree Street, NW, Atlanta, GA 30308; (404) 881–6571

Covenant Care Services, Inc., 352 First Street, Macon, GA 31201; (912) 741–9829

Edgewood Baptist Church, Inc., New Beginning Adoption and Counseling Agency, 1316 Wynnton Court, Suite A, Columbus, GA 31906; (706) 571–3346

Extended Families and Educational Services, 2001 M. L. King Jr. Drive SW, Atlanta, GA 30310; (404) 756–0148

Families First, 1105 W. Peachtree Street, Atlanta, GA 30309; (404) 853–2800

Family Counseling Center/CSRA, Inc., 603 Ellis Street, Augusta, GA 30901; (706) 722–6512

Georgia Association for Guidance, Aid, Placement, and Empathy (AGAPE), Inc., 3094 Mercer University Drive, Suite 200, Atlanta, GA 30341; (404) 452–9995

Georgia Baptist Children's Home and Family Ministries North Area (Palmetto), 9250 Hutchison Ferry Road, Palmetto, GA 30268;(770) 463–3344

The Giving Tree, Inc., 1842 Clairmont Road, Decatur, GA 30033; (404) 633–3383

Greater Chattanooga Christian Services (*see* Tennessee)

Hope for Children, Inc., 1515 Johnson Ferry Road, Suite 200, Marietta, GA 30062; (770) 977–0813

Independent Adoption Center, Inc., 2339 Lawrenceville Highway, Suite 12, Decatur, GA 30033; (404) 321–6900 or (800) 877–6736

Jewish Family Services, Inc., Cradle of Love Adoption Counseling and Services, 4549 Chamblee-Dunwoody Road, Atlanta, GA 30338; (770) 873–2277

LDS Social Services, 4823 N. Royal Atlanta Drive, Tucker, GA 30084; (770) 939–2121

*Lutheran Ministries of Georgia Adoption Program, 756 W. Peachtree Street, NW, Atlanta, GA 30308; (404) 875–0201

*Open Door Adoption Agency, Inc., 403B N. Broad Street, Thomasville, GA 31792; (912) 228–6339

*Partners in Adoption, Inc., 1050 Little River Way, Alpharetta, GA 30201; (770) 720–1967

ROOTS, 5532G Old National Highway, Suite 250, College Park, GA 30349; (770) 209–8311

HAWAII

State Agency: Hawaii Department of Human Services, 810 Richards Street, Suite 400, Honolulu, HI 96813; (808) 586–5698

State Exchange and Photolisting: Central Adoption Exchange of Hawaii (see above)

State Reunion Assistance: Family Court Central Registry Court Management Service, 777 Bunchbowl Street, Honolulu, HI 96811

Independent Adoption: Permitted

Private Agencies

*Adopt International, 900 Fort Street, Pioneer Plaza Building, #1700, Honolulu, HI 96813; (808) 523–1400

*Catholic Services to Families, 200 N. Vineyard Boulevard, 3rd Floor, Honolulu, HI 96817; (808) 537–6321

*Child and Family Services, 200 N. Vineyard Boulevard, Suite 20, Honolulu, HI 96817; (808) 521–2377

*Crown Child Placement International, Inc., P.O. Box 520, Kaaawa, HI 96730; (808) 237–7167

*Hawaii International Child Placement and Family Services, Inc., 1208 Laukahi Street, Honolulu, HI 96824–0468; (808) 377–0881

LDS Social Services Hawaii Honolulu Agency, 1500 S. Beretonia Street, Suite 403, Honolulu, HI 96826; (808) 945–3690

Queen Liliuokalani Children's Center, 1300 Halona Street, Honolulu, HI 96817; (808) 847–1302

IDAHO

State Agency: Idaho Department of Health and Welfare, 5th Floor, Boise, ID 83720–0036; (208) 334–5700

State Exchange and Photolisting: see above

State Reunion Registry: Department of Health and Welfare, Division of Family and Community Services, P.O. Box 83720, Boise, ID 83720; (208) 334–5700

Independent Adoption: Permitted

Private Agencies

Casey Family Program, 6441 Emerald, Boise, ID 83704; (208) 377–1771

Children's Adoption Services, Inc., 2308 North Cole, Suite E, Boise, ID 83704; (208) 376–0558

Family Wellness Center, 420 W. Bannock, Boise, ID 83701; (208) 344–0094

Idaho Youth Ranch Adoption Services, P.O. Box 8538, Boise, ID 83707; (208) 377–2613

LDS Social Services, 10740 Fairview, Suite 100, Boise, ID 83704; (208) 376–0191. There are offices in Burley (208) 678–8200, Idaho Falls (208) 529–5276, and Pocatello (208) 232–7780.

Lutheran Social Services of Washington and Idaho, 2201 Government Way, #J, Coeur d'Alene, ID 83814; (208) 667–1898

*New Hope Child & Family Agency, 5816 E. Sunnyside Road, Idaho Falls, ID 83406; (208) 523–6930 or (800) 574–7705

Northwest Services, 112 S. Kimball Avenue, #140, Caldwell, ID 83605; (208) 459–6772

ILLINOIS

State Agency: Illinois Department of Children and Family Services, 406 E. Monroe Street, Springfield, IL 62701–1498; (217) 524–2422. However, for adoption resources and general information, contact the state exchange (see below).

State Exchange and Photolisting: Adoption Information Center of Illinois (AICI), 188 W. Randolph Suite 600, Chicago, IL 60606; (312) 346–1516 or (800) 572–2390

State Reunion Registry: Illinois Department of Public Health, Office of Vital Records, Adoption Registry, 605 West Jefferson, Springfield, IL 62702; (217) 782–6553

State Confidential Intermediary Service: Confidential Intermediary Service of Illinois, 3166 Des Plaines River Road, Suite 23, Des Plaines, IL 60018; (847) 298–9097

Independent Adoption: Permitted

Private Agencies

*Adoption-Link, Inc., Suite 104, 1145 Westgate, Oak Park, IL 60301; (708) 524–1433

Aunt Martha's Youth Services, 4343 Lincoln Highway, #340, Matteson, IL 60443; (708) 747–2701

Aurora Catholic Social Services, 1700 N. Farnsworth Avenue, Aurora, IL 60505; (708) 892–4366

Baby Fold, 210 Landmark, Suite A, Normal, IL 61761; (309) 454–1770

*Bethany Christian Services, 9730 S. Western, Suite 704, Evergreen Park, IL 60642; (708) 422–9626

Bethany for Children and Families, 1706 Brady Street, Suite 207, Davenport, IA 52803–4708; (319) 324–9169

*Catholic Charities—Chicago Archdiocese, 126 N. DesPlaines, Chicago, IL 60661; (312) 655–7000. There is an office in Round Lake (847) 546–5733.

Catholic Charities—Joliet Diocese, 203 N. Ottawa Street, 2nd Floor, Suite A, Joliet, IL 60432; (815) 723–3053

Catholic Charities—Springfield Diocese, 120 S. 11th Street, Springfield, IL 62703; (217) 525–0500

*Catholic Social Services—Belleville Diocese, 617 S. Belt, West, Belleville, IL 62220; (618) 277–9200

*Catholic Social Services—Peoria Diocese, 413 NE Monroe, Peoria, IL 61603; (309) 671–5720

Catholic Social Services—Rockford Diocese, 921 W. State Street, Rockford, IL 61102; (815) 965–0623

Central Baptist Family Services, 2100 S. Indiana, Suite 360, Chicago, IL 60616; (312) 326–7430

Chicago Child Care Society, 5467 S. University Avenue, Chicago, IL 60615; (773) 643–0452

Chicago Youth Centers, 10 W. 35th Street, Chicago, IL 60616; (312) 225–8200

*Children's Home and Aid Society of Illinois, 1002 College Avenue, Alton, IL 62002; (618) 462–2714. There are offices in Chicago (312) 831–1133, Champaign (217) 359–8815, and Rockford (815) 962–1043.

Childserv, 9415 Western Avenue, Chicago, IL 60620; (773) 233–5100

Christian Family Services, 9955 Bunkham Road, Fairview Heights, IL 62208; (618) 397–7678

Counseling and Family Service, 330 SW Washington, Peoria, IL 61602; (309) 676–2400

*Cradle Society, 2049 Ridge Avenue, Evanston, IL 60201; (847) 475–5800

*Evangelical Child and Family Agency, 1530 N. Main, Wheaton, IL 60187; (630) 653–6400

Family Care Services of Illinois, 234 S. Wabash Avenue, Chicago, IL 60604; (312) 427–8790

*Family Counseling Clinic, Inc., 19300 W. Highway 120, Grayslake, IL 60030; (847) 223–8107

*Family Resource Center, 5828 N. Clark Street, Chicago, IL 60660; (312) 334–2300 or (800) 676–2229

Family Resources, Inc. (*see* Iowa)

*Family Service Agency of Adams County, 915 Vermont Street, Quincy, IL 62301; (217) 222–8254

*Family Service Center of Sangamon County, 1308 S. Seventh Street, Springfield, IL 62703; (217) 528–8406

*Glenkirk, 2501 N. Chestnut, Arlington Heights, IL 60004; (847) 394–2171

Hands Around the World, 1417 E. Miner, Arlington Heights, IL 60004; (847) 255–8309

*Hobby Horse House, 208 S. Mauvaisterre Street, Jacksonville, IL 62651; (217) 243–7708

*Illinois Baptist Children's Home, 4243 Lincolnshire Drive, Mt. Vernon, IL 62864; (618) 242–4944

Illinois Children's Christian Home, P.O. Box 200, St. Joseph, IL 61873; (217) 469–7566

Jewish Children's Bureau, 1 S. Franklin Street, Chicago, IL 60606; (312) 346–6700

LDS Social Services, 1813 N. Mill Street, Suite F, Naperville, IL 60540; (630) 369–0486

*Lifelink Adoption Service, 2324 S. Alpine Road, Rockford, IL 61108–7726; (815) 220–3141. There is an office in Bensenville (630) 766–5800.

*Love Basket, 10314 Lincoln Trail, Suites 204/205, Fairview Heights, IL 62208; (618) 394–1927

Lutheran Child and Family Services, 431 S. Grand Avenue,

West, Springfield, IL 62704; (217) 544–4631. There are offices in River Forest (708) 771–7180, Belleville (618) 234–8904, and Mt. Vernon (618) 242–3284.

Lutheran Social Services, 555 6 Street, Molina, IL 61265; (309) 797–2226

*Lutheran Social Services of Illinois, 701 Devonshire, Suite 204, Box C-9, Champaign, IL 61820; (217) 398–3011. There are offices in Oak Park (708) 445–8341, Peoria (309) 671–0300, and Chicago (773) 239–3700.

*New Life Social Services, 3525 W. Peterson, Suite 215, Chicago, IL 60659; (773) 478–9874

PSI Services, Inc., 111 E. Wacker Drive, Suite 2500, Chicago, IL 60601; (312) 946–0740

*Saint Mary's Services, 717 W. Kirchoff Road, Arlington Heights, IL 60005; (847) 870–8181

*Sunny Ridge Family Center, Inc., 2 S. 426 Orchard Road, Wheaton, IL 60187; (630) 668–5117

Volunteers of America of Illinois, 224 N. Desplaines, Suite 500, Chicago, IL 60661; (312) 707–9477. There is an office in East St. Louis (618) 271–9833.

INDIANA

State Agency: Indiana Division of Family and Children, Family Protection/Preservation, 402 W. Washington Street, Third Floor, W-364, Indianapolis, IN 46204–2739; (317) 233–1743 or (888) 204–7466

State Exchange and Photolisting: *Indiana Adoption Resource Exchange* (see above)

State Reunion Registry: Indiana Adoption History Registry, Registrar—Vital Records Division, P.O. Box 1964, Indianapolis, IN 46206–1964; (317) 383–6280

Independent Adoption: Permitted

Private Agencies

AD-IN, Inc., 8801 N. Meridian Street, Suite 105, Indianapolis, IN 46260; (317) 573–0149

Adoption Alternatives, 116 S. Taylor, South Bend, IN 46601; (219) 232–5843

*Adoption Network Domestic and International, Inc., 4334 Miami, South Bend, IN 46614; (219) 299–9583

Adoption Resources Services, Inc., 810 W. Bristol, Suite R, Elkhart, IN 46514; (219) 262–2499

Adoption Services, Inc., 3050 N. Meridian Street, Indianapolis, IN 46208; (317) 926–6338

Adoption Support Center, 6331 N. Carrolton Avenue, Indianapolis, IN 46220; (317) 255–5916 or (800) 274–1084

*Americans for African Adoptions, Inc., 8910 Timberwood Drive, Indianapolis, IN 46234; (317) 271–4567

Baptist Children's Home, 354 West Street, Valparaiso, IN 46383; (219) 462–4111

*Bethany Christian Services, 6144 N. Hillside Avenue, Suite 10, Indianapolis, IN 46220; (317) 254–8479. There is an office in Schererville (219) 864–0800.

Catholic Charities, 315 E. Washington, Fort Wayne, IN 46802; (219) 439–0242

*Catholic Charities, 120 S. Taylor Street, South Bend, IN 46601; (219) 234–3111 or (800) 686–3112

*Catholic Charities Bureau, 123 NW Fourth Street, Suite 603, Evansville, IN 47708; (812) 423–5456

Catholic Family Services, 973 W. Sixth Avenue, Gary, IN 46402; (219) 882–2723

Catholic Family Services of Michigan City, 1501 Franklin Street, Michigan City, IN 46360–3709; (219) 879–9312

*Childplace, Inc., 2420 Highway 62, Jeffersonville, IN 47130; (812) 282–8248 or (800) 787–9084

*Children's Bureau of Indianapolis, English Foundation Building, 615 N. Alabama Street, Suite 426, Indianapolis, IN 46204; (317) 264–2700

Coleman Adoption Agency, 419 English Foundation Building, 615 N. Alabama Street, Suite 119, Indianapolis, IN 46204; (317) 638–0965

*Compassionate Care, Route 3, Box 12B, Oakland City, IN 47660; (812) 749–4152 or (800) 749–4153

*Families through International Adoption/China's Children, 971A S. Kenmore Drive, Evansville, IN 47715; (812) 479–9900

Family and Children's Services, 655 S. Hebron, Evansville, IN 47414; (812) 471–1776

G.L.A.D., P.O. Box 9105, Evansville, IN 47724; (812) 424–4523

Guardian Angel Adoption Center, 1950 W. 86th Street, Suite 202, Indianapolis, IN 46260; (317) 876–9668

Homes for Black Children, 3131 E. 38th Street, Indianapolis, IN 46218; (317) 545–5281

Independent Adoption Center, Inc., 537 Turtle Creek Drive South, Indianapolis, IN 46337; (317) 788–1039 or (800) 771–3721

Indiana Agency for LDS Social Services (*contact* Salt Lake City, Utah agency)

Jeremiah Agency, P.O. Box 864, Greenwood, IN 46142–0864; (765) 887–2434

Loving Option, 206 S. Main Street, Bluffton, IN 46714; (219) 824–9077

*Lutheran Child and Family Services, 1525 N. Ritter Avenue, Indianapolis, IN 46219; (317) 359–5467

*Lutheran Social Services, 330 Madison Avenue, Fort Wayne, IN 46857–1329; (219) 426–3347. There is an office in Griffith (219) 838–0996.

Open Arms Christian Homes, Highway 54 E., Switz City, IN 47465; (812) 659–3564

Paralegal on Call, Inc., P.O. Box 652, Greenwood, IN 46217

Shults-Lewis Child and Family Services, 150 E. 325 S., Valparaiso, IN 46383; (219) 462–0513

St. Elizabeth's, 2500 Churchman Avenue, Indianapolis, IN 46203; (317) 787–3412. There is an office in New Albany (812) 949–7305.

Sunny Ridge Family Center, Inc., 25426 Orchard Road, Wheaton, IL 60187–8099; (219) 836–2117

Valley Children's Services, One Professional Center, 1801 N. Sixth Street, Suite 600, Terre Haute, IN 47804; (812) 234–0181

The Villages, Inc., 652 N. Girl's School Road, Suite 240, Indianapolis, IN 46214–3662; (800) 874–6880

IOWA

State Agency: Iowa Department of Human Services, Hoover Building, Des Moines, IA 50319–0114; (515) 281–5358

State Exchange and Photolisting: Iowa Adoption Resource Exchange (see above)

State Reunion Registry: None

Independent Adoption: Permitted

Private Agencies

Alternative Services, Inc., 1228 Third Avenue, SE, Cedar Rapids, IA 52406–2425; (319) 364–6185

American Home Finding Association, 217 E. Fifth Street, Ottumwa, IA 52501; (515) 682–3449

Baptist Children's Home and Family Ministries, 224½ NW Abilene Road, Ankeny, IA 50021; (515) 964–0986

*Bethany Christian Services, 6000 Douglas, Suite 230, Des Moines, IA 50322; (515) 270–0824. There are offices in Orange City (712) 737–4831 and Pella (515) 628–3247.

*Bethany for Children and Families, 1706 Brady Street, Suite 207, Davenport, IA 52803–4708; (319) 324–9169

Boys and Girls Home and Family Services, Inc., 2625 Nebraska Street, Sioux City, IA 51104; (712) 277–4031

Bremwood Lutheran Children's Home Society, 106 16th Street SW, Waverly, IA 50677; (319) 352–2630

*Catholic Charities of the Archdiocese of Dubuque, 1229 Mt. Loretta, Dubuque, IA 52004–1309; (319) 588–0558

Catholic Charities of Sioux City, 1601 Military Road, Sioux City, IA 51103; (712) 252–4547

*Catholic Social Service, 601 Grand Avenue, Des Moines, IA 50303; (515) 244–3761

Cedar Valley Family Counseling, Box 150, Swisher, IA 52338; (319) 857–4480

*Children and Families of Iowa, 1111 University Avenue, Des Moines, IA 50314; (515) 288–1981

Children's Square U.S.A., 541 Sixth Avenue, Council Bluffs, IA 51502–3008; (712) 322–3700

*Crittenton Center, 1105 28th Street, Sioux City, IA 51104; (712) 255–4321

Families, Inc., 101 W. Main Street, W. Branch, IA 52358; (319) 643–2532

Families of NE Iowa, 108 W. Maple, Maquoketa, IA 52060; (319) 652–4958

*Family Resources, Inc., 115 W. Sixth Street, Davenport, IA 52803; (319) 323–1853. There is an office in Bettendorf (319) 359–8216.

First Resources Corporation, 109 E. Marion, Sigourney, IA 52591; (515) 622–2543

Four Oaks, Inc., 5400 Kirkwood Boulevard, SW, Cedar Rapids, IA 52406–5216; (319) 364–0259

Francis Lauer Youth Services, 17162 Kingbird Avenue, Mason City, IA 50401; (515) 423–2582

*Gift of Love International Adoptions, Inc., 5750 Columbine Drive, Johnston, IA 50131–1570; (515) 276–9277

Healing the Children, 412 E. Church Street, Marshalltown, IA 50158; (515) 753–7544

*Hillcrest Family Services, 205 12th Street SE, Cedar Rapids, IA 52403–4028; (319) 362–3149

*Holt International Children's Services, Midwest Office, 430 S. 35th Street, Suite 2, Council Bluffs, IA 51501; (712) 328–1224. There is an office in Carter Lake (712) 347–5911.

Integrated Health Services, Inc., 118 S. Main, N. English, IA 52316; (319) 664–3278

Keys to Living, 463 Northland Avenue, NE, Cedar Rapids, IA 52402–6237; (319) 377–2161

LDS Social Services Iowa, 3301 Ashworth Road, W. Des Moines, IA 50265; (515) 226–0484

*Lutheran Family Service, 230 Ninth Avenue, North, Fort Dodge, IA 50501; (515) 573–3138

*Lutheran Social Service of Iowa, 3116 University Avenue, Des Moines, IA 50311; (515) 277–4476

*New Horizons Adoption Agency, Inc., Frost-Bentco Building, Highway 254, Frost, MN 56033; (507) 878–3200

Ralston Adoption Agency, 2208 S. Fifth Avenue, Marshalltown, IA 50158–4515; (800) 304–0219

Tanager Place, 724 N. Third, Burlington, IA 52601; (319) 752–4000

Young House, Inc., 724 N. Third, Burlington, IA 52601; (319) 752–4000

KANSAS

State Agency: Kansas Department of Social and Rehabilitation Services, 300 SW Oakley, West Hall, Topeka, KS 66606; (785) 296–4661

State Exchange and Photolisting: Kansas Families for Kids (KFFK), Suite 206, Topeka, KS 66603; (785) 354–4663 or (800) 210–5387

State Reunion Registry: None

Independent Adoption: Permitted

Private Agencies

A.C.T. (Adoption, Counseling, and Training) Adoption Services, 612½ Main, Lansing, KS 66043; (913) 727–2888

*Adoption and Counseling Services for Families, 10045 Hemlock, Overland Park, KS 66212; (913) 383–8448

Adoption & Fertility Resources, 4500 College Boulevard, Suite 110, Overland Park, KS 66211; (913) 781–8550

Adoption Centre of Kansas, 1831 Woodrow, Wichita, KS 67203; (316) 265–5289

Adoption of Babies & Children, 9303 W. 75th Street, Overland Park, KS 66204; (913) 385–2229

Adoption Option, 7211 W. 98 Terrace, Overland Park, KS 66212; (913) 642–7900

Adoption Works, Inc., 400 N. Woodlawn, Wichita, KS 67208; (316) 687–4393

American Adoptions, 11560 W. 95th, Overland Park, KS 66214; (913) 492–2229

Baumann, Powell, and Stonestreet Independent Adoptions, 5847 SW 29th Street, Topeka, KS 66614; (785) 273–7524

Catholic Charities, Diocese of Dodge City, 2546 20th Street, Great Bend, KS 67530; (316) 792–1393

*Catholic Charities, Diocese of Kansas City, 2220 Central Avenue, Kansas City, KS 66102; (913) 621–1504

*Catholic Charities, Diocese of Salina, 428 West Iron Road, Salina, KS 67402; (785) 825–0208

Catholic Social Service, 437 N. Topeka, Wichita, KS 67202; (316) 264–8344

Christian Family Services of the Midwest, Inc., 10550 Barkley, Suite 100, Overland Park, KS 66212; (913) 383–3337

Family Life Services Adoption Agency, 305 S. Summit, Arkansas City, KS 67005–2848; (316) 442–1688

Gentle Shepherd Child Placement, 6405 Metcalf, Suite 318, Overland Park, KS 66206–3928; (913) 432–1353

Hagar Associates, Inc., 3601 W. 29th Street, Suite 129A, Topeka, KS 66614; (785) 271–6045

Heart of America Adoption Center, 108 Poplar, P.O. Box 1185, Olathe, KS 66051; (913) 764–1888

*Heartland International, 1831 Woodrow Avenue, Wichita, KS 67203–2932; (316) 265–5289

Highlands Child Placement Service, Inc., 5506 Cambridge, Kansas City, KS 64132; (816) 924–6565

*Inserco, Inc., 5120 E. Central, Wichita, KS 67208; (316) 681–3840

Kansas Children's Service League, 1365 N. Custer Street, Wichita, KS 67201; (316) 942–4261. There is an office in Topeka (785) 274–3100 and the Black Adoptions Project in Kansas City (913) 621–2016.

Kaw Valley Center, 4300 Brenner Road, Kansas City, KS 66104; (913) 334–0294

*Lutheran Social Services, 1855 N. Hillside, Wichita, KS 67214–2317; (316) 686–6645

Maude Carpenter Children's Home, 1501 N. Meridian, Wichita, KS 67203; (316) 942–3221

Native American Family Services, Inc., 15434 K Road, Mayetta, KS 66509–9093; (913) 966–2141

*Special Additions, 10985 W. 175th Street, Olathe, KS 66062; (913) 681–9604

Sunflower Family Services, 1503 Vine, Suite E, Hays, KS 67601–8384; (785) 625–4600

The Villages, Inc., 2209 SW 29th Street, Topeka, KS 66611; (785) 267–5900

Wynne Services, Inc., P.O. Box 171221, Kansas City, KS 66117; (913) 621–0665

KENTUCKY

State Agency: Cabinet for Families and Children, 275 E. Main Street, Frankfort, KY 40621; (502) 564–2147; Special Needs Adoption Project (SNAP), 908 W. Broadway, Louisville, KY 40203; (502) 595–4303, and Special Needs Adoption Project (SNAP), Department for Social Services, 710 W. High Street, Lexington, KY 40508; (606) 252–1728

State Exchange and Photolistng: Kentucky Adoption Resource Exchange, Frankfort (see above)

State Reunion Registry: Program Specialist, Adult Adoptees, Department for Social Services Adoptees, 275 East Main Street, Sixth Floor, West, Frankfort, KY 40621; (502) 564–2147

Independent Adoption: Permitted

Private Agencies

A Helping Hand Adoption Agency, 3066 Harrodsburg Road, Lexington, KY 40533; (606) 223–0112

Adopt! Inc., 135 Lackawana Rd., Lexington, KY 40503; (606) 275–5012

Adoptions of Kentucky, 1 River Front Plaza, Suite 1708, Louisville, KY 40202; (502) 585–3005

*Bluegrass Christian Adoption Services, 1309 S. Limestone, Lexington, KY 40503; (606) 276–2222

Catholic Charities, 2911 S. Fourth Street, Louisville, KY 40208; (502) 637–9786

*Catholic Social Service Bureau, 3629 Church Street, Covington, KY 41015; (606) 581–8974

*Catholic Social Service Bureau, 1310 Leestown Road, Lexington, KY 40508; (606) 253–1993

Childplace, Inc., 4500 Westport Road, Louisville, KY 40207; (502) 363–1633

*Children of the Americas, 1890 Lyda Avenue, Bowling Green, KY 42104; (502) 843–0300

*Children's Home of Northern Kentucky, 200 Home Road, Covington, KY 41011–1942; (606) 261–8768

*Chosen Children Adoption Services, Inc., 5227 Bardstown Road, Louisville, KY 40291–1714; (502) 491–6410

Copper Care, Inc. Kentucky, 3031 Dixie Highway, Suite 101F, Edgewood, KY 41017; (606) 331–1785

Hope Hill Children's Home, 10230 Hope-Means Road, Hope, KY 40334; (606) 498–5230

*Jewish Family and Vocational Service, 3640 Dutchmans Lane, Louisville, KY 40205; (502) 452–6341

*Kentucky Baptist Homes for Children, 809 E. Chestnut, Louisville, KY 40204–1014; (502) 568–9115

Kentucky One Church One Child, 1730 W. Chestnut, Louisville, KY 40203; (502) 561–6827 or (800) 248–8671

*Kentucky United Methodist Childrens Home, 193 Phillips Court, Owensboro, KY 42301; (502) 683–3723

LDS Social Services, Inc., 1000 Hurstbourne Lane, Louisville, KY 40224; (502) 429–0077

*Pathways Child Placement Services, Inc., 1579 Bardstown Road, Louisville, KY 40205–1150; (502) 459–2320

St. Elizabeth's Regional Maternity Center, 116 Bauer Avenue, Louisville, KY 40207; (502) 897–7921

St. Joseph's Children's Treatment Center, Southern and Ashland Streets, Covington, KY 41015; (606) 261–4040

The Villages of Kentucky, 435 First Street, Henderson, KY 42420; (502) 826–0281

LOUISIANA

State Agency: Department of Social Services, Office of Community Services, P.O. Box 3318, Baton Rouge, LA 70821; (504) 342–4086

State Exchange and Photolisting: Louisiana Adoption Resource Exchange (LARE) (see above)

State Reunion Registry: Louisiana Voluntary Registry, P.O. Box 3318, Baton Rouge, LA 70821; (504) 342–9922 or (800) 259–2456

Independent Adoption: Permitted

Private Agencies

Acorn Adoption, Inc., 118 Ridgelake Drive, Metairie, LA 70001; (504) 838–0080

The Adoption Center, Inc., 118 Ridgelake, Metairie, LA 70003; (504) 833–8381

*Adoption Options, 1724 N. Burnside, Suite 7, Gonzales, LA 70737; (504) 644–1033

*AMSI International Adoption Service, Inc., 4824 Prytania Street, Suite 201, New Orleans, LA 70115; (504) 895–1118

*Answered Prayer Adoption Services, Inc., 42431 Highway 30, Gonzales, LA 70737; (504) 647–8911

Beacon House Adoption Services, Inc., 750 Louisiana Avenue, Port Allen, LA 70767; (504) 387–6365

*Bethany Christian Services of Louisiana, 8786 Goodwood Boulevard, Baton Rouge, LA 70806–7917; (504) 927–3235

*Catholic Charities Archdiocese of New Orleans, 1231 Prytania Street, New Orleans, LA 70130; (504) 523–3755

*Catholic Community Services Counseling, Maternity, and Adoption Department, 4884 Constitution Avenue, Baton Rouge, LA 70821; (504) 927–4930

*Catholic Social Services of Houma-Thibodaux, 1220 Aycock Street, Houma, LA 70361; (504) 876–0490

Catholic Social Services of Lafayette, 708 W. University, Lafayette, LA 70501; (318) 235–5218

*Children's Bureau of New Orleans, Inc., 1001 Howard Avenue, Suite 2800, Plaza Tower, New Orleans, LA 70113; (504) 525–2366

Gail House, 8676 Goodwood Boulevard, Baton Rouge, LA 70806; (504) 926–0070

*Gladney Center (*see* Texas)

Holy Cross Child Placement Agency, Inc., 929 Olive Street, Shreveport, LA 71104; (318) 222–7892

*Jewish Family Service of Greater New Orleans, 3330 W. Esplanade Ave. S., Suite 600, Metairie, LA 70002–3454; (504) 831–8475

LDS Social Services Pratt Center, 2000 Old Spanish Trail, Suite 115, Slidell, LA 70458; (504) 649–2774

Louisiana Baptist Children's Home, 7200 DeSiard Road, Monroe, LA 71211; (318) 343–2244

Mercy Ministries of America, 804 Spell Street, West Monroe, LA 71291; (318) 388–2040

*Special Delivery Adoption Services, Inc., 7809 Jefferson Highway, Suite D-1, Baton Rouge, LA 70809; (504) 924–2507

*St. Elizabeth Foundation, 8054 Summa Drive, Baton Rouge, LA 70809; (504) 769–8888

St. Gerard's Adoption Network, Inc., 100 S. Vivian Street, Eunice, LA 70535; (318) 457–9048

Sunnybrook Children's Home, Inc. (*see* Mississippi)

*Volunteers of America—Greater New Orleans, 3900 N. Causeway Boulevard, Metairie, LA 70002; 835–3005. There are offices of Volunteers of America in Alexandria (318) 442–8026, Ruston (318) 254–8160, and Shreveport (318) 221–5000.

MAINE

State Agency: Department of Human Services, 221 State Street, Augusta, ME 04333; (207) 287–5060

State Exchange and Photolisting: Northern New England Adoption Exchange (see above)

State Reunion Registry: Maine State Adoption Reunion Registry, Office of Vital Records, 221 State Street, Augusta, ME 04330; (207)287–3131

Independent Adoption: Permitted

Private Agencies

Families & Children Together, 16 Penn Plaza, Bangor, ME 0440l; (207) 941–2347

Good Samaritan Agency, 450 Essex Street, Bangor, ME 04401; (207) 942–7211

International Adoption Services Center, P.O. Box 55, Alna, ME 04535; (207) 586–5058

Maine Adoption Placement Service, 306 Congress Street, Portland, ME 04101; (207) 772–3678

Maine Adoption Placement Services, 6 State Street, Bangor, ME 04402; (207) 941–9500. There is an office in Houlton (207) 532–9358.

Maine Children's Home for Little Wanderers, 34 Gilman Street, Waterville, ME 04901; (207) 873–4253

Sharing in Adoption, 366 US Route 1, Falmouth, ME 04901; (207) 781–3092

St. Andre Home, 283 Elm Street, Biddeford, ME 04005; (207) 282–3351

MARYLAND

State Agency: Social Services Administration , Maryland Department of Human Resources, 311 W. Saratoga Street, Baltimore, MD 21201; (410) 767–7506

State Exchange and Photolisting: Maryland Adoption Resource Exchange (see above); (410) 767–7359

State Reunion Registry: Maryland Mutual Consent Voluntary Adoption Registry, Social Services Administration, 311 West Saratoga, Baltimore, MD 21201; (410) 767–7372

Independent Adoption: Permitted/no paid intermediaries/newspaper advertising allowed

Private Agencies

*Adoption Alliances, 5750 Park Heights Avenue, Baltimore, MD 21215; (410) 466–8439

Adoption Forever, Inc., 5830 Hubbard Drive, Rockville, MD 20852; (301) 468–1818

*Adoption Resource Center, Inc., 6630 Baltimore National Pike, Baltimore, MD 21228; (410) 744–6393

*Adoption Service Information Agency, Inc. (ASIA), 8555 16th Street, Suite 603, Silver Spring, MD 20910; (301) 587–7068

*Adoptions Together, Inc., 10230 New Hampshire, Suite 200, Silver Spring, MD 20903; (301) 439–2900. There is an office in Baltimore (410) 653–3446.

*American Adoption Agency, 4308 Montgomery Road, Bethesda, MD 20814; (301) 572–4002

*Associated Catholic Charities, Archdiocese of Baltimore, 320 Cathedral Street, Baltimore, MD 21201; (410) 547–5498. There are several offices in Baltimore.

*Barker Foundation, 7945 MacArthur Boulevard, Suite 206, Cabin John, MD 20818; (301) 229–8300

*Bethany Christian Services, 1641 Route 3 Northbound, Suite 205, Crofton, MD 21114–2466; (410) 721–2835

Burlington United Methodist Family Services, Inc., St. Pauls United Methodist Church, P.O. Box 477, 318 East Oak Street, Oakland, MD 21550–1504; (301) 334–1285

Catholic Charities Archdiocese of Washington D.C., 1504 St. Camillus Drive, Silver Spring, MD 20903; (301) 434–2550

Children's Choice, Island Professional Park, Suite 200-B, Stevensville, MD 21666; (410) 643–9290. There are offices in Baltimore (410) 576–9225 and Salisbury (410) 546–6106.

*Cradle of Hope Adoption Center, 8630 Fenton Street, Silver Spring, MD 20910; (301) 587–4400

*Creative Adoptions, Inc., 10750 Hickory Ridge Road, Suite 109, Columbia, MD 21044; (301) 596–1521

*Datz Foundation, 16220 Frederick Road, Gaithersburg, MD 20877; (301) 258–0629

Family and Child Services of Washington, D.C., Inc., 5301 76th Avenue, Landover Hills, MD 20784; (301) 459–4121

*Family and Children's Services of Central Maryland, Inc., 204 W. Lanvale Street, Baltimore, MD 21217; (410) 366–1980

Family Building Center, The Mercantile-Towson Building, 409 Washington Avenue, Suite 920, Towson, MD 21204–4903; (410) 494–8112

*Holy Cross Child Placement Agency, Inc., St. John's Episcopal Church, 6701 Wisconsin Avenue, Chevy Chase, MD 20815; (301) 907–6887

*International Families, Inc., 613 Hawkesburg Lane, Silver Spring, MD 20904; (301) 384–2036

*Jewish Family Services, 5750 Park Heights Avenue, Baltimore, MD 21215; (410) 466–9200

*Jewish Social Services Agency of Metropolitan Washington, 6123 Montrose Road, Rockville, MD 20852–4880; (301) 881–3700

Latter Day Saints Social Services—East Coast, 198 Thomas Johnson Drive, Suite 13, Frederick, MD 21702; (301) 694–5896 or (800) 477–6177

Lutheran Social Services of the National Capital Area, Zion Evangelical Lutheran Church, 7410 New Hampshire Avenue, Takoma Park, MD 20017; (301) 434–0080

*New Family Foundation, 5537 Twin Knolls Road, Suite 440, Columbia, MD 21045; (410) 715–4828

New Life Adoption Agency, 9051 Baltimore National Pike, Building 1, Suite 1-D, Ellicott City, MD 21042; (410) 480–0652

*Tressler Lutheran Services of Maryland, 5000 York Road, Baltimore, MD 21212–4437; (410) 532–9600

*Welcome House Social Services of the Pearl S. Buck Foundation, Inc., 1037 Marleigh Circle, Towson, MD 21204; (410) 821–7188

*World Child, Inc., 9300 Columbia Boulevard, Silver Spring, MD 20910; (301) 588–3000

*World Child—Frank Adoption and Assistance, Inc., 1400 Spring Street, Suite 410, Silver Spring, MD 20910; (301) 589–3271

MASSACHUSETTS

State Agency: Massachusetts Department of Social Services, 24 Farnsworth Street, Boston, MA 02210; (617) 727–0900

State Exchange and Photolisting: Massachusetts Adoption Resource Exchange, Inc. (MARE), 45 Franklin Street, Boston, MA 02110–1301; (617) 542–3678 or (800) 882–1176

State Reunion Registry: Adoption Search Coordinator, Massachusetts Department of Social Services (see above)

Independent Adoption: Not permitted/identified adoption possible

Private Agencies

Adoption Center, Inc., 1105 Washington Street, West Newton, MA 02165; (617) 527–6171

*Adoption Resource Associates, 57 Russell Avenue, Watertown, MA 02172; (617) 923–1895

*Adoption Resource Center at Brightside, 2112 Riverdale Street, West Springfield, MA 01089–1099; (413) 788–7366

Adoptions with Love, Inc., 188 Needham Street, Newton, MA 02164; (617) 964–4357 or (800) 722–7731

*Alliance for Children, Inc., 40 William Street, Wellesley, MA 02181–3902; (781) 431–7148

*Beacon Adoption Center, Inc., 66 Lake Buel Road, Great Barrington, MA 01230; (413) 528–2749

*Berkshire Center for Families and Children, 480 West Street, Pittsfield, MA 01201; (413) 448–8281

*Bethany Christian Services, 1538 Turnpike Street, North Andover, MA 01845; (978) 794–9800 or (800) BETHANY

Boston Adoption Bureau, Inc., 14 Beacon Street, Suite 620, Boston, MA 02108; (617) 277–1336

*Boston Children's Services, 271 Huntington Avenue, Boston, MA 02115; (617) 267–3700

*Cambridge Adoption and Counseling Associates, Inc., 111 Mount Auburn Street, Cambridge, MA 02142; (617) 923–0370

*Cambridge Family and Children's Services, 929 Massachusetts Avenue, Cambridge, MA 02139; (617) 876–4210

Catholic Charities, 70 Lawrence Street, Lowell, MA 01852; (978) 452–1421

*Catholic Charities, 79 Elm Street, Southbridge, MA 01550; (508) 765–5936

Catholic Charities Center of the Old Colony Area, 686 N. Main Street, Brockton, MA 02401; (508) 587–0815

*Catholic Charities of Cambridge and Somerville, 270 Washington Street, Somerville, MA 02143; (617) 625–1920

*Catholic Charities of the Diocese of Worcester, 10 Hammond Street, Worcester, MA 01610–1513; (508) 797–5659. There is an office in Fitchburg (508) 343–4879.

Catholic Charities, Merrimack Valley, 430 N. Canal Street, Lawrence, MA 01840; (978) 685–5930

Catholic Charities, North Shore, 9 Margin Street, Peabody, MA 01960; (978) 532–3600

Catholic Family Services of Greater Lynn, 55 Lynn Shore Drive, Lynn, MA 01902; (781) 593–2312

*Catholic Social Services of Fall River, Inc., 783 Slade Street, Fall River, MA 02724; (508) 674–4681

*Children's Aid and Family Services of Hampshire County, Inc., 8 Trumbull Road, Northampton, MA 01060; (413) 584–5690

*Children's International Adoption Project, 22 Washington Street, Norwell, MA 02061; (617) 871–2577

Children's Services of Roxbury, Inc., 2406 Washington Street, Roxbury, MA 02119; (617) 445–6655

*China Adoption with Love, Inc, 159 High Street, Brookline, MA 02146; (617) 731–0798 or (800) 888–9812

*Concord Family Service Society, Inc., 111 Old Road, Concord, MA 01742–4141; (978) 369–4909

DARE Family Services, 17 Popular Street, Roslindale, MA 02131; (617) 469–2311. There is an office in Danvers (508) 750–0751.

Downey Side Families for Youth, 999 Liberty Street, Springfield, MA 01104; (413) 781–2123

Family and Children's Services of Catholic Charities, 53 Highland Avenue, Fitchburg, MA 01420; (508) 343–4879

Family and Children's Services of Greater Lynn, Inc., 111 N. Common Street, Lynn, MA 01902; (781) 598–5517

*Florence Crittenton League, 119 Hall Street, Lowell, MA 01854–3612; (978) 452–9671

*Full Circle Adoptions, 39 Main Street, Northampton, MA 01060; (413) 587–0007

*Gift of Love Adoption Services, Inc., 1087 Newman Avenue, Seekonk, MA 02771; (508) 826–8470

*Hope Adoptions, Inc., 21 Cedar Street, Worcester, MA 01609; (508) 752–1456

Italian Home for Children, Inc., Family Resource Program, 1125 Centre Street, Jamaica Plain, MA 02130; (617) 524–3116

*Jewish Family and Children's Services Adoption Resources, 1340 Centre Street, Newton, MA 02159; (617) 332–2218

*Jewish Family Services of Greater Springfield, Inc., 15 Lenox Street, Springfield, MA 01108

*Jewish Family Services of Metrowest, 14 Vernon Street, Framingham, MA 01701; (508) 875–3100

*Jewish Family Services of the North Shore, 324B Essex Street, Swampscott, MA 01907–1212; (617) 581–1530

Jewish Family Services of Worcester, 646 Salisbury Street, Worcester, MA 01602; (508) 755–3101

La Alianza Hispana, Inc., 409 Dudley Street, Roxbury, MA 02119; (617) 427–7175

LDS Social Services of Massachusetts, Inc., 150 Brown Street, Weston, MA 02193–2604; (603) 889–0148

*Love the Children of Massachusetts, 2 Perry Drive, Duxbury, MA 02332; (617) 934–0036

*Lutheran Social Services of New England, 416 Belmont Street, Worcester, MA 01604; (508) 791–4488

*MAPS International, 400 Commonwealth Avenue, Boston, MA 02115–2813; (617) 267–2222

Massachusetts Society for the Prevention of Cruelty to Children, 130 Liberty Street, Brockton, MA 02401; (508) 586–2660

*New Bedford Child and Family Services, 1061 Pleasant Street, New Bedford, MA 02740; (508) 996–8572

*New England Home for Little Wanderers, 161 S. Huntington Avenue, Boston, MA 02130; (617) 232–8610

*Protestant Social Service Bureau, 776 Hancock Street, Quincy, MA 02170; (617) 773–6203

*Southeastern Adoption Services, Inc. (SEAS), 585 Front Street, Marion, MA 02738; (508) 996–6683

Special Adoption Family Services, 418 Commonwealth Avenue, Boston, MA 02215; (617) 572–3678

United Homes for Children, 1147 Main Street, Tewksbury, MA 01876; (508) 640–0089. There is an office in Dorchester (617) 825–3300.

*Wide Horizons for Children, 38 Edge Hill Road, Waltham, MA 02154; (617) 894–5330

Worcester Children's Friend Society, 21 Cedar Street, Worcester, MA 01609; (508) 753–5425

MICHIGAN

State Agency: Family Independence Agency, P.O. Box 30037, Lansing, MI 48909; (517) 373–4021

State Exchange and Photolisting: Kinship/Family Adoption Registry, 30215 Southfield Road, Southfield, MI 48076; (248) 443–0306 or (800) 267–7144 and Michigan Adoption Resource Exchange, P.O. Box 6128, Jackson, MI 49204–6128; (517) 783–6273 or (800) 589–6273

State Reunion Registry: Central Adoption Registry, Family Independence Agency Adoption Services, 235 South Grand, Suite 412, Lansing, MI 48909

Independent Adoption: Not permitted/identified adoptions possible

Private Agencies

*Adoption Associates, Inc, 13535 State Road, Grand Ledge, MI

48837–9626; (517) 627–0805. There are offices in Jenison (616) 667–0677 and St. Clair Shores (810) 294–1990.

Adoption Cradle, 554 Capital Avenue, SW, Battle Creek, MI 49015; (616) 963–0794

Alternatives for Children and Families, 644 Harrison, Flint, MI 48502; (810) 235–0683

*Americans for International Aid and Adoption (AIAA), 877 S. Adams Road, Suite 106, Birmingham, MI 48009–7026; (248) 645–2211

*Bethany Christian Services, 901 Eastern Avenue NE, Grand Rapids, MI 49501–0294; (616) 224–7610. There are offices in Fremont (616) 924–3390, Holland (616) 396–0623, Kalamazoo (616) 384–0202, Madison Heights (248) 588–9400, and Paw Paw (616) 657–7096.

Binogii Placement Agency/Anishnabeck Community & Family Services, 1529 Marquette Avenue, Sault Ste. Marie, MI 49783; (906) 635–6538

Catholic Family Services, 1819 Gull Road, Kalamazoo, MI 49001; (616) 381–9800

Catholic Family Services of the Diocese of Saginaw, 710 N. Michigan Avenue, Saginaw, MI 48602; (517) 753–8446. There are offices in Midland (517) 631–4711 and Bay City (517) 892–2504.

Catholic Human Services, 154 S. Ripley Boulevard, Alpena, MI 49707; (517) 356–6389

Catholic Human Services, 111 S. Michigan, Gaylord, MI 49735; (517) 732–6761

Catholic Human Services, 1000 Hastings Street, Traverse City, MI 49686; (616) 947–8110

Catholic Social Services of Flint, 202 E. Boulevard Drive, Suite 210, Flint, MI 48503; (810) 232–9950

Catholic Social Services of Kent County, 1152 Scribner, NW, Grand Rapids, MI 49504; (616) 456–1443

Catholic Social Services of Macomb County, 235 S. Gratiot Avenue, Mount Clemens, MI 48043; (810) 468–2616

Catholic Social Services of Marquette, 347 Rock Street, Marquette, MI 49855; (906) 228–8630

Catholic Social Services of Monroe County, 16 E. Fifth Street, Monroe, MI 48161; (313) 242–3800. There is an office in Temperance (313) 847–1523.

Catholic Social Services of Oakland County, 26105 Orchard Lake Road, Suite 303, Farmington Hills, MI 48334; (248) 471–4140. There is an office in Pontiac (248) 333–3700.

Catholic Social Services of St. Clair, 2601 13th Street, Port Huron, MI 48060; (810) 987–9100

Catholic Social Services of the Diocese of Muskegon, 1095 Third Street, Suite 125, Muskegon, MI 49441; (616) 726–4735

Catholic Social Services of Upper Michigan, 500 S. Stephenson Avenue, Suite 400, Iron Mountain, MI 49801; (906) 774–3323

Catholic Social Services of Washtenaw, 4925 Packard, Ann Arbor, MI 48108–1521; (313) 971–9781

Catholic Social Services of Wayne County, 9851 Hamilton Avenue, Detroit, MI 48202; (313) 883–2100

Catholic Social Services, St. Vincent Home, 2800 W. Willow Street, Lansing, MI 48917; (517) 323–4734

Child and Family Capitol Area, 4801 Willoughby Road, Suite 1, Holt, MI 48842; (517) 699–2749

Child and Family Services of Northeast Michigan, 1044 U.S. 23, North Alpena, MI 49707; (517) 356–4567

Child and Family Services of Northwestern Michigan, 3785 Veterans Drive, Traverse City, MI 49684; (616) 946–2104

*Child and Family Services of Saginaw County, 2806 Davenport, Saginaw, MI 48602–3734; (517) 790–7500

Child and Family Services of Southwestern Michigan, 2000 S. State Street, St. Joseph, MI 49085; (616) 983–5545

Child and Family Services of the Upper Peninsula, Inc., 104 Colds Drive, Marquette, MI 49855; (906) 226–2516. There is an office in Houghton (906) 482–4488.

Child and Family Services of Western Michigan, 321 S. Beechtree Street, Grand Haven, MI 49417; (616) 846–5880. There is an office in Holland (616) 396–2301.

Child and Parent Services, 30600 Telegraph, Suite 2215, Bingham Farms, MI 48025; (248) 646–7790

*Children's Hope Adoption Services, 7823 S. Whiteville Road, Shepherd, MI 48883; (517) 828–5842

Christ Child House, 15751 Joy Road, Detroit, MI 48228; (313) 584–6077

Christian Cradle, 416 Frandor, Suite 205, Lansing, MI 48912; (517) 351–7500

Christian Family Services, 17105 W. 12 Mile Road, Southfield, MI 48076; (248) 557–8390

D. A. Blodgett Services for Children and Families, 805 Leonard, NE, Grand Rapids, MI 49503; (616) 451–2021

Eagle Village, Family Living Program, 4507 170th Avenue, Hersey, MI 49639; (616) 832–2234

*Eastern European Adoption Services, 22233 Genesis, Woodhaven, MI 48183; (313) 479–2348

Ennis Center for Children, 20100 Greenfield Road, Detroit, MI 48235; (248) 342–2699. There are offices in Flint (810) 233–4031 and Pontiac (810) 333–2520.

*Evergreen Children's Services, 10421 W. Seven Mile Road, Detroit, MI 48221; (248) 862–1000. There is an office in Southfield (810) 557–5800.

*Family Adoption Consultants, 421 W. Crosstown Parkway, Kalamazoo, MI 49005; (248) 343–3316. There is an office in Rochester (810) 652–2842.

Family and Children's Service of Calhoun and Barry Counties, 182 W. Van Buren Street, Suite 208, Battle Creek, MI 49017; (616) 965–3247

Family and Children's Service of Midland, 1714 Eastman Avenue, Midland, MI 48641–2086; (517) 631–5390

Family and Children's Service of the Kalamazoo Area, 1608 Lake Street, Kalamazoo, MI 49001; (616) 344–0202

Family Counseling and Children's Service of Lenawee County, 213 Toledo Street, Adrian, MI 49221; (517) 265–5352

*Family Service and Children's Aid of Jackson County, P.O. Box 6128, Jackson, MI 49204; (517) 787–7920

Homes for Black Children, 2340 Calvert, Detroit, MI 48206; (313) 869–2316

Huron Service for Youth, Inc., 27676 Cherry Hill Road, Garden City, MI 48135; (313) 422–5401

Huron Services for Youth, Child, & Family Services, 124 Pearl Street, Ypsilanti, MI 48197; (313) 480–1800

Interact Family Services, 1260 Woodkrest Drive, Flint, MI 48532

*International Adoption Association, Inc., 517 Baldwin, Jenison, MI 49428; (616) 457–6537 or (800) 419–0289

*Jewish Family Service, 24123 Greenfield Road, Southfield, MI 48075; (248) 559–1500

Judson Center, 23077 Greenfield, Suite 107, Southfield, MI 48075; (248) 443–5000

Keane Center for Adoption, 930 Mason, Dearborn, MI 48124; (313) 277–4664

LDS Social Services, 37634 Enterprise Court, Farmington Hills, MI 48331; (248) 553–0902

Lula Belle Stewart Center, 11000 W. McNichols, Detroit, MI 48221; (313) 862–4600

Lutheran Adoption Service, 6019 W. Saginaw Road, Bay City, MI 48707; (517) 686–3170. There are offices in Lansing (517) 886–1380 and Southfield (248) 423–2770.

Lutheran Social Service of Wisconsin and Upper Michigan, 1009 W. Ridge, Marquette, MI 49855; (906) 226–7410

Methodist Children's Home Society, 26645 W. 6 Mile Road, Detroit, MI 48240; (313) 531–6191

Michigan Indian Child Welfare Agency, 1345 Monroe Avenue, NW, Suite 220, Grand Rapids, MI 49505; (616) 454–9221. There are offices in Lansing (517) 393–3256, Sault St. Marie (906) 632–8062, Baraga, (906) 353–6178, and Wilson (906) 466–2881.

*Morning Star Adoption Resource, Inc., 26711 Woodward Street, Suite 209, Huntington Woods, MI 48070; (248) 399–2740

Oakland Family Services, 114 Orchard Lake Road, Pontiac, MI 48341; (248) 858–7766

*Orchards Children's Services, 30215 Southfield Road, Southfield, MI 48076–1360; (248) 433–8653

Sault Tribe Binogii Placement Agency, 2864 Ashmun Street, Sault St. Marie, MI 49783; (906) 632–5250

Spaulding for Children, 16250 Northland Drive, Suite 120, Southfield, MI 48075; (248) 443–0300

Spectrum Human Services, 34000 Plymouth Road, Livonia, MI 48150; (313) 552–8020. There is an office in Southfield (248) 552–8020.

St. Francis Family Services, 17500 W. 8 Mile Road, Southfield, MI 48075; (248) 552–0750

St. Vincent-Sarah Fisher Center, 27400 W. 12 Mile Road, Farmington Hills, MI 48334; (248) 626–1087

Teen Ranch—Port Huron, 3815 Lapeer Road, Port Huron, MI 48060; (810) 987–6111

Teen Ranch Family Services, 2861 Main Street, Marlette, MI 48453; (517) 635–7511. There is an office in Southfield (248) 443–2900.

*Touch of Hope Adoption Center, 12 S. Center Street, Hartford, MI 49057; (616) 621–2411

Whaley Children's Center, 1201 N. Grand Traverse, Flint, MI 48503; (810) 234–3603

Youth Living Centers, 30000 Hiveley, Inkster, MI 48141; (313) 728–3400

MINNESOTA

State Agency: Minnesota Department of Human Services, Family & Children's Services, 444 Lafayette Road, Human Services Building, St. Paul, MN 55155–3832; (612) 296–3740

State Exchange and Photolisting: Minnesota Adoption Resource Network; 2409 West 66th Street, Minneapolis, MN 55423; (612) 861–7115

State Reunion Registry: Minnesota Department of Human Services, Adoption/Guardianship Section, 444 Lafayette Road, St. Paul, MN 55155–3831; (612) 296–2795

Independent Adoption: Yes

Private Agencies

*Bethany Christian Services, 3025 Harbor Lane, North, Suite 223, Plymouth, MN 55447–5138; (612) 553–0344

*Caritas Family Services, 305 North Seventh Avenue, Suite 100, St. Cloud, MN 56303; (320) 252–4121

Catholic Charities, Diocese of Crookston, P.O. Box 610, Crookston, MN 56716; (218) 281–4224

*Catholic Charities of the Diocese of Winona, 11 Riverfront, Winona, MN 55987; (507) 454–2270. There is an office in Rochester (507) 287–2047.

*Children's Home Society of Minnesota, 2230 Como Avenue, St. Paul, MN 55108; (612) 646–6393 or (800) 952–9302

Christian Family Life Services, Inc (*see* North Dakota)

*Crossroads Adoption Services, 4620 W. 77th Street, Suite 105, Minneapolis, MN 55435; (612) 831–5707

Downey Side Minnesota, 400 Sibley Street, Suite 560, St. Paul, MN 55101; (612) 228–0117

Family Alternatives, Inc., 416 E. Hennepin Avenue, Minneapolis, MN 55414; (612) 379–5341

*Forever Families International Adoption Agency, 2004 Highway 37, Eveleth, MN 55734; (218) 744–4734

*Hope Adoption and Family Services, Inc., 421 S. Main Street, Stillwater, MN 55082; (612) 439–2446

*International Adoption Service/American Program, 4940 Viking Drive, Suite 338, Minneapolis, MN 55435; (612) 893–1343

LDS Social Services, 1813 N. Mill Street, Suite F, Naperville, IL 60563; (708) 369–0486

*Love Basket, 3902 Minnesota, Duluth, MN 55802; (218) 720–3097

Lutheran Home Christian Family Service, 611 West Main Street, Belle Plain, MN 56011; (612) 873–2215

*Lutheran Social Service of Minnesota, 2414 Park Avenue, South, Minneapolis, MN 55404; (612) 871–0221 or (888) 205–3769

*New Horizons Adoption Agency, Frost-Benico Building, Highway 254, Frost, MN 56033; (507) 878–3200

New Life Family Services, 1515 E. 66th Street. Minneapolis, MN 55423–2674; (612) 866–7643

North Homes, Inc., 924 City Home Road, Grand Rapids, MN 55744; (218) 327–3055

PATH, 2324 University Avenue, Suite 101, St. Paul, MN 55114; (612) 646–3221

*Reaching Arms International, Inc., 11409 Ridgemount Avenue, West, Minnetonka, MN 55305; (612) 541–0370

*Seton Catholic Charities of the Archdiocese of Minneapolis—St. Paul, 1600 University Avenue, Suite 400, St. Paul, MN 55104; (612) 641–1180

Summit Adoption Home Studies, Inc., 1389 Summit Avenue, St. Paul, MN 55105; (612) 645–6657

Wellspring Adoption Agency, 1219 University Avenue SE, Minneapolis, MN 55414; (612) 379–0980

MISSISSIPPI

State Agency: Department of Human Services, Adoption Unit, 750 North State Street, Jackson 39202; (601) 359–4981

State Exchange and Photolisting: Mississippi Adoption Resource Exchange, P.O. Box 352, Jackson, MS 39205; (601) 359–4407 or (800) 821–9157

State Reunion Registry: None

Independent Adoption: Permitted

Private Agencies

Adoption Centre, 128 English Village Drive, Long Beach, MS 39560; (601) 863–0011 or (800) 544–9106

Adoption Ministries of Mississippi, P.O. Box 20346, Jackson, MS 39289–0346; (601) 352–7888

AGAPE Child and Family Services (*see* Tennessee)

*Bethany Christian Services, 2618 Southerland Drive, Jackson, MS 39216; (601) 366–4282. There is an office in Hattiesburg, (601) 264–4984.

*Catholic Charities, 748 North President Street, Jackson, MS 39205; (601) 355–8634

Catholic Social and Community Services, P.O. Box 1457, Biloxi, MS 39530–1457; (601) 374–8316

Jewish Family Services (*see* Tennessee)
Latter Day Saints Social Services (*see* Louisiana)
*Lutheran Ministries of Georgia (*see* Georgia)
Mississippi Band of Choctaw Indians Agency, P.O. Box 6010, Philadelphia, MS 39350; (601) 656–5251
Mississippi Children's Home Society, 1801 North West Street, Jackson, MS 39205; (601) 352–7784
New Beginnings of Tupelo, 144 East Main Street, Tupelo, MS 38802; (601) 842–6752
*Southern Adoption Agency, 420 Crockett Avenue, Philadelphia, MS 39350; (601) 693–3933
Sunnybrook Children's Home, Inc., 222 Sunnybrook Road, Ridgeland, MS 39157; P.O. Box 4871, Jackson, MS 39296–4871; (601) 856–6555

MISSOURI

State Agency: Missouri Department of Social Services, 615 Howerton Court, Jefferson City, MO 65103–0088; (573) 751–8981
State Exchange and Photolisting: Missouri Adoption Exchange, Division of Family Services, P.O. Box 88, Jefferson City, MO 65103–0088; (573) 751–2502 or (800) 554–2222
State Reunion Registry: Adoption Information Registry (see above); (573) 751–317
Independent Adoption: Permitted

Private Agencies
*Adoption Advocate, 3100 Broadway, Suite 218, Kansas City, MO 64111; (816) 753–1711
*Adoption and Counseling Services (*see* Kansas)
Adoption and Fertility Resources, 144 Westwoods Drive, Liberty, MO 64068; (816) 781–8550
Adoption Option, 200 SE Douglas, Lee's Summit, MO 64063; (816) 224–1525

Associates in Adoption Counseling, 6915 NW 77th Terrace, Kansas City, MO 64152; (816) 746–4279

*Bethany Christian Services, 500 Northwest Plaza, Suite 1016, St. Ann, MO 63074–2225; (314) 209–0909

Catholic Charities of Kansas City, 1112 Broadway, Kansas City, MO 64111; (816) 221–4377

Catholic Services for Children and Youth, 4140 Lindell Boulevard, St. Louis, MO 63108; (314) 371–4980

Central Baptist Family Services, 7750 Clayton Road, Suite 305, Richmond Heights, MO 63117; (314) 644–4548

Children's Home Society of Missouri, 9445 Litzsinger Road, Brentwood, MO 63144; (314) 968–2350

*China's Children, 10245 Chaucer, Suite 4, St. Louis, MO 63114; (314) 890–0086

Christian Family Life Center, 7700 Clayton Road, Suite 102, St. Louis, MO 63105; (314) 946–1700

Christian Family Services of the Midwest, Inc., 6000 Blue Ridge Boulevard, Raytown, MO 64133; (913) 383–3337

*Christian Family Services, Inc., 8039 Watson Road, Suite 120, Webster Groves, MO 63119; (314) 968–2216

*Creative Families, 9378 Olive Street Road, Suite 320, St. Louis, MO 63122; (314) 567–0707

Family Therapy Center of the Ozarks, 1345 E. Sunshine, Suite 108, Springfield, MO 65804; (417) 882–7700

*Gentle Shepherd Child Placement Agency, 6405 Metcalf, Suite 318, Overland Park, KS 66202–3928; (913) 432–1353

*Highlands Child Placement Services, P.O. Box 300198, Kansas City, MO 64130–0198; (816) 924–6565

James A. Roberts Agency, 8301 State Line Road, Suite 216, Kansas City, MO 64114; (816) 523–4440

Jewish Family and Children's Services, 9385 Olive Boulevard, Olivette, MO 63044; (573) 993–1000

Kansas Children's Service League, 3200 Wayne, Kansas City, MO 64109; (913) 621–2016

*LDS Social Services, 517 W. Walnut, Independence, MO 64050; (816) 461–5512

The Light House, 1409 E. Meyer Boulevard, Kansas City, MO 64131; (816) 361–2233

*Love Basket, 4472 Goldman Road, Hillsboro, MO 63050; (314) 797–4100

*Lutheran Family and Children's Services, 4201 Lindell Boulevard, Suite 400, St. Louis, MO 63108; (314) 534–1515

Lutheran Social Services of Kansas, 3031 Holmes, Kansas City, MO 64109; (816) 931–0027

Missouri Baptist Children's Home, 11300 St. Charles Rock Road, Bridgeton, MO 63044; (314) 739–6811

Provident Counseling, 2650 Olive Street, St. Louis, MO 63103; (314) 371–6500

Salvation Army Hope Center, 3740 Marine Avenue, St. Louis, MO 63118; (314) 773–0980

*Small World Adoption Foundation, Inc., 1270 Fee Fee Road, St. Louis, MO 63146; (314) 858–9050

United Methodist Children and Family Services, 110 N. Elm, Webster Groves, MO 63119; (314) 961–5718

*Universal Adoption Services, 124 E. High Street, Jefferson City, MO 64101; (573) 634–3733

*Worldwide Love for Children, 1601 W. Sunshine, Suite L, Springfield, MO 65807; (417) 869–3151

MONTANA

State Agency: Montana Department of Public Health and Human Services, P.O. Box 8005, Helena, MT 59604; (406) 444–5919

State Exchange and Photolisting: Montana Adoption Resource Center, Post Adoption Center, P.O. Box 634, Helena, MT 59624; (406) 449–3266; and Treasure Book Photo Listing, Helena, MT; (888) 937–5437

State Reunion Registry: None

Independent Adoption: Permitted

Private Agencies

*Catholic Social Services, 25 S. Ewing, Helena, MT 59601; (406) 442–4130

*Catholic Social Services for Montana, 1222 N. 27th St, Suite 101, Billings, MT 59101

LDS Social Services, 2001 11th Avenue, Helena, MT 59601; (406) 443–1660

Lutheran Social Services, P.O. Box 1345, Great Falls, MT 59403; (406) 761–4341

NEBRASKA

State Agency: Division of Protection & Safety , Nebraska Health & Human Services, P.O. Box 95044, Lincoln, NE 68509; (402) 471–9331

State Exchange and Photolisting: Nebraska Adoption Resource Exchange (see above)

State Reunion Registry: Search/Reunion Contact Person (see above); (402) 471–9254

Independent Adoption: Permitted

Private Agencies

*Adoption Links Worldwide, 6901 Dodge Street, Suite 101, Omaha, NE 68132; (402) 556–2367

Black Homes for Black Children, 115 S. 46th Street, Omaha, NE 68132; (402) 595–2912

*Catholic Charities, 3300 N. 60th Street, Omaha, NE 68104; (402) 554–0520

*Catholic Social Service Bureau, 237 S. 70th Street, Suite 220, Lincoln, NE 68510; (402) 489–1834

*Child Saving Institute, 115 S. 46th Street, Omaha, NE 68132; (402) 553–6000

*Holt International Children's Services, Midwest Office (*see* Iowa)

Jewish Family Services, 333 S. 132nd Street, Omaha, NE 68154; (402) 330–2024

LDS Social Services (*see* Missouri)

*Lutheran Family Services of Nebraska, Inc., 120 S. 24th Street, Omaha, NE 68102; (402) 342–7007

*Nebraska Children's Home Society, 3549 Fontenelle Boulevard, Omaha, NE 68144; (402) 451–0787

Nebraska Christian Services, Inc., 11600 W. Center Road, Omaha, NE 68144; (402) 334–3278

NEVADA

State Agency: Division of Child and Family Services, 6171 W. Charleston Boulevard, Building 15, Las Vegas, NV 89158; (702) 486–7650

State Exchange and Photolisting: Nevada Adoption Exchange, Division of Child and Family Services, 610 Belrose Street, Las Vegas, NV 89158; (702) 486–7800

State Reunion Registry: Division of Child and Family Services, Adoption Registry, Capitol Complex, 711 E. Fifth Street, Carson City, NV 89710–1002; (702) 687–4968

Independent Adoption: Permitted

Private Agencies

Catholic Charities of Southern Nevada, 531 N. 30th Street, Las Vegas, NV 89101; (702) 385–3351

Catholic Community Services of Northern Nevada, 275 E. 4th Street, Reno, NV 89513–5415; (702) 322–7073

Jewish Family Service Agency, 3909 S. Maryland Parkway, Suite 205, Las Vegas, NV 89119; (702) 732–0304

LDS Social Services, 513 S. Ninth Street, Las Vegas, NV 89101; (702) 385–1072

*New Hope Child and Family Agency, 1515 E. Tropicana, Suite 570; Las Vegas, NV 89119; (702) 734–9665

*New Hope Child and Family Agency, 440 Ridge Street, Reno, NV 89502; (702) 323–0122

NEW HAMPSHIRE

State Agency: New Hampshire Division for Children, Youth and Families, 6 Hazen Drive, Concord, NH 03301; (603) 271–4721

State Exchange and Photolisting: (see above)

State Reunion Registry: None

Independent Adoption: Permitted

Private Agencies

Adoptive Families for Children, 26 Fairview Street, Keene, NH 03431; (603) 357–4456

*Bethany Christian Services, P.O. Box 320, Candia, NH 03034–0320; (603) 483–2886

Casey Family Services, 105 Loudon Road, Concord, NH 03301; (603) 224–8909

Child and Family Services of New Hampshire, 99 Hanover Street, Manchester, NH 03105; (603) 668–1920 or (800) 642–6486

*Creative Advocates for Children and Families, P.O. Box 1703, Manchester, NH 03105; (603) 623–5006

LDS Social Services of Massachusetts, Inc. (*see* Masschusetts)

*Lutheran Child and Family Services of New Hampshire, 85 Manchester Street, Concord, NH 03301; (603) 224–8111

New Hampshire Adoption Bureau, 71 W. Merrimack Street, Manchester, NH 03103; (800) 338–2224

*New Hampshire Catholic Charities, Inc., 215 Myrtle Street, Manchester, NH 03105; (603) 669–3030 or (800) 562–5249

*New Hope Christian Services, 210 Silk Farm Road, Concord, NH 03301; (603) 225–0992

*Vermont Children's Aid Society (*see* Vermont)

*Wide Horizons for Children (*see* Massachusetts)

NEW JERSEY

State Agency: New Jersey Division of Youth and Family Services, 50 E. State Street, Trenton, NJ 08625–0717; (609) 292–9139

State Exchange and Photolisting: Division of Youth and Family Services, Adoption Exchange Operations Support Unit, 50 E. State Street, Trenton, NJ 08625; (609) 984–5453

State Reunion Registry: (see above; for placements by NJ DYFS only)

Independent Adoption: Permitted

Private Agencies

Adoption ARC, Inc (*see* Pennsylvania)

*Adoptions from the Heart, 451 Woodland Avenue, Cherry Hill, NJ 08002; (609) 465–4481

*Adoptions International (*see* Pennsylvania)

Adoption Services Associates (*see* Texas)

Bethanna (*see* Pennsylvania)

*Bethany Christian Services, 1120 Goffle Road, Hawthorne, NJ 07506; (201) 427–2566

*Bethany Christian Services (*see* Pennsylvania)

*Better Living Services, Inc., Suite C, 560 Springfield Avenue, Westfield, NJ 07090–2969; (908) 654–0277

Brookwood Child Care (*see* New York)

*Catholic Charities, Diocese of Metuchen, 101 North Gaston Avenue, Somerville, NJ 08876; (908) 704–8252

Catholic Charities, Diocese of Trenton, 115 W. Pearl Street, Burlington, NJ 08016; (609) 386–6221

*Catholic Community Services of Newark, 499 Belgrove Drive, Kearny, NJ 07032; (201) 991–3770

*Catholic Family and Community Services, 476 17th Avenue, Paterson, NJ 07501; (201) 523–9595

Catholic Home Bureau for Dependent Children *(see* New York)

Catholic Social Services *(see* Pennsylvania)

Catholic Social Services of the Diocese of Camden, 810 Montrose Street, Vineland, NJ 08360; (609) 691–1841

Child and Home Study Associates *(see* Pennsylvania)

*Children of the World, 685 Bloomfield Avenue, Suite 201, Verona, NJ 07044; (973) 239–0100

Children's Adoption Network, Inc. *(see* Pennsylvania)

Children's Adoption Services, Inc. *(see* Idaho)

*Children's Aid and Family Services, Inc., 575 Main Street, Hackensack, NJ 07601; (201) 487–2022. There are offices in Morristown (201) 285–0165 and Orange (201) 673–6454.

The Children's Aid Society *(see* New York)

Children's Choice, Inc., 151 Fries Mill Road, Turnersville, NJ 08012; (609) 228–5223

*Children's Home Society of New Jersey, 929 Parkside Avenue, Trenton, NJ 08618; (609) 695–6274. There is an office in Clinton (908) 852–5825.

Chosen Children Adoption Services, Inc. *(see* Kentucky)

*Christian Homes of Children, 275 State Street, Hackensack, NJ 07601; (201) 342–4235

Downey Side Families for Youth, 1610 S. Broad Street, Hamilton Township, NJ 08610; (609) 392–7300

*Family and Children's Services, 40 North Avenue, Elizabeth, NJ 07207; (908) 352–7474

*Family Focus *(see* New York)

*Family Options, P.O. Box 447, Lincroft, NJ 07738; (908) 946–0880

Friends In Adoption (*see* Vermont)

Golden Cradle, 1050 N. Kings Highway, Suite 201, Cherry Hill, NJ 08034; (609) 667–2229

Graham-Windham Child Care (*see* New York)

*Growing Families, Inc., 178 South Street, Freehold, NJ 07728; (908) 431–4330

Harlem Dowling Children Services (*see* New York)

*Holt International Children's Services, 340 Scotch Road, Trenton, NJ 08638; (609) 882–4972

*Homestudies and Adoption Placement Services, Inc., 668 American Region Drive, Teaneck, NJ 07666; (201) 836–5554

*Jewish Child Care Association (*see* New York)

Jewish Family and Children's Agency (*see* Pennsylvania)

Jewish Family and Children's Services, Suite 150, 1301 Springdale Road, Cherry Hill, NJ 08003; (609) 424–1333

Jewish Family Services of Central New Jersey, 655 Westfield Avenue, Elizabeth, NJ 07208; (908) 352–8375

Jewish Family Services of Metro West, 256 Columbia Turnpike, Suite 105, Florham Park, NJ 07932–0825; (973) 674–4210

Jewish Family Services of Monmouth County, 705 Summerfield Avenue, Asbury Park, NJ 07712; (908) 774–6886

Juvenile Justice Center (*see* Pennsylvania)

LDS Social Services (*see* New York)

*Louise Wise Services (*see* New York)

*Lutheran Social Ministries of New Jersey, 120 Route 156, Yardville, NJ 08620; (609) 585–0303

Marian Adoption Services (*see* Pennsylvania)

*New Beginnings Family and Children's Services, Inc. (*see* New York)

New York Catholic Guardian Society (*see* New York)
*The New York Foundling Hospital (*see* New York)
*Seedlings, Inc., 1 Tall Timber Drive, Morristown, NJ 07960; (201) 605–1188
Sheltering Arms Children's Services (*see* New York)
Small World Agency (*see* Tennessee)
*Spence-Chapin Services to Families and Children (*see* New York)
St. Dominic's Home (*see* New York)
Tabor Children's Services (*see* Pennsylvania)
*The Gladney Center (*see* Texas)
United Family and Children's Society, 305 W. Seventh Street, Plainfield, NJ 07060; (908) 755–4848
*Voice for International and Domestic Adoptions (*see* New York)
*Welcome House Social Services of the Pearl S. Buck Foundation (*see* Pennsylvania)
*Wide Horizons for Children, Inc. (*see* Massachusetts)
Women's Christian Alliance (*see* Pennsylvania)

NEW MEXICO

State Agency: New Mexico Children, Youth and Families Department, P.O. Drawer 5160, Santa Fe, NM 87502; (505) 827–8456
State Exchange and Photolisting: New Mexico Adoption Exchange (see above); (505) 827–8422
State Reunion Registry: None
Independent Adoption: Permitted

Private Agencies

*A.M.O.R. Adoptions, Inc., 4208 Rancho Centro, NW, Albuquerque, NM 87120; (505) 897–1112 or (800) 596–2273

Adoption Assistance, 10609 Antonio NE, Albuquerque, NM 87122; (505) 821–0088

Adoptions Plus, 6022 Constitution, Suite 5, Albuquerque, NM 87110; (505) 262–0446

Catholic Social Services, Inc., 1234 San Felipe Avenue, Santa Fe, NM 87505–0443; (505) 982–0441

*Chaparral Maternity and Adoptions, 1503 University Boulevard, NE, Albuquerque, NM 87102; (505) 243–2586

Child-Rite/Adopt a Special Kid (AASK) of New Mexico, 5345 Wyoming, #105, Albuquerque, NM; (505) 797–4191. There are offices in Santa Fe (505) 988–5177 and Taos (505) 758–0343.

Christian Child Placement Services, 1356 NM 236, Portales, NM 88130; (505) 356–4232

Family for Children, 6209 Hendrex NE, Albuquerque, NM 87110; (505) 881–4200

La Families Placement Services, Suite 103, 707 Broadway NE, Albuquerque, NM 87102; (505) 766–9361

LDS Social Services, 3807 Atrisco, NW, Suite C, Albuquerque, NM 87120; (505) 836–5947. There is an office in Farmington (505) 327–6123.

*Rainbow House International, 19676 Highway 85, Belen, NM 87002; (505) 861–1234

Triad Adoption Services, Inc., 2811 Indian School Road, NE, Albuquerque, NM 87106; (505) 266–0456

NEW YORK

State Agency: New York State Department of Social Services, 40 N. Pearl Street, Albany, NY 12243; (518) 474–9406

State Exchange and Photolisting: New York State Adoption Service (see above); (518) 473–1512 or (800) 345-KIDS

State Reunion Registry: Adoption Information Registry, Department of Health, Public Health Representative, Corning Tower, Room 208, Albany, NY 12237; (518) 474–1746

Independent Adoption: Permitted

Private Agencies

Abbott House, 100 North Broadway, Irvington, NY 10533; (914) 591–3200

Adoption and Counseling Services, Inc., 1 Fayette Park, Syracuse, NY 13202; (315) 471–0109

*Americans for International Aid and Adoption, P.O. Box 290, Plainville, NY 13137–0290; (315) 638–9449

Angel Guardian Home, 6301 12th Avenue, Brooklyn, NY 11219; (718) 232–1500

Association to Benefit Children—Variety House, 404 E. 91st Street, New York, NY 10128; (212) 369–2010

Astor Home for Children, P.O. Box 5005, Rhinebeck, NY 12572; (914) 876–4081

Baker Victory Services, 790 Ridge Road, Lackawanna, NY 14218; (716) 828–9510

*Bethany Christian Services, Warwick Reformed Church, 16 Maple Avenue, Warwick, NY 10990; (914) 987–1453

*Brookwood Child Care, 25 Washington Street, Brooklyn, NY 11201; (718) 596–5555

Cardinal McCloskey School and Home, 2 Holland Avenue, White Plains, NY 10603; (914) 997–8000

*Catholic Charities of Buffalo, 525 Washington Street, Buffalo, NY 14203; (716) 856–4494

*Catholic Charities of Cortland, 33–35 Central Avenue, Cortland, NY 13045; (607) 756–5992

*Catholic Charities of Ogdensburg, P.O. Box 296, 716 Caroline Street, Ogdensburg, NY 13669–0296; (315) 393–2660.

There are offices in Malone (518) 483–1460 and Watertown (315) 788–4330.

Catholic Charities of Oswego, 181 West 2nd Street, Oswego, NY 13126; (315) 343–9540

Catholic Charities of Plattsburgh, 151 S. Catherine Street, Plattsburgh, NY 12901; (518) 561–0470

Catholic Charities of Rome, 212 W. Liberty Street, Rome, NY 13440; (315) 337–8600

Catholic Charities of Syracuse, 1654 W. Onondaga Street, Syracuse, NY 13204; (315) 424–1871

*Catholic Family Center, 25 Franklin Street, Rochester, NY 14604; (716) 262–7134

Catholic Guardian Society of New York, 1011 First Avenue, New York, NY 10022; (212) 371–1000

*Catholic Home Bureau for Dependent Children, 1011 First Avenue, New York, NY 10022; (212) 371–1000

*Catholic Social Services of Broome County, 232 Main Street, Binghamton, NY 13905; (607) 729–9166

*Catholic Social Services of Utica/Syracuse, 1408 Genesee Street, Utica, NY 13502; (315) 724–2158

Central Brooklyn Coordinating Council, 1958 Fulton Street, Brooklyn, NY 11233; (718) 778–1400

Child and Family Services, 678 W. Onondaga Street, Syracuse, NY 13204; (315) 474–4291

Child and Family Services of Erie, 107 Statler Towers, Suite 555, Buffalo, NY 14202; (716) 856–3802

Child Development Support Corporation, 352–358 Classon Avenue, Brooklyn, NY 11238; (718) 398–2050

Children's Aid Society, 150 E. 45th Street, New York, NY 10017; (212) 949–4955

Children's Home of Kingston, 26 Grove Street, Kingston, NY 12401; (914) 331–1448

Children's Home of Poughkeepsie, 91 Fulton Street, Poughkeepsie, NY 12601; (914) 452–1420

Children's Village, Echo Hills, Dobbs Ferry, NY 10522; (914) 693–0600

Coalition for Hispanic Family Services, 315 Wyckoff Avenue, Brooklyn, NY 11237; (718) 497–6090

Community Maternity Services, 27 N. Main Avenue, Albany, NY 12203; (518) 438–2322

Concord Family Services, 1313 Bedford Avenue, Brooklyn, NY 11216; (718) 398–3499

Downey Side Families for Youth, P.O. Box 2139, New York, NY 10003; (212) 629–8599

*Edwin Gould Services for Children, 41 E. 11th Street, New York, NY 10003; (212) 598–0051

Episcopal Mission Society, 18 W. 18th Street, New York, NY 10011–4607; (212) 675–1000

Family and Children's Services of Broome County, Binghamton, NY 13905; (607) 729–6206

Family and Children's Services of Ithaca, 204 N. Cayuga Street, Ithaca, NY 14850; (607) 273–7494

*Family and Children's Services of Schenectady, 246 Union Street, Schenectady, NY 12305; (518) 393–1369

Family Connections, 20 Hyatt Street, Cortland, NY 13045; (607) 756–6574

*Family Focus, 54–40 Little Neck Parkway, Suite 3, Little Neck, NY 11362; (718) 224–1919

Family Service of Utica, Suite 201, 401 Columbia Street, Utica, NY 13502; (315) 735–2236

Family Service of Westchester, 1 Summit Avenue, White Plains, NY 10606; (914) 948–8004

Family Support Systems Unlimited, 2530 Grand Concourse, Bronx, NY 10458; (718) 220–5400

*Family Tree, 1743 Route 9, Clifton Park, NY 12065; (518) 371–1336

Forestdale, Inc., 67–35 112 Street, Forest Hills, NY 11375; (718) 263–0740

Friendship House of Western New York, Inc., 90 Dona Street, Lackawanna, NY 14218; (716) 826–1500

From the Heart, 145 N. Main Street, Mechanicville, NY 12118–1619; (518) 664–5988

Graham-Windham Child Care, 33 Irving Place, New York, NY 10003; (212) 529–6445

Green Chimneys, Caller Box 719, Putnam Lake Road, Brewster, NY 10509–0719; (914) 279–2996

Harlem Dowling Children's Services, 2090 Seventh Avenue, New York, NY 10027; (212) 749–3656

Heartshare Human Services, 191 Joralemon Street, Brooklyn, NY 11201; (718) 330–0639

Hillside Children's Center, 1337 E. Main Street, Rochester, NY 14609; (716) 654–4529

International Social Service American Branch, Inc., 95 Madison Avenue, 3rd Floor, New York, NY 10016; (212) 532–5858

Jewish Board of Family and Children Services, 120 W. 57th Street, New York, NY 10019; (212) 582–9100

*Jewish Child Care Association, 575 Lexington Avenue, New York, NY 10022; (212) 371–1313

Jewish Family Services of Erie County, 70 Barker Street, Buffalo, NY 14209; (716) 883–1914

Jewish Family Service of Rochester, 441 E. Avenue, Rochester, NY 14607; (716) 461–0110

Lakeside Family and Children's Services, 185 Montague Street, Brooklyn, NY 11201; (718) 237–9700

LDS Social Services of New York, 2 Jefferson Street, #205, Poughkeepsie, NY 12601; (914) 485–2755

Leake and Watts Children's Home, 463 Hawthorne Avenue, Yonkers, NY 10705; (914) 963–5220

Little Flower Children's Services, 186 Remsen Street, Brooklyn, NY 11201; (718) 875–3500

Louise Wise Services, 12 E. 94th Street, New York, NY 10128; (212) 876–3050

Lutheran Service Society of New York, 2500 Kensington Avenue, Buffalo, NY 14226; (716) 839–3391

Lutheran Social Services, Inc., 27 Park Place, Suite 400, New York, NY 10007; (212) 406–9110

*MAPS New York, P.O. Box 26920, Rochester, NY 14626; (716) 723–8773

McMahon Services for Children, 305 Seventh Avenue, New York, NY 10001; (212) 243–7070

Mercy Home for Children, 310 Prospect Park, West, Brooklyn, NY 11215; (718) 467–2564

Miracle Makers, Inc., 510 Gates Avenue, Brooklyn, NY 11216; (718) 385–2273

Mission of the Immaculate Virgin, 6581 Hylan Boulevard, Staten Island, NY 10309; (718) 317–2627

New Alternatives for Children, 37 W. 26th Street, New York, NY 10010; (212) 696–1550

*New Beginnings Family and Children's Services, Inc., 141 Willis Avenue, Mineola, NY 11501; (516) 747–2204

New Hope Family Services, 3519 James Street, Syracuse, NY 13206; (315) 437–8300

*New Life Adoption Agency, Suite 301, E. Genesee Street, Syracuse, NY 13202; (315) 422–7300

New York Catholic Guardian Society, 1011 First Avenue, New York, NY 10022; (212) 371–1000

*New York Foundling Hospital, 590 Avenue of the Americas, New York, NY 10011; (212) 727–6828

Ohel Children's Home and Family Services, 4510 16th Avenue, 4th Floor, Brooklyn, NY 11204; (718) 851–6300

Open Arms Adoption and Family Center, 27 Ericson Drive, Greenfield Center, NY 12833; (518) 893–7442

*Parsons Child and Family Center, 60 Academy Road, Albany, NY 12208; (518) 426–2600

Pius XII Youth/Family Services, 188 W. 230 Street, Bronx, NY 10463; (718) 562–7855

PRACA Child Care, 53 Broadway, New York, NY 10003; (212) 673–7320

Salvation Army Foster Home, 132 W. 14th Street, New York, NY 10011; (212) 807–6100

Sheltering Arms Children Services, 122 E. 29th Street, New York, NY 10016; (212) 679–4242

Society for Seamen's Children, 25 Hyatt Street, 4th Floor, Staten Island, NY 10301; (718) 447–7740

*Spence-Chapin Adoption Services, 6 E. 94th Street, New York, NY 10128–0612; (212) 369–0300

St. Augustine Center, 1600 Filmore Avenue, Buffalo, NY 14211; (716) 897–4110

St. Christopher Ottilie, 12 Main Avenue, Sea Cliff, NY 11579; (516) 759–1844. There are offices in Jamaica (718) 526–7533, Brooklyn (718) 935–9466, and Brentwood (516) 273–2733.

St. Christopher's/Jennie Clarkson, 71 S. Broadway, Dobbs Ferry, NY 10522; (914) 693–3030

St. Dominics Home, 343 E. 137th Street, Bronx, NY 10454; (718) 993–5765

St. Joseph's Children's Services, 540 Atlantic Avenue, Brooklyn, NY 11217–1982; (718) 858–8700

St. Mary's Child and Family Services, 525 Convent Road, Syosset, NY 11791; (516) 921–0808

St. Vincent's Services, 66 Boerum Place, P.O. Box 174, Brooklyn, NY 11202; (718) 522–3700

Talbot-Perkins Children Services, 116 W. 32nd Street, New York, NY 10001; (212) 736–2510

Urban League of Rochester, Minority Adoption Program, 265 North Clinton Ave, Rochester, NY 14605; (716) 325–6530

*Voice for International and Domestic Adoptions (VIDA), 345 Allen Street, Hudson, NY 12534; (518) 828–4527

NORTH CAROLINA

State Agency: North Carolina Department of Health and Human Services, Division of Social Services, 325 N. Salisbury Street, Raleigh, NC 27603–5905; (919) 733–3801

State Exchange and Photolisting: North Carolina Adoption Resource Exchange (see above)

State Reunion Registry: None

Independent Adoption: Permitted

Private Agencies

Another Choice for Black Children, P.O. Box 494, Sanford, NC 27330; (919) 774–3534 or (800) 774–3534

Association for Guidance, Aid, Placement, and Empathy (AGAPE), 302 College Road, Greensboro, NC 27410; (910) 855–7107

*Bethany Christian Services, Inc., P.O. Box 15569, Asheville, NC 28813–0569; (704) 274–7146

Caring for Children, P.O. Box 19113, Asheville, NC 28815; (704) 253–0241

*Carolina Adoption Services, Inc., 1000 N. Elm Street, Greensboro, NC 27401; (910) 275–9660

Catholic Social Ministries of the Diocese of Raleigh, Inc., 400 Oberlin Road, Suite 350, Raleigh, NC 27605; (919) 832–0225

Catholic Social Services of the Diocese of Charlotte, Inc., 1524 E. Morehead Street, Charlotte, NC 28236; (704) 343–9954

Children's Home Society of North Carolina, Inc., 740 Chestnut Street, Greensboro, NC 27415–4608; (910) 274–1538

*Christian Adoption Services, 624 Matthews-Mint Road, Suite 134, Matthews, NC 28105; (704) 847–0038

*Datz Foundation of North Carolina, 875 Walnut Street, Cary, NC 27511; (919) 319–6635

Family Services, Inc., 610 Coliseum Drive, Winston-Salem, NC 27106–5393; (919) 722–8173

*Gladney Center, 1811 Sardis Road, North, Charlotte, NC 28270; (704) 849–2003

*International Adoption Society, 3803B Computer Drive, Suite 201, Raleigh, NC 27609; (919) 510–9135

LDS Social Services, 5624 Executive Center Drive, Suite 109, Charlotte, NC 28212–8832; (704) 535–2436

*Lutheran Family Services in the Carolinas, Inc., 505 Oberlin Road, Raleigh, NC 27605; (919) 832–2620

NORTH DAKOTA

State Agency: North Dakota Department of Human Services, State Capitol Building, 600 E. Boulevard, Bismarck, ND 58505; (701) 328–4805

State Exchange and Photolisting: see above; (701) 328–2316

State Confidential Intermediary Service: Adoption Search/Disclosure (see above)

Independent Adoption: Not permitted

Private Agencies

Catholic Family Service, 1223 S. 12th Street, Bismarck, ND 58504–6633; (701) 255–1793. There are offices in Fargo (701) 235–4457, Grand Forks (701) 775–4196, and Minot (701) 852–2854.

*Christian Family Life Services, 203 S. Eighth Street, Fargo, ND 58103; (701) 237–4473

LDS Social Services, P.O. Box 3100, Bismarck, ND 58502; (701) 342–3500

Lutheran Social Services, 211 S. Third Street, Grand Forks, ND 58201; (701) 772–7577. There are offices in Minot (701) 838–7800 and Bismarck (701) 223–1510.

*Lutheran Social Services of North Dakota, 1325 S. 11th Street, Fargo, ND 58107–0389; (701) 235–7341

*New Horizons Foreign Adoption Service, 2823 Woodland Place, Bismarck, ND 58504; (701) 258–8650

Village Family Service Center, 1223 S. 12th, Bismarck, ND 58501. (701) 255–1165. There are offices in Fargo (701) 235–6433, Grand Forks (701) 746–8062, Minot (701) 852–3328, and Williston (701) 774–3328.

OHIO

State Agency: Office of Family & Child Services, Ohio Department of Human Services, 65 E. State Street, 5th Floor, Columbus, OH 43266–0423; (614) 466–9274

State Exchange and Photolisting: Southwest Ohio Adoption Exchange, Department of Human Services, 628 Sycamore Street, Cincinnati, OH 45202; (513) 632–6366; and Ohio Adoption Photo Listing (OAPL), Bureau of Children Services, Adoption Services Section, 65 E. State Street, Columbus, OH 43266–0423; (614) 466–1213

State Reunion Registry: Adoption Registry, Ohio Department of Health, Vital Statistics, P.O. Box 15098, Columbus, OH 43266–0588; (614) 644–5635

Independent Adoption: Permitted

Private Agencies

A Place to Call Home, Inc., 4864 Whisper Cove Court, Gahanna, OH 43230; (614) 476–0850

Adopt a Special Kid (AASK) of the Midwest, 1025 N. Reynolds Road, Toledo, OH 43615; (419) 534–3350

Adoption at Adoption Circle, 2500 E. Main Street, Suite 103, Columbus, OH 43209; (614) 237–7222 or (800) 927–7222

Adoption by Gentle Care, 17 Brickel Street, Columbus, OH 43215; (614) 469–0007

The Adoption Center, Inc., 12151 Ellsworth Road, North Jackson, OH 44451; (330) 547–8255

Adriel School, Inc., 414 North Detroit Street, West Liberty, OH 43357; (937) 465–0010

Advantage Adoption and Foster Care, 1342 West Fourth Street, Mansfield, OH 44906; (419) 528–4411

Agape for Youth, Inc., 914 Senate Drive, Dayton, OH 45459; (513) 439–4406

American International Adoption Agency, 7045 County Line Road, Williamsfield, OH 44093; (330) 876–5656

Applewood Centers, Inc., 2525 East 22nd Street, Cleveland, OH 44115–3266; (216) 781–2043

Bair Foundation, 5249 Belmont Avenue, Youngstown, OH 44505–1023; (330) 759–7272

Baptist Children's Home and Family Ministries, Inc., 1934 S. Limestone Street, Springfield, OH 45505; (937) 322–0006

Beech Acres, 6881 Beechmont Avenue, Cincinnati, OH 45230; (513) 231–6630

Beech Brook/Spaulding for Children, 3737 Lander Road, Pepper Pike, OH 44124; (216) 831–2255

Bellefaire Jewish Children's Bureau, 22001 Fairmount Boulevard, Shaker Heights, OH 44118; (216) 932–2800

Berea Children's Home, 202 E. Bagley Road, Berea, OH 44017; (216) 234–7501

Building Bridges, 2157 Salem Avenue, Dayton, OII 45406; (513) 274–6619

*Catholic Charities Diocese of Toledo, 1933 Spielbusch Avenue, Toledo, OH 43624; (419) 244–6711

Catholic Charities Services Corp/Catholic Social Services of Lake County, 8 N. State Street, Suite 455, Painesville, OH 44077; (216) 946–7264

Catholic Community Services, 1175 Laird Avenue, Warren, OH 44483; (330) 393–4254

Catholic Community Services of Stark County, Inc., 625 Cleveland Avenue, NW, Canton, OH 44702; (330) 455–0374

Catholic Service League of Ashtabula County, 4200 Park Avenue, Ashtabula, OH 44004–6857; (216) 992–2121

*Catholic Social Services, Inc., 197 E. Gay Street, Columbus, OH 43215–3229; (614) 221–5891

Catholic Social Service of Cuyahoga County, 7800 Detroit Avenue, Cleveland, OH 44102; (216) 631–3499

Catholic Social Services of Lorain County, 2136 N. Ridge Road, Elyria, OH 44035; (216) 324–2614

*Catholic Social Services of Southwestern Ohio, 100 E. Eighth Street, Cincinnati, OH 45202; (513) 241–7745

*Catholic Social Services of the Miami Valley, 922 W. Riverview Avenue, Dayton, OH 45407–2400; (937) 223–7217

Children's Home of Cincinnati, Ohio, 5050 Madison Road, Cincinnati, OH 45227; (513) 272–2800

Children's Protective Service of the Ohio Humane Society, 2400 Reading Road, Cincinnati, OH 45202; (513) 721–7044

Christian Children's Home of Ohio, 2685 Armstrong Road, Wooster, OH 44691; (330) 345–7949

Clear Creek Valley of Ohio, 9280 Ridge Road, Amanda, OH 43102–0338; (330) 345–7949 or (800) 643–9073

Colgan Foundation, 1930 Maple Avenue, Zanesville, OH 43701; (614) 453–9089

Crittenton Family Services, Inc., 1414 E. Broad Street, Columbus, OH 43205; (614) 251-0103

Diversion, 101 E. Sandusky Street, Suite 200, Findlay, OH 45840; (419) 422–4770

European Adoption Consultants, 9800 Boston Road, North Royalton, OH 44133; (440) 237–3554

*Family Adoption Consultants, 8536 Crow Drive, Macedonia, OH 44056; (216) 468–0673

*Family Service Association, 226 N. 4th Street, Steubenville, OH 43952; (614) 283–4763

*Family Services of Summit County, 212 E. Exchange Street, Akron, OH 44304; (330) 376–9494

Focus Network, 799 S. Main Street, Lima, OH 45804; (419) 222–1168

Focus on Youth, Inc., 2718 East Kemper Road, Cincinnati, OH 45241; (513) 771–4710

Hannah's Hope Adoption by Cathedral Ministries, 5225 Alexis Road, Sylvania, OH 43560; (419) 882–8463

HARAMBEE, Services for Black Families, 11811 Shaker Boulevard, Cleveland, OH 44120; (216) 791–2229

Harbor House Maternity Home, 119 E. Fayette Street, Celina, OH 45822; (419) 586–8961

The House of New Hope, 951 B Buckeye Avenue, Newark, OH 43055–2520; (614) 345–5437

Inner Peace Homes, 136½ South Main Street, Bowling Green, OH 43402; (419) 354–6525

Jewish Family and Children's Services, 517 Gypsy Lane, Youngstown, OH 44504; (330) 746–7929

*Jewish Family Service, 4501 Denlinger Road, Dayton, OH 45426; (937) 854–2944. There are offices in Akron (330) 867–3388 and Sylvania (419) 885–2561.

Jewish Family Services/Adoption Connection, 11223 Cornell Park Drive, Cincinnati, OH 45242; (513) 489–1616

KARE, Inc. (Kids Are Really Essential), 3453 W. Siebenthaler Avenue, Dayton, OH 45406; (513) 661–0084

LDS Social Services, 4431 Marketing Place, Groveport, OH 43125; (614) 836–2466

Lutheran Children's Aid and Family Services, 4100 Franklin Boulevard, Cleveland, OH 44113; (216) 281–2500

*Lutheran Social Services of Central Ohio, 750 East Broad Street, Columbus, OH 43205–1000; (614) 228–5200

Lutheran Social Services of Northwestern Ohio, Inc., 2149 Collingwood Boulevard, Toledo, OH 43620; (419) 243–9178

Lutheran Social Services of the Miami Valley, 3131 South Dixie Drive, Dayton, OH 45439; (937) 643–0020

Marycrest, 8010 Brookside Road, Independence, OH 44131; (216) 524–5280

Mathis Care, 435 Dayton Street, Cincinnati, OH 45214; (513) 926–4522

Mid-Western Children's Home, 4581 Long Spurling Road, Pleasant Plain, OH 45162; (513) 877–2141

New Hope Adoptions International, 101 W. Sandusky Street, Findlay, OH 45840; (419) 423–0760

Newstart Foundation, Inc., 119 Main Street, Chardon, OH 44024; (216) 286–1155

Ohio Youth Advocate Program, Inc., 3780 Ridge Mill Drive, Hilliard, OH 43026–9231; (614) 777–8777

Options for Families and Youth, 5133 West 140th Street, Brookpark, OH 44017; (216) 234–3247

Pressley Ridge Schools, 2368 Victory Parkway, Cincinnati, OH 45206; (513) 559–1402

Private Adoption Services, 3411 Michigan Avenue, Cincinnati, OH 45208; (513) 871–5777

Rosemont Center, 2440 Daylight Avenue, Columbus, OH 43211; (614) 471–2626

Specialized Alternatives for Families and Youth, 10100 Elida Road, Delphos, OH 45833; (419) 695–8010 or (800) 532–7239

St. Aloysius Orphanage, 4721 Reading Road, Cincinnati, OH 45237; (513) 242–7600

St. Joseph Children's Treatment Center, 650 St. Paul Avenue, Dayton, OH 45410; (937) 254–3562

SYMBIONT, 27 West Church Street, Newark, OH 43055; (614) 345–3862

V. Beacon Agency, 743 South Bryne Road, Toledo, OH 43609; (419) 382–3572

Westark Family Services, Inc, 325 Third Street SE, Massillon, OH 46646; (330) 832–5043

World Family Adoption Studies, Inc., 552 Linwood Avenue, Columbus, OH 43205; (614) 258–5247

Youth Engaged for Success, 3930 Salem Avenue, Dayton, OH 45406; (937) 275–0762

Youth Services Network of Southwest Ohio, 4124 Linden Avenue, Dayton, OH 45432; (937) 256–9113

OKLAHOMA

State Agency: Department of Human Services, P.O. Box 25352, Oklahoma City, OK 73125; (405) 521–2475

State Exchange and Photolisting: None

State Reunion Registry: Voluntary Adoption Reunion Registry and Confidential Intermediary Search Program (see above); (405) 521–4373

Independent Adoption: Permitted

Private Agencies

Adoption Affiliates, 6136 E. 32nd Place, Tulsa, OK 74135; (918) 664–2275 or (800) 253–6307

Adoption Center of Northeastern Oklahoma, 6202 S. Lewis, Tulsa, OK 74136; (918) 582–5467

Associated Catholic Charities, 1501 N. Classen Boulevard, Oklahoma City, OK 73106; (405) 523–3000

Baptist Children's Home, 16301 S. Western, Oklahoma City, OK 73170; (405) 691–7781

*Baptist General Convention, 3800 N. May Avenue, Oklahoma City, OK 73112; (405) 942–3800

Bethany Adoption Service, 3940 N. College, Bethany, OK 73008–0531; (405) 789–5423

*Bless This Child, Inc., Route 4, Box 1005, Checotah, OK 74426; (918) 473–7045

*Catholic Charities, 739 N. Denver, Tulsa, OK 74148; (918) 585–8167

Chosen Child Adoption Agency, P.O. Box 55424, Tulsa, OK 74155–5424; (918) 298–0082

*Christian Homes of Abilene, 802 N. 10th, Duncan, OK 73533; (405) 252–5131

Christian Services in Oklahoma, P.O. Box 36000, Oklahoma City, OK 73136–2000; (405) 478–3362

Cradle of Lawton, 902 NW Kingwood, Lawton, OK 73505; (405) 355–1730

Crisis Pregnancy Outreach, 11604 E. 58th Street, Tulsa, OK 74146; (918) 252–9897

Deaconess Home, 5300 N. Grand Boulevard, Oklahoma City, OK 73112; (405) 949–4200

*Dillon International Inc., 3530 East 31st Street, Tulsa, OK 74135–1519; (918) 749–4600

*Edna Gladney Center, 6403 N. Grand Boulevard, Suite 1040, Oklahoma City, OK 73116; (405) 848–8433

*For the Love of a Child Adoption Services Inc., 11212 N. May Avenue, Suite 200, Oklahoma City, OK 73120; (405) 749–0400

Hannah's Prayer Adoption Agency, 8621 S. Memorial, Tulsa, OK 74133; (918) 254–0189

*Heartland International, 1221 Sun Valley, Midwest City, OK 73110; (405) 741–1526

*Heritage Family Services, P.O. Box 4646, Tulsa, OK 74159; (918) 584–3700

LDS Social Services, 4500 S. Garnett, Tulsa, OK 74102; (918) 665–3090

*Lutheran Social Services, 3000 United Founders Boulevard, Suite 141, Oklahoma City, OK 73112–4279; (405) 848–1733

Lutheran Social Services of Tulsa, 3223 E. 31st Street, Suite 111, Tulsa, OK 74105; (918) 587–9439

*Project Adopt, 3000 United Founders Boulevard, Suite 141, Oklahoma City, OK 73112; (405) 848–0592

*Small Miracles International, 105 Mid-America Boulevard, Suite 3, Midwest City, OK 73110; (405) 732–7295

Women Care, 1216 Rankin, Edmond, OK 73034; (405) 359–1400

OREGON

State Agency: Office for Services to Families and Children, 500 Summer Street NE, 2nd Floor, South HRB, Salem, OR 97310; (503) 945–5677

State Exchange and Photolisting: Oregon Adoption Exchange (see above); (503) 945–5998

State Reunion Registry: Department of Human Resources, Children's Services Division, 198 Commercial Street, SE, Salem, OR 97310–0450; (503) 378–4452

Independent Adoption: Permitted

Private Agencies

Adventist Adoption and Family Services Program, 6040 SE Belmont Street, Portland, OR 97215; (503) 232–1211

*Albertina Kerr Center for Children, 424 NE 22nd Avenue, Portland, OR 97232; (503) 239–8101

*All God's Children International, 4114 NE Fremont Street, Portland, OR 97212; (503) 282–7652

*Associated Services for International Adoption (ASIA), 17647 Hill Way, Lake Oswego, OR 97035; (503) 697–1004

Bethany Christian Services, 149 E. 3rd Avenue, Suite 200, Hillsboro, OR 97123–4018; (503) 693–6873

*Boys and Girls Aid Society of Oregon, 18 SW Boundary Court, Portland, OR 97201–3985; (503) 222–9661

Bridges Adoption and Family Services, Inc., Portland, OR 97219; (503) 246–2445

Caring Connections, 5439 SE Bantam Court, Milwaukie, OR 97267; (503) 282–3663

*Cascade International Children's Services, Inc., 3439 NE Sandy, Portland, OR 97232; (503) 230–9450 or (800) 566–9450

Casey Family Program, 3910 SE Stark Street, Portland, OR 97214; (503) 239–9977

*Catholic Charities, Inc., 231 SE 12th Avenue, Portland, OR 97214; (503) 231–4866

*China Adoption Services Agency, Inc., P.O. Box 19764, Portland, OR 97280; (503) 245–0976

Columbia Counseling, Inc., 1445 Rosemont Road, West Linn, OR 97068; (503) 655–9470

*Dove Adoption International, Inc., 3735 SE Martins, Portland, OR 97202; (503) 775–0469

Families Are Forever, 4114 NE Fremont Street, Portland, OR 97212; (503) 282–7652

First American Adoptions, P.O. Box 69622, Portland, OR 97201; (503) 223–7930

Give Us This Day, Inc., P.O. Box 11611, Portland, OR 97211; (503) 288–4335

*Heritage Adoptions, 516 SE Morrison Street, Suite 714, Portland, OR 97214; (503) 233–1099

*Holt International Children's Services, P.O. Box 2880, Eugene, OR 97402; (541) 687–2202

*International Children's Care (*see* Washington)

*Journeys of the Heart Adoption Services, P.O. Box 482, Hillsboro, OR 97123; (503) 681–3075

LDS Social Services, 530 Center Street, Suite 706, Salem, OR 97301; (503) 581–7483

Lutheran Family Services, 605 SE 39th Avenue, Portland, OR 97214; (503) 231–7480

Medina Children's Services (*see* Washington)

New Hope Child & Family Agency, 4370 NE Halsey Street, Suite 215, Portland, OR 97213; (800) 228–3150

Northwest Adoptions and Family Services, 2695 Spring Valley Lane, NW, Salem, OR 97304; (503) 581–6652

Open Adoption & Family Services, Inc., 2950 SE Stark Street, Suite 230, Portland, OR 97214; (503) 233–9660. There is an office in Eugene (541) 343–4825.

*Orphans Overseas, 10226 SW Park Way, Portland, OR 97225; (503) 297–2006

*PLAN International Adoption Services, P.O. Box 667, McMinnville, OR 97128; (503) 472–8452

PENNSYLVANIA

State Agency: Pennsylvania Department of Public Welfare, Health & Welfare Building, P.O. Box 2675, Harrisburg, PA 17105; (717) 787–7756

State Exchange and Photolisting: Statewide Adoption Network, 5021 E. Trindle Road, Mechanicsburg, PA 17055; (800) 445–2444; and Statewide Adoption Network (see above); (717) 772–7040

State Reunion Registry: Pennsylvania Adoption Medical History Registry, P.O. Box 2675, Harrisburg, PA 17105; (717) 772–7015 or (800) 227–0225

Independent Adoption: Permitted

Private Agencies

A Second Chance, 204 North Highland Avenue, Pittsburgh, PA 15206; (412) 665–2300

*Adopt-A-Child, 6315 Forbes Avenue, Pittsburgh, PA 15217; (412) 421–1911

*Adoption ARC, Inc., 4701 Pine Street, #J-7, Philadelphia, PA 19143; (215) 844–1082 or (800) 884–4004

Adoption by Choice, 2312 West 15th Street, Erie, PA 16505; (814) 459–4050

Adoption Connection, 709 Third Avenue, New Brighton, PA 15066; (412) 846–2615

Adoption Home Study Associates of Chester County, 1014 Centre School Way, West Chester, PA 19382; (215) 431–7862

*Adoption Horizons, 899 Petersburg Road, Carlisle, PA 17103; (717) 249–8850

Adoption Resource Center, 4701 Pine Street, Philadelphia, PA 19143; (215) 844–1082

*Adoption Services, Inc., 28 Central Boulevard, Camp Hill, PA 17011; (717) 737–3960

Adoption Services, Inc., 115 South St. John's Drive, Camp Hill, PA 17011; (717) 737–3960

*Adoption Unlimited, 2770 Weston Road, Lancaster, PA 17603; (717) 872–1340

Adoption World, Inc., 3246 Birch Road, Philadelphia, PA 19154; (215) 632–4479

*Adoptions Abroad, 67 Old Clairton Road, Pittsburgh, PA 15236; (412) 653–5302

*Adoptions from The Heart, 76 Rittenhouse Place, Ardmore, PA 19003; (215) 642–7200. There are offices in Lancaster (717) 691–9686 and Greensburg (412) 853–6533.

*Adoptions International, 601 S. 10th Street, Philadelphia, PA 19147; (214) 627–6313

Alliance Adoption Agency, 341 Park Road, Ambridge, PA 15003; (412) 266–3600

American Friends of Children, 619 Gawain Road, Plymouth Meeting, PA 19464; (610) 828–8166

*Asian Angels (Angels of the World, Inc.), 11 Bala Avenue, Bala Cynwyd, PA 19004; (610) 668–7952

*Asociacion Puertorriquenos en Marcha, 445–47 Luray Street, Philadelphia, PA 19122; (215) 235–6788

*Baby Adoption International, 2473 Napfle Street, Philadelphia, PA 19152; (215) 677–2808

Bennett and Simpson Enrichment Services Adoption, 4300 Monument Road, Philadelphia, PA 19131; (215) 877–1925

Best Nest, 325 Market Street, Williamsport, PA 17701; (717) 321–1969. There is an office in Philadelphia (215) 546–8060.

Bethanna, 2160–13 Lincoln Highway East, Lancaster, PA 17602; (717) 299–1926. There is an office in Southampton (215) 355–6500.

Bethany Christian Services, 1681 Crown Avenue , Suite 203, Lancaster, PA 17601–6303; (717) 399–3213. There are offices in Fort Washington (215) 628–0202 and Philadelphia (215) 247–5473.

*Bethany Christian Services of Western Pennsylvania, 694 Lincoln Avenue, Pittsburgh, PA 15202–3421; (412) 734–2662

Capital Area Adoption Services, 514 Landsvale Street, Marysville, PA 17053; (717) 957–2513

*Catholic Charities Agency of the Diocese of Greensburg, 115 Vannear Avenue, Greensburg, PA 15601; (412) 837–1840

Catholic Charities Counseling and Adoption Services, 90 Beaver Drive, Suite 111B, Dubois, PA 15801–2424; (814) 371–4717. There are offices in Erie (814) 456–2091 and Sharon (412) 346–4142.

*Catholic Charities of the Diocese of Harrisburg, 4800 Union Deposit Road, Harrisburg, PA 17105; (717) 657–4804

Catholic Charities of the Diocese of Pittsburgh, Inc., 212 Ninth Street, Pittsburgh, PA 15222–3507; (412) 471–1120

Catholic Social Agency, 928 Union Boulevard, Allentown, PA 18103; (610) 435–1541. There is an office in Reading (610) 370–3378.

Catholic Social Services, 81 South Church Street, Hazleton, PA 18201; (717) 485–1521. There are offices in Tunkhannock and Stroudsburg (717) 476–6460.

Catholic Social Services of Luzerne County, 33 E. Northhampton Street, Wilkes-Barre, PA; (717) 822–7118

Catholic Social Services of Lycoming County, 1015 Washington Boulevard, Williamsport, PA 17701; (717) 322–4220

*Catholic Social Services of the Archdiocese of Philadelphia, 222 N. 17th Street, Philadelphia, PA 19103; (215) 587–3900

*Catholic Social Services of the Diocese of Altoona-Johnstown, 1300 12th Avenue, Altoona, PA 16603; (814) 944–9388

*Catholic Social Services of the Diocese of Scranton, 400 Wyoming Avenue, Scranton, PA 18503; (717) 346–8936

CATY Services, 415 Gettysburg Street, Pittsburgh, PA 15206; (412) 362–3600

*Child and Home Study Associates, 1029 Providence Road, Media, PA 19063; (215) 565–1544

*Children's Adoption Network, 130 Almshouse Road, Richboro, PA 18954; (215) 942–9900

Children's Aid Home Programs of Somerset County, 574 E. Main Street, Somerset, PA 15501; (814) 445–2009

Children's Aid Society in Clearfield County, 1004 S. Second Street, Clearfield, PA 16830; (814) 765–2685

Children's Aid Society of Franklin County, 225 Miller Street, Chambersburg, PA 17201–0353; (717) 263–4159

Children's Aid Society of Mercer County, 350 W. Market Street, Mercer, PA 16137; (412) 662–4730

*Children's Aid Society of Montgomery County, 1314 DeKalb Street, Norristown, PA 19401; (215) 279–2755

Children's Choice, 4814 Joneston Road, Harrisburg, PA 17109; (717) 541–9809. There are offices in Selinsgrove (717) 743–0505, Chester (610) 872–6200, and Philadelphia (610) 521–6270.

Children's Home of Pittsburgh, 5618 Kentucky Avenue, Pittsburgh, PA 15232; (412) 441–4884

The Children's Home Society of New Jersey, 771 North Pennsylvania Avenue, Morrisville, PA 19067; (215) 736–8550

Children's Services, 1315 Walnut Street, Philadelphia, PA 19107; (215) 546–3503

*Chinese Adoption Services, 322 Sue Drive, Hummelstown, PA 17036; (717) 564–7478

Choices—An Adoption Agency, 527 Swede Street, Norristown, PA 19401; (215) 884–1414

Church of the Brethren Youth Services, 1417 Oregon Road, Leola, PA 17540; (717) 656–6580

*Common Sense Adoption Services, 5021 E. Trindle Road, Mechanicsburg, PA 17055; (717) 766–6449

Community Adoption Services of Heavenly Vision Ministries, 6513 Meadow Street, Pittsburgh, PA 15206; (412) 661–4774

Concern, 1 W. Main Street, Fleetwood, PA 19522; (610) 944–0445. There is an office in Fort Washington (215) 654–1963.

Council of Spanish Speaking Organizations, 705–709 North Franklin Street, Philadelphia, PA 19123; (215) 627–3100

Covenant Family Resources, 743 Roy Road, King of Prussia, PA 19406; (610) 354–0555

Eckels Adoption Agency, 915 Fifth Avenue, Williamsport, PA 17701; (717) 323–2520

Families Across Boundaries, 5208 Library Road, Bethel Park, PA 15102; (412) 854–0330

Families Caring for Children, 96 Front Street, Nanticoke, PA 18634; (717) 735–9082

Families Caring for Children Mercy Medical Arts, 8 Church Street, Wilkes-Barre, PA 18702; (717) 823–9823

Families International Adoption Agency, 1205 Farragut Street, Pittsburgh, PA 15217; (412) 681–7189

Families United Network, 54 South Brown Street, Elizabethtown, PA 17022; (717) 367–9798

Family Adoption Center, 625 Stanwix Street, Pittsburgh, PA 15222; (412) 288–2138

Family Health Council, Inc., 960 Penn Avenue, Suite 600, Pittsburgh, PA 15222; (412) 288–2130

*Family Service, 630 Janet Avenue, Lancaster, PA 17601; (717) 397–5241

*Family Services and Children's Aid Society of Venango County, 716 E. Second Street, Oil City, PA 16301; (814) 677–4005

*Family Services of Northwestern Pennsylvania, 5100 Peach Street, Erie, PA 16509; (814) 864–0605

FIMEL—Family Institute for More Effective Living, 3605 Geryville Pike, Greenlane, PA 18054; (215) 679–5609

Friends Association for the Care and Protection of Children,

206 N. Church Street, West Chester, PA 19381; (215) 431–3598

Genesis of Pittsburgh, 185 Dakota Street, Pittsburgh, PA 15202; (412) 766–2693

ILB Adoption Agency, 2705–2709 Murray Avenue, Pittsburgh, PA 15217; (412) 421–7133

Infant and Youth Care, 54 South Brown Street, Elizabethtown, PA 17022; (717) 367–9798. There is an office in Philadelphia (215) 424–1144.

Institute for Human Resources and Services, 250 Pierce Street, Kingston, PA 18704; (717) 288–9386

*International Assistance Group, 21 Brilliant Avenue, Pittsburgh, PA 15215; (412) 781–6470

*International Families, 518 S. 12th Street, Philadelphia, PA 19147; (215) 557–7797

Jewish Family and Children's Agency, 10125 Verree Road, Philadelphia, PA 19116; (215) 698–9950

Jewish Family and Children's Service, 5743 Barlett Street, Pittsburgh, PA 15217; (412) 683–4900

Jewish Family Service, 3333 N. Front Street, Harrisburg, PA 17110; (717) 233–1681

Juvenile Justice Center, 100 West Coulter Street, Philadelphia, PA 19144; (215) 849–2112

*Kaleidoscope of Family Services, Inc., 355 Lancaster Avenue, Haverford, PA 19041; (215) 473–3991

Kidspeace National Centers for Kids in Crisis, 1650 Broadway, Bethlehem, PA 18015; (215) 867–5051

La Vida Adoption Agency, 1265 Drummer Lane, Wayne, PA 19087; (610) 647–8008. There are offices in King of Prussia (215) 647–8008 and Malvern (215) 296–7699.

LDS Social Services, 46 School Street, Greentree, PA 15205; (412) 921–8303. There is an office in Harrisburg (717) 694–5896.

Living Hope Adoption Agency, 3205 Meetinghouse Road, Telford, PA 18969; (215) 672–7471

*Love the Children, 221 W. Broad Street, Quakertown, PA 18951; (215) 536–4180

Lutheran Children & Family Service of Eastern Pennsylvania, 1256 Easton Road, Roslyn, PA 19001; (215) 951–6850

Lutheran Home at Topton, 1 S. Home Avenue, Topton, PA 19562; (610) 682–1504

Lutheran Service Society of Western Pennsylvania, 1011 Old Salem Road, Greensbury, PA 15601; (412) 837–9385

Madison Adoption Associates, 619 Gawain Road, Plymouth Meeting, PA 19462; (215) 459–0454

Marian Adoption Services, 3138 Butler Pike, Plymouth Meeting, PA 19462; (610) 941–0910 or (800) 525–9944

National Adoption Network, Ltd., 15–31 Morris Avenue, Bryn Mawr, PA 19010; (215) 649–5046

New Beginnings Family and Children's Services, 8 Pennsylvania Avenue, Matamoras, PA 18336; (516) 747–2204

Northeast Treatment Center, 836–50 North Third Street, Philadelphia, PA 19123; (215) 574–9500

PAACT, 703 N. Market Street, Liverpool, PA 17045; (717) 444–3629

Permanency Planning Services Inc. (PPSI), 1633 Beechwood Boulevard, Pittsburgh, PA 15217; (412) 421–8288

Pinebrook Services for Children & Youth, 1033 Sumner Avenue, Whitehall, PA 18052; (610) 432–3919

Plan-It For Kids, PC, 501 Main Street, Berlin, PA 15530; (814) 267–3182

Presbyterian Children's Village, 452 S. Roberts Road, Rosemont, PA 19010; (610) 525–5400

Pressley Ridge Youth Development Extension Program, 801 Beaver Street, Sewickley, PA 15143; (412) 740–1310

Project STAR of Permanency Planning Advocates of Western Pennsylvania, 6301 Northumberland Street, Pittsburgh, PA 15217; (412) 521–9000

PSI Services, 1617 JFK Boulevard, Suite 1700, Philadelphia, PA 19103; (215) 569–1206

Rainbow Project, 200 Charles Street, Pittsburgh, PA 15238; (412) 782–4457

Rehabilitation Auditing and Placement Services (RAP), 100 West Mall Plaza, Carnegie, PA 15106; (412) 278–8550

St. Joseph's Center, 2010 Adams Avenue, Scranton, PA 18509; (717) 342–8379

Tabor Children's Services, 601 New Britain Road, Doylestown, PA 18901–4248; (215) 348–4071

Three Rivers Adoption Council/Black Adoption Services, 307 4th Avenue, Pittsburgh, PA 15222; (412) 471–8722

Tressler Lutheran Services, 836 S. George Street, York, PA 17403; (717) 845–9113. There are offices in Williamsport (717) 327–9195 and Mechanicsburg (717) 795–0300.

*Welcome House Social Services of the Pearl S. Buck Foundation, 520 Dublin Road, Perkasie, PA 18944–0181; (215) 249–1516

Women's Christian Alliance, 1610 N. Broad Street, Philadelphia, PA 19121; (215) 236–9911

Your Adoption Agency, Germantown Road, R.D. 2, Susquehanna, PA 18847; (717) 853–2022

RHODE ISLAND

State Agency: Department for Children and Their Families, 610 Mt. Pleasant Avenue, Providence, RI 02908; (401) 457–4790

State Exchange and Photolisting: Adoption Rhode Island, 500 Prospect Street, Pawtucket, RI 02860; (401) 724–1910

State Reunion Registry: State of Rhode Island and Providence Plantations, Family Court Juvenile Division, 1 Dorrance Plaza, Providence, RI 02903; (401) 277–3352

Independent Adoption: Permitted

Private Agencies

*Alliance for Children, Inc. (*see* Massachusetts)

*Alliance for Children, 500 Prospect Street, Pawtucket, RI 02860; (401) 725–9555

*Bethany Christian Service, P.O. Box 1017, E. Greenwich, RI 02818–0964; (401) 245–2960

Friends in Adoption, 224 5th Street, Providence, RI 02906; (401) 831–1120 or (800) 982–3678

*Gift of Life Adoption Services, P.O. Box 40864, Providence, RI 02940; (401) 826–8420

*International Adoptions, Inc., 259 Eddie Dowling Highway, North Smithfield, RI 02895; (401) 765–8200

*Jewish Family Services/Adoption Options, 229 Waterman Avenue, Providence, RI 02906; (401) 331–5437

Little Treasures Adoption Services, P.O. Box 255, Cranston, RI 02920; (401) 828–7747

Urban League of Rhode Island, Inc., 246 Prairie Avenue, Providence, RI 02905; (401) 351–5000

*Wide Horizons, 116 Andre Avenue, Wakefield, RI 02879; (401) 783–4537. There is an office in North Southfield (401) 766–9197.

SOUTH CAROLINA

State Agency: Department of Social Services, Division of Adoption and Birth Parent Services, P.O. Box 1520, Columbia, SC 29202–1520; (803) 734–6095 or (800) 922–2504

State Exchange and Photolisting: South Carolina Seedlings, P.O. Box 1453, Greenville, SC 29602–1453; (864) 239–0303

State Reunion Registry: South Carolina Department of Social Services, Adoption Reunion Registry (see above)

Independent Adoption: Permitted

Private Agencies

*A Loving Choice Adoption Agency, 1535 Sam Rittenburg Boulevard, Charleston, SC 29407; (803) 556–3391. There is an office in Spartanburg (864) 576–7033.

*Adoption Center of South Carolina, 1600 Marian Street, Columbia, SC 29202; (803) 771–2272

*Bethany Christian Services, 712 Richland Street, Columbia, SC 29201–2300; (803) 779–0541. There are offices in Florence (803) 629–1177, Greenville (864) 235–2273, and Myrtle Beach (803) 236–5433.

Catholic Charities of Charleston, 1662 Ingram Road, Charleston, SC 29407; (803) 769–4466

Children Unlimited, Inc., 1825 Gadsden Street, Columbia, SC 29211; (803) 799–8311

*Christian Family Services, 5072 Tara Tea Drive, Tega Cay, SC 29715; (803) 548–6030

*Christian World Adoption, Inc., 669 N. Marina Drive, Wando, SC 29492; (803) 856–0305

Epworth Children's Home, 2900 Millwood Avenue, Columbia, SC 29250; (803) 256–7394

LDS Social Services, 5624 Executive Center Drive, Charlotte, NC 28212–8832; (704) 535–2436

*Lutheran Family Services, 1329 Atlantic Drive, Columbia, SC 29210–7901; (803) 750–0034

Southeastern Children's Home, Inc., 155 Children's Home, Duncan, SC 29334; (864) 439–0259

*World Wide Adoptions, 205 Overland Drive, Spartanburg, SC 29307; (864) 583–6981

SOUTH DAKOTA

State Agency: Department of Social Services, 700 Governors Drive, Pierre, SD 57501; (605) 773–3227

State Exchange and Photolisting: None

State Reunion Registry: Reunion Registry (see above)

Independent Adoption: Permitted

Private Agencies

Bethany Christian Services, 1719 West Main Street, Rapid City, SD 57702; (605) 343–7196. There is an office in Sioux Falls (605) 336–6999.

Catholic Family Services, 3200 West 41 Street, Sioux Falls, SD 57105; (605) 336–3326. There is another office in Rapid City (605) 348–6086.

Child Protection Program, Sisseton Wahpeton Dakota Nation, P.O. Box 509, Agency Village, SD 57262; (605) 698–3911

Children's Home Society, 801 North Sycamore Avenue, Sioux Falls, SD 57101; (605) 334–6004

Christian Counseling Service, 231 South Phillips Avenue, Sioux Falls, SD 57102; (605) 336–6999

LDS Social Services, 2525 West Main Street, Rapid City, SD 57702; (605) 342–3500

Lutheran Social Services, 600 West 12 Street, Sioux Falls, SD 57104; (605) 336–3347

New Horizons Adoption Agency, 27213 473rd Avenue, Sioux Falls, SD 57104; (605) 332–0310

Yankton Sioux Tribal Social Services, P.O. Box 248, Marty, SD 57361; (605) 384–3804

TENNESSEE

State Agency: Department of Children's Services, 436 Sixth Avenue, North, Cordell Hull Building 8th Floor, Nashville, TN 37243–1290; (615) 532–5637

State Exchange and Photolisting: Resource Exchange for Adoptable Children in Tennessee, 201 23rd Avenue, North, Nashville, TN 37203–9000; (615) 321–3867

State Reunion Registry: None

Independent Adoption: Permitted

Private Agencies

Adoption Connection, 2412 North Park Boulevard, Knoxville, TN 37917; (423) 522–0704

Adoption Counseling Services, 2185 Wickersham Lane, Germantown, TN 38139; (901) 753–9089

Adoption Home Studies and Social Services, 909 Oak Street, Chattanooga, TN 37403; (423) 756–3134

Adoption Resource Center, 8529 Timberlock Cove, Cordova, TN 38018; (901) 754–7902

All God's Children, 6227 Lee Highway, Chattanooga, TN 37421; (615) 499–6428

*Associated Catholic Charities of East Tennessee, 119 Dameron Avenue, Knoxville, TN 37917; (423) 971–3560

Associated Catholic Charities of the Diocese of Memphis, St. Peter Home, 1805 Poplar Avenue, Memphis, TN 38104; (901) 725–8240

Association for Guidance, Aid, Placement, and Empathy (AGAPE), 4555 Trousdale Drive, Nashville, TN 37204–4513; (615) 781–3000

Association for Guidance, Aid, Placement, and Empathy (AGAPE), Child and Family Services, 1881 Union Avenue, Memphis, TN 38111; (901) 272–7339

*Bethany Christian Services of Tennessee, Inc., 4719 Brainerd Road, Chattanooga, TN 37411–3842; (423) 622–7360.

There are offices in Nashville (615) 297–5229 and Memphis (901) 454–1401.

*Catholic Charities of Tennessee, Inc., 30 White Bridge Road, Nashville, TN 37205; (615) 352–3087

*Child and Family Services of Knox County, 901 E. Summit Hill Drive, Knoxville, TN 37915; (423) 524–7483

*Christian Counseling Services, 515 Woodland Street, Nashville, TN 37206; (615) 254–8336

Church of God Home for Children, 449 McCarn Circle, Sevierville, TN 37864; (423) 453–4644

East Tennessee Christian Services, Inc., 4638 Chambliss Avenue, Knoxville, TN 37919; (423) 584–0841

Family and Children's Services, 201 23rd Avenue, North, Nashville, TN 37203; (615) 320–0591

Family and Children's Services of Chattanooga, Inc., 300 E. Eighth Street, Chattanooga, TN 37403; (423) 755–2822

Free Will Baptist Family Ministries, 90 Stanley Lane, Greeneville, TN 37743; (423) 693–9449

Greater Chattanooga Christian Services, 400 Vine Street, Chattanooga, TN 37403; (615) 756–0281

Guardian Angel International Adoption Agency, 116 Pulaski, Lawrenceburg, TN 38464; (615) 766–5277

Guidance Center, Connections Program, 1338 West College, Murfreesboro, TN 37129; (615) 893–0803

Happy Haven Homes, Inc., 998 County Farm Road, Cookeville, TN 38501; (615) 526–2052

*Heaven Sent Children, Inc., 316 West Lytle Street, Murfreesboro, TN 37130; (615) 898–0803

*Holston United Methodist Home for Children, Inc., P.O. Box 188, Greeneville, TN 37743; (423) 638–4171

International Assistance and Adoption Project, 405 James Boulevard, Signal Mountain, TN 37377; (423) 886–6986

*Jewish Family Services, 6560 Poplar Avenue, Memphis, TN 38138; (901) 767–8511

Life Choices, Inc., 3297 Park Avenue, Memphis, TN 38111; (901) 323–5433

Madison Children's Home, 616 N. Dupont Avenue, Madison, TN 37116–0419; (615) 860–3240

Mercy Ministries, Inc., 15328 Old Hickory Boulevard, Nashville, TN 37215–0829; (615) 831–6987

Mid-Cumberland Children's Services, Inc., 106 N. Mountain Street, Smithville, TN 37166; (615) 597–7134

Mid-South Christian Services, 3100 Walnut Grove Road, Memphis, TN 38111; (901) 454–1401

Miriam's Promise, 900 Glendale Lane, Nashville, TN 37204; (615) 292–3500

Omni Visions, 101 Lea Avenue, Nashville, TN 37210; (615) 726–3603

Porter-Leath Children's Center, 868 N. Manassas Street, Memphis, TN 38107; (901) 577–2500

Senior Citizen's Services, Inc., Stepping Stones, 4700 Poplar Avenue, Memphis, TN 38117; (901) 766–0600

*Small World Ministries, Inc., 401 Bonnaspring, Nashville, TN 37076; (615) 883–4372

Tennessee Baptist Children's Homes, Inc., P.O. Box 728, Brentwood, TN 37024; (615) 371–2000. There are offices in Chattanooga (423) 892–2722, Johnson City (423) 929–2157, and Spring Hill (615) 486–2274.

Tennessee Conference Adoption Services, 900 Glendale Lane, Nashville, TN 37204; (615) 292–3500

West Tennessee Children's Home, #20 Redbud, Jackson, TN 38301; (901) 423–4851

*Williams-Illien Adoptions, Inc., 3439 Vinson Drive, Memphis, TN 38315; (901) 373–6003

Youth Villages, 3354 Perimeter Hill, Suite 140, Nashville, TN

37211; (615) 333–0060. Another office is in Memphis (615) 528–9771.

TEXAS

State Agency: Department of Protective and Regulatory Services, P.O. Box 149030, MCE–559, Austin, TX 78717–9030; (512) 438–3302

State Exchange and Photolisting: Texas Adoption Resource Exchange (see above); (800) 233–3405

State Reunion Registry: Texas Department of Health, Bureau of Vital Statistics, 1100 W. 49th Street, Austin, TX 78756–3191; (512) 834–4485

Independent Adoption: Permitted

Private Agencies

AAA—Alamo Adoption Agency, 8930 Four Wind, San Antonio, TX 78239; (210) 226–4124

AAMA Host Home Project, 204 Clifton, Houston, TX 77011; (713) 926–4756

ABC Adoption Agency, Inc., 417 San Pedro Avenue, San Antonio, TX 78212; (210) 227–7820

About Life, Inc., 4131 N. Central, Dallas, TX 75204; (214) 369–5433

Abrazo Adoption Associates, 10010 San Pedro, San Antonio, TX 78216; (210) 342–5683 or (800) 454–5683

Adopt a Special Kid (AASK) of Texas, 1060 W. Pipeline Road, Hurst, TX 76053; (817) 595–0497

Adoption—A Gift of Love, P.O. Box 50384, Denton, TX 76206; (817) 387–9311

Adoption Access, 8340 Meadow Road, Dallas, TX 75231; (214) 750–4847

Adoption Advisory, Inc., 3607 Fairmount, Dallas, TX 75219; (214) 520–0004

Adoption Advocates, 328 W. Mistletoe, San Antonio, TX 78212; (210) 734–4470

Adoption Affiliates, Inc., 215 W. Olmos Drive, San Antonio, TX 78212; (210) 824–9939

*Adoption Alliance, 7303 Blanco Road, San Antonio, TX 78216; (210) 349–3991

*Adoption as an Option, 12611 Kingsride Lane, Houston, TX 77024; (713) 468–1053

Adoption Information and Counseling, 2020 Southwest Freeway, Houston, TX 77098; (713) 529–5125

Adoption Resource Consultants, P.O. Box 1224, Richardson, TX 75083; (214) 517–4119

Adoption Service Associates, 8703 Wurzbach Road, San Antonio, TX 78240; (210) 699–6094 or (800) 648–1807

*Adoption Services, Inc., 3500 Overton Park, West, Fort Worth, TX 76109; (817) 921–0718

Adoptive Family Services, 13140 Coit Road, Dallas, TX 75240; (972) 437–9950

All-Church Home for Children, 1424 Summit Avenue, Fort Worth, TX 76102; (817) 335–4041

*Alternatives In Motion, 20619 Aldine Westfield Road, Humble, TX 77338; (713) 821–6508

Andrel Adoptions, 3908 Manchaca, Austin, TX 78704; (512) 448–4605

Associated Catholic Charities, 3520 Montrose, Houston, TX 77006–4350; (713) 526–4611

Baptist Children's Home, 7404 Highway 90, West, San Antonio, TX 78227; (210) 674–3010

Blessed Trinity Adoptions, Inc., 8503 Havner Court, Houston, TX 77037; (713) 855–0137

*Bright Dreams International, 2929 Carlisle, Dallas, TX 75204; (214) 953–1616

*Buckner Adoption, 5204 S. Buckner Boulevard, Dallas, TX 75227; (214) 321–4506

Buckner Baptist Children's Home, 129 Brentwood Avenue, Lubbock, TX 79416–1601; (806) 795–7151

Care Connection, Inc., 400 Harvey Street, San Marcos, TX 78666; (512) 396–8111

Caring Choices, Inc., 1438 Campbell Road, Suite 102, Houston, TX 77055; (713) 722–8100

Caring Family Network, 12233 N. FM 620, Austin, TX 78750; (512) 918–2992

Catholic Charities, 2903 W. Salinas Street, San Antonio, TX 78207; (210) 734–5054

Catholic Counseling Services, 3725 Blackburn, Dallas, TX 75219; (214) 526–2772

Catholic Family Service, P.O. Box 15127, Amarillo, TX 79105; (806) 376–4571

Catholic Social Services, 2669 Burchill Road, Fort Worth, TX 76105; (817) 536–6857

Catholic Social Services of Laredo, P.O. Box 3305, Laredo, TX 78044; (956) 722–2443

Child Placement Center, 2212 Sunny Lane, Killeen, TX 76541; (254) 690–5959

Children & Family Institute, 4200 S. Freeway, Fort Worth, TX 76115; (817) 922–9974

*Children's Home of Lubbock, P.O. Box 2824, Lubbock, TX 79408; (806) 762–0481

Chosen Heritage, 121 NE Loop 820, Hurst, TX 76053; (817) 589–7899

*Christian Homes of Abilene, Inc., P.O. Box 270, Abilene, TX 79604; (915) 677–2205 or (800) 592–4725

Christian Services of East Texas, 1810 Shiloh Road, Tyler, TX 75703; (903) 509–0558

Christian Services of the Southwest, 6320 LBJ Freeway,

Dallas, TX 75240; (214) 960–9981

*Christ's Haven for Children, P.O. Box 467, Keller, TX 76248; (940) 431–1544

Coastal Bend Youth City, Inc., P.O. Box 268, Driscoll, TX 78351; (512) 387–4513

Covenant Children, Inc., P.O. Box 474, Bertram, TX 78605; (512) 355–3081

*Cradle of Hope, 311 N. Market Street, Dallas, TX 75202; (214) 747–4500

Cradle of Life Adoption Agency, 245 N. Fourth Street, Beaumont, TX 77701; (409) 832–3000

DePelchin Children's Center, 100 Sandman Street, Houston, TX 77007; (713) 861–8136

El Paso Adoption Services, 604 Myrtle, El Paso, TX 79901; (915) 542–1086

El Paso Center for Children, 3700 Altura Boulevard, El Paso, TX 79930; (915) 565–8361

*Friends Adoptions International, 700 S. Friendswood Drive, Friendswood, TX 77546; (281) 992–4677

Gift of Love Adoption Agency, 1341 W. Mockingbird, Dallas, TX 75247; (214) 819–2424

*Gladney Center, 2300 Hemphill Street, Fort Worth, TX 76110; (817) 926–3304

*Great Wall China Adoption, 5555 N. Lamar Boulevard, Austin, TX 78751; (512) 323–9595

Harmony Family Services, 1626 N. Third, Abilene, TX 79601; (915) 672–8820

*Heart International Adoption Services, 1319 Alabama Road, Wharton, TX 77488; (713) 532–1774

*High Plains Children's Home and Family Services, Inc., P.O. Box 7448, Amarillo, TX 79114–7448; (806) 355–6588

Homes of Saint Mark, 3000 Richmond, Houston, TX 77098; (713) 522–2800

*Hope Cottage, 4209 McKinney Avenue, Dallas, TX 75205; (214) 526–8721

Inheritance Adoptions, P.O. Box 2563, Wichita Falls, TX 76307; (940) 322–3678

*International Child Placing Agency, P.O. Box 112, Los Fresnos, TX 78566; (956) 233–5705

J & B Kids, Inc., Placing Agency, Route 1, Box 173 F, Yorktown, TX 78164; (512) 564–2964

Jester Adoption Services, P.O. Box 280, Denton, TX 76202; (940) 380–1010

LDS Social Services-Texas, 1100 W. Jackson Road, Carrollton, TX 75006; (214) 242–2182

Lee and Beulah Moor Children's Home, 1100 Cliff Drive, El Paso, TX 79902; (915) 544–8777

Life Anew Adoption Agency, 3435 Pine Mill Road, Paris, TX 75460; (903) 785–7701

Living Waters Inc., 1106 Clayton Lane, Austin, TX 78723; (512) 302–1260

*Los Ninos International Adoption Center, 1600 Lake Front Circle, The Woodlands, TX 77380–3600; (713) 363–2892

Loving Alternatives Adoptions, P.O. Box 131466, Tyler, TX 75713; (903) 581–7720

*Lutheran Social Services of Texas, Inc., P.O. Box 49589; Austin, TX 78765; (512) 459–1000. There is an office in Houston (713) 521–0110.

Marywood Maternity and Adoption Services, 510 W. 26th Street, Austin, TX 78705; (512) 472–9251 or (800) 251–5433

Methodist Home, 1111 Herring Avenue, Waco, TX 76708; (254) 753–0181

Methodist Mission Home, 6487 Whitby Road, San Antonio, TX 78240; (210) 696–2410

New Life Children's Services, 19911 Tomball Parkway, Houston, TX 77070; (713) 955–1001

Nuestros Ninos, 710 N. Post Oak Road, Houston, TX 77024–3832; (713) 613–5235

PAC Child Placing Agency, 4655 S FM 1258, Amarillo, TX 79118–7219; (806) 335–9138

Placement Services Agency, P.O. Box 799004, Dallas, TX 75379–9004; (972) 387–3312

Read Adoption Agency, Inc., 718 Myrtle, El Paso, TX 79901; (915) 533–3697

Smithlawn Maternity Home and Adoption Agency, 711 76th Street, Lubbock, TX 79413; (806) 745–2574

Spaulding for Children, 710 N. Post Oak Road, Houston, TX 77024–3832; (713) 681–6991

Texas Baptist Children's Home, P.O. Box 7, Round Rock, TX 78664; (512) 388–8256

Texas Baptist Home for Children, P.O. Drawer 309, Waxahachie, TX 75165; (214) 937–1321

*Texas Cradle Society, 8600 Wurzbach Road, San Antonio, TX 78240–4334; (210) 614–0299

*Trinity Adoption Services International, 7610 Club Lake Drive, Houston, TX 77095; (713) 855–0042

UTAH

State Agency: Utah Department of Human Services Division of Child & Family Services, 120 North, 200 West #225, Salt Lake City, UT 84103; (801) 538–3993

State Exchange and Photolisting: Department of Human Services Division of Child & Family Services, P.O. Box 45500, Salt Lake City, UT 84145–0500; (801) 538–4100

State Reunion Registry: Department of Health, Director of Vital Statistics, 288 North 1460 West, Salt Lake City, UT 84145–0500; (801) 538–6105

Independent Adoption: Permitted

Private Agencies

Adoption Center of Choice, Inc., 241 West, 520 North, Orem, UT 84057; (801) 224–2440

Alternative Options, 11638 High Mountain Drive, Sandy, UT 84092; (801) 572–6360

*Catholic Community Services, 2300 West 1700 South, Salt Lake City, UT 84104; (801) 977–9119

*Children's Aid Society of Utah, 652 26th Street, Ogden, UT 84401; (801) 393–8671

Children's Service Society, 12450 South, 400 East, Salt Lake City, UT 84111; (801) 355–7444 or (800) 839–7444

*Chosen Children Adoption Agency, 3043 Arthurs Court, Salt Lake City, UT 84102; (801) 969–5395

*Families for Children, P.O. Box 521192, Salt Lake City, UT 84152–1192; (801) 487–3916

*Families International, Suite 510, 139 East South Temple, Salt Lake City, UT 84111; (801) 537–1508

LDS Social Services, 350 East, 300 North, American Fork, UT 84003; (801) 756–5217

LDS Social Services, 563 West, 500 South, Bountiful, UT 84010; (801) 298–5700

*LDS Social Services, 16 West, 535 South, Cedar City, UT 84701; (435) 586–4470

LDS Social Services, 95 West, 100 South, Logan, UT 84321; (801) 752–5302

LDS Social Services, 1525 Lincoln Avenue, Ogden, UT 84404; (801) 621–6510

LDS Social Services, 294 East, 100 South, Price, UT 84501; (801) 637–2991

LDS Social Services, 1190 North, 900 East, Provo, UT 84604; (801) 378–7620

LDS Social Services, 55 North, 100 West, Richfield, UT 84701; (801) 896–6446

LDS Social Services, 10 E. South Temple, Salt Lake City, UT 84111; (801) 240–6500

LDS Social Services, 625 East, 8400 South, Sandy, UT 84701; (801) 566–2556

Utah Adoption Services for Women, 715 East, 3900 South, Salt Lake City, UT 84107; (801) 262–7999

*Wasatch International Adoptions, 2580 Jefferson Avenue, Ogden, UT 84401; (801) 334–8683

West Sands Adoption and Counseling, 461 East, 2780 North, Provo, UT 84604; (801) 377–4379

VERMONT

State Agency: Department of Social and Rehabilitation Services, 103 S. Main Street, Waterbury, VT 05671; (802) 241–2142

State Exchange and Photolisting: Northern New England Adoption Exchange, Department of Human Services, 221 State Street, Augusta, ME 04333; (207) 287–5060

State Reunion Registry: Vital Records Division, Vermont Department of Health, 108 Cherry Street, Burlington, VT 05402; (802) 241–2122

Independent Adoption: Permitted

Private Agencies

Adoption Advocates, 28 Webster Road, Shelburne, VT 05482; (802) 985–8289

Adoption Resource Services, Inc., 1904 North Avenue, Burlington, VT 05401; (802) 863–5368

*Bethany Christian Services (*see* Massachusetts)

Casey Family Services, 7 Palmer Court, White River Junction, VT 05001–3323; (802) 649–1400

Friends in Adoption, P.O. Box 7270, Middletown Springs, VT 05757; (802) 235–2312

LDS Social Services (*see* New Hampshire)

*Lund Family Center, P.O. Box 4009, Burlington, VT 05406–4009; (802) 864–7467 or (800) 639–1741

*Vermont Catholic Charities, 351 North Avenue, Burlington, VT 05401; (802) 658–6110

*Vermont Children's Aid Society, 79 Weaver Street, Winooski, VT 05404–0127; (802) 655–0006

*Wide Horizons for Children (*see* Massachusetts)

VIRGINIA

State Agency: Department of Social Services, 730 E. Broad Street, Richmond, VA 23219–1849; (804) 692–1290

State Exchange and Photolisting: Adoption Resource Exchange of Virginia (AREVA) (see above); (804) 692–1280 or (800) 362–3678

State Reunion Registry: None

Independent Adoption: Permitted

Private Agencies

*ABC Adoption Services, Inc., 4725 Garst Mill Road, Roanoke, VA 24018; (540) 989–2845

*Adoption Center of Washington, 100 Daingerfield Road, Alexandria, VA 22314; (202) 452–8278 or (800) 452–3878

*Adoption Service Information Agency, Inc. (ASIA), 7659 Leesburg Pike, Falls Church, VA 22043; (202) 726–7193

*American Adoption Agency, Inc., 9070 Euclid Avenue, Manassas, VA 22110; (202) 638–1543

*Barker Foundation, Inc., 1495 Chain Bridge Road, McLean, VA 22101; (703) 536–1827. There is an office in Norfolk (804) 626–3594.

*Bethany Christian Services, Inc., 11212 Waples Mill Road, Fairfax, VA 22030; (703) 385–5440. There are offices in

Fredericksburg (540) 373–5165 and Virginia Beach (757) 499–9367.

Catholic Charities of Hampton Roads, Inc., 1301 Colonial Avenue, Norfolk, VA 23517; (757) 625–2568. There are offices in Chesapeake (757) 484–0703, Newport News (757) 875–0060, Virginia Beach (757) 467–7707, and Williamsburg (757) 253–2847.

*Catholic Charities of Southwestern Virginia, Inc., 820 Campbell Avenue, SW, Roanoke, VA 24016; (540) 344–5107. There is an office in Blacksburg (540) 552–0664.

*Catholic Charities of the Diocese of Arlington, Inc., 3838 N. Cathedral Lane. Arlington, VA 22203; (703) 841–2531. There are offices in Burke (703) 425–0100, Fredericksburg (540) 371–1124, and Wincester (540) 667–7940.

Children's Home Society of Virginia, Inc., 4200 Fitzhugh Avenue, Richmond, VA 23230; (804) 353–0191. There is an office in Roanoke (540) 344–9281.

*Commonwealth Catholic Charities, 1512 Willow Lawn Drive, Richmond, VA 23230; (804) 285–5900

*Coordinators/2, Inc., 5204 Patterson Avenue, Richmond, VA 23226–1507; (804) 288–7595 or (800) 690–4206

*Datz Foundation, 404 Pine Street, Vienna, VA 22180; (703) 242–8800

*Families United through Adoption, 4609 Heather Court, Charlottesville, VA 22911; (804) 978–2861

Family and Child Services of Washington, D.C., Inc., 5249 Duke Street, Alexandria, VA 22304; (703) 823–2656

Family Life Services, 1000 Villa Road, Lynchburg, VA 24503; (804) 384–3043

Family Services of Tidewater, Inc., 222 19th Street, West Norfolk, VA 23517; (757) 622–7017

*Frost International Adoptions, 5205 Leesburg Pike, Falls Church, VA 22041; (703) 671–3711 or (888) 823–2090

*Jewish Family Services, Inc., 6718 Patterson Avenue, Richmond, VA 23226; (804) 282–5644

Jewish Family Service of Tidewater, Inc., 7300 Newport Avenue, Norfolk, VA 23505; (757) 489–3111. There are offices in Newport News (757) 489–3111 and Virginia Beach (757) 473–2695.

Jewish Social Service Agency, Inc., 7345 McWhorter Place, Annandale, VA 22003; (703) 750–5400

LDS Social Services of Virginia, Inc., 8110 Virginia Pine Court, Richmond, VA 23237; (804) 743–0727

Lutheran Family Services, Inc., Route 1, Box 417, McGaheysville, VA 22804; (540) 289–6141

Lutheran Social Services of the National Capital Area, Inc., Family and Children's Services, 7401 Leesburg Pike, Falls Church, VA 22043; (703) 698–5026

*New Family Foundation (*see* Washington, D.C.)

Nurturing Family Growth, 207 Pearson Drive, Lynchburg, VA 24502; (804) 237–4195

Rainbow Christian Services, Inc., 6004 Artemus Road, Gainesville, VA 22065; (703) 754–8516

Shore Adoption Services, Inc., 113 Holly Crescent, Virginia Beach, VA 23451; (757) 422–6361

*United Methodist Family Services of Virginia, Inc., 6335 Little River Turnpike, Alexandria, VA 22312; (703) 941–9008. There are offices in Richmond (804) 353–4461 and Virginia Beach (757) 490–9791

Virginia Baptist Children's Home and Family Services, Mount Vernon Avenue, Salem, VA 24153; (540) 389–5468. There are other offices in Annandale (703) 750–3660, Richmond (804) 231–4466, and Newport News (757) 826–3477.

*Welcome House Social Services of the Pearl S. Buck Foundation, Inc., 5905 W. Broad Street, Richmond, VA 23230; (804) 288–3920

WASHINGTON

State Agency: Department of Social and Health Services, P.O. Box 45713, Olympia, WA 98504; (360) 902–7968

State Exchange and Photolisting: Northwest Adoption Exchange, 1809 Seventh Avenue, Seattle, WA 98101; (206) 292–0092; and Washington Adoption Resource Exchange (see above); (360) 753–2178

State Reunion Registry: None

Independent Adoption: Permitted

Private Agencies

*Adoption Advocates International, 401 E. Front Street, Port Angeles, WA 98362; (360) 452–4777

*Adventist Adoption and Family Services, 1207 E. Reserve Street, Vancouver, WA 98661; (360) 693–2110

*Americans Adopting Orphans, 12345 Lake City Way, Seattle, WA 98125; (206) 524–5437

*Americans for International Aid and Adoption (AIAA), P.O. Box 6051, Spokane, WA 99207; (509) 489–2015

*Bethany Christian Services, 19936 Ballinger Way, NE, Seattle, WA 98155–1223; (206) 367–4604 or (800) 733–4604. There are offices in Bellingham (360) 733–6042 and Tacoma (253) 383–5333.

Catholic Children and Family Services of Walla Walla, Drumheller Building , Walla Walla, WA 99362; (509) 525–0572

Catholic Children's Services of Northwest Washington, P.O. Box 5704, Bellingham, WA 98227–5704; (360) 733–5800

Catholic Children's Services of Tacoma, 5410 N. 44th, Tacoma, WA 98407; (253) 752–2455

Catholic Community Service, King County, 100 23rd Avenue, South, Seattle, WA 98144; (206) 323–6336

Catholic Community Service, Snohomish County, Commerce Building, Everett, WA 98201; (425) 259–9188

Catholic Family and Child Service of Ephrata, Columbia, Basin Branch, 121 Basin, NW, Ephrata, WA 98823; (509) 754–2211

Catholic Family and Child Service of Grandview, 302 Division, Grandview, WA 98930; (360) 882–3050

Catholic Family and Child Service of Wenatchee, 23 S. Wenatchee, Wenatchee, WA 98801; (509) 662–6761

*Catholic Family and Child Service of Yakima, 5301-C Tieton Drive, Yakima, WA 98908; (509) 453–8264

Catholic Family and Child Services, 518 W. Clark, Pasco, WA 99301; (509) 545–6145

Catholic Family and Child Services, P.O. Box 1504, Richland, WA 99352; (509) 946–4645

Catholic Family Counseling Center, 410 W. 12th, Vancouver, WA 98860; (360) 694–2631

*Children's Home Society of Washington, Central Area, 321 E. Yakima Avenue, Yakima, WA 98901; (509) 457–8139

*Children's Home Society of Washington, Northeast Area, 4315 Scott Street, Spokane, WA 99203; (509) 747–4174

*Children's Home Society of Washington, Northwest Area, 3300 NE 65th Street, Box 15190, Seattle, WA 98115–0190; (206) 524–6020

*Children's Home Society of Washington, Southeast Area, 6 W. Alder, Walla Walla, WA 99362; (509) 459–2130

*Children's Home Society of Washington, Southwest Area, 1105 Broadway, Vancouver, WA 98660; (360) 695–1325

*Children's Home Society of Washington, West Central Area, 201 S. 34th, Tacoma, WA 98408; (253) 472–3355

Church of Christ Homes for Children, 30012 S. Military

Road, Auburn, WA 98003; (253) 839–2755

*Faith International Adoptions, 535 E. Dock Street, Tacoma, WA 98402; (253) 383–1928

Family Foundation, 424 N. 130th, Seattle, WA 98133; (206) 367–4600

Family Foundation, 1229 Cornwall Avenue, Bellingham, WA 98225; (360) 676-KIDS

*International Children's Care, P.O. Box 4406, Vancouver, WA 98662; (360) 573–0429

*International Children's Services of Washington, Inc., 3251 107th, SE, Bellevue, WA 98004; (206) 451–9370

Jewish Family Services, 1214 Boylston Avenue, Seattle, WA 98101; (206) 461–3240

LDS Social Services, 220 S. Third Place, Renton, WA 98055; (206) 624–3393

Lutheran Social Services of Washington, 4040 S. 188th, Seattle, WA 98188; (206) 246–7650

Lutheran Social Services of Washington and Idaho, 6920 220th Street SW, Mountlake Terrace, WA 98043; (206) 672–6009. There is an office in Spokane (509) 327–7761.

Lutheran Social Services of Washington, Southeast Area, 320 N. Johnson Street, Kennewick, WA 99336; (509) 783–7446

Lutheran Social Services of Washington, Southwest Area, 223 N. Yakima, Tacoma, WA 98403; (253) 272–8433

*Medina Children's Services, Black Child Adoption Program, 123 16th Avenue, Seattle, WA 98122; (206) 461–4538

*New Hope Child and Family Agency, 2611 NE 125th St., Seattle, WA 98125; (206) 363–1800

Open Adoption and Family Services, 1150 23rd Avenue, Seattle, WA 98125–5210; (206) 723–1011

Regular Baptist Child Placement Agency, P.O. Box 16353, Seattle, WA 98116; (206) 938–1487

Seattle Indian Center Infant Adoption and Family Services, 611 12th Avenue, South, Seattle, WA 98144; (206) 329–8700

The Adoption of Special Children (TASC), 123 16th Avenue, Seattle, WA 98122; (206) 461–4520

*World Association for Children and Parents (WACAP), 315 S. Second Street, Renton, WA 98055; (206) 575–4550

WEST VIRGINIA

State Agency: Department of Health and Human Resources, DHHR Capital Complex, Building 6, Room B-850, Charleston, WV 25305; (304) 558–7980

State Exchange and Photolisting: West Virginia's Adoption Resource Network (see above); (304) 558–2891

State Reunion Registry: West Virginia Mutual Consent Voluntary Adoption Registry (see above); (304) 558–2891

Independent Adoption: Permitted

Private Agencies

Adoption Services, Inc. (PA), 115 South Street John's Drive, Camp Hill, PA 17011; (717) 737–3960

*Burlington United Methodist Family Services, Route 3, Box 346A, Grafton, WV 26354; (304) 265–1338. There are offices in Keyser (304) 788–2342 and Scott Depot (304) 757–9127.

*Childplace, Inc., 1602 Stonehenge Road, Charleston, WV 25314; (304) 344–0319

*Children's Home Society, 432 Oakland Street, Morgantown, WV 26505; (304) 599–6505

*Children's Home Society of WV, 1145 Greenbriar Street, Charleston, WV 25311; (304) 345–3894. There is an office in Princeton (304) 425–8438.

Family Services Association, Overbrook Tower, 500 Cove Road, Weirton, WV 26062; (304) 797–0444

LDS Social Services (*see* Ohio)
*Voice for International and Domestic Adoptions (VIDA) (*see* New York)

WISCONSIN

State Agency: Department of Health and Family Services, P.O. Box 8916, Madison, WI 53708–8916; (608) 266–3595
State Exchange and Photolisting: Wisconsin Adoption Information Exchange, Special Needs Adoption Network, 1126 S. 70th Street, Milwaukee, WI 53214; (414) 475–1246 or (800) 762–8063
State Reunion Registry: Adoption Search Coordinator, Division of Children and Family Services, P.O. Box 8916, Madison, WI 53708–8916; (608) 266–7163
Independent Adoption: Permitted

Private Agencies
*Adoption Advocates, Inc., 2601 Crossroads Drive, Madison, WI 53718–7923; (608) 246–2844
*Adoption Choice, 924 E. Juneau Avenue, Milwaukee, WI 53202–2748; (414) 276–3262
*Adoption Option, 1804 Chapman Drive, Waukesha, WI 53186; (414) 544–4278
*Adoption Services of Green Bay & The Fox Valley, 911 N. Lynndale Drive, Appleton, WI 54914; (414) 735–6750
*Bethany Christian Services, 20 Forest Avenue, Fond du Lac, WI 54935–4182; (414) 923–6577
*Bethany Christian Services of Wisconsin, 2312 N. Grandview Boulevard, Waukesha, WI 53188–1606; (414) 547–6557
Catholic Charities, 3501 South Lake Drive, Milwaukee, WI 53207–0912; (414) 769–3400
Catholic Charities Bureau, Inc., 1416 Cumming Avenue, Superior, WI 54880; (715) 394–6617

*Catholic Charities, Inc., 4905 Schofield Street, Madison, WI 53716–2640; (608) 221–2000

*Catholic Charities/Milwaukee Region, 2021 N. 60th Street, Milwaukee, WI 53208; (414) 771–2881

Catholic Charities/North Region, 503 Wisconsin Avenue, Sheboygan, WI 53801; (414) 458–5726. There is an office in West Bend (414) 334–0886.

Catholic Charities/South Region, 2711 19th Street, Racine, WI 53403–2314; (414) 637–8888. There is an office in Kenosha (414) 658–2088.

Catholic Charities/Waukesha Region, 741 North Grand Avenue, Waukesha, WI 53186; (414) 547–2463

*Catholic Residential Services, Inc., 505 King Street, La Crosse, WI 54601–4062; (608) 782–5323

Catholic Social Services, 1825 Riverside Drive, Green Bay, WI 54305–3825; (920) 437–7531

Catholic Social Services, 3311 Prairie Avenue, Beloit, WI 53511; (608) 365–3665

Catholic Social Services, Fox Cities Area Office, 921 W. Midway Road, Menasha, WI 54952–0256; (920) 725–3066

Catholic Social Services, Diocese of Green Bay, 1203 North 16th Street, Manitowoc, WI 54220; (920) 684–6651

Catholic Social Services, Marinette Area Office, 844 Pierce Avenue, Marinette, WI 54143; (715) 735–7802

Catholic Social Services/Oshkosh, 201 Ceape Avenue, Oshkosh, WI 54801; (414) 235–6002

Center for Child and Family Services, Inc., 4456 North 28th Street, Milwaukee, WI 53209; (414) 442–4702

*Children's Home Society of Minnesota (*see* Minnesota)

*Children's Service Society of Wisconsin, 4915 Monona Drive, Madison, WI 53716; (608) 221–3511. There are offices in Oshkosh (920) 633–3591, West Allis (414)

453–1400, and Wisconsin Rapids (715) 421–0480.

*Community Adoption Center, 3701 Kadow Street, Manitowoc, WI 54220; (920) 682–9211. There is an office in Janesville (608) 756–0405.

Douglas Memorial Center, 8018 W Capitol Drive, Milwaukee, WI 53222–1918; (414) 445–5953

*Evangelical Child and Family Agency—District Office, 1617 S. 124th Street, New Berlin, WI 53151; (414) 789–1881 or (800) 686–3232

Family Service Association of Sheboygan, 1930 North 8th Street, Sheboygan, WI 53081; (414) 458–3784

*Hope International Family Services, Inc. (*see* Minnesota)

Institute for Child and Family Development, 4206 W. Capital Drive, Milwaukee, WI 53216; (414) 449–2274

LDS Social Services, 1711 University Avenue, Madison, WI 53705; (608) 238–5377

Lutheran Counseling and Family Service, 1119 Regis Court, Eau Claire, WI 54701; (715) 832–7615. There are offices in Shawano (715) 524–4840, Wausau (715) 845–6289, Appleton (920) 731–5651, Sheboygan (414) 457–4011, and Wauwatosa (414) 536–8333.

Lutheran Social Services, 1101 W. Clairmont Avenue, Eau Claire, WI 54701; (715) 833–0992. There are offices in Superior (715) 394–4173, Wausau (715) 842–5577, Madison (608) 277–2970, La Crosse (608) 788–5090, and Appleton (920) 734–4326.

*Lutheran Social Services of Wisconsin and Upper Michigan, 4143 S. 13th Street, Milwaukee, WI 53214; (414) 281–4400

*Pauquette Children's Services, Inc., 315 W. Conant Street, Portage, WI 53901–0162; (608) 742–8004

Special Beginnings, 237 South Street, Waukesha, WI 53186; (414) 896–3600

*Special Children, Inc., 910 N. Elm Grove Road, Elm Grove, WI 53122; (414) 821–2125

*Van Dyke, Inc., 1224 Weeden Creek Road, Sheboygan, WI 53081–8285; (414) 452–5358

WYOMING

State Agency: Department of Family Services, 2300 Capitol Avenue, Cheyenne, WY 82002; (307) 777–3570

State Exchange and Photolisting: The Adoption Exchange, 925 S. Niagara, Denver, CO 82204; (303) 333–9845

State Confidential Intermediary Service: Wyoming Confidential Adoption Intermediary Services (see above); (307) 777–3570

Independent Adoption: Permitted

Private Agencies

*Bethany Christian Services, 3001 Henderson Drive, Cheyenne, WY 82001; (307) 635–2032

*Catholic Social Services, P.O. Box 1026, Cheyenne, WY 82003–1026; (307) 638–1530 or (800) 788–4606. There are offices in Casper (307) 237–2723, Cody (307) 587–6694, Gillette, and Rock Springs (307) 362–7823.

*Focus on Children, P.O. Box 323, Cokeville, WY 83114–0323; (307) 279–3557

*Global Adoptions, 1425 S. Thurmond, Sheridan, WY 82801; (307) 672–7605

LDS Social Services, 7609 Santa Marie Drive, Cheyenne, WY 82009; (307) 637–8929. There is an office in Cody (307) 587–9413.

*Wyoming Children's Society, 716 Randall Ave., Cheyenne, WY 82003–0105; (307) 632–7619

*Wyoming Parenting Society, P.O. Box 2468, Jackson, WY 83001; (307) 733–7771

APPENDIX C

FOR FURTHER REFERENCE

◆

There is a vast and evolving literature about adoption and infertility. The **National Adoption Information Clearinghouse** (see appendix A) will do a customized search for you on a particular adoption topic.

◆

You can order books by mail from:

Adoptive Families of America, 2309 Como Avenue, St. Paul, MN 55108; (800) 372–3300 or (612) 645–9955

Child Welfare League of America, 440 First Street NW, Washington, DC 20001; (202) 638–2952; http://www.cwla.org. Publishes the journal *Child Welfare*.

Perspectives Press, P.O. Box 90318, Indianapolis, IN 46290; (317) 872–3055; http://www.perspectivespress.com (specialty publisher focusing on infertility and adoption books).

Tapestry Books, P.O. Box 359, Ringoes, NJ; (800) 765–2367 or (908) 806–6695; http://www.tapestrybooks.com

You'll also discover innumberable listings at online bookstores such as **Amazon.com** (http://www.amazon.com).

◆

If you're interested in subscribing to an adoption magazine, there are many choices. The National Adoption Information Clearinghouse has a variety of bibliographic lists you can request. Among the choices:

Adoptalk, NACAC, 970 Raymond Avenue, St. Paul, MN 55114; (612) 644–3036

Adopted Child, Box 9362, Moscow, ID 83848; (208) 882–1794 (e-mail: lmelina@moscow.com)

Adoption Medical News, 1921 Ohio Street NE, Palm Bay, FL 32907; (407) 725–6379

Adoptive Families, which grew out of the bimonthly *OURS* (published by Adoptive Families of America)

FACE Facts, FACE, Box 28058, Northwood Station, Baltimore, MD 21239l; (410) 488–2656

International Concerns for Children Newsletter, 911 Cypress Drive, Boulder, CO 80303; (303) 494–8333

Open Adoption, National Federation for Open Adoption Education, 391 Taylor Boulevard, Pleasant Hill, CA 94523; (510) 827–2229

Open Adoption Birthparent, 721 Hawthorne Street, Royal Oak, MI 48067; (810) 543–0997

Roots and Wings, P.O. Box 638, Chester, NJ 07930; (908) 637–8828

◆

A more scholarly publication is *Adoption Quarterly,* The Haworth Press Inc., 10 Alice Street, Binghamton, NY 13904; 800–HAWORTH.

If you prefer to get your information by listening to audio cassettes or watching videotapes, you'll find that the basic adoption resources have their own collections and can direct you to others.

The **National Adoption Information Clearinghouse** (see appendix A) publishes an *Adoption Videos and Tapes Catalogue* that is updated annually.

Adoptive Families of America, for example, sells *Mr. Rogers' Neighborhood Adoption Video* and *Reading Rainbow Adoption Video*.

Lois Melina has developed a series of audiotapes, available through *Adopted Child* magazine (see above).

Keep in mind that parent groups and agencies purchase audio- and videotapes and lend them out to interested families. And don't forget to check out your local video store for movies that touch on adoption.

◆

The list that follows is a sampling of the books and pamphlets available. I have tried to mix some of the older books, which may be out-of-print but still found in libraries, with more contemporary readings. The listings, with brief descriptions, are intended to whet your appetite and stimulate thought. It is not comprehensive, but singles out books that I believe will be of interest to adults and children. You'll want to update this list as you discover new works.

ADOPTION: INFORMATION AND ISSUES

Chris Adamec, *The Complete Idiot's Guide to Adoption* (New York: Alpha Books, 1998). Part of the "Complete Idiot Guides" how-to books.

Christine A. Adamec, *There ARE Babies to Adopt* (New York: Pinnacle Books, 1991). Basic how-to information for adopting an infant.

Colleen Alexander-Roberts, *The Legal Adoption Guide: Safely Navigating the System* (Dallas: Taylor Publishing Company, 1996). Discussion of independent adoption issues, including the role of an attorney, birth parent rights, open adoption, and the hospital experience.

Jayne Askin, *Search–A Handbook for Adoptees and Birthparents* (Phoenix: Oryx Press, 1992). A resource book that takes interested people through the stages of the search—what's involved and how to go about it.

Elizabeth Bartholet, *Family Bonds: Adoption and the Politics of Parenting* (Boston: Houghton Mifflin, 1993). An examination of infertility and adoption policies as well as the author's personal experiences.

Laura Beauvais-Godwin and Raymond Godwin, *The Complete Adoption Book: Everything You Need to Know to Adopt The Child You Want in Less Than 1 Year* (Holbrook: Adams Media Corporation, 1997). An earlier version of this book focused on independent adoption and the authors are strongest here, since Raymond is an attorney and Laura is the director of Adoption and Home Studies Services.

Peter L. Benson, Anu R. Sharma, and Eugene C. Roehlkepartain, *Growing Up Adopted: A Portrait of Adolescents & Their Families* (Minneapolis, Minnesota: Search Institute, 1994). This study, drawing upon a survey of 715 families, concludes that typical adopted teenagers, who were adopted as infants, have a positive identity, are strongly attached to their families, accept adoption as a fact of life, and are in good mental health.

Linda Bothun, *When Friends Ask about Adoption: Question & Answer Guide for Non-Adoptive Parents and Other Caring Adults* (Chevy Chase, Maryland: Swan Publications, 1987). Answers to "Do you love her like your own?" and the other questions that adoptive parents inevitably hear.

David M. Brodzinsky and Marshall D. Schechter, eds., *The Psychology of Adoption* (New York: Oxford University Press, 1990). This scholarly collection of essays by well-known adoption researchers highlights the problems facing adoptees, adoptive parents, and birth parents. Note the editors: "Our goal was to provide an overview of current work in adoption, with a focus primarily on mental health issues."

David M. Brodzinsky, Marshall D. Schechter, and Robin Marantz Henig, *Being Adopted: The Lifelong Search for Self* (New York: Doubleday, 1992). Drawing upon their clinical research and the accounts of adoptees, the authors "map out what it is like to be adopted" over the life cycle of the individual. The book uses a developmental perspective, based on Erik Erikson's seven-stage life cycle, to examine how the search for self and the experience of loss influence the adoptee's psychological development over time. A thought-provoking, invaluable resource.

E. Wayne Carp, *Family Matters: Secrecy and Disclosure in the History of Adoption* (Cambridge: Harvard University Press, 1998). Historian Carp had access to the records of the Children's Home Society of Washington and used them, along with a multitude of published sources, to examine the history of disclosure. His discovery: openness, not secrecy, was the norm in adoption until the post–World War II era. A fascinating account—and one which takes the discussion of openness into the nineties.

William Feigelman and Arnold R. Silverman, *Chosen Children*. (New York: Praeger Publishers, 1983). A research study that examines new patterns of adoptive relationships. Among its subjects: the differences in attitudes between infertile couples and "preferential adopters" (fertile couples, singles), adjustments of black children adopted by white families, adaptation of transracially adopted Korean-born adolescents, and adjustment of Colombian-born children adopted by white families.

Carol Hallenbeck, *Our Child: Preparation for Parenting in Adoption* (Wayne, Pennsylvania: Our Child Press, 1988). An instructor's guide to creating a class for adoptive parents.

Andrew Harnack, *Adoption: Opposing Viewpoints* (San Diego: Greenhaven Press, 1995). Collection of essays of opposing points of view on such topics as adoption rights, foster care, agency policies, transracial adoptions, and confidential adoptions.

Mary Hopkins-Best, *Toddler Adoption: The Weaver's Craft* (Indianapolis, Indiana: Perspectives Press, 1997). Focuses on the decision to adopt a children between the ages of one and three, the special preparations families need to make, and the adjustment process. Observes the author: "A child who is adopted as a toddler needs parents who understand both his developmental needs and the effect of his early life experiences on that development."

Claudia Jewett, *Adopting the Older Child* (Harvard: Harvard Common Press, 1978). A landmark book that introduces people to the adoption of older children. Jewett follows the history of several children and their adoptive families, starting before the adoption and continuing through to the postplacement period.

Patricia Irwin Johnston, *An Adoptor's Advocate* (Fort Wayne: Perspectives Press, 1984). Linking infertility and adoption, the book seeks to "bring out into the open some of those most carefully concealed fears and doubts that preadoptive parents experience, to help couples and counselors understand the emotional processes that connect infertility and adoption, and to offer some suggestions for improving the system for the benefit of all concerned."

Patricia Irwin Johnston, *Launching a Baby's Adoption: Practical Strategies for Parents and Professionals* (Indianapolis, Indiana: Perspectives Press, 1997). This guide is intended to provide guidance in preparing for the arrival, and smoothing the transitional year, of an adopted infant. It is not a how-to-adopt but rather a look at the emotional and psychological issues in adoption.

H. David Kirk, *Adoptive Kinship: A Modern Institution in Need of Reform* (Toronto: Butterworth, 1981). This book extends the argument that Kirk set forth in his *Shared Fate: A Theory and Method of Adoptive Relationships* (New York: Free Press, 1964), that the adoptive situation is different from the family whose bonds are based on birth. People involved in adoption must acknowledge the differences as they build their family relationships.

Miriam Komar, *Communicating with the Adopted Child* (New York: Walker and Company, 1991). How to talk with your adopted children, including sample conversations.

Betty Jean Lifton, *Journey of the Adopted Self: A Quest for Wholeness* (New York: Basic Books, 1994). Ruminations on the adoptee's search for identity and the problems the adoptee faces in the closed adoption system. Her discussions of the reunion process are interesting but adoptive parents beware: the stridency of her argument, her drawing upon Greek myth and psychoanalytic theory, and particularly her explication of the adopted child syndrome can be off-putting.

Betty Jean Lifton, *Lost and Found: The Adoption Experience*, rev. ed. (New York: Harper & Row, 1988). Focuses on the adoptee's struggle for a sense of identity using extensive interviews with members of the adoption triangle. Her chapter, "Rights and Responsibilities for Everyone in the Adoption Circle," is one of the most cogent statements that I have seen.

Cynthia D. Martin and Dru Martin Groves, *Beating the Adoption Odds: Using Your Head and Your Heart to Adopt* (Orlando: Harcourt Brace, 1998). Cynthia Martin, in collaboration with her adopted daughter, has revised her *Beating the Adoption Game*. A wide-ranging book whose strengths lie in infant adoptions.

Lois Ruskai Melina, *Making Sense of Adoption: A Parent's Guide* (New York: Harper & Row, 1989). Through sample conversations, the book covers the questions adoptees ask and provides answers that adoptive parents may use. There are also sample activities, such as making your own adoption storybook.

Lois Ruskai Melina, *Raising Adopted Children: A Manual for Adoptive Parents* (New York: HarperCollins, 1998). A comprehensive guide that looks at the special circumstances of adoptive parenting. Melina begins with "instant family" and takes you through the teenage years. Topics covered in the book include: adjustment of the family, bonding and attachment, talking to your child about adoption, sexuality, behavior problems, and the importance of family history.

Stanley B. Michelman and Meg Schneider with Antonia van der Meer, *The Private Adoption Handbook: A Step-by-Step Guide to the Legal, Emotional, and Practical Demands of Adopting a Baby* (New York: Villard Books, 1988). Written by an attorney who has specialized in independent adoptions and an adoptive mother who used him for her attorney, the book provides an overview of the process. There's a heavy emphasis on the role that the attorney plays, how newspaper advertising works, installing a babyphone, and the other methods that Michelman's clients used.

Julia L. Posner with James Guilianelli, *CWLA's Guide to Adoption Agencies and Adoption Resources* (Washington, D.C.: Child Welfare

League of America, 1990). A state-by-state listing of agencies and their services, including the wait, the children, the requirements, the costs. For some states there's a 100 percent response by agencies, for others much less.

Judith Schaffer and Christina Lindstrom, *How to Raise an Adopted Child* (New York: Crown Publishers, 1989). The authors see their book as the adoptive parents' Dr. Spock: adoption information is grafted onto general parenting information. Helpful questions and answers, modeled on an advice column, accompany each chapter.

Dorothy W. Smith and Laurie Nehls Sherwen, *Mothers and their Adopted Children—The Bonding Process* (New York: Tiresias Press, 1983). Based on a survey and interviews, the book looks at how bonding takes place.

Jerome Smith, *The Realities of Adoption* (Lanham, Maryland: Madison Books, 1997). Discussion of issues and research in contemporary adoption, including Smith's role in the Baby Jessica case.

Jerome Smith, *You're Our Child: A Social/Psychological Approach to Adoption* (Washington, D.C.: University Press of America, 1981). Looks at the psychological tasks faced by adoptive parents and adoptees.

Arthur D. Sorosky, Annette Baran, and Reuben Pannor, *The Adoption Triangle: Sealed or Open Records: How They Affect Adoptees, Birth Parents, and Adoptive Parents*, rev. ed. (New York: Anchor Press/Doubleday, 1984). Examines the effect of the sealed record on adoptees, birth parents, and adoptive parents and sets forth the belief that adoption is a lifelong process. The authors called for reevaluation of current adoption practices towards more openness.

Jean A. S. Strauss, *Birthright: The Guide to Search and Reunion for Adoptees, Birthparents and Adoptive Parents* (New York: Penguin Books, 1994). Based on both her experience and those of other members of the adoption triad, Strauss covers the decision to search, the process, the emotional turbulence in the wake of a reunion, and the impact that search has on adoptive parents.

Marianne Takas and Edward Warner, *To Love A Child: A Complete Guide to Adoption, Foster Parenting, and Other Ways to Share Your Life with Children* (Reading, Massachusetts: Addison-Wesley, 1992). A general survey with a particularly useful discussion of foster parenting.

Holly van Gulden and Lisa M. Bartels-Rabb, *Real Parents, Real Children: Parenting the Adopted Child* (New York: The Crossroad Publishing Company, 1993). Practical, and sensitive, advice on handling adoption issues from infancy through young adulthood. The authors write: "by understanding how your child understands, interprets, and feels about adoption and why, you can do much to help him or her through these struggles." This book distinguishes itself from other books on raising adopted children by offering detailed discussions in several chapters on what happens when children are moved at different stages of their development.

Mary Watkins and Susan Fisher, *Talking with Young Children about Adoption* (New Haven: Yale University Press, 1993). In this scholarly work the authors offer guidance on what parents need to do to discuss adoption with their younger children. You'll also gain insight into interpreting what young children have shared through play and their talking about their understanding of adoption. Most fascinating: accounts by adoptive parents of the conversations they've had with their children concerning adoption and adoption issues.

Lawrence Wright, *Twins and What They Tell Us about Who We Are* (New York: John Wiley, 1997). Ever wonder how much of people's makeup—character, intelligence, and lifestyle—result from their genes? Since many of the twin studies have focused on identical twins who were adopted by different families and raised apart, you'll find the book irresistible reading. Not an adoption book per se but it gets you thinking about the impact of "nature vs. nurture."

FOR CHILDREN AND ADOLESCENTS

Suzanne Bloom, *A Family for Jamie* (New York: Clarkson Potter, 1991). A simple picture book that describes how a family waited to adopt a baby. Fiction.

Brian Boyd, *When You Were Born in Korea: A Memory Book for Children Adopted from Korea* (St. Paul, Minnesota: Yeong & Yeong Book Company, 1993). Photos and text that focus on the foster care and adoption process for infants in South Korea. Nonfiction.

Anne Braff Brodzinsky, *The Mulberry Bird* (Fort Wayne, Indiana: Perspectives Press, 1986). How a mother bird realizes that she cannot raise her baby bird and finds a new family for her child.

There is a 1996 edition as well. Some adoptive parents prefer the earlier edition. Fiction.

Catherine and Sherry Bunin, *Is That Your Sister? A True Story of Adoption* (New York: Pantheon Books, 1976). Illustrated with photographs of her family and narrated by six-year-old Catherine, this book tells her family's adoption story—the building of a transracial family. Presents questions that children may hear from others. Nonfiction.

Betsy Byars, *The Pinballs* (New York: Harper & Row, 1977). The tale of three children who find themselves in foster care and how they build a friendship. Fiction.

Jeannette Caines, *Abby* (New York: Harper & Row, 1973). Picture book for preschoolers. Abby, who was adopted when she was an infant, likes to look at her baby book and hear the story of her arrival in her family. Fiction.

Joanna Cole, *How I Was Adopted* (New York: Morrow Junior Books, 1995). Picture book narrated by Samantha who tells her adoption story. An unusual feature: depiction of a pregnant birth mother with her uterus delineated and illustrations on how a baby emerges through the birth canal. Fiction.

Jamie Lee Curtis, *Tell Me Again about the Night I Was Born* (New York: HarperCollins, 1996). Simple picture book in which a young adoptee asks her mother to tell her the details about her birth and arrival into her family. Fiction.

Nancy D'Antonio, *Our Baby from China: An Adoption Story* (Niles, Illinois: Albert Whitman & Co., 1997). A family's journey to China told in photos. Nonfiction.

Sara Dorow, *When You Were Born in China* (St. Paul, Minnesota: Yeong & Yeong Book Company, 1997). Focuses on the care of babies in orphanages and the adoption process. Nonficiton.

Iris L. Fisher, *Katie-Bo: An Adoption Story* (New York: Adama Books, 1987). Charming story recounted by older brother of how their Korean sister Katie-Bo comes into their family. Fiction.

Susi Gregg Fowler, *When Joel Comes Home* (New York: Greenwillow Books, 1993). In this picture book a young girl talks about her excitement that friends are adopting a baby and her plans, including having the chance to hold him, for his welcome. Includes an airport scene with flowers and balloons. Fiction.

Susan Gabel, *Filling in the Blanks: A Guided Look at Growing Up Adopted*

(Indianapolis, Indiana: Perspectives Press, 1988). A workbook, designed for children ages ten to fourteen, with pages to fill in about "My Birth Family," "My Adoption Process," "My Adoptive Family," and "My Self." Nonfiction.

Susan Gabel, *Where the Sun Kisses the Sea* (Indianapolis, Indiana: Perspectives Press, 1989). Picture-book story of a young boy in a Korean orphanage and his joining a family in the United States. Fiction.

Linda Walvoord Girard, *Adoption is for Always* (Niles, Illinois: Albert Whitman & Co., 1986). A young girl has questions about why she was adopted. Fiction.

Linda Walvoord Girard, *We Adopted You, Benjamin Koo* (Niles, Illinois, Albert Whitman & Co., 1989). The story of Benjamin and his feelings about adoption. Fiction.

Shirley Gordon, *The Boy Who Wanted a Family* (New York: Harper & Row, 1980). The fears, hopes, and experiences of seven-year-old Michael during the one-year waiting period before the finalization of his adoption. The account takes him from his foster home, the last of many, to his home with his single adoptive mother. Fiction.

Karen Gravelle and Susan Fischer, *Where Are My Birth Parents? A Guide for Teenage Adoptees* (New York: Walker and Company, 1993). A discussion of adolescent adoptees' searching—how to do it and the emotions they feel. Nonfiction.

James Howe, *Pinky and Rex and the New Baby* (New York: Atheneum, 1993). Howe's many books delight youngsters and this one is no exception: a straightforward tale about the friendship between Pinky and Rex and how their families handle the adoption of Rex's baby brother Matthew. There's a comfortable, familiar ring, complete with three "I'm the Big Sister" T-shirts, an explanation of "Where Did the Baby Come From?," and a party to celebrate the adoption. Fiction.

Keiko Kasza, *A Mother for Choco* (New York: G. P. Putnam's Sons, 1992). Picture-book tale of a bird's search for a mother and how Mrs. Bear adopts him even though they don't look alike. Fiction.

Karen Katz, *Over the Moon: An Adoption Tale* (New York: Henry Holt, 1997). Influenced by her daughter's adoption from Guatemala, Katz creates an exuberant, fanciful picture book: "Your baby has been born! She is wonderful. Come quickly and get her." Joyful reading. Fiction.

Holly Keller, *Horace* (New York: Greenwillow Books, 1991). Horace's parents have stripes; he has spots. Every night his mama told him, "We chose you when you were a tiny baby because you had lost your first family and needed a new one. We liked your spots, and we wanted you to be our child." One day Horace decides to find a family with spots. Herein lies the charming picture-book tale. Fiction.

Phoebe Koehler, *The Day We Met You* (New York: Bradbury Press, 1990). Simple picture book with lush illustrations about the activities and feelings of a couple on the day they first saw their baby. Fiction.

Irina Korschunow, *The Foundling Fox* (New York: Harper & Row, 1984). Picture book telling how a young fox, whose mother had been killed by hunters, got a new mother. Fiction.

Jill Krementz, *How It Feels to be Adopted* (New York: Alfred A. Knopf, 1982). Nineteen children, ages eight to sixteen, shared their feelings with Krementz. Photographs of the children, alone and with their parents and family, are an integral part of the book. A book for parents of young children to read and think about; for older children to read; for families to share together. Nonfiction.

Betty Jean Lifton, *I'm Still Me* (New York: Alfred A. Knopf, 1981). The book starts out: "It may sound weird to say that your whole life changed because of an American history assignment. But that's the way it was. . . ." When teenaged Lori Elkins is asked to prepare a family tree, she has to deal with the issues of adoption, origins, and feelings. In this engrossing novel, teenager Lori Elkins decided to search. A book that's not for teenagers only. Fiction.

Patricia MacLachlan, *Mama One, Mama Two* (New York: Harper & Row, 1982). Simple children's picture book that tells the story of a little girl's entry into foster care. Fiction.

Joyce McDonald, *Mail-Order Kid* (New York: G. P. Putnam's Sons, 1988). Ten-year-old Flip purchases a fox through a mail-order catalog. As he tries to tame it, he comes to understand the process of acculturation that his newly adopted brother Todd, age six, has been going through. Fiction.

Elisabet McHugh, *Raising a Mother Isn't Easy* (New York: Greenwillow Books, 1983); *Karen's Sister* (New York: Greenwillow Books, 1983); and *Karen and Vicki* (New York: Greenwillow Books, 1984). Tales told by Korean adoptee Karen about her family.

Karen's Sister highlights adoption issues, since it recounts the arrival and adjustment of five-year-old Meghan from South Korea. Fiction.

Kathryn Ann Miller, *Did My First Mother Love Me? A Story for an Adopted Child* (Buena Park, California: Morning Glory Press, 1994). Picture book that is essentially a letter from a birth mother to the child she placed for adoption: "My dearest child, To your parents I have given the precious gift of you." Fiction.

Jean Davies Okimoto, *Molly by Any Other Name* (New York: Scholastic, 1990). In this sensitively written story, teenager Molly, with the support of her parents, initiates a search for her birth mother. The author tells the story from both Molly's and her birth mother's perspective. Fiction.

Katherine Paterson, *The Great Gilly Hopkins* (New York: Thomas Y. Crowell, 1978). Eleven-year-old Gilly has been shuffled around. When she lands in her latest foster home, she schemes against everyone who tries to befriend her. Fiction.

Fred Rogers, *Let's Talk About It: Adoption* (New York: G. P. Putnam's Sons, 1994). Part of a series of simple photo books, depicting a variety of families and what it means to belong. Nonfiction.

Maxine B. Rosenberg, *Being Adopted* (New York: Lothrop, Lee & Shephard, 1984). Using the photographs of George Ancona, Rosenberg profiles a few youngsters: Rebecca, seven, who is part black; Karin, eight, who is Korean; and Andrei, ten, who is Indian. Nonfiction.

Maxine B. Rosenberg, *Growing Up Adopted* (New York: Bradbury Press, 1989). The author asked fourteen adoptees—older children and adults—to talk about their experiences being adopted. Nonfiction.

Allen Say, *Allison* (Boston: Houghton Mifflin Company, 1997). Award-winning illustrator Say has created a picture book about a young girl, Allison, who's adopted and trying to understand how families are formed. Fiction.

Jane T. Schnitter, *William Is My Brother* (Indianapolis, Indiana: Perspectives Press, 1991). A picture book whose message is: "Some people tell William that he is special because he was adopted. William is not special because he was adopted. William is special because he is William." Fiction.

Harriet Langsam Sobol, *We Don't Look Like Our Mom and Dad* (New

York: Coward-McCann, 1984). Photo-essay about two Korean adoptees and their family. Nonfiction.

Susan and Gordon Adopt a Baby (New York: Random House/Children's Television Workshop, 1986). For those who missed the big day on Sesame Street when Susan and Gordon adopted baby Miles, there's a book chronicling the event. Big Bird is jealous and herein lies the tale. A picture book for Sesame Street aficionados without a preachy adoption message. Fiction.

Theodore Taylor, *Tuck Triumphant* (New York: Doubleday, 1991). Part of a series of stories about Helen and her Labrador Friar Tuck Golden Boy. In this book Helen's parents adopt a six-year-old boy Chok-Do from South Korea and discover that he is deaf. How the family deals with his disability is the book's focus. Fiction.

Ann Turner, *Through Moon and Stars and Night Skies* (New York: HarperCollins, 1990). A young Korean boy tells the story of his adoption from South Korea, his flight to the United States, and his meeting with his adoptive parents in this handsomely illustrated picture book. Fiction.

Valentina Wasson, *The Chosen Baby* (New York: J. B. Lippincott Co, 1977). The classic adoption story with updated pictures and text. Fiction.

Marjorie Ann Waybill, *Chinese Eyes* (Scottdale, Pennsylvania: Herald Press, 1974). A picture book that tells the story of a first-grade Korean adoptee's encounter with prejudice—"There's little Chinese eyes!" The book looks at her feelings and her mother's explanation of differences and similarities. Fiction.

INFERTILITY

Gay Becker, *Healing the Infertile Family: Strengthening Your Relationship in the Search for Parenthood* (New York: Bantam Books, 1990). A look at how men and women react—what happens to their identities and their relationship—when confronted with impaired fertility and guidance on coping.

Gary S. Berger, M.D., Marc Goldstein, M.D., and Mark Fuerst, *The Couple's Guide to Fertility*, rev. ed. (New York: Doubleday, 1995). A rundown of the medical facts of infertility and the various treatments, including the new reproductive technologies. One distinctive feature: lists of questions throughout the book that you should be asking yourself and your physician.

Stephen L. Corson, M.D., *Conquering Infertility: A Guide for Couples* (New York: Prentice Hall Press, 1990). Detailed medical explanations with an emphasis on female fertility problems.

Robert R. Franklin, M.D. and Dorothy Kay Brockman, *In Pursuit of Fertility: A Fertility Expert Tells You How to Get Pregnant,* 2nd edition (New York: Henry Holt, 1995). Written by an infertility specialist, a detailed overview of the causes of infertility and an explanation of the popular treatments. There's a look at "infertility breakthroughs," such as IVF, GIFT and ZIFT, AID, and surrogate motherhood.

Ellen S. Glazer, *The Long-Awaited Stork: A Guide to Parenting after Infertility* (Lexington, Massachusetts: Lexington Books, 1990). People's feelings of loss and of being different do not vanish because of a successful pregnancy or adoption. How the emotional impact of infertility spills over into parenting is at the heart of this book.

Ellen Sarasohn Glazer and Susan Lewis Cooper, *Without Child: Experiencing and Resolving Infertility* (Lexington, Massachusetts: Lexington Books, 1988). A collection of essays, many of them firsthand accounts, and poems about infertility, pregnancy loss, the new reproductive technologies, adoption, child-free living, and parenting after infertility.

Michael Gold, *And Hannah Wept: Infertility, Adoption, and the Jewish Couple* (Philadelphia: The Jewish Publication Society, 1988). Using Jewish texts, Rabbi Gold explores infertility and adoption from the Jewish point of view. The book is intended as a resource for rabbis, social workers, and other professionals, as well as for Jewish families.

Patricia Irwin Johnston, *Taking Charge of Infertility* (Indianapolis: Perspectives Press, 1994). Uses a "can-do" approach to help couples communicate better, access information, budget their time and energy, so that they take charge, rather than drift, through the infertility experience.

Brian Kearney, *High-Tech Conception: A Comprehensive Textbook for Consumers* (New York: Bantam Books, 1998). For people who are considering IVF or one of the other new reproductive technologies.

Joan Liebmann-Smith, *In Pursuit of Pregnancy: How Couples Discover, Cope with and Resolve Their Fertility Problems* (New York: Newmarket Press, 1987). Through the personal stories of three couples, the book highlights how infertility affects the individual. You'll find it hard to put the book down since it captures the basic, raw emotions.

Dr. Richard Marrs, Lisa Friedman Bloch, and Kathy Kirtland Silverman, *Dr. Richard Marrs' Fertility Book: America's Leading Fertility Expert Tells You Everything You Need to Know about Getting Pregnant* (New York: Delacorte Press, 1997). Comprehensive discussion of the reproductive process, causes and cures for infertility, and emotional impact.

Barbara Eck Menning, *Infertility: A Guide for the Childless Couple* (New York: Prentice Hall Press, 1988) Focuses on the experience of infertility and how it affects people. Written by the founder of Resolve (see appendix A), this book looks at the psychological and social toll that infertility takes.

Debby Peoples and Harriette Rovner Ferguson, *What to Expect When You're Experiencing Infertility: How to Cope with the Emotional Crisis and Survive* (New York: W. W. Norton & Company, 1998). Through examples and a Q&A approach, the book looks at the medical, financial, and emotional issues, moving from crisis to acceptance to resolution.

Linda P. Salzer, *Surviving Infertility: A Compassionate Guide through the Emotional Crisis of Infertility* (New York: HarperCollins, 1991). Salzer attacks head-on the emotional pressure that infertility places on a relationship. Writes Salzer: "'Do you have children?' Such an ordinary question—but for the couple facing infertility, it brings thoughts of temperature charts, doctors' appointments, marital conflict, and sex on schedule. The struggle to have a child can turn your life on end and change a calm, well-adjusted person into a bundle of nerves. I know—I've been there." There's a resonance in this book that makes it required reading if you're in pain.

Sherman J. Silber, *How To Get Pregnant* (New York: Warner, 1991). A basic guide discussing infertility, particularly strong in explaining the reproductive system. Silber emphasizes that infertility is a problem shared by a couple, hence treatment must be directed at both husband and wife.

Harriet Fishman Simons, *Wanting Another Child: Coping with Secondary Infertility* (New York: Lexington Books, 1995). It is estimated that secondary infertility, which occurs after a couple or woman has already had a biological child, affects as many as 1.4 million

American couples. This book is for them, touching on the special social and emotional issues that arise, the unique parenting issues, and strategies that will help them work with medical providers and get through the experience.

INTERCOUNTRY ADOPTION

Myra Alperson, *The International Adoption Handbook: How To Make Foreign Adoption Work for You* (New York: Henry Holt and Company, 1997). Brief, general overview.

Howard Altstein and Rita J. Simon, eds. *Intercountry Adoption: A Multinational Perspective* (New York: Praeger, 1991). A research volume with essays that describe the experiences of foreign-born adoptees in the United States, Canada, Norway, the Netherlands, Denmark, West Germany, and Israel.

Barbara Bascom and Carole McKelvey, *The Complete Guide to Foreign Adoption: What to Expect and How to Prepare for Your New Child* (New York: Pocket Books, 1997). Thc book focuses largely on the Romanian adoption experience. A strong description of the orphanage system and the impact that orphanage life can have on children.

Frances M. Koh, *Oriental Children in American Homes: How Do They Adjust?* (Minneapolis: East-West Press, 1981). A study of culture and adoption. Koh analyzes the differences between Asian and American society in social relations, methods of discipline, education, and personality development, and discusses their effects on the adjustment of Asian children in American homes.

AnneMarie Merrill, ed., *Report on Intercountry Adoption*, produced by the International Concerns for Children (see appendix A). Issued annually, this report takes a country-by-country, agency-by-agency look at intercountry adoption. Chock-full of valuable information, including short essays reprinted from other publications. A subscription entitles you to updates that are mailed throughout the year.

Margi Miller and Nancy Ward, *With Eyes Wide Open: A Workbook for Parents Adopting International Children Over Age One* (Minneapolis, Minnesota: LN Press, Inc., 1996). A workbook created by the Children's Home Society of Minnesota that helps prospective parents prepare for a child and the adjustment issues they will face. Not just for parents of children over the age of one—helpful for all adoptive parents.

Jean Nelson-Erichsen and Heino R. Eirchsen, *How to Adopt Internationally: A Guide for Agency-Directed and Independent Adoptions* (Fort Worth, Texas: Mesa House Publishing, 1997). The Erichsens, founders of Los Ninos International Adoption Center, have created a basic nuts-and-bolts guide to adoption. This guide reproduces many of the basic documents you'll encounter and takes you through basic procedures.

Cheri Register, *Are Those Kids Yours?: American Families with Children Adopted from Other Countries* (New York: The Free Press, 1991). Any parent of a child adopted from abroad has heard that question. A broad-ranging book on the issue of international adoption that asks and answers many questions. Says Register: "My intention in writing this book is to identify some of the ethical issues raised by international adoption and to show how they are played out in the actual day-to-day experience of adoptive families."

O. Robin Sweet and Patty Bryan, *Adopt International: Everything You Need to Know to Adopt a Child from Abroad* (New York: Farrar, Strauss and Giroux, 1996). A general discussion of intercountry adoption, including appendices that have extensive country-by-country details on adoption, listings of agencies by country and by state, support groups and other details. If the information you find seems familiar, that's because you've seen it collected elsewhere.

Eileen M. Wirth and Joan Worden, *How to Adopt a Child from Another Country* (Nashville: Abingdon Press, 1993). Written by an adoptive parent and the director of an adoption agency, the book blends thoughtful advice with personal experience, including the return of Worden's daughter to South Korea to meet her birth family.

OPEN ADOPTION

Suzanne Arms, *To Love and Let Go* (New York: Alfred A. Knopf, 1983.) A group of profiles: birth mothers who relinquished their children, an adult adoptee's search, an adoption attorney, and prospective adoptive families. Arms vividly describes several open infant adoptions, including one in which the parents were present at the child's birth. The adoptions that she witnessed occurred through independent placement, and the book is a strong plea for more openness in adoption. In 1990 Celestial Arts in Berkeley issued a revised, updated, and expanded edition, entitled *Adoption: A Handful of Hope*. I prefer the first edition and suggest you check for it at your library.

Lincoln Caplan, *An Open Adoption* (New York: Farrar, Straus & Giroux, 1990). A close-up, engrossing account of how twenty-year-old Peggy Bass in Maryland chose Dan and Lee Stone in Massachusetts as the adoptive parents of her child. Interwoven with this is a more general account of open adoption.

James L. Gritter, ed., *Adoption without Fear* (San Antonio: Corona, 1989). Seventeen couples who adopted through Community, Family and Children Services in Traverse City, Michigan, tell their story. You'll get a sense of how adoptive parents and birth parents feel when they first meet.

James L. Gritter, *The Spirit of Open Adoption* (Washington, D.C.: CWLA Press, 1997). A unique work by an open adoption expert who wants to "stimulate thought about ways to transform adoption into a healthy institution."

Dion Howells with Kären Wilson Pritchard, *The Story of David* (New York: Delacorte Press, 1997). The Howells developed a close, very open relationship with their son's birth mother. The book offers insight into the process, including their experience as foster parents who weren't sure if their son's placement would lead to adoption.

Jeanne Warren Lindsay, *Open Adoption: A Caring Option* (Buena Park, California: Morning Glory Press, 1987). An extensive discussion of open adoption. Lindsay shares the experiences of birth parents and adoptive parents and describes a variety of programs.

Lois Ruskai Melina and Sharon Kaplan Roszia, *The Open Adoption Experience: A Complete Guide for Adoptive and Birth Families—From Making the Decision through the Child's Growing Years* (New York: HarperCollins, 1993). The book, which alternates between providing advice to birth and adoptive parents, focuses on fully open adoptions and how they evolve over time. The advice covers the nuts and bolts of carrying through an open adoption as well as the emotional issues it raises.

Bruce Rappaport, *The Open Adoption Book: A Guide to Adoption without Tears* (New York: Macmillan, 1992). Written by the director of the Independent Adoption Center, the book focuses on people's fears of open adoption and the realities they will encounter.

Kathleen Silber and Patricia Martinez Dorner, *Children of Open Adoption* (San Antonio: Corona, 1990). A chronicling, based on case studies, of the effect that open adoption has on the children from infancy through the teen years. While there's some how-to information, the book is primarily anecdotal.

Kathleen Silber and Phylis Speedlin, *Dear Birthmother* (San Antonio: Corona, 1991). The letters exchanged between adoptive parents and birth parents as well as the letters sent from birth parents to their children form the backbone of this book. The letters are used to hammer away at four myths: (1) birth parents don't care about their children; (2) adoption must be a strictly confidential matter; (3) birth parents will forget about their children; and (4) if the adoptee loved her parents, she would not have to search for her birth parents.

Mary Stephenson, *My Child Is a Mother* (San Antonio: Corona Publishing, 1991). A birth grandmother offers her account of her daughter's unplanned pregnancy and the open adoption that followed.

PERSONAL ACCOUNTS/FAMILY PROFILES

Paulette Bates Alden, *Crossing the Moon* (New York: Penguin Books, 1996). A memoir of infertility and the author's sharp turn away from motherhood. As she notes at its conclusion, "I thought it was important for people to hear from others who had survived infertility and who were okay without a child."

J. Douglas Bates, *Gift Children: A Story of Race, Family, and Adoption in a Divided America* (New York: Ticknor & Fields, 1993). Oregonians Gloria and Doug Bates adopted two African-American girls: four-year-old Lynn in 1970 and three-year-old Liska in 1972. Bates, drawing upon interviews with his family and letters written by the girls, chronicles the family's joys, setbacks, and challenges with transracial adoption.

Barbara J. Berg, *Nothing to Cry about* (New York: Bantam Books, 1983). A moving account of the author's experiences (she suffered two late miscarriages before successfully giving birth). One chapter chronicles her daughter's adoption through an independent placement. Berg's technique involved spreading the word through résumés.

Jill Bralosky and Helen Schulman, eds., *Wanting A Child: Twenty-Two Writers on Their Difficult but Mostly Successful Quests for Parenthood in a High-Tech Age* (New York: Farrar Straus and Giroux, 1998). A collection of personal essays and fiction about the dream of having a child. The collection includes tales of surrogacy, in vitro fertilization, pregnancy after multiple miscarriages, and adoption.

Joseph Blank, *Nineteen Steps Up the Mountain: The Story of the DeBolt Family* (New York: Lippincott, 1976). Biography of the DeBolts who built a large family of special-needs children and later founded AASK (Adopt a Special Kid; see appendix A).

Mary Earle Chase, *Waiting for Baby: One Couple's Journey through Infertility to Adoption* (New York: McGraw Hill, 1990). From infertility, inseminations, and psychics to a successful private adoption. And some how-to-adopt appended for good measure.

Maggie Francis Conroy, *A World of Love* (New York: Kensington Books, 1997). How the Conroy family expanded from one child to four through intercountry adoption from the former Soviet Union and Colombia. Conroy's story captures the pleasures—and the challenges—of adopting older, special-needs children.

Gay Courter, *I Speak for This Child: True Stories of a Child Advocate* (New York: Crown Publishers, 1995). Couter's compelling memoir recounts her experience as a Guardian ad Litem in Florida. The children she represents are trapped in the foster care system and her book chillingly reveals the tumult in their lives. Says she: "To the system, children are 'trouble units' in need of beds. One of the things I do is fight for them as people."

Patty Dann, *The Baby Boat: A Memoir of Adoption* (New York: Hyperion, 1998). The chronicle of the author's journey to Lithuania to adopt their infant son.

Elaine DePrince, *Cry Bloody Murder: A Tale of Tainted Blood* (New York: Random House, 1997). The author's intention was to write the story of how her family was devastated by AIDS, which her children contracted through the contaminated blood plasma they needed to control their hemophilia. *Cry Bloody Murder,* although not found on adoption bookshelves, is a heartbreaking tale of the special-needs adoption of three hemophiliac boys.

Michael Dorris, *The Broken Cord* (New York: HarperCollins, 1989). Chronicle of a single adoptive father's day-to-day experience raising a son affected by fetal alcohol syndrome. You'll understand why this eloquent, absorbing book was a bestseller.

Lorraine Dusky, *Birthmark* (New York: M. Evans and Company, 1979.) Birth mother's account of her pregnancy, her relinquishment of her child, and her postpartum feelings. The book appeared some thirteen years after the birth of her child. Dusky searched for—and eventually found—her daughter.

Florence Fisher, *The Search for Anna Fisher* (New York: Arthur Fields, 1973). A landmark personal chronicle of an adoptee's search for her birth family. Fisher was instrumental in the creation of the adoptee group, Adoptees' Liberty Movement Association (ALMA; see appendix A).

Anne Taylor Fleming, *Motherhood Deferred: A Woman's Journey* (New York: Fawcett Columbine, 1994). A memoir of infertility, of choices made, dreams deferred, comingled with the story of coming of age in the fifties and sixties.

Tim Green, *A Man and His Mother: An Adopted Son's Search* (New York: Regan Books, 1997). Tale of a popular sportscaster's search.

Bertha Holt, *The Seed from the East and Outstretched Arms*. (Eugene, Oregon: Reprinted by Industrial Publishing Company, 1983). The story of the development of the Holt adoption program in South Korea. If you're the parent of a child from South Korea, particularly if your child came from the Holt agency in the United States or in South Korea, you'll enjoy reading this family's story. Check with Holt International Children's Services (see appendix B under Oregon) about their availability.

Dion Howells with Karen Wilson Pritchard, *The Story of David* (New York: Delacorte Press, 1997). Chronicle of an open adoption, including the birth mother's ambivalence.

Betty Jean Lifton, *Twice Born* (New York: McGraw-Hill, 1975). An autobiography focusing on how Lifton felt as an adoptee, her search and meeting with her birth mother, and the relationship that developed following her search. The emotional complexities of adoption, rather than any legal barriers set up in Lifton's path, form the heart of the book.

Charlotte Lopez with Susan Dworkin, *Lost in the System: Miss Teen USA's Triumphant Fight to Claim a Family of Her Own* (New York: Simon & Schuster, 1996). Autobiography of a Vermont teen who spent her youth in the foster care system. The book offers a valuable perspective for foster and adoptive parents.

Ann Kimble Loux, *The Limits of Hope: An Adoptive Mother's Story* (Charlottesville: University of Virginia Press, 1997). A disturbing cry of despair from the trenches about the adoption of two preschoolers out of the foster care system. Loux's story begins in 1974 and continues through the present.

Katrina Maxtone-Graham, *An Adopted Woman* (New York: Remi Books, 1983). An autobiography describing the author's search and the many barriers thrown up in her path. Her account raises questions about the policy of closed records and particularly the reluctance of one agency to provide even non-identifying information.

Jacquelyn Mitchard, *Mother Less Child: The Love Story of a Family* (New York: W. W. Norton, 1985). The pace of this book is dizzying: from an ectopic pregnancy in the summer of 1982, through infertility and psychological and marital crises, tubal surgery, to choosing not to parent one newborn through a private adoption and accepting another by January 1984. Mitchard has since written more on adoptive parenthood, as well as best-selling fiction.

Margaret Moorman. *Waiting to Forget* (New York: W. W. Norton, 1996). A birthmother remembers.

Marguerite Ryan, *Adoption Story: A Son is Given* (New York: Rawson Associates, 1989). How one independent adoption ended up in a bitter court battle for several years.

Carol Schaefer, *The Other Mother: A Woman's Love for the Child She Gave Up for Adoption* (New York: Soho, 1991). Secrecy, shame, guilt, and pain are key ingredients in the moving chronicle of this birth mother. You'll cringe when you read her account of the months spent in a Catholic home for unwed mothers in the 1960s.

Susan Sheehan, *Life for Me Ain't Been No Crystal Stair* (New York: Pantheon, 1993). The engrossing story of Crystal Taylor and her family as they weave in and out of the New York City foster care system.

Gail Sheehy, *Spirit of Survival* (New York: William Morrow, 1986). The story of how the child Phat Mohm survived Pol Pot's Cambodia and came to live in America as Sheehy's adopted daughter. A fascinating chronicle of the day-to-day building of a relationship and how the survivor must come to terms with her past.

Barbara Shulgood and Lynne Sipiora, *Dear Barbara, Dear Lynne: The True Story of Two Women in Search of Motherhood* (Boston: Addison-Wesley, 1992). Correspondence between two women who struggle with infertility, adoption, and their feelings.

Jill Smolowe, *An Empty Lap: One Couple's Journey to Parenthood* (New York: Pocket Books, 1997). Ride the roller-coaster of infertility, grapple with depression, feel the push and pull of a couple heading in two directions, and finally, discover the sunlight of adoption.

Susan Wadia-Ellis, ed., *The Adoption Reader: Birth Mothers, Adoptive Mothers and Adopted Daughters Tell Their Stories* (Seattle, Washington: Seal Press, 1995). A collection of personal writings.

Jan L. Waldron, *Giving Away Simone: A Memoir* (New York: Times Books, 1995). An engrossing memoir of the experience of adoption through several generations. Waldron is particularly strong in describing her experience as a birth mother, the opening up of her child's adoption, and the ups and downs of open adoption for many years following.

Jana Wolff, *Secret Thoughts of an Adoptive Mother* (Kansas City: Andrews and McMeel, 1997). A journey through snippets, reading almost like diary entries, of the adoption process. Wolff's chapter headings say it all: "Could We Love Somebody Else's Child?" "If This is the Happiest Day of My Life, Why am I so Sad?" "Can We Return This Child," "Mother and Child Reunion: Is She Going to Kiss Him or Kidnap Him?"

POETRY

Patricia Irwin Johnston, comp., *Perspectives on a Grafted Tree: Thoughts for Those Touched by Adoption* (Fort Wayne, Indiana: Perspectives Press, 1983). Poetry written by adoptive parents and birth parents that touches on parts of the adoption process—"beginnings and endings," "the grafting," "reactions," "attachments," "motherspeakings," "identities," and "reflections." A unique book.

SPECIAL-NEEDS ADOPTION

L. Anne Babb and Rita Laws, *Adopting and Advocating for the Special Needs Child* (Westport, Connecticut: Bergin & Garvey, 1997). An overview of the special-needs adoption process and its complex issues by two adoption experts. Chapters focus on the adoption process, attachment issues, the day-to-day realities of living with special-needs children, including financial and educational challenges, and failed and wrongful adoptions.

John Hubner and Jill Wolfson, *Somebody Else's Children: The Courts, the Kids, and the Struggle to Save America's Troubled Families* (New

York: Crown Publishers, Inc., 1996). A study of the children and families who enter San Jose, California's family court, the book offers a compelling glimpse of the lives of children in foster care. Among the profiles: Nicky Delgato, nine weeks premature and testing positive at birth for drugs, whose foster parents want to adopt him while his birth parents try to regain him.

Gregory C. Keck and Regina M. Kupecky, *Adopting the Hurt Child: Hope for Families with Special-Needs Kids* (Colorado Springs, Colorado: Pinon Press, 1995). Practical advice, including discussions of attachment issues, dreams and realities, the adjustment process, the effects that adoption have on the birth children, therapy—and when adoption fails.

Bernard McNamara and Joan McNamara, *The SAFE-TEAM Parenting Workbook* (Greensboro, North Carolina: Family Resources, 1990). A workbook for adoptive families with sexually abused children.

Bernard McNamara and Joan McNamara, eds., *Adoption and the Sexually Abused Child* (Portland, Maine: University of Southern Maine, 1990). An anthology of essays that examine adoption and the sexually abused child.

Deborah H. Minshew and Chrisan Hooper, *The Adoptive Family as a Healing Resource for the Sexually Abused Child* (Washington, D.C.: Child Welfare League of America, 1990). A training manual for professionals.

Katherine Nelson, *On the Frontier of Adoption: A Study of Special-Needs Adoptive Families* (New York: Child Welfare League of America, 1985). Examines the experiences of 177 families and the types of services they needed. The book is designed to help adoption professionals and families understand the problems they will face.

SPECIAL PARENTING ISSUES

Jay Belsky and John Kelly, *The Transition to Parenthood: How a First Child Changes a Marriage* (New York: Delacorte Press, 1994). The tales told in this book are of new families created through pregnancy, but the experiences will resonate with all families.

Melissa Ludtke, *On Our Own: Unmarried Motherhood in America* (New York: Random House, 1997). This engrossing study looks at both teens and older women who choose to raise a child on their own. If you are an older woman contemplating single parenthood, Ludtke's examination of the decision to parent, the ways women structure their lives, and the issues these women face as parents offers an interesting perspective. As the author, who adopted a daughter from China, notes in her prologue: "I hope to offer a deeper appreciation of the personal dimension of this decision and the action it can entail."

Hope Marindin, ed., *The Handbook for Single Adoptive Parents* (Chevy Chase, Maryland: National Council for Single Adoptive Parents, 1997). Available through the National Council for Single Adoptive Parents (see appendix A). Although written for the single considering adoption, this book, which is periodically revised, updated, and enlarged, contains much valuable information for anyone contemplating adoption. There is a nice mix of practical information (the mechanics of adoption, affording an adoption, and managing single parenthood) with personal experiences. Grab it!

April Martin, *The Lesbian and Gay Parenting Handbook: Creating and Raising Our Families* (New York: HarperCollins, 1993). This book walks the reader through the special concerns of gays and lesbians: from the decision to parent, the different options, how to navigate adoption roadblocks, legal concerns, family relationships, children's needs over time, and where to turn for further information.

Jane Mattes, *Single Mothers by Choice: A Guidebook for Single Women Who are Considering or Have Chosen Single Motherhood* (New York: Times Books, 1994). This overview, written by the founder of the national support organization, offers a discussion of adoption as well as the "daddy" issue and other special concerns of children of single mothers.

NOTES

CHAPTER ONE:

1. This section comes from interviews with adoptive parents and birth parents. For a more extended discussion of Sara and Matt's experience, see Lois Gilman, "I Gave Up My Baby," *YM*, November 1990.
2. I have used statistics appearing in *Adoption Statistics—A Brief Overview,* a factsheet created by the National Adoption Information Clearinghouse.
3. Michael D. Lemonick, "The New Revolution in Making Babies," *TIME*, 1 December 1997, pp. 45–50.
4. Sherman J. Silber, *How To Get Pregnant* (New York: Scribner's, 1980), p. 5.
5. Linda P. Salzer, *Surviving Infertility* (New York: HarperCollins, 1991), p. 360.
6. Marcia Stamell, "Infertility: Fighting Back," *New York*, 21 March 1983.
7. Jill Smolowe, *An Empty Lap: One Couple's Journey to Parenthood* (New York: Pocket Books, 1997), pp. 101–2.
8. Ibid., pp. 116–7.
9. These questions are based on an interview with Linda Salzer. For a fuller discussion, see her chapter "The Crossroads of Infertility," in Salzer, *Surviving Infertility*, which gives a similar set of questions.
10. With Amy Rackear's permission, I have adapted an essay by her "Adoption: Another Kind of Miracle," which appeared in Resolve's newsletter and has been reprinted by them.
11. L. Anne Babb, "The Internet's 'Believe It or Not,'" *Adoptive Families*, May/June 1997, pp. 10–11.

CHAPTER TWO:

1. April Martin, *The Lesbian and Gay Parenting Handbook: Creating and Raising Our Families* (New York: HarperCollins, 1993), p. 134.
2. Peter Slavin, "So You Want To Adopt," *Air Force Times*, 13 February 1989.
3. Smith-Pliner is quoted in Kelly Costigan, "Going It Alone," *Town & Country*, June 1993, p. 117.
4. Debra Smith, "Foster Parent Adoption: What Parents Should Know," National Adoption Information Clearinghouse fact-sheet.

CHAPTER THREE:

1. Lois Gilman, "Adoption: How to Do It on Your Own," *Money*, October 1985, pp. 161–8.
2. This list takes as its starting point "Choosing Birthparents: The Ten Red Flags," which appears in Families for Private Adoption, *Successful Private Adoption*! (Washington, D.C.: Families for Private Adoption, 1996). I have truncated the items, dropped some, and rephrased others. I have also incorporated information from additional sources.
3. Mark T. McDermott, "Avoiding Contested Adoptions," *RESOLVE of the Washington Metropolitan Area, Inc.*, November/December 1993, p. 9.
4. For an interesting discussion, see Terry O'Neill, "Special Report: Birthfather Rights," *Adoptive Families*, September/October 1994, p. 11. There is also an extended discussion of various cases in the *Duke Journal of Gender Law & Policy* 2, no. 1 (spring 1995).
5. *OURS* magazine, January/February 1993, p 32.
6. Dorothy Kalins, "Babyhunt: The Agony and the Ecstasy of Our Private Adoption," *New York* 26, no. 29, p. 30.
7. I have drawn my examples from the section on "Financial Considerations," in Families for Private Adoption, *Successful Private Adoption!*
8. I have relied on the section "Obtaining Background and Medical Information" in Families for Private Adoption, *Successful Private Adoption!* There are sample forms that you can use.
9. Lois Gilman and Susan Freivalds, "How To Realize the Joy of Adopting a Child," *MONEY,* November 1997.

CHAPTER FOUR:

1. There are many definitions of open adoption, and the definitions keep changing. When *Dear Birthmother* by Kathleen Silber and Phylis Speedlin first appeared in 1982, the authors talked about the "process of accepting the responsibility of raising an individual who has two sets of parents"—and called for different practices: sharing names, sharing letters, sharing photographs, meeting face to face. As this chapter shows, open adoption has moved beyond that. I have relied on experts such as Kathleen Silber, Jim Gritter, and Sharon Kaplan and on my interviews with adoptive parents and birth parents who have been participating in open adoptions to help me more fully understand what they are experiencing. I have tried to read the currently available literature and attended adoptive parents' preparation sessions.

   Finally, it should be noted that, with the cooperation of Catholic Social Services of Green Bay, Wisconsin, I first conducted extensive telephone interviews with birth mothers and with adoptive parents in 1983 for the first edition of *The Adoption Resource Book*. While the names Joan Smith, Sharon Blair, and Donna King are pseudonyms, these three women have kept in touch with me over the years and I have had the opportunity to update their stories. This book is their beneficiary.
2. Beverly Fritz, "Healing the Past," *OURS*, November/December 1989.
3. Kathleen Silber and Patricia Martinez Dorner, *Children of Open Adoption* (San Antonio: Corona, 1990), pp. 85–6.
4. Ibid., p. 15.
5. Ibid., p. 15.
6. Jeanne Warren Lindsay, *Open Adoption: A Caring Option* (Buena Park, Calif.: Morning Glory Press, 1987), p. 180.
7. Ruth G. McRoy, Harold D. Grotevant, and Susan Ayers Lopez, *Changing Practices in Adoption* (Austin, Texas: Hogg Foundation for Mental Health, 1994), p.16.
8. Lois Gilman, "I Gave Up My Baby," *YM*, November 1990. I have quoted from the article as well as drawn from an unpublished interview with the adoptive mother Becky Miller. The names used are pseudonyms.

9. McRoy, Grotevant, and Lopez, *Changing Practices,* p. 20.
10. Ibid., p. 21
11. The story of the Dredges is chronicled in Lois Gilman, "The Miracle of Adoption," *Cosmopolitan,* February 1995.
12. Lois Ruskai Melina and Sharon Kaplan Roszia, *The Open Adoption Experience* (New York: HarperCollins, 1993), p. 318.
13. McRoy, Grotevant, and Lopez, *Changing Practices,* p. 6.
14. Ibid., p. 29.
15. Amy Silverberg, "Open Adoption: Is It Legally Enforceable? Should It Be?," *Adoptive Families.* November/December 1996, pp. 14–16.
16. Sharon Harrigan, "Problems You May Face," *OURS,* November/December 1989.
17. This list is derived from my interviews concerning open adoption and my participation in the orientation process at Lutheran Social Services in Denver in 1990. You'll find a similar list in the personal workbook accompanying the video/audiotape collection *Winning at Adoption* (The Family Network, Studio City, California) and in Melina and Roszia's *The Open Adoption Experience.*
18. While I interviewed Kathleen Silber for this book, this opinion was also expressed in *Open Adoption: The Experts Speak Out,* a video produced by Carol Land and Sharon Kaplan.
19. McRoy, Grotevant, and Lopez, *Changing Practices,* p. 22.

CHAPTER FIVE:

1. John Hubner and Jill Wolfson, *Somebody Else's Children: The Courts, the Kids, and the Struggle to Save America's Troubled Children* (New York: Crown Publishers, 1996), pp. 28–9
2. From National Adoption Information Clearinghouse factsheet, *Adoption Statistics—A Brief Overview.* The figures were for April-September 1996 and were collected by the Children's Bureau, U.S. Department of Health and Human Services.
3. Chasnoff has been following a group of children since 1986. He has spoken about his research at several conferences and his findings have been reported in the press.
4. Lois Melina, "Researchers are optimistic about drug-exposed children; prospective parents are apprehensive," *Adopted Child,*

November 1997. The Evan B. Donaldson Adoption Institute held a meeting on this topic in October 1997.

5. These anecdotes come from the newsletter, *Growing with FAS,* January 1990, p. 3, and Sandra Blakeslee's "Child-Rearing is Stormy When Drugs Cloud Birth," *New York Times,* 19 May 1990.
6. This anecdote comes from an unpublished manuscript of the Jenkinses, "Koko, an AIDS Baby Story," that the family generously shared with me.
7. Based on material in the newsletter of Alabama Friends of Adoption (Birmingham), 1982.
8. Connecticut Adoption Resource Exchange, *Second Annual Report,* 1 July 1981–30 June 1982, p. 30.
9. Rita Laws, "Between the Lines," *Adoptive Families,* September/October 1995, pp. 34–5.

CHAPTER SIX:

1. The Immigration and Naturalization Service and the U.S. Department of State keep track of the number of "immigrant orphans" admitted annually and do country-by-country breakdowns. Figures come from published sources, including those posted by the National Adoption Information Clearinghouse and the Joint Council on International Children's Services.
2. From Holt International Children's Services, *Adoption—A Family Affair* (Eugene, Oregon: Holt International Children's Services).
3. This was originally published in *FACE Facts* (see appendix C). Reprinted in Barbara Holtan and Laurel Strassberger, eds., *They Became Part of Us* (Maple Grove, Minn.: Mini-World, 1985), p. 180.
4. *GIFT,* Summer 1982.
5. Maggie Francis Conroy, *A World of Love* (New York: Kensington Books, 1997), p. 107.
6. Dr. Dana Johnson, "Adopting an Institutionalized Child: What are the Risks?" *Adoptive Families,* May/June 1997, p. 27.
7. Margaret K. Hostetter, M.D., Sandra Iverson, R.N., Kathryn Doyle, O.T.R., and Dana Johnson, M.D., Ph.D., "Unsuspected

Infectious Diseases and Other Medical Diagnoses in the Evaluation of Internationally Adopted Children," *Pediatrics* 83, no. 4, April 1989, p. 559.

8. Lisa H. Albers, M.D., M.P.H., Dana E. Johnson, M.D., Ph.D., Margaret K. Hostetter, M.D., Sandra Iverson, R.N., Laurie C. Miller, M.D., "Health of Children Adopted from the Former Soviet Union and Eastern Europe," *JAMA Abstracts*, 17 September 1997; Dr. Albers was quoted in a Reuters report of 16 September 1997 about the article.
9. I have chronicled Carrie's and Bob and Dawna's stories in Lois Gilman, "The Miracle of Adoption," *Cosmopolitan*, February, 1995. I have added in this chapter and elsewhere information that I gathered from them in my interviewing.
10. Michael Robbins, "The Right Way to Adopt A Baby From Abroad," *MONEY*, November 1997.
11. Article by Dr. Jenista in *ICCC Newsletter*, 1988. Dr. Jenista shared the manuscript with me.
12. Ibid.

CHAPTER 7:

1. Thomas D. Morton, "Practice Issue: The Home Study," *Adoption Report*, 1982.
2. "The Adoption Homestudy: From the Client's Viewpoint–A Learning Experience," *Adoption Dialogues* (newsletter of the Networking Adoption Program of Jewish Child Care Association), Fall 1997.
3. Morton, *Adoption Report*, p. 5.
4. Pat Shirley, *FACE Facts*, November 1982.
5. I have drawn from *What To Do If You Get Stuck*, a factsheet prepared in the early eighties by the now-defunct Sonoma County, Calif. chapter of OURS.
6. Shirley, *FACE Facts*, November 1982.
7. Based on Kenneth J. Hermann, Jr., *Adoption: Questions, Resources and Readings* (New York: OURS of Western New York, 1983); *What To Do If You Get Stuck*; interviews I conducted in the nineties; and suggestions from adoption experts.

CHAPTER 8:

1. National Center for Health Statistics website, *How To Obtain Birth, Death, Marriage, and Divorce Certificates,* December 1997. The website is updated several times a year. You can also contact the National Center for Health Statistics to get an older printed publication.
2. A detailed, current book, written for use by attorneys, is *Adoption Law and Practice,* published by Matthew Bender and Company. The National Adoption Information Clearinghouse can provide you with summaries of state laws free of charge.
3. Maureen Evans, "Fingerprinting Changes," *The Bulletin of the Joint Council on International Children's Services,* Winter 1997/98.
4. Laura Rittenhouse, "Post China Paperwork," Families with Children from China newsletter.

CHAPTER 9:

1. Barbara Shulgold and Lynne Sipiora, *Dear Barbara, Dear Lynne: The True Story of Two Women in Search of Motherhood* (Reading, Mass.: Addison-Wesley Publishing, 1992), p. 75.
2. From the newsletter of New York Singles Adopting Children, December 1990.
3. Claudia L. Jewett, *Adopting the Older Child* (Harvard, Mass.: Harvard Common Press, 1978), p. 53.
4. *New York Times,* 2 November 1983.
5. Gilman and Freivalds, "How To Realize the Joy of Adopting a Child," *MONEY,* November 1997.
6. Dana Johnson, "Medical Issues in International Adoption," *Adoptive Families,* January/February 1997. There is a growing specialized medical adoption literature that you can dip into. Check with the National Adoption Information Clearinghouse for citations.
7. Dana E. Johnson and Margaret Hostetter, "Post-Arrival Evaluations," *Adoptive Families,* March/April 1997.
8. You will find these tests recommended in several sources, including the articles by Dr. Johnson. You can also obtain information from the American Academy of Pediatrics.
9. Johnson and Hostetter, "Post-Arrival Evaluations."

10. There are several centers around the country that now focus on the health-care concerns of internationally adopted children; the National Adoption Information Clearinghouse as well as Adoptive Families of American and your local adoptive parent group can refer you to local physicians. Health professionals can also obtain an article on the "Medical Supervision of Internationally Adopted Children," through the Gerber Products' Company hotline (*Pediatric Basics* 77, Summer 1996; telephone: 800–595–0324)
11. Jewett, *Adopting the Older Child,* p. 99–100. Claudia Jewett Jarratt also spoke with me in 1991 and reviewed portions of the manuscript. Some of these questions, as well as additional comments from her, come from our discussions.
12. Lois Melina, "Cocaine and Alcohol Affect Unborn Babies," *Adopted Child,* November 1988; and Judith Schaffer, *Cocaine Use during Pregnancy: Its Effects on Infant Development and Implications for Adoptive Parents* (New York: New York State Citizens' Coalition for Children, 1989).
13. Cheri Register, *Are Those Kids Yours? American Families with Children Adopted from Other Countries* (New York: Free Press, 1991), pp. 78–79.
14. Comments made to Jack Frank at the Adoptive Parents Committee adoption conference, "Adoption: Directions for the 80s," November 20, 1983.
15. Jewett, *Adopting the Older Child,* p. 81.
16. James L. Gritter, ed., *Adoption without Fear* (San Antonio: Corona, 1989), pp. 138, 145.
17. *PLAN,* July/August 1984. Reprinted in *FAIR,* October 1982, p. 11.
18. Lois Melina, *Raising Adopted Children: A Manual for Adoptive Parents* (New York: Harper & Row, 1986), p. 12.
19. Lois Melina, "Don't Re-name Even a Young Child," *Adopted Child,* July 1982, pp. 1, 4. Another interesting article on the subject is Joyce S. Kaser and R. Kent Boesdorfer, "What Should We Name This Child? The Difficulties of Naming Older Adopted Children," *Children Today,* November/December 1981, p. 8.

20. Gloria Peterson, ed., *The Special Student* (Illinois Council on Adoptable Children, 1982), p. 1.
21. Comments by Jack Frank at the Adoptive Parents Committee Adoption Conference, "Adoption: Directions for the '80s," November 20, 1983.
22. For a discussion of how grandparents feel about adoption, see Lois Gilman, "A Special Kind of Love," *New Choices*, February 1990.
23. Melina, *Raising Adopted Children*, p. 35.

CHAPTER TEN:

1. Jana Wolff, *Secret Thoughts of an Adoptive Mother* (Kansas City: Andrews and McMeel, 1997), pp. 57, 59.
2. *Buena Vista*, May 1983. Many adoptive parents talked with me about their adjustment experiences. Where the anecdote is based on a published source, I have footnoted the source. Otherwise the information comes from my interviews.
3. David M. Brodzinsky, "Adjustment to Adoption: A Psychological Perspective," *Clinical Psychology Review* 7 (1987), p. 32.
4. Barbara Shulgold and Lynne Sipiora, *Dear Barbara, Dear Lynne: The True Story of Two Women in Search of Motherhood* (Reading, Mass.: Addison-Wesley Publishing, 1992), pp. 116, 128.
5. Originally printed in *FACE Facts*, April 1983. Reprinted in Barbara Holtan and Laurel Strassberger, eds., *They Became Part of Us* (Maple Grove, Minn.: Mini-World, 1985).
6. Gail Steinberg, "When You Don't Fall in Love Right Away: How Adoption Affects Bonding and Attachment with Your Child," *OURS*, January/February 1994, p. 25.
7. *Clark Adoption Resources Newsletter*, June 1983.
8. Ann Kimble Loux, *The Limits of Hope: An Adoptive Mother's Story* (Charlottesville: University of Virginia Press, 1997), p. 23.
9. Shulgold and Sipiora, *Dear Barbara, Dear Lynne*, p. 161.
10. Holly van Gulden and Lisa M. Bartels-Rabb, *Real Parents, Real Children: Parenting the Adopted Child* (New York: The Crossroad Publishing Company, 1993), pp. 75–6.

11. Jay Belsky and John Kelly, *The Transition to Parenthood: How a First Child Changes a Marriage* (New York: Delacorte Press, 1994), p. 263.
12. Ibid., pp. 155–6.
13. Ibid., p. 156.
14. Cheri Register, *Are Those Kids Yours? American Families with Children Adopted from Other Countries* (New York: Free Press, 1991), p. 111.
15. Jill Krementz, *How It Feels To Be Adopted* (New York: Alfred A. Knopf, 1982), p. 16.
16. Maxine B. Rosenberg, *Growing Up Adopted* (New York: Bradbury Press, 1989), pp. 91–5.
17. John Bowlby, quoted in Robert Karen, *Becoming Attached: Unfolding the Mystery of the Infant-Mother Bond and Its Impact on Later Life* (New York: Warner Books, 1984), p. 4. I have paraphrased the examples of the theorists from Karen's excellent book.
18. Ibid., p. 440.
19. "Infant Adoption: Two Families Experiences with Intercountry Adoption," *Children Today*, November/December 1980, pp. 2–5. All quotations about Jane are taken from this article.
20. Brazelton is quoted in Lois Gilman, "Adoption—Big Adjustments, Big Rewards," *Mothers Today*, September/October 1984, p. 31.
21. Barbara Bascom and Carole McKelvey, *The Complete Guide to Foreign Adoption: What to Expect and How To Prepare for Your New Child* (New York: Pocket Books, 1997), p. 150.
22. Ibid., p. 152.
23. Barbara Holtan, "Are We Having Fun Yet?" *Report on Foreign Adoption*, 1991, p. 34.
24. Ibid.
25. Laurie Flynn, "Why Would Anyone Adopt a Teenager," *Change*, Fall 1980, pp. 7–8. All quotations of Flynn are from this article.
26. Gregory C. Keck and Regina M. Kupecky, *Adopting the Hurt Child: Hope for Families with Special-Needs Kids* (Colorado Springs, Colo.: Pinon Press, 1995), pp. 82–3.

27. When discussing the grieving process, experts often refer to Elisabeth Kübler-Ross, *On Death and Dying* (New York: Macmillan, 1969). You might also want to read Claudia L. Jewett's *Helping Children Cope with Separation and Loss* (Harvard, Mass.: Harvard Common Press, 1982).
28. Claudia Jewett, *A Parent's Guide to Adopting an Older Child* (pamphlet produced by the Open Door Society of Massachusetts), p. 21.
29. Keck and Kupecky, *Adopting the Hurt Child*, p. 100.
30. Jewett, *Adopting the Older Child*, p. 288.
31. "Looking Back at Disruption." Materials developed at a 1975 "Disruption" workshop in conjunction with the annual meeting of Spaulding for Children. The quoted material is excerpted from a section entitled "Disruption."
32. Trudy Festinger, "Adoption Disruption: Rates and Correlates," in David Brodzinsky and Marshall D. Schechter, eds., *The Psychology of Adoption* (New York: Oxford University Press, 1990), p. 217.
33. Keck and Kupecky, *Adopting the Hurt Child*, p. 177.
34. Ibid., p. 128.

CHAPTER ELEVEN:

1. All quotations are from Katrina Maxtone-Graham, *An Adopted Woman* (New York: Remi Books, 1983).
2. Jill Krementz, *How It Feels To Be Adopted* (New York: Alfred A. Knopf, 1982), p. 8.
3. Betty Jean Lifton, *Lost and Found: The Adoption Experience* rev. ed. (New York: Harper & Row, 1988), pp. 205–6.
4. David Brodzinsky and Marshall D. Schechter, eds., *The Psychology of Adoption* (New York: Oxford University Press, 1990), p. 14. See also David M. Brodzinsky, Marshall D. Schechter, and Robin Marantz Henig, *Being Adopted: The Lifelong Search for Self* (New York: Doubleday, 1992).
5. Peter L. Benson, Anu R. Sharma, and Eugene C. Roehlkepartain, *Growing Up Adopted: A Portrait of Adolescents & Their Families* (Minneapolis, Minn.: Search Institute, 1994), p. 24.

6. Brodzinsky, Schechter, and Henig, *Being Adopted,* p. 64.
7. Mary Watkins and Susan Fisher, *Talking with Young Children about Adoption* (New Haven: Yale University Press, 1993), p. 61.
8. David H. Brodzinsky, Dianne Schechter, and Anne Braff Brodzinsky, "Children's Knowledge of Adoption: Developmental Changes and Implications for Adjustment," in R. Ashmore and D. Brodzinsky, eds., *Thinking about the Family: Views of Parents and Children* (Hillsdale, N.J.: Erlbaum, 1986), p. 212.
9. Some of this material originally appeared in Lois Gilman, "Adoption: Tackling the Tough Questions," *Parenting,* November 1990. I interviewed both David Brodzinsky and Lois Melina for the *Parenting* article.
10. Brodzinsky, Schechter, and Henig, *Being Adopted,* p. 62.
11. Brodzinsky, Schechter, and Brodzinsky, "Children's Knowledge," pp. 227–8.
12. Brodzinsky, Schechter, and Henig, *Being Adopted,* p. 103.
13. Brodzinsky, Schechter, and Brodzinsky, "Children's Knowledge," pp. 213–14.
14. This point is made in a press release describing the report; in Benson, Sharma, and Roehlkepartain, *Growing Up Adopted,* p. 7; Benson made similar remarks at a conference of Adoptive Families of America (1994).
15. Watkins and Fisher, *Talking with Young Children about Adoption,* p. 63. The authors note that you'll hear discussions of adoption during imaginative play, walks, and baths. The anecdotal stories at the back of their book are filled with such examples.
16. Lois Melina, "Entrustment ceremonies provide benefits to birth families and adoptive families," *Adopted Child,* April 1997, p. 3.
17. For a discussion of Judaism and adoption, see Michael Gold, *And Hannah Wept: Infertility, Adoption, and the Jewish Couple* (Philadelphia: Jewish Publication Society, 1988). Other resources: *The Resource Book, A Guide to Jewish Adoption Issues* (Jewish Family & Children's Service of Greater Philadelphia: 215–698–9950), which includes a description of rituals and prayers; Carolyn Flanders McPherson and Hillel (James E.) Rosenfeld, *Let's Celebrate Adoption: A Guide for the Jewish Community* (produced by the Michigan Post Adoption Services

System Management Team) and Julie Brook Alexander, *Contemporary Adoption: Reform Jewish Perspectives* (a pamphlet published by the Union of American Hebrew Congregations)

18. Maxine B. Rosenberg, *Growing Up Adopted* (New York: Bradbury Press, 1989), p.8.
19. Lois Melina, "*Adoption Day* ritual acknowledges significant day for child, family," *Adopted Child,* December 1995, p. 1. You'll also find a discussion of adoption ritual in *Adoptive Families* magazine. See, for example, Judye Heitfeld, "Arrival Celebrations," *Adoptive Families,* September/October 1994; and Holly van Gulden and Lisa Bartels-Rabb, "Anniversary Days," *Adoptive Families,* March/April 1995.
20. Lifton, *Lost and Found,* p. 20.
21. Pat Tobin, "Blessing in a Back Street," in FACE Booklet, *Family Building Through Adoption.*
22. Lois Melina, *Making Sense of Adoption: A Parent's Guide* (New York: Harper & Row, 1989), p. 113.
23. Lifton, *Lost and Found,* pp. 205–6.
24. Krementz, *How It Feels to Be Adopted,* pp. 79–80.
25. Melina, *Making Sense of Adoption,* p. 37.
26. Excerpted from Lois Melina, "Even Well Adjusted Parents Can be Uneasy Disclosing Adoption," *Adopted Child,* January 1991.
27. Lois Melina, *Raising Adopted Children: A Manual for Adoptive Parents* (New York: Harper & Row, 1986), p. 81.
28. Portions of the discussion on school appeared in Lois Gilman, "School Savvy: How to Help Your Child Avoid Curricular Pitfalls," *Adoptive Families,* September/October 1995. Also helpful will be the Nancy Sheehan Ng and Lansing Wood *Adoption and the Schools* (available from FAIR, P.O. Box 51436, Palo Alto, CA 94303; 650–328–6832); the National Adoption Information Clearinghouse's factsheet *Adoption and School Issues*"; the various writings of Lois Melina; *The Adopted Child in Elementary School* by the Adoptive Family Network (P.O. Box 7, Columbia, MD 21045; 301–984–6133), *Adoption Education: A Multicultural/Family Curriculum* by the Illinois Committee for Adoption (721 North LaSalle Street, Chicago, Illinois 60610; 312–655–7596).
29. H. David Kirk, *Shared Fate* (New York: Free Press, 1964), pp. 30, 35.

30. *New York Times,* 9 November 1997.
31. Van Gulden and Bartels-Rabb, *Real Parents, Real Children: Parenting the Adopted Child* (New York: The Crossroad Publishing Company, 1993), pp. 177–8.
32. Ronny Diamond, "Secrecy vs. Privacy," *Adoptive Families,* September/October 1995, p. 10.
33. Article in the newsletter of Holt International Children's Services, January/March 1982.
34. Ruth Chamberlin, "Conference Review: Adoptees Talk About Transracial Adoption," *Adoptalk,* October 1982.
35. Judith Schaffer and Christina Lindstrom, *How to Raise an Adopted Child* (New York: Crown, 1989), pp. 280–81.
36. Holt International Children's Services, *A Family Affair.*
37. Holt newsletter, 1982.
38. Holt newsletter, 1982.
39. *New York Times,* 1 November 1990.
40. Jean A. S. Strauss, *Birthright: The Guide to Search and Reunion for Adoptees, Birthparents and Adoptive Parents* (New York: Penguin Books, 1994), pp. 5, 8.
41. Arthur D. Sorosky, Annette Baran, Reuben Pannor, *The Adoption Triangle: Sealed or Open Records: How They Affect Adoptees, Birth Parents, and Adoptive Parents,* rev. ed. (New York: Anchor Press/Doubleday, 1984), p. 201.
42. Brodzinsky, Schechter, and Henig, *Being Adopted,* p. 113.
43. Ibid., p. 118.
44. J. Douglas Bates, *Gift Children: A Story of Race, Family, and Adoption in a Divided America* (New York: Ticknor & Fields, 1993), p. 256–7.
45. Lois Melina, "Middle Childhood May Be Time To Contact Birth Parents," *Adopted Child,* December 1990, p. 4.
46. Jan Waldron, *Giving Away Simone: A Memoir* (New York: Times Books, 1995), pp. xiv, 235.

INDEX